Marcia Adams'

HEIRLOOM
RECIPES

Marcia Adams' HEIRLOOM RECIPES

YESTERDAY'S FAVORITES TOMORROW'S TREASURES

Photographs by Raymond Bial

CLARKSON POTTER/PUBLISHERS
NEW YORK

ALSO BY MARCIA ADAMS

Christmas in the Heartland

Heartland

Cooking from Quilt Country

Excerpt from "The Current" in *Farming: A Hand Book*,
copyright © 1969 by Wendell Berry, reprinted by permission of Harcourt Brace & Company.

Published by Clarkson Potter/Publishers,
201 East 50th Street, New York, New York 10022. Member of the Crown Publishing Group.

Random House, Inc. New York, Toronto, London, Sydney, Auckland

CLARKSON N. POTTER, POTTER,
and colophon are trademarks of Clarkson N. Potter, Inc.

Manufactured in the United States of America

Design by
DONNA AGAJANIAN

Library of Congress Cataloging-in-Publication Data
Adams, Marcia.
Marcia Adams' heirloom recipes: yesterday's favorites,
tomorrow's treasures/by Marcia Adams;
photographs by Raymond Bial. — 1st ed.
p. cm.
1. Cookery, American.   I. Title.
TX715.A2246   1994
641.5973—dc20 94-7662
CIP
ISBN 0-517-59347-5

10 9 8 7 6 5 4 3 2 1

First Edition

To The Learned Society
Who have done their share in furthering civilization:

BETSY CHAPMAN

JOAN FACKLER-GERBERDING

SUZANNE HALL

HOLLEY HOBBS

LADONNA HUNTLEY-JAMES

JUDY LEE

ELAINE SHULTZ

CAROL VER WIEBE

With appreciation and gratitude for their friendship

Having once put his hand into the ground,
seeding there what he hopes will outlast him,
a man has made a marriage with his place,
and if he leaves it his flesh will ache to go back.
                              From "The Current,"
                              Wendell Berry

ACKNOWLEDGMENTS

How do I acknowledge thee, Let me count thy names. . . . I feel somewhat like Browning as I think about all the people who make my books happen and help them find their way into the reader's hands.

My husband, Dick, deserves so much credit for making this book a reality; he was with me every step and every line of the way. For the two of us, this cookbook has been a warmly shared experience. Pam Krauss is the very definition of a good editor—what a lucky day it was for me when I was assigned to her care. The staff at Clarkson Potter so graciously responded to my questions and requests—Anne Tamsberg, Gail Shanks, Phyllis Fleiss, Jane Treuhaft, Howard Klein, Libby Kessman, and all the others; I am so grateful to you. Later, Tina Constable and Nancy Maloney scheduled publicity and complex book tours with great efficiency and attention to detail.

Photographer Raymond Bial from Urbana, Illinois, captured the precious images that make this book so handsome. It is an exhilarating experience when the author and photographer share the same vision, and that happened here. We were efficiently assisted by Lois Hamilton, who gathered and arranged all the props for the photography.

This has been an ambitious book to research and libraries all over the United States responded to my calls; here in Fort Wayne, Laura McCaffrey at the Allen County Library coordinated it all, and at my office, Susan Raver kept the computer humming as the material and recipes came together in a manuscript. Unfailingly organized and pleasant, her assistance was invaluable. My agent, Chris Tomasino, provided good practical advice and Carl DeSantis, my attorney, assisted time and again with astute business guidance.

At Bowling Green State University, where the series was taped, a crew of forty people spent two and a half months translating the written word to tape, which is now aired around the world. Denise Kisabeth, my director and co-producer, is a very special person in my life, and I feel so fortunate that we have had the opportunity to work together. The cooking crew, Doris Kisabeth, Cindy Tyrell, Diana Bruns, and food and prop stylist Lois Hamilton, prepared dish after dish, day after day; it is a miracle of sorts, and I marveled at their energy and willingness to tackle it all. Joan Fackler-Gerberding gathered together all the antiques and provided the research for them as well. The Indiana State Museum generously supplied Amish quilts from the Pottinger Collection.

A viewer once called the station and wanted to buy the whole TV set—curtains, baker's rack, kitchen cabinets, accessories, and all. That says something about Jan Bell and Debbie Bewley, who created the set. Tim Smith conjures up clever publicity. Tim Westhoven and Mark Henning create marvelous location segments and never tell me "it can't be done." Scott Kisabeth and Fred Dickinson always make things work in the studio, working in concert with the special skills of many others. And overseeing it all are Ron Gargasz, Patrick Fitzgerald, and Chris Sexton; they all help create a series that brings pleasure and information to our viewers.

I especially wish to thank Amelia's Fine Things in Fort Wayne, which provided the lovely dishes and accouterments as well as the show's generous sponsors, Minute Tapioca, Patricia R. Miller and Barbara Bradley Backgaard of Vera Bradley Designs, and The Fremont Company, makers of Frank's Sauerkraut and SnowFloss Sauerkraut, who gave us an opportunity to tell the book's story to so many people.

Doing what I love—the writing and the television work—is such a privilege, but none of it would happen without the support of my readers and viewers—thank you, thank you so very much.

CONTENTS

The Glories of Autumn

Winter's Pleasures

Marcia Adams'
HEIRLOOM
RECIPES

INTRODUCTION

"I learn by going where I have to go."
Theodore Roethke
from "The Waking"

I have always been attracted to what I call "attic receipts," those old recipes found on dog-eared and yellowing bits of paper stored in the attic in Aunt Sarah's long-forgotten trunk. From the time I began cooking as a young bride, I found these culinary heirlooms quite wonderful; they were appealing in flavor and generally simple to make, often using ingredients readily on hand in my kitchen. And the stories that accompanied them were absolutely fascinating. These recipes served me well, helping me provide my growing family with nourishing, economical meals. When I used them for entertaining, my delighted guests would say, after enjoying a serving of brisket and sauerkraut or gooseberry fool, "I haven't eaten this in ages. May I please have the recipe?" Later, when I began writing about food for publication, I discovered that because we are a country obsessed with the "new," many of these older recipes had not been in print for years and were on their way to oblivion.

Many of the current generation of cooks have missed the opportunity to work alongside a parent or grandparent in the kitchen. They have not had the pleasure of learning to prepare favored family dishes from an oral tradition. And it is certainly now rare for several generations to work together in the kitchen, enjoying the fellowship and sharing culinary knowledge and family food-ways as they preserved the harvest or created a holiday repast.

As a civilization, we have always prepared food in celebration of life's memorable events, both happy and sad. The memories of those gatherings and the foods we shared link us to our past and collective traditions and, in some cases, what we perceive to be better times. In our kitchens, as we prepare these attic "receipts" to serve to our families and friends, we are able to reinvoke those precious earlier days. These evocative recipes connect us with one another across the years and across the country. Now, more than ever, I feel our family recipes bond us to one another; as the oral tradition fades into obscurity, it is imperative to have them recorded.

Since the publication of my first cookbook, which contained many of these older recipes, I have received more and more requests for them. It gives me so much pleasure when I am told by a reader, "I have been looking for that recipe for years, and here it was, in your book." It makes me feel I have returned a precious and very tangible part of that person's family history.

I am far from finished with my search for these receipts and will doubtless be tracking them down the rest of my life. I live in Indiana, but my quest for old recipes has taken me and my husband, Dick, all over the country, like recipe detectives, seeking out the old worn recipe books and the cooks who prepare these dishes and know their stories. It is like being a passionate collector of antiques, only the antiques we look for are not furniture or even dishes, but recipes. We bring our culinary quarry back to Indiana, where they are tested and retested to make sure they work in today's kitchens. I want them to have a new life in new surroundings.

Dick and I have thoroughly enjoyed our sleuthing and have learned so much about the history of our country and how its settlement influenced our foodways. As always, when we prepare to go on trips, I did a great deal of prior research, especially into the history of the regions we would be visiting. This investigation helps me understand how certain food styles and recipes developed; inevitably there is a direct linkage to the land and water.

Yet I don't consider this a regional cookbook, nor is it arranged in that fashion. This is for two very good reasons. First, I recognized that certain old dishes, or heirloom recipes, had been around for generations and were served in every state and often in much the same way (homemade ice cream is an Independence Day tradition from coast to coast, for example). Fried chicken and corn bread, though admittedly in different versions, as well as meat loaf popped up everywhere. Certain ethnic influences crisscrossed regional demarcations as well—German, Scandinavian, Italian, and Mexican have left their culinary mark in many states. Secondly, the book was written over a period of a year and evolved as we traveled, passing from one region to the next in a somewhat arbitrary route using early wagon train trails as our map. Throughout the book you'll find notes and observations from our culinary quest, as well as mentions

of other notable sights we took in along the way.

Finding beloved but forgotten recipes was not too difficult; my best source has always been small-town libraries, where librarians have thoughtfully preserved locally written cookbooks and generally know the town's best cooks. Newspaper food editors around the country were also knowledgeable about their community's food history and whom to contact for more information. And because of my earlier books and the television shows, I have a network of correspondents across the country who share my enthusiasm for heirloom recipes, and I made appointments to see them as we traveled. Everyone we met was so helpful and welcoming; it reinforced my belief that we are an open, warmhearted nation.

My interest in American literature and writers, as well as gardens, occasioned several detours along the way and as often as not led us to some fine old recipes at the same time. Whenever people discovered we were looking for older recipes, they happily volunteered examples of their own. Some, we were told, were "just served at family meals"; others were prepared for special occasions only once or twice a year. Most were linked to the past and to the cooks who created them. These recipes are part of what I call the ribbon of memory, reminding us of who we are and where we've been. And these are the recipe traditions we want to pass on to our children.

As Dick and I crisscrossed the country over the course of four seasons (returning home to Indiana periodically to regroup), we encountered a broad spectrum of dishes, ranging from Joe Frogger cookies in the East to chili spareribs in the West. Occasionally, I would find a more contemporary recipe that seemed destined to be an heirloom recipe of tomorrow, and felt it should be included here, though sadly there are precious few of those.

This is the story of our culinary odyssey: a journal of our travels and impressions of the places we visited, what we learned, and most important, a record of the enduring and beloved old recipes we encountered along the way.

Signs of SPRING

WAKEN TO A NEWLY minted slant of light streaming into the bedroom. Perceptibly and overnight, spring has announced itself and with it comes a fanfare of wild flowers—purple violets and pink trillium, and the flowering trees—graceful redbud and bridal-white dogwood, a hosanna of color in the new feathery green of the woods.

In the garden, we uncover the strawberries and finish planting onion sets and radishes. With spring comes the progression of delectable foods for our table—morel mushrooms, dandelion greens, tiny lamb chops, and in another few weeks, we will enjoy rhubarb cream pie and platters of crisp asparagus. Strawberries and jade-green gooseberries will soon follow.

Our travel arrangements for New England, New York City, and Baltimore are all made and we leave tomorrow morning. References in my research to Joe Frogger cookies and apple slump have truly piqued my interest.

Later, we take the cats, Edith and Emily, out for an evening stroll; in the gathering dusk we hear the first spring peepers preparing for concert, their sound arising from a nearby pond in the woods. The primeval tune will go on until the flickering dawn.

Scooping up the cats, we go inside to finish up the packing. The van is nearly loaded already with my research books and files, laptop computer, needlepoint, and maps. Tomorrow, we'll add the suitcases and a picnic lunch, and head east.

The Greening of the
COUNTRY

DRIVING THROUGH THE eastern and mid-Atlantic region of the country, Dick and I revel in the newness of spring. Golden forsythia and daffodils sway and nod in country farmyards.

From year to year, I forget how good the land, well, smells. As the soil warms and becomes friable, its scent is strong and fresh, indicating it is time to plant. We see small squares of garden already seeded with lettuce, radishes, spinach, peas, and in some places, potatoes. Tender plants, such as tomatoes, squash, and green bell peppers, will be safely transplanted after the last full moon in May.

Among the old letters and journals written by early pioneer women, references to past gardens and to the gardens they were attempting literally to carve out of the tough prairie soil fill many pages. Many of them had carried slips of favorite roses and shrubs as a reminder of home.

They also wrote of the first bunch of rhubarb, the pan of new peas, the thinnings of the lettuce and spinach added to new young dandelion leaves for wilted salad. An emphasis on seasonal cooking is very popular now, but early cooks knew no other way. It wasn't until the science of food preservation was developed, plus a transportation system that could move foodstuffs across the continent, that we began preparing dishes out of season.

The old recipes that have evolved from this season reflect the calendar. The unexpected southwestern coupling of asparagus with pine nuts; new red-skinned potato salad; wilted greens and fiddleheads; and desserts made from maple syrup and rhubarb were all spring specialties of early cooks.

As we motor along the back roads, we find the lowlands and bogs aglow with tall yellow water iris and marsh marigolds. By this time, the woods are lined with purple rocket and wild phlox. We stop the van and clamber out to enjoy a plowman's lunch. A nearby apple orchard is in bloom, the pink-white billowing trees marching up green meadows dotted with dandelions. As I cut into the fresh crusty bread and prepare to top the slices with local cheese and salami, Dick says, "It doesn't get much better than this."

*A*sparagus with Pine Nuts *S*pring Asparagus with Cream Sauce *W*ilted Green Salad with Sweet-Sour Bacon Dressing *C*reamy Coleslaw with Boiled Dressing *M*aple Upside-Down Cake *A*mish Rhubarb Pudding *R*hubarb Custard Pie *G*ooseberry Fool *B*lack Cherry Cookies *M*aple Custard Ice Cream *S*trawberry Shortcake, Biscuit Style *V*iolet Syrup *H*aymakers' Switchel

SPARAGUS WITH PINE NUTS

SERVES 4

*You can serve this hot as a side dish or at room temperature as a salad. Either way, it is an aristocratic dish.
The white pine nuts enhance the green asparagus, and the two textures play off each
other nicely. Though fresh asparagus (my grandfather called it "sparrowgrass") is best, you can substitute frozen.
Toast the pine nuts and make the dressing in advance.
Pine nuts grow inside the pine cone, which has to be heated to release the nut, a tedious process,
which explains why these delicious morsels are so costly. I buy mine in bulk at a food co-op and, since they are
a high-fat nut, store them in the freezer.*

DRESSING
3 tablespoons olive oil
1 tablespoon fresh lemon juice
1 garlic clove, mashed
2 teaspoons minced fresh oregano, or
  ¼ teaspoon dried
2 teaspoons minced fresh basil, or
  ¼ teaspoon dried
Salt and freshly ground pepper to taste

1½ pounds fresh asparagus
2 tablespoons toasted pine nuts
  (see Note)

In a small jar with a tight lid, shake together the oil, lemon juice, garlic, oregano, basil, and salt and pepper. Pour into a small saucepan and set aside.

Wash the asparagus and snap off the tough ends; place the spears in a vegetable steamer over boiling water and steam, covered, until the asparagus is crisp-tender, approximately 7 to 10 minutes. Drain and arrange on an oval serving dish; cover to keep warm. Over medium heat, bring the dressing to a boil. Immediately pour the hot dressing over the asparagus, then sprinkle with the toasted pine nuts. Serve immediately or at room temperature.

NOTE: *To toast pine nuts, place them in a heavy, dry skillet over medium-high heat. Cook, shaking often, just until fragrant and golden brown.*

$\mathscr{S}$PRING ASPARAGUS WITH CREAM SAUCE

SERVES 6 TO 8

*Fresh asparagus is very good with just a bit of butter and lemon
juice served over it, but this delicate cream sauce, lightly seasoned with lemon, Dijon mustard, and
nutmeg, really dresses it up. The sauce is also good with broccoli and green beans.*

SAUCE

3 tablespoons butter	¼ teaspoon Dijon mustard
1 rounded tablespoon all-purpose flour	¼ teaspoon ground nutmeg
1 cup milk	⅛ teaspoon ground white pepper
2 large egg yolks, well beaten	2 teaspoons minced parsley, chervil, or chives
1 tablespoon lemon juice	
1 tablespoon sugar	2 pounds fresh asparagus
1 teaspoon grated lemon zest	

Make the sauce: In a small saucepan, melt the butter over medium heat. Whisk in the flour to make a smooth paste. Gradually add the milk, whisking constantly until creamy. Turn off the heat, then add the egg yolks, lemon juice, sugar, lemon zest, mustard, nutmeg, and pepper and whisk until well blended. Turn the heat to medium and cook, stirring constantly, until the mixture is thickened, about 5 minutes; but do not allow it to boil. Stir in the herbs, turn the heat to low, and keep warm until the asparagus is cooked.

   Meanwhile, prepare the asparagus: Snap the tough stem ends off the asparagus and steam or microwave until tender but firm, about 7 to 10 minutes. (The time will depend on the size of the asparagus spears.) Drain well on paper towels and place on a heated platter. Pour the sauce over the asparagus or pass it separately.

PHOTO POST CARD

AMERICA 25

CONCORD, MASSACHUSETTS

I am delighted to be back in New England, partly because I am so fond of Yankee cookery! We try to stop at the old inns and village taverns, some of which have an unbroken history of feeding travelers for 200 years, and still serve traditional foods of the region. Many still have their own vegetable gardens, and right now, the lettuces are just perfect for salads. The old timers called green vegetables "garden sass" and this included the first asparagus, which most early cooks served in a cream sauce. Will be in Concord tommorow.

WILTED GREEN SALAD WITH SWEET-SOUR BACON DRESSING

SERVES 8

*Bacon and a sweet-and-sour dressing enhance early spring lettuces. However, for texture, I
like also to include some curly endive, spinach, and tender dandelion greens. Allow the dressing to cool
slightly before pouring it over the greens. This old recipe is a legacy from our early German settlers.
The dressing can be made in advance and reheated in a
double boiler over simmering water. It is also very good on young dandelion greens alone.*

12 cups lightly packed torn
    assorted greens
6 to 8 slices of lean bacon,
    cut into 1-inch pieces
8 scallions
1 large egg

½ teaspoon ground mustard
¼ cup sugar
¼ cup water
¼ cup cider vinegar
Freshly ground pepper to taste

Wash, dry, and chill the greens. (This can be done up to a day in advance.)

In a large skillet, sauté the bacon until crisp, stirring often. Transfer the bacon to paper toweling with a slotted spoon, leaving the drippings in the skillet. Chop the scallions thinly, including some of the green, and set aside.

In a small bowl, beat the egg slightly. Whisk in the mustard, sugar, water, vinegar, and pepper. Pour off all but ¼ to ⅓ cup of the bacon drippings and add the scallions. Cook over medium heat, stirring, for about a half minute. Lower the heat and whisk in the egg mixture. Cook and whisk until the mixture is thickened and hot, about 3 minutes. Allow the mixture to cool to lukewarm, about 5 to 8 minutes. Place the chilled greens in a heatproof bowl. Pour the dressing over the greens, toss quickly, sprinkle with the reserved bacon, and serve immediately.

Wooden slaw cutters make short work of shredding cabbage

CREAMY COLESLAW WITH BOILED DRESSING

Of all the salads eaten across the United States, coleslaw is the perennial favorite. Cabbage was always an important staple for pioneer cooks, for it kept well into early winter if stored in the cool root cellar, and large amounts of it found its way into kraut. So it was not uncommon to serve coleslaw in some form nearly year-round. Before the days of canned mayonnaise and blenders, slaw was prepared with boiled dressing. Add some carrot and parsley to the cabbage, plus a bit of celery and mustard seed, and this is a fine treat twelve months of the year.

DRESSING	COLESLAW
2 large eggs	6 cups shredded cabbage (about 1¾ pounds)
3 tablespoons sugar	1 large shredded carrot (about ¾ cup)
1½ tablespoons all-purpose flour	1 celery stalk, finely chopped (about ½ cup)
1¼ teaspoons salt	1 small onion, finely chopped (about ¼ cup)
½ teaspoon ground mustard	½ green bell pepper, finely chopped (about ½ cup)
¼ cup cider vinegar	¼ cup minced parsley
¼ cup water	1½ teaspoons celery seed
1 tablespoon butter or olive oil	1 teaspoon mustard seed
3 tablespoons cream or milk	½ teaspoon coarsely ground pepper

In a small saucepan, beat the eggs thoroughly; add the sugar, flour, salt, and mustard. Combine the vinegar and the water and beat into the egg mixture, then add the butter or oil. Cook over low heat, stirring constantly until thick, about 5 to 8 minutes. The mixture will become very lumpy-looking (not to worry); beat it to smoothness. When very thick, remove from the heat and beat in the cream or milk. Cool. (This can be made a day in advance and refrigerated.)

In a large bowl, combine all of the coleslaw ingredients. Add the cooled dressing and toss lightly to coat with the dressing.

NOTE: *If you'd rather not make a boiled dressing, you can make a reasonable substitute by combining 1 cup commercial mayonnaise, ½ cup sugar, and ¼ cup cider vinegar; pour over the slaw ingredients and toss.*

 MAPLE UPSIDE-DOWN CAKE

SERVES 6 TO 8

Every spring in New England, the word goes out: "Sap's running!" At the sugar bush, farmers tap the maple trees and hang buckets on the rough gray-brown trunks to collect the sap. The sap is boiled down for hours in evaporator pans set, ideally, over wood fires; the smoke will flavor the syrup. Thirty gallons of sap make just one gallon of syrup and once the buds on the trees become plump and temperatures remain above freezing at night, the season is over. Be sure to buy enough syrup in season to last you all year. Store it in the refrigerator or freeze it, so you can make this very old-fashioned New England treat anytime. It is not overly sweet, and the cake's texture is a bit coarse, which is quite perfect with the topping.

1 tablespoon butter, at room temperature	**Speck of salt**
3 tablespoons sugar	**½ cup milk**
1 large egg, beaten	**1 cup maple syrup**
1 cup all-purpose flour	**½ cup chopped walnuts**
2 teaspoons baking powder	
½ teaspoon grated nutmeg	**Whipped Cream Topping (page 286)**

Preheat the oven to 400° F. Butter an 8-inch round cake pan.

In a large mixer bowl, combine the butter and sugar and beat for 7 minutes, until light and fluffy. Add the egg and beat 3 minutes longer, or until the batter is lemon colored. In a medium mixing bowl, whisk together the flour, baking powder, nutmeg, and salt. Add the flour mixture to the butter mixture alternately with the milk, beginning and ending with the dry ingredients; blend well.

In a small saucepan, bring the maple syrup to a boil. Pour the syrup into the cake pan, sprinkle in the nuts, then slowly pour the batter over the syrup and nuts, patting it into the pan with a rubber spatula. (If you have trouble with this, don't worry; the cake will bake out to the edges, just as it should.) Bake the cake for 30 minutes, or until it is golden brown and the syrup is bubbling up around the edges. Cool in the pan for 10 minutes, then invert onto a plate. Serve warm with Whipped Cream Topping.

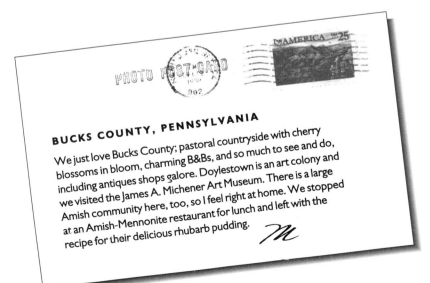

PHOTO POST CARD

AMERICA 25

BUCKS COUNTY, PENNSYLVANIA

We just love Bucks County; pastoral countryside with cherry blossoms in bloom, charming B&Bs, and so much to see and do, including antiques shops galore. Doylestown is an art colony and we visited the James A. Michener Art Museum. There is a large Amish community here, too, so I feel right at home. We stopped at an Amish-Mennonite restaurant for lunch and left with the recipe for their delicious rhubarb pudding.

M

AMISH RHUBARB PUDDING

SERVES 12

*This nostalgic old recipe is a real treat at rhubarb time. A cake batter is spread on the
bottom of a flat deep pan (use one a bit larger than the conventional glass 9 × 13-inch dish—it is too
shallow and the batter runs out into your oven—messy), then chopped rhubarb, sugar, and boiling
water are poured over the batter. During baking, the moist tender cake comes to the top and underneath
remains a lovely pink pudding. And the warm cream sauce really makes this
an unrepentantly good dessert. The cream sauce is also perfect as a gingerbread topping.
This is a typical Amish recipe: just a few
common ingredients, but combined in a different way that makes the dish very special.*

1 large egg	WARM CREAM SAUCE
2½ cups granulated sugar	¾ cup granulated sugar
2 cups all-purpose flour	2 tablespoons all-purpose flour
2 teaspoons baking powder	1 teaspoon grated orange zest
1 teaspoon ground nutmeg	2 cups milk
1 teaspoon vanilla extract	2 tablespoons (¼ stick) butter,
½ teaspoon salt	at room temperature
1 cup milk	1 teaspoon vanilla extract
4 cups finely chopped rhubarb	¼ teaspoon ground nutmeg
2½ cups boiling water	Speck of salt
½ cup packed light brown sugar	
⅛ teaspoon red food coloring	

Preheat the oven to 375° F. Butter a 10 × 14-inch pan.

In a large mixer bowl, slightly beat the egg. Add 1 cup of granulated sugar and combine well. Add the
flour, baking powder, nutmeg, vanilla, salt, and milk; blend. Pour the batter into the pan. Set aside.

In another large bowl, mix together the rhubarb, boiling water, the remaining sugars, and the food coloring. Pour this *over* the batter, making sure the rhubarb is evenly distributed. (Admittedly, it looks like a
rather questionable success here, but not to worry, it comes out all right.)

Bake for 45 to 50 minutes, or until the top is golden brown and bubbly and the cake is done in the center; insert a toothpick—it should come out clean.

Meanwhile, prepare the cream sauce: In a small saucepan over medium-high heat, combine the sugar,
flour, and orange zest. Gradually add the milk, whisking until smooth. Bring the mixture to a boil, then
lower the heat to medium-low and cook for 3 minutes, whisking constantly. Remove the saucepan from
the heat and whisk in the remaining ingredients.

Remove the pudding from the oven and cool to lukewarm. (It can be reheated in the microwave.) Cut
into squares and serve topped with the Warm Cream Sauce.

RHUBARB CUSTARD PIE

MAKES ONE 8-INCH PIE

*Pies were such a culinary staple in Colonial times that early brick ovens were described in
terms of their pie-baking capacity, from a modest ten-pie–size oven up to a colossal twenty-pie oven. Pies were baked
in quantity to last the week, then stored in the cold pantry, or even frozen out in the snow.
In the spring rhubarb pies were popular, for every garden had a rhubarb plant or two in it. Rhubarb
was also one of the cherished plants the pioneer women carried West.
This is a delicate pink custard pie; during baking, the fruit rises to the top, forming a tart layer atop the
smooth custard. This pie can also be made with frozen rhubarb.*

1 cup finely diced rhubarb,	1 cup evaporated milk
fresh or unthawed frozen	1 large egg, beaten
One 8-inch unbaked pie shell (page 284)	Red food coloring (optional)
1 heaping tablespoon all-purpose flour	
1 cup sugar	Garnish: cinnamon or nutmeg

Preheat the oven to 425° F. Place the rhubarb in the pie shell.

In a medium bowl, combine the flour and sugar and gradually stir in the milk. Add the egg and mix with a rotary hand beater or whisk to blend. If desired, add enough food coloring to tint the mixture pale pink and pour it over the rhubarb. Sprinkle the top with either cinnamon or nutmeg. Bake for 15 minutes, then lower the heat to 350° F. and bake 25 minutes longer. Cool completely before cutting.

GOOSEBERRY FOOL

SERVES 6

*Gooseberries are a bit hard to find, but shop around at farmer's markets and have them reserve several quarts
for you; they freeze very well. At our house, we are inordinately fond of them in pie, but gooseberry fool, that ethereal
creamy dessert, is another way I like to prepare these round, firm green berries that turn a bit pink as they ripen.
Fools are old, old desserts, dating back to Shakespeare's time. For another traditional country touch, you can toss in a
few elderberry blooms foraged from a country roadside with the gooseberries while they are cooking.
That is quite optional. And if you don't have gooseberries, you can substitute strawberries, blackberries, or raspberries.*

1 pound ripe gooseberries	1 teaspoon grated orange rind
3 elderberry flower heads (optional)	1½ cups heavy cream
¼ cup water or sweet white wine	
1 cup sugar	Garnish: fresh mint leaves

Top and tail the gooseberries, and rinse them in a colander under running water. Place the berries, the elderberry flowers (if you are using them), and the water or white wine in a heavy saucepan. Cook, uncovered, over low heat until the fruit is very tender and squashy, about 15 minutes. Remove the flower heads and discard.

Add the sugar and orange rind and stir until the sugar has dissolved. Cool the mixture, then transfer to a food processor and process until the gooseberries are pureed. Chill the mixture in the refrigerator.

In a large chilled mixer bowl, whip the cream until thick but not terribly stiff. Fold the cold fruit puree into the whipped cream and transfer either to individual sherbet glasses or a large glass bowl. Garnish with mint leaves just before serving.

BLACK CHERRY COOKIES

MAKES 32 COOKIES

Michigan is the country's number one producer of cherries, and when I was in East Lansing to do a book signing there was a cherry dessert and cookie contest going on.
This was the prize winner, the creation of Dr. Louella Snow, who teaches anthropology at nearby Michigan State University. We met later for dinner and to swap stories and recipes. It seemed to us that an interest in old recipes goes hand in hand with anthropology, and it was a most stimulating evening.
These cookies boast cheese among their ingredients, which gives them a very good flavor and texture.

1½ cups all-purpose flour	**½ cup (1 stick) butter**
1 teaspoon baking powder	**1 cup shredded mild cheddar cheese**
¼ teaspoon salt	**1 cup black cherry jam**
1½ tablespoons dark brown sugar	**½ cup finely chopped toasted**
1½ tablespoons granulated sugar	**walnuts (see Note)**

Preheat the oven to 350° F.

In a medium mixing bowl, whisk together the flour, baking powder, salt, and the sugars. With a pastry blender, cut in the butter until the mixture resembles crumbs. Add the cheese and toss to combine. Remove ¾ cup of the mixture and set aside. Press the remaining mixture evenly into the bottom of a greased 8-inch square baking pan. Spread the jam evenly over the crust. Sprinkle the nuts over the jam and top with the reserved crumb mixture, pressing the crumbs gently into the jam. Bake for 25 to 30 minutes, or until golden. Cool completely in the pan, then cut into 1 × 2-inch bars. Cover with plastic wrap and store in the refrigerator.

N O T E : *To toast walnuts, bake them in a shallow pan at 375° F. for 5 to 6 minutes.*

MAPLE CUSTARD ICE CREAM

SERVES 8

The Indians were gathering maple sap in New England long before the Pilgrims set foot on shore.
They gouged the trees to start the sap running and the liquid drained into buckskin bags attached to the tree.
The bags then were dropped into hot coals to reduce the liquid to syrup.
Today during the "sugaring off" season, plastic tubing is attached to the trees and the sap drains directly
into the sugaring house, where it is evaporated in long pans over wood-stoked fires. Traveling in Vermont in the spring,
one sees steam puffing out of the small shacks on the hillsides, the tubing resembling tentacles as it snakes down
the hill—very twentieth-century. However, this divinely smooth ice cream is not a twentieth-century recipe. Serve it
with a bit more maple syrup poured over the top and add a few chopped toasted pecans.

3 large eggs	1½ cups half-and-half
One 14-ounce can sweetened	¼ teaspoon maple extract
condensed milk	Speck of salt
½ cup maple syrup	2 cups heavy cream

In a heavy saucepan, beat the eggs with the condensed milk and maple syrup; stir in the half-and-half, maple extract, and salt. Over the lowest possible heat and stirring constantly, cook until the mixture thickens, approximately 15 to 20 minutes; watch carefully to make sure it doesn't scorch. Remove from the heat and stir in the cream, then cool to room temperature. Pour into the freezer can of an ice cream maker and process according to the manufacturer's instructions.

NOTE: *See Note on page 97 if using an old-fashioned freezer.*

travel Notes FROM NEW ENGLAND

I am always so pleased to visit New England—the small towns are picturesque and tidy, Boston is brimming with historical associations and stimulating architecture.

I belong to the school that considers New England the cradle of American cookery, and in fact there are those who maintain that our cooking and our taste buds haven't progressed much since the days of the Pilgrims. We are still cooking English food; the folks from the British Isles were our first immigrants and their foodways influence us today. There may be new interpretations as the recipes move across regions and from cook to cook, chef to chef, and that is appropri-

ate; eating the foods indigenous to the regions in which we live is the best of all possible worlds!

Those early colonists didn't understand this when they first reached our shores, and because of their stiff-necked attitudes and just plain helplessness, they nearly perished. Of the hundred worn-out men, women, and children that staggered off the <u>Mayflower</u> in that gray December of 1620, only half lived to see the spring. Inadvertently, they had landed at the wrong place and because the winter season had so far advanced, they had no choice but to stay. They settled at Plymouth, Massachusetts, on the site of a deserted Indian village. Visiting this place today, it is easy to imagine the difficulty of their new life. They learned to cope with the harsh climate and difficult soil, and from that particular crucible of

STRAWBERRY SHORTCAKE, BISCUIT STYLE

SERVES 6

California claims to be the strawberry capital of the world, but many other states (including New York and New Jersey) have large strawberry crops as well. And certainly strawberry shortcake is one of the country's most beloved desserts. These biscuits are good-sized (well, that's all right—one doesn't have shortcake that often!), moist, and rich, with a hint of orange. Try them with fresh peaches and other fresh fruits.

1 cup cake flour	**¼ cup whole milk**
1 cup all-purpose flour	**1 tablespoon grated orange zest**
3 tablespoons sugar	**1 teaspoon vanilla extract**
2 teaspoons cream of tartar	**6 cups cleaned, sweetened, partially**
1 teaspoon baking soda	**crushed strawberries**
½ teaspoon salt	
¼ teaspoon grated nutmeg	**Garnish: Whipped Cream Topping**
½ cup (1 stick) very cold butter	**(page 286) or heavy cream**
½ cup heavy cream	

Preheat the oven to 400° F.

In a large bowl, whisk together the flours, sugar, cream of tartar, soda, salt, and nutmeg. Cut the butter into slices and work it into the flour mixture with a pastry blender until a coarse meal forms. In a medium bowl, combine the cream, milk, orange zest, and vanilla and add all at once to the flour mixture. Combine quickly, forming a stiff dough; don't overwork it.

Turn the dough out onto a lightly floured surface and divide the dough into 6 parts. Flour your hands and quickly form the portions into 3-inch circles ¾ inch thick. Place on an ungreased cookie sheet and bake 12 to 15 minutes, or until the biscuits are a light golden brown. To serve, place in a shallow bowl or deep plate and top with the sweetened berries. Dollop on the Whipped Cream Topping or pass a pitcher of cream.

learning the New England attitude of tenacity, hard work, and "making do" as well as Yankee foodways, evolved.

Finally accepting the Indians' help, and especially with the assistance of one named Squanto (he was the first chef-in-residence), the colonists of Plymouth Rock learned to appreciate the great Indian triad of foods, corn, beans, and squash, that remain favorites in New England today.

However, we must not overlook the bounty of the sea and its relationship to this region's cookery. In Boston, above Faneuil Hall, a weathervane in the shape of the silver codfish turns in the wind, a reminder of this fish's importance to New England; fresh or salted, the cod was the cornerstone of New England's cookery and commerce for years.

Traveling about New England this cool spring, we pass through numerous small towns, their streets abloom with ancient but still fragrant purple lilac trees. At Deerfield, an impeccably restored Colonial village, we are reminded of those brave, determined, badly prepared, and ill-equipped people who first settled our land. These towns, some still surrounded by crumbling stone fences, are tangible reminders of a time when those walls were all that separated wilderness from civilization.

VIOLET SYRUP

MAKES SCANT 1½ CUPS

In the spring in many parts of the country, purple violets carpet our native woodlands; their intensely colored blooms make charming little bouquets. Since they are edible, the blossoms can be scattered over fresh green salads as a garnish. Eating flowers is not a new idea; Native Americans were eating daylily buds a long time before the English arrived, and roses and violets were part of the European diet for centuries before the recent craze for them started here.

Sometimes, just before a party, I dig up whole violet plants and pot them in foil-lined silver bowls; they will wilt in a few hours, however, so this is something that has to be done at the last minute. It's a pity their season is so short, but you can make a beautiful violet syrup that is a very nice accompaniment to rice puddings, Pavlova, or even vanilla ice cream. The syrup will keep up to a month in the refrigerator, or it can be frozen for up to a year. And the best part of this recipe is gathering the violets.

200 spring violets, stems removed	**2 teaspoons fresh lemon juice**
1½ cups distilled water (no substitutes)	**2 cups sugar**

Place the violet blooms in a glass pint jar. In a small saucepan, bring the water to a boil and pour over the violets; cool. Cover and allow the mixture to stand for 24 hours. Strain the violet water solution into a small saucepan and add the lemon juice (this will lighten the color a bit). Add the sugar and boil for 7 minutes, washing down the sides with a wet paper towel wrapped around a wooden spoon handle to prevent sugar crystals from forming during the boiling period.

Pour the hot syrup into a glass jar or container. Cool and refrigerate or freeze until serving time.

HAYMAKERS' SWITCHEL

SERVES 6 TO 8

This is an early Colonial drink, quite common, in fact, and made from ingredients that were easy to come by. It was a beverage to take to the men working in the fields, and to them, a welcome sweet-and-sour refreshment, a seventeenth-century Gatorade, if you will. This recipe also appears in old Santa Fe cookbooks.

1 quart cold water	**½ cup light molasses**
1 cup dark brown sugar	**1 tablespoon ground ginger**
1 cup cider vinegar	

In a large pitcher, combine all the ingredients and stir well. Chill and serve.

Early nineteenth century paste ware

Greet the
MORNING

Until recently a light continental breakfast was never America's style. But now the meal that was once the backbone of our citizenry's workday has evolved into something quickly prepared and consumed on the run. On weekends, however, we are more apt to reinvoke those sustaining meals of yesteryear.

Starting the day with a substantial meal was imperative in the early years of America's history. We read of the earliest cooks preparing simple but filling breakfasts of cornmeal mush sweetened with maple syrup, served in wooden trenchers. In the beginning, eggs were a luxury and meat, generally pork, was carefully rationed. Eventually, as livestock flourished and farms yielded more crops, the settler's breakfast menu improved. Hominy was popular and in the Colonial South breakfasts were ample, even luxurious, beginning with mint juleps and progressing on to ham, eggs, grits, cold turkey, breads of all kinds, tea, coffee, and chocolate.

For the pioneers moving West in the 1800s by prairie schooner—the name given the wagons whose high white canopies resembled a ship sailing through a sea of grass—breakfast was generally a hurried affair of biscuits, cold salt pork from the night before, and coffee. However, during the Victorian period, the emerging upper classes ate sumptuously at breakfast time, as did most farm families, who had a choice of dairy and produce selections right outside their kitchen door. In New Orleans, creole rice fritters called calas were sold on street corners, and in the Southwest, scrambled eggs were rolled in tortillas.

A hearty weekend breakfast (or brunch if you prefer) allows the family, either by themselves or with friends, to come together in a less hurried way than during the week. It is a luxury to have the time to stir up pancakes or fritters and read the paper over innumerable cups of coffee. Perhaps this is the most sustaining aspect of breakfast after all.

Glazed Bacon Bites Broiled Grapefruit Rice Batter Pancakes German Pancake Sourdough Pancakes Cottage Cheese Pancakes Pumpkin Puff Pancakes with Cider Sauce Baked French Toast Casserole Buttermilk Biscuit Sandwich Squares with Scrambled Egg and Bacon Filling Brunch Corned Beef with Orange Sauce Popovers with Mushrooms and Bacon Delicate Corn Fritters Calas Sautéed Chicken Livers with Mushrooms Frizzled Beef Raspberry–Cream Cheese Coffee Cake

LAZED BACON BITES

SERVES 6

This is an unexpected sort of brunch snack, which is very easy to prepare. The bacon
gets quite crisp and rather caramelized at the same time. The sweetness and crunchiness of the pork
provides a nice contrast with Bloody Marys. The total baking time is 25 minutes.

½ **pound thickly sliced bacon**	1 **tablespoon German-style**
(approximately 9 slices)	**grainy mustard**
½ **cup packed light brown sugar**	2 **tablespoons orange juice**

Preheat the oven to 350° F. Place the bacon strips in a single layer on a foil-lined jelly roll pan. Bake the bacon for 10 minutes.

Meanwhile, in a small bowl, combine the sugar, mustard, and orange juice; set aside.

Remove the bacon from the oven and drain off the fat. Push the slices together (they will have shrunk) and with a teaspoon, spread half the glaze over the bacon. Return the bacon to the oven and bake 5 minutes longer. Turn the bacon strips, cover with the remaining glaze, and bake 10 minutes longer. Transfer the strips to wax paper. Cool slightly and with a scissors, cut each strip into thirds. Serve warm or cooled.

ROILED GRAPEFRUIT

SERVES 4

This is the one of the quickest and most stylish ways to prepare breakfast grapefruit-
it's rather like a grapefruit brûlée. The fruit can be prepared the night before (for this takes a while),
tightly wrapped with plastic wrap, and refrigerated. Put the sugar topping on just before broiling.
This is my father's recipe; he was an excellent cook and he always prepared this for holiday breakfasts.
At our house, it is still a Christmas morning tradition.

2 **large pink grapefruits, halved**	**Butter**
4 **to** 6 **generous tablespoons**	**Ground cinnamon**
dark brown sugar	

Preheat the broiler, placing the broiler pan as high as it will go. With a grapefruit knife, cut the grapefruits into segments, then detach the segments from the membrane, discarding the membrane and leaving the grapefruit in the shells. Sprinkle each grapefruit half with brown sugar, top with bits of butter and with cinnamon.

Place the fruit on a foil-lined jelly roll pan (juices will run out) and broil about 2 inches from the heat until the grapefruits are browned and bubbly, about 3 to 5 minutes. Transfer to serving bowls or footed compotes and serve immediately.

RICE BATTER PANCAKES

MAKES TWELVE 3-INCH PANCAKES, OR 4 SERVINGS

*As soon as the rice industry began to flourish in the South, New Englanders happily
added this grain to their diet, though it never replaced corn in their affections. However, these rice pancakes
are hard to beat. They are pale golden and delicately flavored, with a firm texture. Serve
them with thickly sliced bacon on a lazy Sunday morning for a substantial meal that will last you all day.*

¾ cup all-purpose flour
2 teaspoons baking powder
1 teaspoon salt
1 large egg
½ cup milk
1 tablespoon honey

1 cup cooked rice
1 teaspoon butter, melted
Vegetable oil for frying
 (I prefer corn oil for this)

Butter, maple syrup, or sorghum

Preheat a griddle or electric skillet to 375° F.

In a small mixing bowl, whisk together the flour, baking powder, and salt. In a medium mixing bowl,
beat the egg; add the milk and honey, mixing well. By hand, gently blend in the flour mixture, then gradually add the rice and butter; don't overbeat.

Add about 2 teaspoons of oil to the skillet and when hot, drop the batter into the oil by tablespoons.
When the cakes are golden brown on one side and bubbles begin to form on top, about 3 to 5 minutes,
use a metal spatula to turn the cake over and fry until the other side is golden, about 2 minutes. Transfer
to a heated platter and place in a warm (200° F.) oven; continue frying until all the batter is used. Serve
with butter, maple syrup, or sorghum.

GERMAN PANCAKE

(ABENKATER)

SERVES 6

*More than any other group save the English, the German immigrants have left their
mark on American cookery. In the 1800s, German communities sprang up all over the Midwest, the South,
and even in Texas. Their foods were satisfying and practical.
I first ate this puffy, bacon-topped pancake in Circleville, Ohio; the hostess has German antecedents and is
working on her own family cookbook. I especially like this dish because it is a total breakfast in
one skillet. It falls the minute you cut into it like a giant popover, so serve it immediately. I like to serve it
topped with thick fruit toppings; Knudsen makes really good ones that taste homemade.*

4 large eggs, at room temperature
1 cup milk, at room temperature
1 teaspoon vanilla extract
1 cup all-purpose flour

1 teaspoon salt
6 strips of bacon or turkey bacon

Maple syrup or pourable fruit topping

Preheat the oven to 375° F.

In a large mixing bowl, beat the eggs thoroughly (I use an electric hand mixer), add ½ cup of the milk and the vanilla, then beat in the flour and salt, and finally the remaining milk.

Pour the batter into a greased 8-inch square pan and place the bacon strips on top of the batter. Bake for 45 to 60 minutes, or until the top is golden brown and puffy. Cut in 6 pieces and serve immediately with maple syrup or fruit topping.

Sourdough Pancakes

MAKES TEN 4- TO 5-INCH PANCAKES, OR 3 TO 4 SERVINGS

I've prepared many a pancake in my time, but I do believe these are the best! Puffy, golden, and quite high, they have the texture of a cake and a pronounced yeast flavor. They are good enough for company, so I hope you'll serve them to your best friends.
But first, you must make the starter, so plan a week in advance for this and then mix up part of the batter the night before. You'll agree, these pancakes are worth the extra effort of making the starter. However, after the starter is going, these are very quick to prepare, and I often serve them as an emergency lunch or Sunday night supper.

1 cup unbleached all-purpose flour
1 cup sourdough starter (page 126)
½ cup milk
1 large egg, beaten
1 tablespoon sugar
2 tablespoons vegetable oil

1½ teaspoons baking powder
½ teaspoon salt
¼ to ½ teaspoon baking soda
   (depending on the sourness of the starter)

Butter and maple syrup

The night before serving, in a large bowl (not metal) whisk together the flour, starter, and milk. Cover loosely with plastic wrap and allow to stand unrefrigerated at least 12 hours.

When ready to fry the pancakes, preheat a griddle or a 10- or 12-inch electric fry pan to 375° F. In a small bowl, beat the egg and whisk in the sugar, oil, baking powder, salt, and soda. Add to the starter mixture and whisk until smooth. The batter will be very springy and light.

Generously grease the griddle with oil or bacon fat. Pour the batter in ⅓-cup portions onto the griddle or pan, spacing about 1½ inches apart (a 12-inch skillet will hold 3 cakes). Cook until bubbles form on top of the pancakes and the bottoms are browned, about 1 minute. Turn with a wide spatula; cook until brown on the bottom, about 1 minute longer. Serve hot with butter and maple syrup.

Cottage Cheese Pancakes

*Every culture has its own version of pancakes, ranging from Jewish blintzes to palacintas,
the thin Hungarian pancake that is served for dessert or as an entrée, depending on its filling. In America, we call
them griddle cakes, flannel cakes, hoecakes, flapjacks, and so on. Most of us associate them with
breakfast, and a plate of golden griddle cakes is a special way to begin a day. The following recipe is Mormon
and very, very good. Serve it with sausage or bacon and fruit or maple syrup.*

¾ cup all-purpose flour

2 tablespoons wheat germ

½ teaspoon baking soda

½ teaspoon salt

½ cup plus 1 ½ tablespoons
    sour cream

3 tablespoons milk or more

2 large eggs

½ cup small curd cottage cheese

Vegetable oil for frying

Maple syrup and butter

In a small bowl, whisk together the flour, wheat germ, soda, and salt. Spoon the sour cream into a 1-cup
glass measuring cup and add 3 tablespoons of milk, or enough to make ¾ cup of thinned sour cream. In a
large mixing bowl, beat the eggs until frothy, then whisk in the cottage cheese and thinned sour cream
until well blended. Add the dry ingredients gradually, combining by hand with a large spoon.

    Preheat an electric fry pan to 325° F. Lightly grease the bottom of the skillet with oil. Pour the batter by
heaping ⅛ cupfuls onto the hot skillet, spreading each one out thinly. Fry the pancakes until they are gold-
en brown underneath and just starting to bubble, about 3 minutes, then turn and fry the other side until
golden, about 2 minutes. Serve warm with maple syrup and butter.

NEWBURYPORT, MASSACHUSETTS

This was the home of author John P. Marquand, who said of
Newburyport, "It is not a museum piece, although it sometimes
looks like it." American Federalist houses abound, built by affluent
shipowners and sea captains. Built at the mouth of the Merrimack
River, there are good antiques shops, bookstores, excellent small
restaurants, and an exceptional breakfast place, Ann's Bakery,
where the menu boasts an extraordinary selection of pancakes.

PUMPKIN PUFF PANCAKES WITH CIDER SAUCE

SERVES 4

Pumpkin was a most important crop for the Indians and early settlers alike.
In New England especially, we find many recipes using this subtly flavored vegetable in dishes other than pie.
These light puffy pancakes, faintly orange, are enhanced by an aromatic cider sauce.
It's a delightfully new brunch dish; serve it with Brunch Corned Beef with Orange Sauce (page 29).

CIDER SAUCE

¾ cup cider or apple juice
½ cup packed light brown sugar
½ cup light corn syrup
2 tablespoons (¼ stick) butter
1 teaspoon fresh lemon juice
¼ teaspoon ground cinnamon
⅛ teaspoon ground nutmeg

PANCAKES

1 cup sifted all-purpose flour
1 tablespoon granulated sugar
2 teaspoons baking powder
½ teaspoon salt
½ teaspoon ground cinnamon
2 large eggs, separated
1 cup milk
½ cup canned pumpkin
2 tablespoons (¼ stick)
  butter, melted

A small amount of vegetable oil
  for frying

In a medium saucepan, combine all of the cider sauce ingredients and bring to a boil. Lower the heat to low and simmer, uncovered, for 12 to 15 minutes. Keep warm until ready to serve.

Preheat a griddle or fry pan to 360° F. Into a medium bowl, sift together the flour, sugar, baking powder, salt, and cinnamon. In a large bowl, beat the egg yolks and add the milk, pumpkin, and butter. Add the dry ingredients all at once, stirring just until the flour is moistened. In a separate bowl, beat the egg whites until stiff, then fold them gently into the flour mixture.

Add a little bit of oil to the skillet. Using about ⅓ cup of batter for each pancake, cook 4 cakes at a time. When holes appear on top of the pancake, turn and cook on the other side until golden brown.

BAKED FRENCH TOAST CASSEROLE

SERVES 6 TO 8

*Most of us have grown up eating French toast for breakast, not knowing it
has a fine history. It does indeed come to us from the French, who called it pain perdu, or lost bread.
But the English can also lay claim to French toast, which they know as poor knights of
Windsor. In medieval England, one of the differences between gentry and common folk was that gentry served
dessert at dinner. Now, knights were gentry, but not all knights were rich. Those who couldn't afford
to serve dessert would serve a version of this recipe with jam, keeping their status intact.
This version will enhance any cook's status—a baked puffy French toast with a praline glaze, it is out of this world,
and being able to make it the day before gives it extra marks in my book. This is the ultimate brunch dish.*

1 loaf of French bread (13 to 16 ounces)
8 large eggs
2 cups half-and-half
1 cup milk
2 tablespoons granulated sugar
1 teaspoon vanilla extract
¼ teaspoon ground cinnamon
¼ teaspoon ground nutmeg
Speck of salt

PRALINE TOPPING
1 cup (2 sticks) butter, at room temperature
1 cup packed light brown sugar
1 cup chopped pecans
2 tablespoons light corn syrup
½ teaspoon ground cinnamon
½ teaspoon ground nutmeg

Maple syrup or honey

Slice the French bread into twenty 1-inch slices. (Use any extra bread for garlic toast or crumbs.) Arrange the slices in a generously buttered 9 × 13-inch flat baking dish in 2 rows, overlapping the slices. In a large bowl, combine the eggs, half-and-half, milk, sugar, vanilla, cinnamon, nutmeg, and salt and beat with a rotary beater or whisk until blended but not too bubbly. Pour over the bread slices, making sure all are covered evenly with the milk-egg mixture, spooning some of the mixture in between the slices too. Cover with foil and refrigerate overnight.

The next day, preheat the oven to 350° F.

Combine the praline topping ingredients in a medium bowl and spread it evenly over the bread. Bake for 40 minutes, until puffed and lightly golden. Serve with maple syrup or honey.

Hand-wrought wire egg basket

ℬUTTERMILK BISCUIT SANDWICH SQUARES WITH SCRAMBLED EGG AND BACON FILLING

SERVES 9

Have houseguests and need a breakfast dish that won't take a lot of time and dishes? This egg sandwich fills the bill. Made in advance and frozen, then reheated, it is practically a one-dish meal, instantly produced. Your family will appreciate it too. Serve a platter of these with a choice of assorted juices and/or a bowl of fresh fruit and coffee, and everyone will be fed and you'll be out of the kitchen in no time. Fry the bacon and make the biscuits in advance to speed up preparation. The eggs can be fried singly or 3 at a time, then cut in 3 wedges.

BISCUITS
2 cups all-purpose flour or more
3 tablespoons dry
   powdered buttermilk
2 teaspoons baking powder
2 teaspoons sugar
½ teaspoon baking soda
1 teaspoon salt
⅓ cup vegetable shortening
1 cup water

FILLING
9 large eggs
Finely minced parsley
Salt and pepper to taste
Hot red pepper sauce
1½ teaspoons vegetable oil
   for frying each egg
9 slices fried or baked bacon,
   halved and set aside

Preheat the oven to 450° F.

In a large mixer bowl, mix together the flour, powdered buttermilk, baking powder, sugar, soda, and salt. With a pastry blender, cut in the shortening until the mixture resembles cornmeal. Add the water and mix until the dough leaves the sides of the bowl and forms a ball. Add a bit more flour if necessary, but do not overmix. Turn the dough onto a lightly floured surface and knead lightly for about 30 seconds (20 to 25 times). If the dough is still too sticky, sprinkle on a tiny bit more flour. Roll the dough into a ½-inch-thick 9 × 9-inch rectangle and transfer to an ungreased cookie sheet. Cut into three 3-inch rectangles and bake for 8 to 10 minutes, or until the biscuits are golden brown. Remove from the oven and allow the biscuits to cool completely, about 20 minutes. Slice each biscuit in half horizontally with a serrated knife.

Prepare the filling: In a small bowl, with a fork, lightly combine 1 egg, a bit of parsley, a speck of salt and pepper, and a tiny dash of hot red pepper sauce. In a small heavy skillet, melt the butter over medium heat. Pour in the egg; cook stirring lightly. Flip the egg over with a spatula and cook the other side. Fold the cooked egg to fit in a biscuit (this doesn't have to be perfect) and transfer to a biscuit half; add 2 pieces of bacon and top with the remaining biscuit half. Repeat until the biscuits are all filled. These can be eaten immediately or cooled, then freezer wrapped and reheated later in the microwave for 2 minutes on High.

ℬRUNCH CORNED BEEF WITH ORANGE SAUCE

SERVES 8

I think the brisket cut of beef is too frequently overlooked. It has so much flavor, can be cooked in advance and reheated, and combines well with so many menus. The early settlers valued it, and it was one of their favored cuts for brining or corning. This recipe evolved in my own kitchen when I was looking for a meat dish to serve with the Baked French Toast Casserole (page 26); it is a perfect accompaniment.

One 4- to 5-pound piece of
   corned beef
½ teaspoon dried rosemary
1 bay leaf
6 whole cloves
1 medium onion, cut into chunks
2 celery stalks, cut into chunks
½ orange, unpeeled,
   cut into chunks

SAUCE
One 16-ounce can low-salt chicken broth
½ cup fresh lemon juice
   (approximately 4 large lemons)
½ cup fresh orange juice
   (approximately 1 large orange)
¼ cup (½ stick) butter
1 tablespoon sugar
Salt and freshly ground pepper to taste

Garnish: chopped chervil or parsley

In a large stockpot, combine the beef, rosemary, bay leaf, cloves, onion, celery, and orange and cover with warm water. Bring the liquid to a boil and simmer the beef, covered, over medium-low heat for 40 minutes per pound, approximately 2½ hours. The meat should be tender but not falling apart.

Remove the beef from the broth, cover, and cool. Refrigerate overnight. When the meat is cold, slice it very thinly and arrange it in overlapping slices in a 9 × 13-inch serving dish. Cover and refrigerate.

Make the sauce: In a medium saucepan, reduce the chicken broth over medium-high heat, uncovered, to ½ cup, about 20 to 25 minutes. Add the fruit juices and butter. Continue simmering until the sauce is thick enough to coat a spoon, about 5 more minutes. Stir in the sugar and add the salt and pepper. The sauce can be refrigerated at this point.

About 45 minutes before serving, preheat the oven to 350° F. Pour the sauce over the sliced beef and bake, covered, for 25 to 30 minutes, or until heated through. Sprinkle with the chervil or parsley and serve warm.

POPOVERS WITH MUSHROOMS AND BACON

SERVES 8

Really innovative brunch recipes are hard to come by, and we keep serving the same old thing.
This recipe, however, is a standout—tall, golden-brown, old-fashioned popovers filled with a well-seasoned mushroom
and bacon filling. Popovers deserve to be more popular—they are dramatic, quick to prepare, and low in fat.
The mushroom and bacon mixture with its hint of savory can be made in advance so
there is really not a lot to do the day of serving.
This recipe is from Philadelphia, a great food town. One of my viewers, Hilda Lodge, sent it to me, with the note that
mushrooms are highly prized in that city since there is a large mushroom farm in the area at Kennett Square.

FILLING
1 pound thickly sliced bacon,
   cut into 1-inch pieces
¼ cup (½ stick) butter
1 medium onion, finely chopped
1½ pounds mushrooms,
   including stems, thinly sliced
¾ teaspoon dried savory
   or 2 teaspoons minced fresh
½ cup chopped parsley
3 tablespoons chopped red pimiento

4 shakes of hot red pepper sauce
Salt and pepper to taste

POPOVERS
4½ teaspoons vegetable oil
1¼ cups milk, at room temperature
1¼ cups all-purpose flour
¾ teaspoon salt
⅛ teaspoon ground red pepper
3 jumbo eggs, at room temperature

Make the filling: In a 10-inch skillet or sauté pan, cook the bacon over medium heat until it is crisp, about 10 minutes. With a slotted spoon, remove the bacon and drain on paper towels; set aside.

Discard all but a tablespoon or so of the bacon fat, add the butter and onions to the skillet, and cook over medium-high heat until the onions begin to brown, about 5 minutes. Add the mushrooms and sauté until they begin to brown and all the liquid has evaporated, about 10 minutes, stirring in the savory for the last couple of minutes. Remove from the heat and add the parsley, pimiento, and seasonings. Set aside or refrigerate, still keeping the bacon separate.

Make the popovers: Preheat the oven to 450° F. Put ½ teaspoon vegetable oil in each of 9 sections of a muffin tin. Place the tin in the oven and heat until very hot, about 3 to 5 minutes.

Place the milk, flour, salt, red pepper, and eggs in a food processor bowl and process for 20 seconds. Scrape down the sides of the bowl and process 5 seconds longer. Remove the hot muffin tins from the oven and with a half-cup measuring cup, pour the batter into the heated tins, filling them about two-thirds full. Bake the popovers until crisp and browned, about 25 minutes. Don't open the oven door during this period. Meanwhile, reheat the mushroom mixture (this can be done in the microwave) and just before serving time, fold in the reserved bacon.

To serve, the minute you take the popovers from the oven, transfer them from the tin to serving plates. Make a well in the center of each popover by slitting open the top. Fill the depression liberally with the mushroom mixture and serve immediately.

NOTE: *If perchance the popovers have to wait a few minutes, turn off the oven, open the door completely, and let them cool gradually. They will not fall as soon. Also, this recipe makes 9 popovers, giving you leeway for one to be a flop, which one probably will.*

DELICATE CORN FRITTERS
SERVES 4

Author Edith Wharton was considered an impeccable hostess and entertained with great style.
She came from a privileged New York background, and had the opportunity to observe how to run a household
properly. In her autobiography, A Backward Glance, *she writes of the cooks who worked in the*
family kitchen: "Ah, what artists they were . . . who will ever again taste anything in the whole range of
gastronomy to equal their corned beef, their boiled turkeys with stewed celery and oyster sauce,
their fried chicken, corn fritters, stewed tomatoes, rice griddle cakes, strawberry shortcake, and vanilla ices?"
I do think this recipe for corn fritters would equal those of her memories.

Vegetable oil for deep-frying	**2 teaspoons baking powder**
2 large eggs, slightly beaten	**1½ cups all-purpose flour**
¼ teaspoon salt	**Confectioners' sugar for dusting**
⅛ teaspoon white pepper	
One 16-ounce can cream-style corn	**Maple syrup**

Preheat the oil to 350° F. in a deep fryer or a deep electric skillet. There should be at least 2 inches of oil.
In a large bowl, beat the eggs, salt, and pepper together. Add the corn and blend thoroughly. Add the
baking powder and flour, but do not overstir; some of the flour should be visible. Drop the batter by
tablespoons into the hot oil and fry for 2 to 3 minutes on each side, or until a light brown. Drain on paper
towels and sprinkle immediately with sifted confectioners' sugar. Serve with warmed maple syrup.

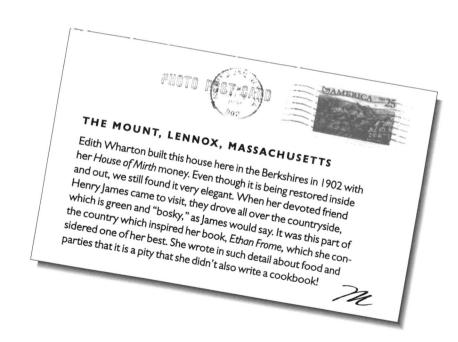

THE MOUNT, LENNOX, MASSACHUSETTS

Edith Wharton built this house here in the Berkshires in 1902 with her *House of Mirth* money. Even though it is being restored inside and out, we still found it very elegant. When her devoted friend Henry James came to visit, they drove all over the countryside, which is green and "bosky," as James would say. It was this part of the country which inspired her book, *Ethan Frome*, which she considered one of her best. She wrote in such detail about food and parties that it is a pity that she didn't also write a cookbook!

Calas

(CREOLE RICE FRITTERS)

MAKES 34 TO 36 CALAS, OR 6 SERVINGS

When discussing the cookery of New Orleans, we hear a lot about beignets, the rectangular powdered
doughnuts traditionally served with café au lait, but a fritter I find more interesting is the calas. The name is thought
to have come from the African word for rice, and years ago these deep-fried rice fritters were
sold by African-American women to churchgoers in the French Quarter to take home for their breakfast. I was
delighted to come upon this easy recipe when we were on our New Orleans jaunt.
This is a very delicate yellow cakelike fritter, and the unexpected texture of the rice makes it very unusual.

Peanut oil for frying	**½ cup plus 2 tablespoons**
2 cups cold cooked rice	**all-purpose flour**
3 large eggs, well beaten	**3 teaspoons baking powder**
¼ teaspoon vanilla extract	
½ teaspoon grated nutmeg	**Garnish: confectioners'**
½ cup granulated sugar	**sugar for dusting**
¾ teaspoon salt	

Preheat at least 2 inches of oil in an electric skillet to 375° F.

In a large mixing bowl, combine the rice, eggs, vanilla, and nutmeg; mix well. In a small mixing bowl, whisk together the sugar, salt, flour, and baking powder; stir into the rice mixture. Drop level tablespoonfuls of the batter into the hot oil and fry until golden brown, about 1 minute on one side; turn over and brown 1 minute longer. Drain on paper towels, then sprinkle with confectioners' sugar and serve hot.

travel Notes FROM THE MID-ATLANTIC

We leave New England quite reluctantly; we could have managed to eat more lobster, I think, and I was sorry I didn't get to see poet May Sarton while in Maine. (She was in Boston, giving a lecture.) Nonetheless, New York City beckons; that place where everything happens first—in food, fashion, art, business, theater, publishing—has always seduced us.

New York City deserves to be designated its own region. Nowhere else in the United States can one find such a glorious assortment of ethnic traditions and ingredients. I tend to forget that Manhattan is an island, and not a big one at that. But from the beginning, whatever happened here in the food world was a harbinger of what the rest of the country would be copying within the year. The Dutch and English settlers who lived here

Sautéed Chicken Livers with Mushrooms

SERVES 4

A special treat for brunch is this savory chicken liver sauté; it can be served with scrambled eggs or over lemon rice or buttered fine noodles. It is a dusky brown dish, so garnish it liberally with minced parsley or chervil.

¼ cup (½ stick) butter or vegetable oil
1 large onion, coarsely chopped
1 pound fresh mushrooms,
    coarsely sliced
1 pound chicken livers, fat and
    connective membranes trimmed away,
    rinsed and drained in a colander

⅓ cup dry sherry
¼ rounded teaspoon dried thyme, or
    2 teaspoons minced fresh
Dash of hot red pepper sauce
Salt and pepper to taste
¼ cup minced fresh parsley or chervil

In a large skillet, heat 2 tablespoons of butter or oil over medium heat; add the onions and mushrooms and sauté until the mushrooms begin to brown and all of their liquid has evaporated, about 10 to 15 minutes. Remove the mushroom mixture from the skillet with a slotted spoon to a medium bowl; set aside.

In the same skillet, heat the remaining butter or oil, add the chicken livers, and brown over medium heat, turning once, cooking about 5 minutes on each side. Return the mushroom-onion mixture to the skillet, then add the sherry, thyme, hot red pepper sauce, and salt and pepper. Simmer over medium-low heat about 5 minutes to blend the flavors and cook off the alcohol. Remove from the heat and stir in the parsley or chervil. Serve immediately, or transfer the mixture to a serving dish and keep hot in a warm oven.

enjoyed local fish, oysters, and pork from the hogs that might often be seen in the gutters on Broadway. By 1800, this little harbor community of 4,000 people growing vegetables and sheltering chickens in their backyards had swelled to a metropolis of 60,000 inhabitants. Among this swelling population was a burgeoning class of affluent professionals who began to patronize restaurants serving food more attuned to their rising position in society. Today restaurants represent one of the city's most thriving industries.

After three days in Manhattan, seeing two plays, going to four art museums, racing through several department stores, and sampling the best of the ethnic restaurants (we can mostly thank the immigrants who flowed into New York City through Ellis Island for that), we headed for Baltimore.

FRIZZLED BEEF

SERVES 6

*Dried beef has saved many a pioneer and cowboy along the way, and some
soldiers, too (not to mention tourists). It never goes out of style.*

6 tablespoons (¾ stick) butter

5 ounces dried beef, julienned

3 tablespoons minced onion

7 tablespoons all-purpose flour

4 cups milk

¾ cup grated sharp cheddar
 or Colby cheese

⅛ teaspoon ground white pepper

3 shakes of hot red pepper sauce

6 English muffins or biscuits

In a sauté pan, melt the butter over medium heat, add the beef and onion, and sauté until the onion begins to color, about 5 minutes. Sprinkle in the flour, lower the heat slightly, and continue to cook, stirring frequently, for another 5 minutes, or until you can see the fat and flour bubbling on the meat.

   Add the milk all at once, turn the heat up to medium-high, and cook and stir for another 8 minutes, or until the mixture is thickened. Sprinkle in the cheese and add the pepper and hot red pepper sauce. Serve hot over toasted English muffins or biscuits.

PHOTO POST CARD

AMERICA 25

PHELPS MANSION INN, NEWBURGH, INDIANA

When Mary Ann and Walter Norton returned from a sojourn in Saudi Arabia, the Midwest and its changing seasons looked especially good to them. Mary Ann fell in love with this handsome Georgian house, and was determined to make it into a bed and breakfast. The inn has become a destination spot, handsomely decorated with furnishings from Arabia, India, and Africa, plus a smattering of antiques. We were cosseted from the time we arrived, and the next morning, there was an outstanding breakfast, which included "frizzled" beef in a rich cheese sauce.

RASPBERRY–CREAM CHEESE COFFEE CAKE

SERVES 8 TO 10

*Bed-and-breakfast establishments are a relatively new thing in the Midwest, but the concept
is booming. Nestled in twenty-six acres of fruit trees is the Apple Orchard Inn in Missouri Valley, a pretty spot with
a 1930s decor. One of the special treats on their breakfast table is this outstanding coffee cake with
a cream cheese and raspberry jam topping. It's quite irresistible.*

2¼ cups all-purpose flour
1 cup sugar
½ cup plus 2 tablespoons (1¼ sticks)
   unsalted butter, at room temperature
½ teaspoon baking powder
½ teaspoon baking soda
¼ teaspoon salt

¾ cup sour cream
1 teaspoon almond extract
2 large eggs
One 8-ounce package cream cheese, softened
½ cup raspberry preserves
½ cup sliced almonds

Preheat the oven to 350° F. Grease and flour the bottom and sides of a 9-inch springform pan.

In a large bowl, combine the flour and ¾ cup of the sugar. Using a pastry blender or fork, cut in the butter until the mixture resembles coarse crumbs. Reserve 1 cup and set aside.

To the remaining crumb mixture, add the baking powder, soda, salt, sour cream, almond extract, and 1 egg. Blend well. With oiled hands, gently pat the dough over the bottom and 1½ inches up the sides of the springform pan; the mixture will be a little sticky.

In a small bowl, combine the cream cheese, the remaining ¼ cup sugar, and 1 egg. Blend well. Pour into the batter-lined pan. In a small saucepan, warm the preserves. Carefully spoon the preserves evenly over the cream cheese mixture. Stir the sliced almonds into the reserved crumb mixture and sprinkle over the preserves. Bake for 45 to 55 minutes, or until the cream cheese filling is set and the crust is deep golden brown. Cool on a rack for 15 minutes, then remove from the pan. The cake can be served warm or cool, but it should be stored in the refrigerator.

Mother's Day
TEA

HENRY JAMES, the former Bostonian-turned-Englishman, observed, "There are few hours in life more agreeable than the hours dedicated to the ceremony known as afternoon tea." I agree with him wholeheartedly, and entertaining with tea, little sandwiches, some sweets, and sherry is a very civilized way to bring people together for companionship and conversation. For a time, in Colonial America, teatime was fashionable in wealthy families, and men and women alike enjoyed "a dish of tea" in the parlor. In recent years our interest in serving tea has been revived, although in the Midwest and the South it has remained a popular way to entertain since Victorian times.

And what could be nicer than having a tea to honor one's mother on her special day? In this country, Julia Ward Howe was the first to suggest designating a day to honor mothers in 1872, and for several years she held an annual Mother's Day meeting in Boston. Other leaders around the country began promoting the celebration, and in 1912, the General Conference of the Methodist Episcopal Church in Minneapolis also endorsed it. Finally, in 1914, President Woodrow Wilson signed a joint resolution of Congress recommending the government observe Mother's Day on the second Sunday of May on an annual basis. The day is observed in a multitude of different ways. A gift or breakfast in bed are traditional in many homes, and at the little Methodist church where I attended Sunday school, it was the custom for the women who had living mothers to wear colored carnations; if one's mother was deceased, a white carnation was worn. A reception honoring the mothers followed the service.

Teas can be simple or elaborate, and now that we are offering tea more often, we see a reemergence of some of the enticing older recipes that have long been gone from our cookbooks. While tea may not be a tradition in your home, once you (and your mother) have enjoyed its genteel pleasures, it will become one.

The Ubiquitous English Nonsoggy Cucumber Sandwich *Cream* Cheese and Walnut Sandwiches
Salmon Paste for Tea Sandwiches or Canapés *Mexican* Sandwiches *Mini* Crab Cakes
Minced Ham Hors d'Oeuvre *Irish* Buttermilk Scones *Clotted* Cream *Lemon* Cream Puffs with
Apricot Sauce *Onion*-Cheese Loaves *Melting* Moments Cookies *Transparent* Puddings

THE UBIQUITOUS ENGLISH NONSOGGY CUCUMBER SANDWICH

SERVES 5 TO 6

You can't have a real tea without cucumber sandwiches! Even Algernon in Oscar Wilde's The Importance of Being Earnest *knew that. The best ones I have ever eaten were served at an afternoon tea in Stratford, Ontario. The hostess did not use a recipe but described to me how she prepared them. This is her method; the seasoned butter and marinated cucumber slices give this tea sandwich added zip.*

FILLING
1 cucumber, peeled
Salt
1 tablespoon olive oil
1 tablespoon fresh lemon juice
Scant teaspoon sugar
Pinch of white pepper

SEASONED BUTTER
½ cup (1 stick) or more butter,
    at room temperature
½ teaspoon Dijon mustard
Juice of ½ lemon
Salt
White pepper

20 slices of thin white bread,
    crusts removed

Two hours in advance, slice the cucumber as thinly as possible. Very lightly salt the slices and transfer them to a colander. Place a plate on top of the cucumbers and weigh down the plate (a can of tomatoes works well). Press the plate periodically to squeeze out the excess juices.

In a medium bowl, combine the oil, lemon juice, sugar, and pepper. Add the well-drained cucumbers and toss. Set aside.

In a small bowl, cream the butter with the mustard, lemon juice, and a dash of salt and pepper. Spread the bread rather lavishly with the butter mixture.

Drain the cucumbers on paper towels. Arrange the cucumbers on top of 10 slices of the bread; top with the remaining 10 slices. Cut each sandwich into 3 finger sandwiches or 4 squares. If not serving immediately, cover lightly with a tea towel dipped in water and very thoroughly wrung out, then cover all with plastic wrap and refrigerate.

Victorian tea strainer and dessert forks

CREAM CHEESE AND WALNUT SANDWICHES
SERVES 10 TO 12

*Old cookbooks are a treasure trove of recipes like this one, intended especially for teas. I might
add, it makes a good lunch sandwich too. When planning tea parties, allow 3 to 4 finger sandwiches per person.*

12 ounces cream cheese, softened
½ cup ground toasted walnuts (see Note)
2 tablespoons finely minced parsley
1 tablespoon finely minced green pepper
1 tablespoon finely minced onion
1 teaspoon fresh lemon juice

¼ teaspoon grated nutmeg (or more to taste)
Salt and white pepper to taste

24 slices of very thin white bread,
   crusts removed
Softened butter

In a mixer bowl, beat the cream cheese, walnuts, parsley, green pepper, onion, lemon juice, nutmeg, and
salt and pepper together until well blended. Spread each piece of bread lightly with butter. Top the buttered side of 12 pieces of the bread with some of the cream cheese mixture, and top with the remaining
slices, buttered side down. Cut into triangles or long finger sandwiches. If not serving immediately, cover
lightly with a tea towel dipped in water and very thoroughly wrung out, then cover all with plastic wrap
and refrigerate.

NOTE: *To toast walnuts, bake them in a shallow pan at 375° F. for 5 to 6 minutes.*

SALMON PASTE FOR TEA SANDWICHES OR CANAPÉS
SERVES 6 TO 8

*This old Victorian recipe is surprisingly easy to prepare and, spread between pieces of thin rye bread,
is very pleasing when combined with sandwiches made of white bread. A well-seasoned mixture of cream cheese,
red salmon, and seasonings, including chopped stuffed olives, this filling can be used any number of ways—
pipe it into endive leaves, onto cucumber slices, or serve it as a dip with crackers.*

8 ounces cream cheese, softened
One 8-ounce can red salmon, drained,
   skin and bones removed
2 tablespoons minced onion
2 tablespoons finely chopped
   stuffed olives
1 tablespoon finely minced parsley
2 teaspoons fresh lemon juice

1 teaspoon Worcestershire sauce
½ teaspoon dried tarragon or
   2 teaspoons minced fresh

Softened butter
24 slices of very thin dark bread,
   crusts removed

In a large mixer bowl, combine all of the ingredients except the butter and bread until well blended.
Transfer to a pint container, cover, and refrigerate until needed.

Spread the butter on one side of each piece of bread. Spread the buttered side of 12 slices with some of the salmon mixture, and top with the remaining slices, buttered side down. Cut into triangles or long finger sandwiches. Serve immediately or cover tightly with a tea towel well dampened in water and very thoroughly wrung out, then cover all with plastic wrap and refrigerate.

MEXICAN SANDWICHES

SERVES 10 TO 12

When I first married and moved to a small town to live, I was occasionally asked to substitute at my mother-in-law's bridge club. The quality of the bridge playing was outstanding and the food they always served at the end of the evening was too. One of the hostesses, Willa Wagoner, was always requested to make her "Mexican" sandwiches when we went to her house. This was long before southwestern or Mexican food was on the scene, and as I view this recipe today, I can see there is nothing Mexican about it at all. It is seasoned with a lot of red pepper, so maybe that is why it was so inappropriately named.

The original recipe called for bacon and that did make a smooth, unctuous filling. However, in the spirit of lightening the amount of fat in our diet, I substitute turkey bacon and it turns out very well indeed. This filling, with just four ingredients and one seasoning, has a lot of personality, and makes a tea sandwich with real zip.

1 pound smoked or cold boiled ham
1 pound raw turkey bacon
4 medium onions
  (approximately 2 cups chopped)
4 cups fresh chopped tomatoes,
  or four 1-pound cans whole tomatoes,
  very well drained (see Note)

1½ teaspoons ground red pepper
  (use a scant 2 teaspoons if you like
  highly seasoned food)

24 slices of thin white bread
Softened butter

Using the food processor, chop the meats finely and transfer to a large sauté pan. Chop the onions in the food processor and add to the meat. Place the tomatoes in the food processor, chop coarsely, and add to the meat mixture. Add the red pepper according to taste and mix well.

Bring the mixture to a boil over high heat, lower the heat to medium, and simmer uncovered, for 1 hour, stirring frequently. If the mixture is too liquidy toward the end of the cooking time, turn up the heat. You want most of the tomato liquid to cook away, but the meat should not brown. Cool and refrigerate until the mixture is cold.

Remove the crusts from the bread. Butter one side of each slice of bread. Using approximately ⅓ cup of filling per sandwich, make 12 sandwiches. Cut in fourths and serve.

N O T E : *I prefer tomatoes canned in tomato puree; they have lots more flavor than water-packed ones.*

MINI CRAB CAKES

SERVES 8

To complement small tea sandwiches I sometimes serve crab cakes made in a dainty size. And I find this smaller size makes a perfect cocktail tidbit. The recipe is from Maryland, where there are many interpretations of this dish. One ingredient common to all of them is a mayonnaise base. This version is seasoned perfectly. Allow the mixture to stand overnight before you sauté the cakes for serving.

2 extra large eggs, slightly beaten
¼ cup seasoned dry bread crumbs
2 tablespoons minced parsley
2 tablespoons fresh lemon juice
2 tablespoons mayonnaise
1 tablespoon Worcestershire sauce
4 tablespoons minced chives

Salt and freshly ground white pepper to taste
3 liberal dashes of hot red pepper sauce
1 pound fresh crabmeat, picked over for shells
Corn oil

Garnish: lemon wedges

In a large mixing bowl, combine the eggs, bread crumbs, parsley, lemon juice, mayonnaise, Worcestershire, chives, salt and pepper, and hot red pepper sauce. Mix thoroughly, then gently mix in the crab, keeping the pieces as large as possible. Place in a covered plastic container and chill at least 8 hours and up to 24 hours before cooking.

Stir the mixture occasionally to help the bread crumbs absorb the liquids. The mixture will be quite loose and will just hold together during cooking.

In a 9-inch heavy skillet, heat ½ inch oil over medium-high heat. Drop 5 teaspoon-sized dollops of crab mixture into the hot fat and cook 1 to 2 minutes. Turn over with a slotted spoon and repeat. The crab cakes should be irregular in shape, the size of a half dollar, and golden brown. Don't fry more than 5 at a time, since they cook quickly. Drain on paper towels and serve immediately with lemon wedges.

Croquette molders

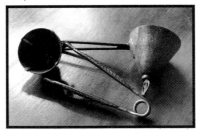

MINCED HAM HORS D'OEUVRE

SERVES 12 TO 16

*This can either be served as a sandwich or molded and turned out onto a platter with crackers
so guests can serve themselves. It is very savory and good. A version of an old English potted ham recipe served
at teatime, it is an ideal use for leftover baked ham. Grinding the ham in the food processor gives the
meat a fine texture and the horseradish and parsley give it flavor and color. Packed into a ring or other decorative
mold, this is a fine cocktail accompaniment or luncheon buffet dish.*

1 tablespoon olive oil	3 tablespoons finely chopped parsley
3 tablespoons finely chopped onion	2 teaspoons prepared horseradish
1 envelope unflavored gelatin	½ teaspoon hot red pepper sauce
½ cup boiling water	¼ teaspoon Worcestershire sauce
2 cups ground ham	Vegetable oil cooking spray
1 cup heavy cream	

In a small sauté pan, heat the oil over medium heat. Add the onions and cook until golden, about 3 to 4 minutes, but do not allow to brown; set aside.

In a medium mixing bowl, dissolve the gelatin in the boiling water. Add the ham and sautéed onions; set aside to cool. In another bowl, beat the cream until stiff peaks form. Stir in the parsley, horseradish, hot red pepper sauce, and Worcestershire, then fold into the meat-onion mixture.

Coat a 1-quart mold with vegetable oil cooking spray, then spoon in the mixture; smooth the top, then cover and refrigerate for at least 3 hours or overnight. With a thin knife, loosen the edges of the mold, rap it smartly on a firm surface, and invert it onto a serving plate. Spread on buttered bread, cut into decorative shapes, or serve with crackers or garlic toasts.

IRISH BUTTERMILK SCONES

MAKES 12 SCONES

*These scones are very similar to the ones my mother made, and she served them frequently.
I regret to say that her recipe has long since been lost, but I still think of her whenever I am cutting them out, one
of those ribbons of memory that we cherish as we cook. Her maiden name was Manahan so we did
have an occasional Irish dish at our table.*

2 cups all-purpose flour

2 tablespoons sugar

1 tablespoon baking powder

⅛ teaspoon baking soda

6 tablespoons (¾ stick) butter, chilled

1 large egg, beaten

½ cup (or a bit more) cold buttermilk

1 large egg beaten with 1 tablespoon
  water for wash (optional)

Clotted Cream (recipe follows)

Strawberry or cherry preserves

Preheat the oven to 350° F.

In a large bowl, whisk together the flour, sugar, baking powder, and soda. Cut in the butter with a pastry blender until it resembles large peas, using your fingers if necessary. Make a well in the center of the flour mixture and pour in the egg and buttermilk. Stir well to combine, then, working quickly, mix the dough with your hands and bring it together to form a ball. Turn the dough out onto a lightly floured board and gently knead it for a few turns. Divide the dough in half and flatten each piece until it is a uniformly 1-inch-thick circle. Cut the circles into 6 pie-shaped wedges and place on a baking sheet about 2 inches apart. Brush with egg wash if you like (I generally skip that). Bake for about 30 to 35 minutes, or until golden. Serve while warm with clotted cream and fruit preserves.

CLOTTED CREAM

MAKES 1¼ CUPS

1 cup heavy sweet cream

¼ cup sour cream

Speck of confectioners' sugar

Speck of salt

In a cold mixer bowl, beat the heavy cream until it thickens and light peaks form. Add the sour cream, sugar, and salt and beat until thick but still spoonable and soft.

NOTE: *This closely resembles British clotted cream, but we can't duplicate it precisely because the proper cream isn't available in this country.*

LEMON CREAM PUFFS WITH APRICOT SAUCE

MAKES 12 LARGE OR 48 MINIATURE CREAM PUFFS

*If you have never made cream puffs, you will be surprised at how easy they are, and when
filled and topped with apricot sauce, they make a dream dessert! The following recipe looks long, but it is just
detailed to encourage you to try this actually rather simple confection. These puffs can also be filled
with ice cream and frozen until needed and served with sweetened and pureed fresh fruit or topped with
chocolate sauce (page 82). If serving at a tea, include a fork.*

CREAM PUFFS
1 cup hot water
½ teaspoon salt
6 tablespoons (¾ stick) butter,
    at room temperature
1 cup all-purpose flour
4 large or 5 medium eggs,
    at room temperature
Vegetable oil cooking spray

LEMON CUSTARD
4 large egg yolks
2 cups sugar
⅓ cup fresh lemon juice
    (approximately 2 lemons)

1 tablespoon grated lemon zest
Speck of salt
4 rounded tablespoons cornstarch
½ cup cold water
2 cups boiling water

APRICOT SAUCE
1 cup apricot preserves
1 cup orange marmalade
1 teaspoon grated lemon zest
Speck of salt
3 tablespoons Cointreau or other
    orange-flavored liqueur

Confectioners' sugar for sprinkling

Make the Cream Puffs: In a heavy medium saucepan, bring the water, salt, and butter just to a boil—don't
let it overboil, or some of the water will evaporate. Add the flour all at once, reduce the heat to low, and
with a wooden spoon, stir the mixture vigorously for 2 to 3 minutes, or until the mixture leaves the sides
of the pan and forms a ball.

Remove from the stove, transfer immediately to an electric mixer bowl, and allow the mixture to cool
for 2 minutes. Add the eggs one at a time, beating for a minute after each addition. After all the eggs have
been added, beat 3 minutes longer on medium speed, occasionally scraping down the sides of the bowl.
At this point, the texture will resemble mashed potatoes. Cover the bowl with a towel and refrigerate for
1 hour.

At least 10 minutes before baking, preheat the oven to 450° F. Lightly spray 2 large baking sheets with
oil. With a tablespoon or ice cream scoop, drop 6 rounds about 2 inches in diameter onto each baking
sheet. Bake for 15 minutes, then lower the heat to 350° F. and bake 30 minutes longer. *Do not* open the
oven door during the baking period. The puffs should be nicely browned when done. Turn off the oven,
open the oven door completely, and allow the cream puffs to cool in the oven for about 1 hour.

Make the Lemon Custard: In the top of a double boiler, beat the egg yolks thoroughly. Blend in the
sugar, lemon juice, lemon zest, and salt. In a small bowl, combine the cornstarch and cold water until
smooth and dissolved. Pour gradually into the lemon mixture. Gradually pour in the boiling water.

Place the double boiler top over gently simmering water and cook, stirring frequently with a rubber spatula (and whisk, if needed) for 20 minutes, or until the mixture thickens and becomes opaque. Remove from the heat and chill thoroughly.

Make the Apricot Sauce: In a small saucepan, combine all of the ingredients, except the Cointreau. Bring to a boil over low heat and simmer for 5 minutes. Remove from the heat and add the Cointreau. Cool, then store in the refrigerator.

Assemble the puffs: With a small knife, cut one-fourth of the puff off the top and pull out the soft insides with your fingers. Fill with the Lemon Custard, return the lid to the top of the puff, and refrigerate until needed. Do not fill them too soon or they will get soggy. Sprinkle the puffs with a bit of confectioners' sugar. Serve with the Apricot Sauce.

N O T E : *To make mini cream puffs, form ³⁄₄-inch rounds of paste on baking sheets. Bake for 12 minutes at 450° F., then lower the heat to 350° F. and bake 15 to 20 minutes longer. Watch them so they don't get overly brown. Turn off the oven, open the door completely, and allow the puffs to cool in the oven, about 45 minutes.*

ONION-CHEESE LOAVES

MAKES 2 LOAVES

Savory cheese-flavored bread laced with onion is especially delightful as a sandwich base.
These loaves are kept extra moist with the addition of a few mashed potatoes.
I was given this recipe by Tillie Barnes, a friend who lives in Vermont where she and her husband have a dairy farm.
Much of their herd's milk is made into cheese, part of the nearly 100 million pounds the state produces each year.

4½ to 5 cups all-purpose flour	1½ cups water
½ cup mashed potatoes	½ cup milk
2 envelopes active dry yeast	2 tablespoons honey
1 tablespoon ground cumin	¼ cup finely minced onion
2 teaspoons salt	2 tablespoons (¼ stick) butter
2 cups shredded extra-sharp cheddar or Swiss cheese	

Combine 2 cups of the flour, potatoes, yeast, cumin, salt, and cheese in a large mixer bowl. Combine the water, milk, honey, onion, and butter in a saucepan; heat until very warm. Add to the flour and blend with a mixer 30 seconds on low speed. Increase the speed to medium and beat 2 minutes. Stir in the remaining flour to make a stiff dough.

Turn the dough onto a floured surface and knead 8 to 10 minutes, until smooth and satiny. Shape into 2 loaves and place into two 9 × 5 × 3-inch greased bread pans. Cover the loaves with a tea towel and let rise in a warm place until they are light and doubled in size, 1 to 1½ hours.

Preheat the oven to 350° F. for 10 minutes. Bake the bread for 30 to 40 minutes, until deep golden brown and the inner temperature registers 200° F. on an instant-reading thermometer. Tip out of the pans onto a rack and cool before slicing.

MELTING MOMENTS COOKIES

MAKES 3 DOZEN COOKIES

Crisp, buttery, with a taste of almond, this is an unbeatable cookie that melts in your mouth, just as its name suggests. I like the frosting left white, but for special holidays or parties, it can be tinted. The cornstarch contributes to the cookie's crisp texture—it is an old recipe that you'll be delighted to rediscover.

1 cup (2 sticks) butter (no substitutes), at room temperature	**ICING**
⅓ cup confectioners' sugar	2 tablespoons (¼ stick) butter (no substitutes), melted
⅛ teaspoon salt	1 cup confectioners' sugar
¾ cup cornstarch	1 teaspoon almond extract
1 cup all-purpose flour	2 tablespoons half-and-half

In a medium mixing bowl, cream the butter until light, then gradually add the confectioners' sugar and salt. Beat this mixture thoroughly, about 3 minutes; gradually add the cornstarch and flour and blend well. Form the dough into walnut-sized balls and chill in the refrigerator for 1 hour.

Preheat the oven to 350° F.

Transfer the balls to an ungreased cookie sheet and let stand for 20 minutes or until soft, then make a thumbprint on top of each to flatten the cookies. Bake for 15 to 16 minutes, or until the cookies are golden on the bottom. Remove to a rack to cool.

While the cookies cool, make the icing: In a small bowl, combine the butter, confectioners' sugar, almond extract, and half-and-half until creamy. (This may be tinted with food coloring.) Ice the cookies when they are completely cooled. Store in tins, in layers separated by plastic wrap.

PHOTO POST CARD

AMERICA 25

BALTIMORE, MARYLAND

What a nice place to be on Mother's Day! We visited Edgar Allan Poe's grave and the National Aquarium—most impressive. We spent a lot of time strolling around Harborplace, a European-style marketplace comprised of two glassed-enclosed pavilions. Stopping for espresso, it was served with a crisp, frosted cookie, just like the ones my mother used to make. She called them melting moments. "We do too," said the waiter. It seemed appropriate to be eating this particular cookie, on this particular day. *M*

$\mathcal{T}$RANSPARENT PUDDINGS

MAKES 36 SMALL TARTLETS

*These tiny open-faced tarts, rather like miniature chess pies, appear mostly in Kentucky
and Pennsylvania cookbooks and are named "transparent puddings." Their background is English, however,
and a version of this confection appears in Hannah Glasse's Art of Cookery (London, 1796).
This delightful mini-dessert would be perfectly at home on a tea cart, and firm enough to travel well,
so consider it for the cookie swap at Christmas.
These are made in jelly tart pans, not the deep mini muffin pans. The pans can be ordered by mail from
Fantes in Philadelphia, a cookware shop that has everything (page 299).*

1 recipe Perfect Pie Pastry (page 284)	**Speck of salt**
½ cup (1 stick) butter,	**2 large eggs**
at room temperature	**½ teaspoon vanilla extract**
1 cup minus 1 tablespoon sugar	**⅛ teaspoon ground mace**
1 tablespoon light corn syrup	

On a lightly floured cloth, roll out the pie pastry ⅛ inch thick. Using a 3-inch cutter, cut out 36 rounds and gently press into shallow tart pans. Set aside. (You may need to bake them in batches.)

Preheat the oven to 375° F.

In the top of a double boiler, combine the butter, sugar, corn syrup, and salt and mix by hand until well creamed. Add the eggs one at a time, beating well until each egg is incorporated. Add the vanilla and mace and mix well. Place the pan over hot but not boiling water and cook, stirring occasionally, until the sugar is dissolved 10 to 15 minutes; do not overcook. Fill each tart two-thirds full (no more than ½ tablespoon) and bake directly on the oven racks for 15 to 20 minutes, or until golden. Cool slightly in the pans, then remove to wire racks to cool completely. Store in covered containers, the layers separated by paper towels. These can be frozen.

PHOTO POST-CARD

AMERICA 25

PHILADELPHIA, PENNSYLVANIA

When in Philadelphia we never fail to stop by Fantes, an absolutely
wonderful cookware shop in the Italian section of town. As
always, it was a pleasure to see Nick Giovannucci, who seems to
have everything I have ever needed for my kitchen. We carry out
an armload of assorted pans, utensils, and bags of rare coffee
blends and ten miles down the road, I regret what I didn't buy.
Thank goodness they have a mail-order service.

M

Family FAVORITES

*T*HE NUMBER of items in the early housewife's cupboard was limited, but with a handful of staples in the pantry coupled with the provender raised on the land outside the kitchen door she managed to keep her family fed. In fact, old recipe books and journals indicate that earlier generations ate rather well. Many of these old-fashioned dishes were unadorned and straightforward, and that is precisely what we appreciate about them today, when food—and life—can seem so complicated.

Clearly there is less time to spend on cooking today, with combined careers, long commutes, and the demands of outside activities. Yet despite what I read about how few people are cooking anymore and the presumed helplessness in the kitchen of a whole generation, I still encounter many cooks who are creating great meals, week in and week out, for their appreciative families. And it is reassuring to me, as one who honors old recipes, to see how often these busy cooks are turning to the recipes they enjoyed as children.

Most of those recipes are economical to duplicate and can be prepared in advance; our grandmothers were pretty smart people. When we reminisce about our favorite childhood dishes, we mention things like pot roast, mashed potatoes and gravy, chicken and biscuits, stuffed cabbage rolls, and even the rather humble but comforting salmon loaf, a Great Depression classic still remembered by many with fondness.

We never forget these favorite old recipes; they are part of the warp and woof of our memories. More and more families are recognizing the significance of gathering at the table to share a meal and conversation on a daily basis. Breaking bread together has never been more important.

Savory Minced Chicken and Pork Pie Loin of Pork Cooked in Milk Salmon Loaf with Creamy Egg Sauce Tony Packo's Hungarian Stuffed Cabbage Baked Chicken Reuben Beef Pot Roast Simmered in Cider Cincinnati Chili Carrot Puff, from Winterthur Jasper's Corn and Bread Pudding Mashed Potatoes with Chèvre Roasted Root Vegetables Cornmeal Pie Boston Baked Beans Boston Brown Bread German Sweet Rice Blueberry Flummery Louisa May Alcott's Apple Slump Steamed Apple Dumplings Lemon Sponge Pudding Layered Pumpkin Gingerbread with Hot Caramel Sauce

SAVORY MINCED CHICKEN AND PORK PIE

SERVES 8

*Pies were not invented in North America, for every country in the old world encased
foods in dough. There are references in Chaucer's Canterbury Tales to a pie dealer who sold pasties that
"hath been twies hoot and twies coold," intimating that leftover pie, too often served again,
wasn't any more appetizing then than it is now.
Early Colonial cooks made meat pies regularly as a way to use every last snip of butchering
meat and leftovers. The pioneers found meat pies practical for they traveled well, and as a result, this fine
old dish is now common in every state. The combination of chicken, pork, onions, wine, marjoram,
and mace make this meat pie distinctive and it's not bad once hot, then once cold, with apologies to Chaucer.
I like to serve it with Apple Ketchup (page 200), Apple Chutney (page 206),
or Bread-and-Butter Pickles for Threshing Day (page 209).*

Pastry for a 2-crust deep
   9-inch pie (page 284)
2 tablespoons vegetable oil
1 cup chopped onion
1 garlic clove, minced
1 whole chicken breast
   (about 14 ounces), skinned, boned,
   and cut into ¾- to 1-inch pieces
¾ pound lean ground pork
1 tablespoon Worcestershire sauce
½ teaspoon salt

½ teaspoon dried marjoram or
   2 teaspoons minced fresh
¼ teaspoon ground mace
¼ teaspoon ground pepper
2 large eggs
½ cup dry white wine
½ cup minced fresh parsley
½ cup quick-cooking oatmeal

Garnish: paprika

Line a deep 9-inch pie shell with the pastry and cut out a 12-inch round for the top crust; set aside.

Heat the oil in a 12-inch sauté pan and add the onions and garlic; sauté over medium heat for 3 minutes. Add the chicken, pork, Worcestershire, salt, marjoram, mace, and pepper. Continue cooking the mixture, stirring occasionally, for 15 minutes, breaking up the large pork pieces that tend to clump together. There will be a generous amount of pan juices; that is perfectly all right. Cool slightly.

Meanwhile, preheat the oven to 350° F.

In a medium bowl, beat the eggs and wine together. Stir in the parsley and oatmeal, then add the egg mixture to the meat mixture and combine thoroughly.

Fill the pie shell with the meat mixture and top with the pastry round. Crimp the edges, slash the top crust, and sprinkle with paprika. Bake the pie for approximately 1 hour and 15 minutes, or until it is a deep golden brown and the juices are bubbling up in the center of the pie. Remove from the oven and allow to stand for 15 minutes before cutting.

NOTE: *This can be made in advance and reheated on a baking sheet in a 350° F. oven for 15 minutes, or until heated through.*

𝓛OIN OF PORK COOKED IN MILK

SERVES 8

Early cooks often braised pork in milk, discovering all on their own that milk tenderizes meat.
The Amish still cook pork in milk, and so do some Italian and French cooks as well. Seasoning the pork first with
garlic, rosemary, and cinnamon, then sautéing it makes the meat very flavorful.
The milk will cook down and appear curdled; however, that is the way it is supposed to be, and it
makes a most savory gravy.

One 3- to 3½-pound loin of pork,
    rolled and tied (not in a mesh bag)
6 garlic cloves, minced
½ teaspoon dried rosemary, crushed,
    or 1½ teaspoons minced fresh
½ teaspoon coarsely ground pepper
¼ teaspoon ground cinnamon

1 tablespoon vegetable or olive oil
1 large onion, peeled, sliced, and
    separated into rings
1 bay leaf
4 cups whole milk
Salt and pepper to taste

Slash the pork at 1-inch intervals with a long sharp knife. In a small bowl, combine the garlic, rosemary, pepper, and cinnamon. Fill the slashes with the garlic-herb mixture.

Heat the oil in a Dutch oven over medium-low heat; transfer the roast to the pan and sauté on all sides, about 15 minutes. Remove the roast from the pan. Add the onions to the pan drippings and sauté until they are golden, about 5 minutes. Return the roast to the pan and add the bay leaf and milk. Cover the pan and bring the milk to a boil, simmering over medium-low to low heat for 1½ to 2 hours, turning the meat occasionally.

Transfer the pork to a heated platter; cover and keep warm. Bring the milk to a boil; simmer, stirring often, until the mixture is reduced to 1½ cups, about 15 minutes. It will be golden brown and curdled. Season with salt and pepper to taste.

To serve, slice the pork into ¼-inch-thick slices and pass the pan sauce in a gravy boat or bowl to ladle on top of the meat.

travel Notes FROM NORTH CAROLINA

The Blue Ridge mountains hide many secrets. We are told there are still isolated pockets of mountain people in North Carolina, whose folk songs date back to Elizabethan England. I know they've also retained some English food-ways as well, such as pork and apple pie and gooseberry catsup. These recipes can still be found in regional cookbooks.

In the spring, the mountains are welcoming, with frothy white dogwood and the insistent pink of the redbud trees. Asheville has long been a vacation hub for these mountains, and in 1895, George Vanderbilt of New York built a splendid retreat in what is now part of the Pisgah National Forest. Biltmore, like Winterthur in Delaware, is a comprehensive museum of decorative arts, plus superb gardens. We were guided through many of the seventy rooms including the kitchens and servants' quarters. There are thirty-

Salmon Loaf with Creamy Egg Sauce

SERVES 6

*Years ago, housewives along the coast made fish loaves with fish left over from earlier meals.
Later, canned salmon became readily available and salmon loaf made its appearance; it was always considered
an economical dish and was frequently served during the Great Depression. Yet I am surprised to find
out how many people remember this dish with great fondness, even though it was, and still is, associated with hard
times in America. Perhaps the memories of families unified by the goal of survival and meeting together
at dinner in a caring atmosphere give this dish its good reputation and a measure of affection.*

One 15-ounce can red salmon, drained
3 large eggs, separated
¼ cup (½ stick) butter, melted
½ cup fresh bread crumbs
1 medium onion, chopped
2 tablespoons fresh lemon juice
1½ tablespoons minced dill

¼ teaspoon dried tarragon
  or 1 teaspoon minced fresh
3 shakes of hot red pepper sauce
Salt and pepper to taste
Basic White Sauce (page 284)
2 hard-cooked eggs, coarsely chopped

Preheat the oven to 350° F. Grease a 9 × 5 × 3-inch loaf pan and set it aside.

Remove all of the large bones and skin from the salmon and discard. Place the salmon in a large bowl and break it up with a spoon. Add the egg yolks and stir to combine. Add the butter, bread crumbs, onions, lemon juice, dill, tarragon, hot red pepper sauce, and salt and pepper and mix well.

In a large mixer bowl, beat the egg whites until stiff, then fold in the salmon mixture. Spoon the mixture into the pan, set it in a larger pan of hot water, and bake for 45 minutes, or until the dish is lightly browned and crusty looking. While the loaf is baking, make the White Sauce and fold in the chopped egg. Cut the salmon loaf into 6 pieces, and serve topped with the warm sauce.

five acres of gardens, but we concentrated on the rose gardens, which were at their peak.

In town, The Thomas Wolfe Memorial is actually the boardinghouse his parsimonious mother operated and is furnished to look as it would in 1906. Some of his most powerfully written episodes in <u>Look Homeward, Angel</u> used this house as a backdrop. The kitchen appears as it did during the days his mother prepared daily meals for the boarders, serving platters of fried chicken, mashed potatoes, sliced tomatoes, fluffy biscuits,

and regional peaches in cobblers, pies, and crisps.

It feels good to be heading back to Indiana. We drive through Georgia, through red-soiled fields of cotton and tobacco and orchards of peaches, the boughs heavy with ripening fruit. At the pecan groves, which always delight our eye in their symmetry of planting, we stop and buy bags of nut meats to bring home for baking.

We've gathered many new recipes and met some interesting people on this leg of our trip; I'm eager to begin testing as soon as we get home.

ONY PACKO'S HUNGARIAN STUFFED CABBAGE

SERVES 8 TO 12

*One of my college roommates was from Akron, Ohio; her family was Hungarian. When she
fantasized about food (as homesick college students are wont to do), she talked about her mother's
cabbage rolls. When visiting at her house, guess what was served for dinner?
Cabbage rolls. And they were unforgettably good. Those plump spicy rolls were just a memory
until I ate them again at Tony Packo's in Toledo, Ohio.
When you talk about Ohio restaurants, Tony Packo's is one of the first mentioned. They feature not
only the famous cabbage rolls, but chili-topped Hungarian hot dogs, which are really
more like brats, strudel, and lots of other tasty things. This is one of the Packo family's recipes.*

CABBAGE ROLLS

1 head cabbage (about 3 pounds)

2 large eggs

2 medium onions, finely chopped

2 garlic cloves, minced

2 teaspoons salt

2 teaspoons paprika
  (preferably Hungarian)

1 teaspoon pepper

2 pounds lean ground beef
  (or 1 pound ground pork
  and 1 pound ground beef)

1 cup uncooked long-grain rice

1 pound sauerkraut, drained

One 16-ounce can tomatoes, cut up,
  with their juice

One 10¾-ounce can condensed
  tomato soup

2 tablespoons sugar

TOMATO-ONION SAUCE

2 small onions, chopped

1 tablespoon butter

One 16-ounce can tomatoes, cut up,
  with their juice

Bring a large kettle of water to a boil. Core the cabbage, immerse in the boiling water, and cook, uncovered, for about 10 minutes to wilt the leaves. Using a slotted spoon, remove the cabbage from the water; let cool slightly. Remove about 12 large leaves from the cabbage and cut out the large center vein from each with a triangular cut.

In a large bowl, combine the eggs, ½ cup onions, the garlic, 1 teaspoon salt, 1 teaspoon paprika, and ½ teaspoon pepper. Add the meat and rice and mix well. Place about ⅓ cup of the meat mixture on one of the 12 prepared leaves. Fold in the sides, then carefully roll up each leaf. Repeat with the remaining leaves and filling.

Chop the remaining cabbage. In a large bowl, combine the chopped cabbage, sauerkraut, tomatoes with their juice, tomato soup, sugar, and the remaining chopped onion, salt, paprika, and pepper.

In a 6- or 8-quart heavy kettle or Dutch oven, spoon half of the sauerkraut mixture evenly in the bottom. Arrange the cabbage rolls, seam side down, over the sauerkraut mixture. Spoon the remaining sauerkraut mixture over the rolls. Add enough water (or chicken stock) to cover the rolls and bring to a boil, then reduce the heat and simmer, covered, for about 2 hours, adding water as needed to keep the rolls covered.

Meanwhile, prepare the tomato-onion sauce: In a small saucepan, sauté the onions in t
tender. Stir in the tomatoes with their juice; heat through.

To serve, transfer the cabbage rolls and sauerkraut mixture to a serving bowl or platter.
tomato-onion sauce over the cabbage rolls.

BAKED CHICKEN REUBEN

SERVES 4

The modern poultry industry started in Delaware in the 1920s and 1930s and is now
the state's most important commodity; the Blue Hen Chicken is the state bird. Many ways have been devised
to promote the versatile low-calorie bird and among them is the National Chicken Cook-Off,
sponsored every other year by the National Broiler Council. Cooks across the country send in their favorite
recipes, and if you win from your state, you are invited to the big cook-off, which is an absolutely
fascinating experience and loads of fun.
I won the National Chicken Cook-Off with this recipe in 1982. It is a quick dish and quite unlike my
usual cooking style in that is uses all ready-made products, a boon that we should rely on now and then. This is a
first-rate dish—good enough to have merited the $10,000 prize which, incidentally, I used to buy
a badly needed new car. That car was always known as my "chicken car."
This recipe came to me from my dear friend, Yvonne Diamond.

4 small chicken breast halves,
   boned, skin on
¼ teaspoon salt
⅛ teaspoon pepper
One 16-ounce can sauerkraut,
   well drained

4 slices natural Swiss cheese
1¼ cups bottled Thousand
   Island dressing
1 tablespoon chopped fresh parsley

Preheat the oven to 325° F. Place the chicken, skin side up in a greased 9 × 13-inch baking dish. Sprinkle
with salt and pepper. Arrange the sauerkraut over the chicken and top with the Swiss cheese. Pour the
dressing evenly over the cheese. Cover the dish with foil and bake for 1½ hours, or until the chicken is
very tender. Remove the foil, turn up the broiler to brown the cheese, if necessary, and sprinkle top with
parsley.

BEEF POT ROAST SIMMERED IN CIDER

SERVES 6

*Certainly the quintessence of family supper would be pot roast, and it has always been
a comforting, sturdy dish. Goodness knows, these foods that evolved in the early eighteenth century
came from a time when citizens needed such foods. For the tastiest results, buy a
roast with the bone in and allow plenty of time for long, slow cooking—in this case, four hours.
I prefer to sear the meat the night before and also measure out the spices.*

One 3- to 4- pound chuck roast, bone in,
   well trimmed
1 tablespoon vegetable oil
2 cups apple cider
2 small onions, peeled
   and coarsely chopped
1 large celery stalk
½ teaspoon ground allspice
½ teaspoon powdered ginger
1 bay leaf

¼ teaspoon coarsely
   ground pepper
6 whole cloves
6 small potatoes, peeled and halved
6 small carrots, peeled and halved
2 tablespoons (¼ stick) butter, softened
2 tablespoons all-purpose flour

Garnish: chopped fresh parsley

Preheat the oven to 300° F.

In a deep sauté pan or roaster, sauté the roast in the oil until nicely browned on all sides. Add the cider, onions, and celery, then stir in the seasonings. Cover and bake for 2½ hours, turning the meat 2 or 3 times. Add the potatoes and carrots, patting them down into the liquid, and continue baking for another 1½ hours, or until the meat and vegetables are tender.

In a small bowl, blend the butter and flour together to form a smooth paste. With a wide spatula and slotted spoon, remove the meat and vegetables to a heated platter. Place the pan on top of the stove and bring the cider mixture to a boil over high heat; gradually add the butter-flour mixture, whisking the mixture as it thickens. Transfer to a gravy boat. Sprinkle parsley over the meat and vegetables and serve with the cider gravy.

PHOTO POST CARD

AMERICA 25

HISTORIC DEERFIELD, DEERFIELD, MASSACHUSETTS

This is like a tiny Williamsburg, evoking an earlier period; it was New England's northernmost outpost when the colonists settled here in 1669. The town has been very well restored, with many of the eighteenth- and nineteenth-century houses open to the public. The cookery from this period is still in existence: those recipes for pot roasts of beef and pork and even meat pies that were cooked in the fireplace in deep iron pots are still around. And aren't we glad!

M

CINCINNATI CHILI

SERVES 6 TO 8

When my second cookbook, Heartland, *came out, I received a lot of mail regarding the*
Cincinnati chili recipe. A flood of alternative variations streamed in, and all sounded tempting. This one, however,
really piqued my interest, with its touch of honey, pumpkin pie spice, and cardamom. I found it so
different that I felt a second version merited inclusion.
In Cincinnati, chili is served with spaghetti or cheese, or onion, or beans, or all four at one time.
This is the secret Cincinnati code: Three-way is chili with spaghetti and cheese, four-way is three-way plus onion,
and five-way is four-way plus beans. I am sure you understand. All the ways are very, very good.

2 pounds ground beef
2 large onions, chopped
3 garlic cloves, minced
One 15-ounce can tomato sauce
One 8-ounce can tomato paste
One 16-ounce can beef stock
One 5-ounce can V-8 juice
2 tablespoons chili powder
2 squares semisweet chocolate,
  melted in the microwave
2 tablespoons cider vinegar
1 tablespoon honey

1 tablespoon pumpkin pie spice
1 teaspoon salt
1 teaspoon ground cumin
½ teaspoon ground cardamom
¼ teaspoon ground cloves

1 pound spaghetti (spaghettini),
  cooked and drained
2 cups shredded cheddar cheese
One 16-ounce can kidney beans, drained
2 cups chopped onions

Oyster crackers

In a deep stockpot or Dutch oven, combine the beef, onions, and garlic. Cook over medium-high heat until the beef is brown and the onions are tender, 15 to 20 minutes. Drain off the fat and add the tomato sauce, tomato paste, beef stock, V-8 juice, chili powder, melted chocolate, vinegar, honey, pumpkin pie spice, salt, cumin, cardamom, and cloves. Bring to a boil, then reduce the heat to low and simmer for 35 minutes. Skim off any fat.

To serve, place some spaghetti in a shallow bowl and top with a ladle of chili. Add cheese, beans, and/or onions. Serve with oyster crackers.

CARROT PUFF, FROM WINTERTHUR

SERVES 10 TO 12

*Winterthur has its own elegant cookbook (The Culinary Collection, published by Gallison Books)
filled with recipes from famous people and illustrated with gorgeous table settings using the du Ponts' collections;
I have that book and enjoy it thoroughly. However, for this book, I wanted family recipes, and the
Winterthur people graciously sent several, including this one from 1934.
They suggested making it in a ring mold (it would require a 10-cup mold) and filling the center with crab
or shrimp in mushroom sauce. I adapted the recipe to serve in a large round casserole; it is very
appealing and well-seasoned, and ideal for buffet meals. Being more of a timbale than a soufflé, it does
hold its shape after it is removed from the oven.*

6 large eggs, separated	**2 teaspoons ground mustard**
2 cups mashed boiled carrots	**1 teaspoon paprika**
(about 1 pound)	**Salt and pepper to taste**
1 cup soft white bread crumbs	**2 cups half-and-half**
1 tablespoon minced onion	

Preheat the oven to 375° F.

In a large bowl, beat the egg yolks for 1 minute. Add the carrots, bread crumbs, onion, mustard, paprika, and salt and pepper and mix well. Whisk in the half-and-half. In a medium bowl, beat the egg whites
until glossy and stiff but not dry. Fold about one-quarter of the egg whites into the carrot mixture to light-
en, then fold the carrot mixture into the remaining egg whites, leaving some patches of egg white; do not
overmix.

Transfer the carrot mixture to a lightly greased, round, 4-inch-deep, 10-inch-diameter casserole and
bake for 45 minutes, or until the top of the casserole is deep golden brown and puffy. Serve immediately.

PHOTO POST CARD

WINTERTHUR MUSEUM, DELAWARE

For American antiques lovers, this place is heaven! There are
more than 89,000 objects, including furniture, textiles, ceramics,
and silver. Everything is presented in room settings and the table
settings take my breath away. The du Ponts loved to entertain,
and fortunately some family recipes have been kept. The Azalea
Woods are in bloom and are a sight to see—this place is an
American treasure.

JASPER'S CORN AND BREAD PUDDING

SERVES 6 TO 8 AS A SIDE DISH OR 3 TO 4 AS AN ENTRÉE

*One of Boston's favorite new (in comparison to Durgin Park) eating spots is Jasper's, named
after the owner-chef Jasper White, who serves a roster of classic New England dishes that changes with the
seasons. Jasper, who says he is an Irish-Italian transplant from New Jersey, is passionately committed to
New England food, and his restaurant menu reflects his interest in food history as well as preparation. This vegetable
dish, reminiscent of both a corn and a bread pudding, is adapted from one of his favorite recipes.*

3 tablespoons butter

9 slices of thin white bread,
   crusts removed (about 3 cups)

6 ears of corn, kernels cut off and
   cobs scraped (about 3 cups)

1 tablespoon chopped fresh parsley

½ teaspoon salt

½ teaspoon freshly
   ground black pepper

4 large eggs

2 cups whole milk

1 tablespoon sugar

¾ cup grated sharp cheddar cheese

Garnish: paprika

Preheat the oven to 350° F. Place the butter in a 9-inch square pan and melt in the preheating oven.
Meanwhile, cut the bread into ½- to ¾-inch cubes and transfer to a jelly roll pan. Remove the preheated
pan from the oven and swish the butter around the bottom and sides of it, then drizzle the rest over the
bread cubes. Place the bread cubes in the oven and bake 12 to 15 minutes, or until golden brown.

Remove the toasted bread cubes from the oven, and sprinkle the corn, parsley, salt, and pepper over
them; toss to combine. Spread the bread cube mixture evenly in the buttered 9-inch pan.

Beat the eggs, milk, and sugar together briefly and pour over the bread and corn. Let the mixture stand
about 10 minutes, pressing down lightly on the bread 2 or 3 times so that it absorbs the custard.

Sprinkle the cheese over the top and dust with paprika. Place in the oven and bake until done, about 1
hour. Test by inserting a knife in the center; it should come out clean. If the top is brown and the custard is
not completely set, you may wish to cover it loosely with aluminum foil for the last few minutes of baking.
Allow the pudding to stand for at least 5 minutes before cutting into squares.

MASHED POTATOES WITH CHÈVRE

MAKES 8

*My Great-Aunt Belle and Uncle Clarence Manahan raised goats and whenever I went there for a meal,
there was always a pitcher of goat's milk on the table instead of cow's milk. And Belle made mashed potatoes using
the goat's milk as well. The mashed potatoes were piled high in a Haviland bowl with a well of butter in the
center and nutmeg was sprinkled on top. This recipe, with its addition of goat cheese, very much reminds me of those
creamy mashed potatoes at the Manahan farm, oh, so many years ago. This is a first-rate dish.*

3 pounds potatoes, peeled and quartered
¼ cup (½ stick) butter,
    at room temperature
7 ounces fresh soft chèvre, cut into
    thick slices, at room temperature

½ to ¾ cup half-and-half
Salt and white pepper to taste

Garnish: ground nutmeg (optional)

In a large saucepan, cover the potatoes with cold water, cover, and bring to a boil. Lower the heat to medium and cook for 25 to 30 minutes, or until the potatoes are fork-tender. Drain.

Meanwhile, heat the butter, chèvre, and ½ cup half-and-half until the cheese melts. Add the butter mixture to the drained potatoes and mash them until they are smooth, adding more warmed half-and-half if a thinner mixture is desired. Season with salt and pepper, transfer to a serving bowl, and sprinkle nutmeg lightly over the top of the potatoes.

ROASTED ROOT VEGETABLES

SERVES 8

*This Italian family recipe for roasted vegetables may be an earthy and humble
combination of ingredients, but with the slow cooking and gentle seasonings, the vegetables take on a
sweetness that harmonizes richly with the garlic.
Do not omit the parsnips! They are especially good in this dish. Europeans brought this creamy
white root to this country, but for some reason, it has never enjoyed the popularity it deserves. Though available
year-round in some markets, they are best in late spring when they have had a chance to winter over
in the ground and are freshly dug. And consider adding a parsnip or two to a stew—it adds a fine sweet flavor.*

1 pound small red potatoes
1 teaspoon salt
1 pound carrots, peeled
3 medium parsnips, peeled
5 tablespoons olive oil
1 head garlic, separated into
    individual cloves

2 tablespoons balsamic
    or red wine vinegar
1½ teaspoons coriander seeds,
    roughly crushed
1 heaping teaspoon paprika
Salt and freshly ground pepper

Preheat the oven to 400° F.

Peel and cut the potatoes into fourths. Place in a medium saucepan, cover with water and 1 teaspoon salt, and bring to a boil. Reduce the heat and simmer for 5 minutes. Drain the potatoes, reserving 5 tablespoons of the cooking water. Cut the carrots and parsnips into 1-inch chunks. In a 1- to 1½-quart baking dish, add the oil and heat in the oven. Then add the vegetables, including the garlic, and toss gently until all are coated with oil.

In a small bowl, mix the vinegar, coriander, paprika, and salt and pepper with the reserved potato water. Pour over the vegetables, turning 2 to 3 times until well coated. Cover loosely with foil and bake 1 hour. (Check once to make sure the liquid hasn't all evaporated.) Remove the foil and continue baking for approximately 15 minutes, or until the vegetables are tender and browned.

CORNMEAL PIE

SERVES 4

The antecedents of this homey pie are old Yankee. The recipe came to me from my friend,
Yvonne Diamond, who lives in the handsome town of Newburyport, Massachusetts, whose streets are lined
with venerable old sea captains' mansions, many topped with widow's walks.
We love visiting there, for the architecture is a marvel and there are also nice shops and restaurants.
Yvonne, knowing of my affection for old recipes, garnered this one from an old Newburyport cookbook; it was
originally made with leftover cornmeal mush, then topped with cheddar from nearby Vermont, but I
prefer the Parmesan. The pie can be made in advance and baked just before serving.

2 cups chicken broth
¼ teaspoon salt
Scant ¼ teaspoon pepper
Liberal pinch of ground nutmeg
½ cup yellow (not stone-ground)
   cornmeal

2 tablespoons (¼ stick) butter
4 tablespoons grated Parmesan cheese

Garnish: paprika

In a deep medium saucepan, combine the broth, salt, pepper, and nutmeg and bring to a boil. Add the cornmeal in a very slow stream, whisking constantly. Cover and cook over low heat, whisking now and then, for 15 minutes. Stir in the butter. Pour into a well-greased 9-inch pie plate and smooth the top. Sprinkle with the Parmesan, then paprika. Cover and chill the mixture for at least 30 minutes or up to 12 hours.

Preheat the oven to 400° F. Bake the pie for 25 minutes, or until the pie is golden brown. Cut into wedges and serve hot.

$\mathcal{B}$OSTON BAKED BEANS

SERVES 8 TO 10

The stacks at the Schlesinger Library boast dozens of recipes for baked beans, but most of them agree on one thing—no tomatoes! The history of this recipe presumably goes back to those Puritan cooks who had adapted the Old Testament custom of not cooking during the Sabbath. The beans were baked long hours to be ready for Saturday night's meal, then they were served again for Sunday breakfast and appeared once more for Sunday's lunch. Traditionally, the beans are served with Boston Brown Bread. Soak the beans overnight before you start the cooking process and plan on baking the beans for at least 8 hours.

1 pound dried pea or Great Northern beans	½ teaspoon ground pepper
Pinch of baking soda	1 medium onion, studded
¼ cup packed dark brown sugar	with 8 whole cloves
½ cup dark molasses	1 ½-pound piece of salt pork,
1½ teaspoons ground mustard	cut through to the rind in 1-inch squares

Pick over the beans and rinse them well. Place them in a deep kettle with water to cover and soak overnight; do not drain. The next day, bring the water to a boil and add the soda. Lower the heat, skim off the foam, and simmer, partially covered, for about 20 minutes, or until the skins peel back when blown on. Drain and reserve at least 6 cups of the cooking liquid in a separate container.

Preheat the oven to 300° F.

Transfer the beans to a greased 8-cup bean pot or ceramic casserole. Add the sugar, molasses, mustard, and pepper. Stir gently to combine, then tuck the onion in down to the bottom of the beans. Lay the slashed salt pork on top, pushing it down into the beans a bit. Add enough of the reserved cooking water to cover the beans completely.

Cover and bake for 8 hours, checking the pot occasionally to make sure the liquid doesn't cook down—the beans should be covered at all times. Do not stir during cooking. Serve hot with corn bread or Boston Brown Bread.

PHOTO POST CARD

AMERICA 25

THE SCHLESINGER LIBRARY, BOSTON, MASSACHUSETTS

The Schlesinger Library at Radcliffe College is an unsung treasure with books, manuscripts, and periodicals that pertain only to women. On the third floor is the culinary collection of 7,000 cookbooks—all kinds, from tattered and glossy to international and local community ones too. I get euphoric just walking through the stacks. Found many old recipes and stories regarding Boston Baked Beans, including one that maintains this dish was originally a Jewish dish from Africa and did not contain pork!

$\mathcal{M}$

BOSTON BROWN BREAD

MAKES 1 LOAF

This moist, flavorful, and quick-to-prepare brown bread is the traditional accompaniment to Boston Baked Beans. Dating back to Colonial days, it was called "thirded bread" because of the proportions: one-third rye or graham flour, one-third cornmeal, and one-third wheat flour. It is steamed rather than baked, and many recipes recommend using coffee cans for molds, but it is very handsome steamed in a pudding mold.

⅓ cup rye or graham flour
⅓ cup all-purpose flour
⅓ cup yellow cornmeal
⅓ cup dry bread crumbs
1 teaspoon baking soda

½ teaspoon salt
1 cup buttermilk
½ cup dark molasses
⅓ cup dark raisins
Vegetable oil cooking spray

In a medium bowl, whisk together the flours, cornmeal, bread crumbs, soda, and salt. Stir in the buttermilk and molasses: do not overmix. Stir in the raisins. Coat a 1½-quart metal steaming tin with vegetable oil cooking spray. Pour in the batter, run a knife or spatula through the batter to remove any air pockets, and cover tightly with a lid or foil. Place the mold on a rack (if you don't have a rack, canning jar rings work very well) in a deep pot with a tight-fitting lid. Add enough hot water to reach two-thirds up the sides of the mold; cover. Bring the water to a simmer and steam the bread for 2 hours and 15 minutes on low heat. Check the pot from time to time to make sure the water is not boiling away. Remove the mold from the water and allow it to stand for 20 minutes, then turn the bread out onto a rack to cool. To serve, cut in slices and serve with Boston Baked Beans.

GERMAN SWEET RICE

SERVES 4

At one of my book signings in central Ohio, a woman by the name of Catherine Wolken inquired if I'd heard of German sweet rice; I hadn't. This part of Ohio had been settled by Germans from Oldenburg and Hanover, and a few people still speak Low German there, but it is "dying out," she said. Her family, and others who had grown up with the recipe, ate it as a meat accompaniment. And though called "sweet," it really isn't. It is like the rice I remember as a girl—creamy and smooth, with a soft texture. Served as a breakfast cereal, with milk, some brown sugar, and cinnamon, it is very satisfying and filling.

½ cup long-grain rice
2 cups milk

1 tablespoon sugar
Speck of salt

Combine all the ingredients in the top of a double boiler over gently boiling water. Bring to a boil and lower the heat to medium-low. Cook, covered, for 1 hour, stirring gently 3 times during the cooking period. The milk will be totally absorbed and the rice will be very soft.

NOTE: *This recipe does not double well, but it is very good reheated in the microwave.*

BLUEBERRY FLUMMERY

MAKES NINE ¹/₂-CUP SERVINGS

*Flummery is an old English pudding, either made with fruit or cream; the recipe has many variations.
This blueberry version is lightly flavored with orange and almond. Thickened with tapioca, an old Portuguese word
meaning pudding, this refreshing dessert is a satisfying ending to any meal. Serve the flummery in clear dessert
glasses or compotes and top with whipped cream and fruit liberally. This is an extraordinarily
attractive and easy-to-prepare dessert.*

1 quart fresh blueberries or
   32 ounces, frozen
½ cup fresh orange juice
½ cup water
¾ cup sugar
¼ cup Minute Tapioca

1 teaspoon grated orange zest
¼ teaspoon almond extract

Garnish: Whipped Cream Topping
   (page 286), fresh mint leaves, and
   fresh blueberries

Wash the blueberries, drain, and transfer to a medium saucepan saucepan. Add the orange juice, water,
sugar, tapioca, orange zest, and almond extract. Let the mixture stand for 5 minutes. Bring to a full boil,
stirring constantly. Remove from heat and pour into a bowl (if using an antique cut glass dish, place a metal
or silver spoon in the bowl first, then pour in the fruit. The silver will absorb the heat and the bowl will not
crack.) Place plastic wrap directly on the flummery. Refrigerate for 6 hours, or overnight.

   Serve in dessert dishes, topped with whipped cream, and garnished with mint leaves and blueberries.

Victorian berry bowl set

LOUISA MAY ALCOTT'S APPLE SLUMP

SERVES 8 TO 10

*Alcott felt strongly that it was her responsibility to provide for her family. Her father,
a Transcendentalist philosopher, was hardly a good provider. She wrote prodigiously
all her life, and in her journal, recorded, "Goethe put his sorrows and joys into poems. I turn my
adventures into bread and butter." She was also quite domestic and this recipe, changed slightly,
was often served at Orchard House in Concord where she lived.*

APPLES

6 cups peeled, cored, and sliced
   cooking apples, such as yellow
   Delicious, Northern Spy,
   or Red Romes
¾ cup granulated sugar
¼ cup packed light brown sugar
½ teaspoon ground cinnamon
½ teaspoon grated nutmeg
¾ cup cider or one 5-ounce
   can apple juice

SLUMP

1½ cups all-purpose flour
½ cup granulated sugar
2 teaspoons baking powder
¼ teaspoon salt
1 large egg
½ cup milk
½ cup (1 stick) butter, melted

Garnish: granulated sugar,
   grated nutmeg, and half-and-half

Preheat the oven to 350° F.

Place the apples in a greased 3-quart 9 × 13-inch flat baking dish and add the sugars, cinnamon, and nutmeg; toss. Pour over the cider or apple juice and mix again. Cover and bake for 30 minutes, or until the apples are partially tender and puffy.

Meanwhile, prepare the slump: In a large bowl, whisk together the flour, sugar, baking powder, and salt. In a small bowl, beat the egg, then stir in the milk and butter. Make a well in the dry ingredients and pour in the egg mixture. Blend gently just to mix; the batter will be very soft.

Remove the apples from the oven and drop the batter by tablespoonfuls on top of the hot apples—about 15 dollops. With the back of a tablespoon, pat out the batter evenly. Sprinkle a bit of sugar and additional nutmeg on top and return the apples to the oven immediately. Continue baking 30 minutes longer, or until the top of the slump is golden brown and crusty looking. Serve while warm with cream.

STEAMED APPLE DUMPLINGS

SERVES 6

*Madeleine Fisher, a librarian who loves old cookbooks and recipes as much as I do, shared with
me this old recipe of her family's, which she prepares as a nostalgic treat. These dumplings are steamed in individual
bags. Pudding bags were made of muslin or knit out of cotton yarn and resembled a man's stocking cap.
The puddings were frequently steamed on top of the vegetables in the great black iron kettles hanging in the
fireplace, or dropped into boiling water; pudding dishes were called twifflers. Another piece of
whimsical information—fat little boys were sometimes called pudding bags.
This version of apple dumplings is very soft and not overly sweet; it is not a quick recipe, but I know there will
be those who will remember it with affection and be glad to know the recipe is again in print.*

FILLING
2 large cooking apples
6 tablespoons granulated sugar
6 tablespoons packed
    light brown sugar
1 teaspoon ground cinnamon
6 teaspoons butter

DUMPLINGS
2 cups all-purpose flour
4 teaspoons baking powder
½ teaspoon salt

½ teaspoon cream of tartar
3 tablespoons granulated sugar
¾ cup (1½ sticks) butter
½ cup plus 3 tablespoons milk

DUMPLING BAGS
1 yard 45-inch muslin,
    cut into six 10-inch circles
Six 10-inch pieces of kitchen cord

Grated nutmeg
Flour

Peel and core the apples and chop them finely. Set aside (add a little Fruit Fresh to keep them from browning). In a small bowl, combine the sugars with the cinnamon. In a large bowl, whisk together the flour, baking powder, salt, cream of tartar, and sugar. Cut in the ¾ cup of butter until coarse crumbs form. Add the milk and mix until blended; the dough will be stiff but springy. Transfer the dough to a floured surface and roll out ⅜ inch thick to a 15 × 12-inch rectangle. Cut into six 5-inch squares. On top of each square of dough, place a heaping ⅓ cup of the apples; top with 2 tablespoons of the sugar mixture and 1 teaspoon of butter. Bring the dough up around the apples and pinch the edges together to seal.

Meanwhile, fill a large saucepan or Dutch oven 10 inches in diameter half full of water and bring to a boil. Moisten the muslin squares under running water, wring them out well, and spread out on the countertop. Sprinkle each cloth liberally with nutmeg, then flour. With a metal spatula, transfer one dumpling to each muslin square. Bring up the edges of the cloth around the dumplings and tie tightly with kitchen cord, leaving room for the dumplings to puff while cooking. Lower the bagged dumplings into the boiling water, cover the pot, and simmer for 1 hour. Do not peek! (The dumplings might tip over when you drop them in, but that won't hurt them.)

With tongs, remove the bags to a jelly roll pan to catch the drips and untie or cut the strings with scissors. Remove the dumplings from the muslin and place in individual bowls. Serve hot with milk or cream and pass additional sugar (I like to use dark brown sugar) and nutmeg.

A page from one of my mother's hand-written cookbooks

Mix together
2 beaten eggs.
4 T sugar.
salt.
¾ c hot milk
¾ c boiling water
1 tsp vanilla
pour into 4 custard cups
bake 45 m. in

Sugarless Cookies.   (Very soft)

2 c sorghum
1 c lard.
4 beaten eggs.
3 T soda.
salt.
raisins, nuts or chocolate bits
flour enough to make stiff 3½ c

Mush
8 ¼ c hot water
2 ¾ c cold water mixed with -
3 c corn meal + ½ c flour.

Mrs Mems Pickles 109
Helen Kohn Cookies 113
Jubilees 113
Cherry Pudding 212
Peach Pudding 255

LEMON SPONGE PUDDING

SERVES 4 TO 6

*Sponge puddings date back to the Civil War, and at that time, the coconut had to
be hand grated, no small job. This dessert is always a treat with its delicate cakelike layer on top and a
piercingly tart lemon custard underneath.
Sometimes a spot of strawberry jam would be placed on top of each serving, but
that's purely optional. I, myself, prefer it plain.*

2 tablespoons (¼ stick) butter, softened	**½ teaspoon salt**
1 cup sugar	**1¼ cups sweetened, flaked coconut**
4 large eggs, separated	**2 tablespoons all-purpose flour**
⅓ cup fresh lemon juice	**1 cup milk**
1 tablespoon grated lemon zest	

Preheat the oven to 350° F.

In a large mixer bowl, cream the butter, then add the sugar gradually, beating until fluffy. Add the egg yolks and beat well. Add the lemon juice, zest, and salt; blend. Fold in ¾ cup coconut and the flour. Stir in the milk. In another mixer bowl, beat the egg whites until stiff but not dry. Fold into the lemon mixture by hand, using a rubber spatula. Pour into a 1½- to 2-quart round bowl or soufflé dish.

Place in a shallow pan of hot water, which should be deep enough so the water comes up to half the depth of the bowl. Bake for 1 hour, or until the top is puffy and golden brown. Toast the remaining ½ cup coconut in a 350° F. oven for 3 minutes and sprinkle over the baked pudding. Refrigerate and serve cold.

A nutmeg grater

ℒAYERED PUMPKIN GINGERBREAD WITH HOT CARAMEL SAUCE

SERVES 9

Poet Emily Dickinson was in charge of the baking at her house, and her letters and poems
make frequent references to this skill. The neighborhood children remember her making them individual ginger-
breads, which she would then lower out of the window in a basket with a cord attached to the handle.
I wonder what she would think of this gingerbread, with its crispy pale cookie base topped by a delicately flavored
pumpkin cake? Hot caramel sauce is an absolutely marvelous addition.

CAKE
2¼ cups all-purpose flour
½ cup granulated sugar
⅔ cup cold butter
¾ cup finely chopped pecans
1½ teaspoons ground ginger
1 teaspoon baking soda
¼ teaspoon ground cloves
¼ teaspoon salt
½ cup light molasses

½ cup canned pumpkin
1 large egg
1 teaspoon vanilla extract

SAUCE
½ cup (1 stick) butter
1¼ cups packed light brown sugar
2 tablespoons light corn syrup
1 cup half-and-half
1 teaspoon vanilla extract

Preheat the oven to 350° F. (If using a glass dish, lower the heat to 325° F.).

In a large mixer bowl, combine the flour and sugar. Cut in the butter so the mixture resembles fine crumbs. (These first 2 steps can be done in a food processor.) Add the pecans and blend. Press 1¼ cups of the mixture firmly into an ungreased 9 × 9-inch pan; set aside.

To the remaining crumbs, add the rest of the ingredients and mix well; pour evenly over the cookie base. Bake 40 minutes, or until the crust is firm and a tester comes out clean.

Meanwhile, make the sauce: In a saucepan, melt the butter over medium-low heat. Add the brown sugar and corn syrup. Bring the mixture to a boil and cook until the sugar dissolves, stirring frequently, for about 5 minutes. Add the half-and-half, return to a boil, and remove from the heat. Stir in the vanilla.

Serve the warm gingerbread, cut into squares, with the hot caramel sauce over the top.

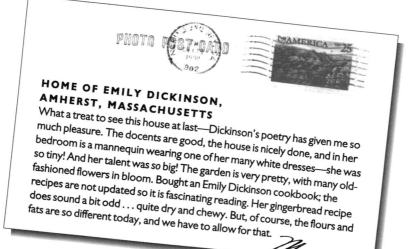

PHOTO POST CARD

AMERICA 25

HOME OF EMILY DICKINSON, AMHERST, MASSACHUSETTS
What a treat to see this house at last—Dickinson's poetry has given me so much pleasure. The docents are good, the house is nicely done, and in her bedroom is a mannequin wearing one of her many white dresses—she was so tiny! And her talent was so big! The garden is very pretty, with many old-fashioned flowers in bloom. Bought an Emily Dickinson cookbook; the recipes are not updated so it is fascinating reading. Her gingerbread recipe does sound a bit odd . . . quite dry and chewy. But, of course, the flours and fats are so different today, and we have to allow for that. *M*

Summer
DAYS

WE RETURN HOME with pleasure, as always. The cats are overjoyed at our return, and there is much meowing and rolling over and displaying of tummies for our attention. We hurry down the steps to see what is happening in the lower garden. We are not disappointed; tall irises dominate the perennial border with their dramatic blue blooms, and next to them, silky pink Oriental poppies have exploded into joyous color.

Gardening friends stop by with a basket of their first blackberries and tiny zucchini and yellow squash. I look forward to trying a new recipe or two, and phone the hardware store to reserve several boxes of canning jars in various sizes. They go fast, and I must have plenty on hand as the blueberries, elderberries, and harvest apples ripen. After we return from this midwestern jaunt, the tomatoes will be ready.

Traveling in the Midwest in the summer is such a treat, for the farmland is so reassuringly verdant and the horizon goes on and on. The still existing tidy white farmhouses with the red barns comfort me, country girl that I am and always will be. From Missouri, we'll swing south, an unusual choice for this time of year, but it will be fun to see how the Fourth of July is celebrated in New Orleans. And the thought of those pralines. . . .

In the evening, after the van has been repacked and we are ready for bed, I lower the blinds against the gathering dark. The elderberry bushes, their trusses of bloom gleaming white in the distance, are incandescent in the night. An a cappella cricket chorus tunes up in the copse of trees at the end of the garden. The cats stretch out on our beds, purring with satisfaction. All's well with the world.

Fourth of
JULY

A FAMILY REUNION and fireworks" is the inevitable response when American cooks are asked how they celebrate the Fourth. The foods served frequently reflected the part of the country where I was doing the interviews, though hot dogs and hamburgers were popular everywhere.

If any food has been linked historically to this holiday, it must be barbecue fare. In New York City, old-timers recall pig roasts, the tender juicy meat sold from booths lining Broadway. Many small towns and villages celebrated the same way, followed by a concert in the park, where local musicians played in a Victorian-designed bandstand. In Maine, a traditional Fourth of July meal is poached salmon with new potatoes and peas, accompanied by an egg sauce. In Texas, it is grilled steak, accompanied by hash brown potatoes and a pot of highly seasoned pinto beans. Lemonade is a favorite beverage everywhere, and many families get out the old-fashioned ice cream freezer.

My earliest memory of Independence Day was at my paternal grandfather's farm, named Twin Oaks Farm by my grandmother, who had planted oak trees on either side of the driveway. The menu varied from year to year; sometimes there was fried chicken, sometimes ham. Of course, there would be potato salad, and doubtless cucumber and onions from the garden. But we always had homemade ice cream and pies and cakes, and fruit cobblers of some sort—this was the season for blackberries and currants, as well as fireworks.

My grandfather bought large boxes of fireworks from the hardware store in town, and we could hardly wait until dark. The fireflies would arrive, winking gently, signaling the end of day and the beginning of the fireworks display. We children were permitted to run about with sparklers and whirligigs, but that was small stuff. The real show began modestly with cherry bombs, ladyfingers, and zebras, with the best saved until last, the Roman candles and the ominously named M-80, which ended the night with a real flourish.

Grilled Chili-Crusted Sirloin Steak Grilled Turkey Burgers Panfried Fish with Roasted Pecan Butter Leah Chase's Southern Fried Chicken Potato Salad with Mustard Dressing Baked Ham Amish Escalloped Tomatoes Sweet Potato Hash Browns with Bacon and Onions Sautéed Squash Salad with Basil and Mint Praline Ice Cream Really Good Chocolate Sauce Blackberry Cobbler with Lemon Curd Sauce Cherry-Pecan Crumble

GRILLED CHILI-CRUSTED SIRLOIN STEAK

SERVES 6 TO 8

It is considered impolite to ask a Texas rancher how many acres of land he owns; this would be the equivalent of asking how much money he had in his savings account. So if you are invited to a Texas barbecue, mind your tongue. What these folk call a barbecue, we would call a cookout. In the Lone Star State, seasoning a piece of locally raised meat with a spicy rub, then gathering around an open fire to cook it was an early cowboy tradition. Today, barbecuing or grilling is still a popular way to feed a group, small or large. The meat is prepared on fifty-gallon oil drums, which have been cut in half lengthwise, and mesquite branches are laid on the fire to add a regional flavor. This spicy rub should be applied to the sirloin 24 hours before broiling; it gives grilled steak real style.

1 tablespoon kosher salt
1 teaspoon coarsely ground black pepper
2 teaspoons chili powder
1¼ teaspoons dried oregano

1 teaspoon ground cumin
¼ teaspoon ground red pepper
3 to 3½ pounds top sirloin, approximately 2 inches thick

In a small bowl, combine the salt, black pepper, chili powder, oregano, cumin, and red pepper. Trim all the fat off the meat and rub the mixture onto both sides of the steak. Place the meat in a shallow glass dish, cover tightly with plastic wrap, and refrigerate overnight.

Remove the steak from the refrigerator about 2 hours before grilling. Light a charcoal fire, and when the coals are covered with fine ash, grill the steak about 6 inches from the heat. Grill for about 25 minutes for rare, 30 minutes for medium-rare, turning once. Slice thinly and serve.

A ceramic salt box

GRILLED TURKEY BURGERS

SERVES 4

For most American families, Fourth of July celebrations are synonymous with backyard cookouts.
Hot dogs and hamburgers are inevitably on the menu at such gatherings. Ground turkey gives us a new, more
healthful twist to an old favorite. I like it grilled over charcoal, like a hamburger, and have found
that ground turkey is enhanced by rather assertive seasonings. Serve this with Tomato Chutney (page 207).

1 pound ground turkey
1 large egg white
2 tablespoons finely
   minced onion
2 tablespoons whole wheat
   bread crumbs
2 tablespoons minced parsley
2 tablespoons vermouth,
   broth, or water

1 tablespoon freshly minced sage
   or 1½ teaspoons dried ground
2 teaspoons finely minced fresh
   tarragon or ½ teaspoon dried
1 teaspoon finely minced garlic
Salt and pepper to taste
Dash of hot red pepper sauce

Hamburger buns (optional)

In a large mixing bowl, combine the turkey with the remaining ingredients; mix well. Form into 4 patties and refrigerate for at least 3 hours to give the flavors a chance to develop.

    Preheat the grill or oven broiler and pan for 10 minutes (if using the oven, broil 6 inches from the heat). Broil the burgers on each side for 4 minutes, or until well done. The patties will puff up slightly when done. Serve immediately, either in buns or not.

PANFRIED FISH WITH ROASTED PECAN BUTTER

SERVES 4 TO 6

The Fourth of July signals the beginning of the season for those who summer on a lake.
Cottages are opened up and cleaned, the pier is put in, flags are hung, and it's time for fun. Serious
fishermen go out every morning in the boat and return with bulging creels, and holiday
mornings are no exception. Platters of fried fish are often the entrée for a Fourth of July meal
when the whole family congregates at the cottage.
This southern recipe is always a big hit; the fish are sautéed, then topped with a well-seasoned
Pecan Butter and quickly broiled. Serve with Fresh Tomato and Cucumber Salad
(page 225) and you'll have a fine dinner.

PECAN BUTTER
1 cup dry-roasted pecan pieces
½ cup (1 stick) butter,
cut into 1-inch pieces
2 teaspoons fresh lemon juice
⅛ teaspoon ground red pepper
1 teaspoon minced garlic
1 teaspoon Worcestershire sauce
¼ teaspoon salt

2 cups all-purpose flour
1 teaspoon salt

1 teaspoon sweet paprika
(not Hungarian)
½ teaspoon ground black pepper
⅛ teaspoon ground
red pepper (optional)
Six 4- to 6-ounce fish fillets
(use a firm-fleshed, skinless variety, such
as walleye, trout, blue gill, or red snapper)
Vegetable oil

Garnish: lemon wedges

Prepare the Pecan Butter: In a blender or food processor, combine the pecans, butter, lemon juice, pepper, garlic, Worcestershire, and salt. Process until it has a smooth, pastelike consistency. Set aside at room temperature.

Preheat the broiler.

In a shallow dish, mix together the flour, salt, paprika, and peppers. Dredge each fish fillet until lightly coated, shaking off any excess. In a large sauté pan or electric skillet, heat the oil to 350° F. (Use enough oil to cover the fish at least halfway.) Fry each fillet until golden brown on each side (approximately 4 minutes per side), turning the fillet only once. Remove to paper toweling to drain. When all the fillets are fried, place them on a broiler pan and spread each fillet with 2 to 3 tablespoons of Pecan Butter. Place under the broiler until the butter barely bubbles, about 30 to 45 seconds. Serve immediately with lemon wedges.

*L*EAH CHASE'S SOUTHERN FRIED CHICKEN

SERVES 4

When we think of picnic food, fried chicken immediately comes to mind. This recipe from Leah Chase would
be good anytime, especially for a Fourth of July picnic, for it is just as delicious cold as it is hot.

3 pounds chicken, legs, thighs, and breast halves	**½ cup water**
	2 garlic cloves, finely minced
2 teaspoons salt	**2 cups all-purpose flour**
2 teaspoons pepper	**1 teaspoon paprika**
2 large eggs	**¼ teaspoon dried ground thyme**
½ cup evaporated milk	**1 quart peanut oil for frying**

Season the chicken with salt and pepper and arrange in a flat 9 × 13 inch dish. In a small bowl, beat the eggs and add the milk, water, and garlic. Pour over the chicken and let stand for 5 minutes or up to 2 hours.

In a heavy paper bag, combine the flour, paprika, and thyme. Drop 4 pieces of chicken at a time into the bag and shake well to cover. Place the floured chicken on a piece of wax paper and repeat with the remaining chicken.

In an electric skillet, heat the oil to 350° F. With tongs, place 5 or 6 pieces of chicken in the skillet at one time; do not overcrowd. Fry, turning as the chicken browns. The legs will take about 15 minutes, the breasts and thighs, about 20 minutes; the chicken should be a deep golden brown. Drain the chicken on paper towels, transfer to a platter, and if desired keep warm in a low oven while the remaining chicken is fried. Serve hot or cold.

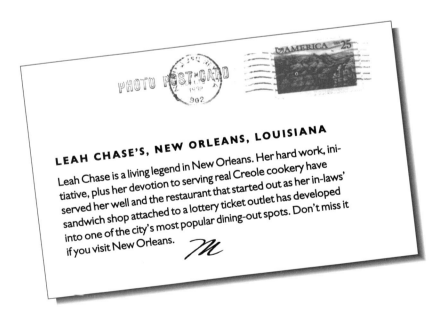

PHOTO POST CARD   AMERICA 25

LEAH CHASE'S, NEW ORLEANS, LOUISIANA

Leah Chase is a living legend in New Orleans. Her hard work, initiative, plus her devotion to serving real Creole cookery have served her well and the restaurant that started out as her in-laws' sandwich shop attached to a lottery ticket outlet has developed into one of the city's most popular dining-out spots. Don't miss it if you visit New Orleans. *M*

$\mathscr{P}$OTATO SALAD WITH MUSTARD DRESSING

SERVES 12

*I enjoy book signings, for I get to meet my readers and viewers, and find out what they are
thinking and cooking. I thoroughly enjoy discovering new bookstores around the
country as well. One of the most successful independent bookstores in the Midwest is Books and Company
in Dayton, Ohio. If you are ever in the area, I do urge you to stop in there, for there is always
something going on, from overnight slumber parties to classes on flower arranging. On my last visit there,
Shirley Partner brought her books to be signed and wanted to know if I would be interested
in her family's recipe for mustard potato salad. "It's just different," she said, "and the recipe is very old.
We always have it at family reunions."
I looked over the recipe, agreed it was different, and knew I would try it. And it is exceptional.
The mustard dressing is very piquant, both sweet and sour. Give the salad plenty of time
to absorb the dressing and prepare it in a shallow bowl or pan. (The celery seed is my addition.) Adding
vinegar to the cooking water keeps the potatoes firm. This salad can be made a day in advance.*

SALAD	DRESSING
5 pounds potatoes, preferably red-skinned, peeled and quartered	**2 large eggs**
2 tablespoons cider vinegar	**1 cup sugar**
½ pound bacon, cut into 1-inch pieces (8 slices)	**⅓ cup yellow ballpark mustard**
¾ cup chopped onion	**½ cup plus 2 tablespoons cider vinegar**
2 teaspoons celery seed	**1 cup less 2 tablespoons water**
1½ teaspoons salt	
1 teaspoon coarsely ground pepper	**Garnish: ¾ cup chopped parsley**

Place the potatoes in a large pot with water to cover. Add the vinegar, cover, and bring to a boil over high heat. Lower the heat to medium and cook for 25 minutes, or until the potatoes are fork-tender. Drain very well and set aside to cool.

Meanwhile, sauté the bacon until crisp. Remove the pan from the heat and set aside. Cube the potatoes and place in a shallow pan (I use a 16-inch round cake pan). Pour the bacon grease and bacon over the potatoes and add the onions, celery seed, salt, and pepper; toss lightly.

Make the dressing: Beat the eggs slightly in a large saucepan. Add the sugar and blend. Beat in the mustard, then add the vinegar and water. Bring to a boil over medium-high heat and cook until the mixture starts to thicken, about 8 to 10 minutes, stirring frequently. The mixture will be quite runny. Pour the hot dressing over the potatoes and combine. Allow the salad to stand for 3 hours to absorb all the dressing, stirring occasionally. Stir in the parsley. Transfer to a serving bowl or storage container.

BAKED HAM

SERVES 10 TO 12

*It isn't surprising that roast pig and smoked hams were favorite foods at early
Independence Day gatherings. Pork was readily available, economical and could be prepared in
large quantities. Baked ham still is frequently served at this holiday, and this recipe from
North Carolina, which marinates for 3 days, yields a moist and fruity ham.*

One 5- to 6-pound smoked ham, fully cooked	**1 cup honey**
¾ cup fresh orange juice	**Whole cloves**
½ cup dry sherry	**1 cup packed dark brown sugar**
	2 tablespoons ground mustard

Trim the skin from the ham, leaving a thin, even layer of fat. With a skewer, poke the ham all over at 2-inch intervals. Place the ham in a large resealable plastic bag and place in a large shallow pan. In a small bowl, combine the orange juice, sherry, and honey; pour over the ham and seal the bag securely. Marinate in the refrigerator for 3 days, turning the ham every 12 hours.

Preheat the oven to 325° F.

Remove the ham from the bag, reserving the marinade. With the ham fat side up, score the fat in a diamond design and stud with cloves. Place the ham, fat side up, on a rack in a shallow roasting pan. Insert a meat thermometer, making sure it does not touch the bone. Pour all but 1 tablespoon of the marinade over the ham. Bake for 1½ hours, or until the meat thermometer registers 130° F.

In a small bowl, combine the brown sugar, mustard, and the tablespoon of reserved marinade and brush the exposed portion of the ham. Cover with a tent of aluminum foil and bake an additional 15 minutes, or until the meat thermometer registers 140° F. Remove from the oven and allow the meat to stand for 10 minutes, then slice thinly and serve.

Bone-handled serving set

On the first day of our quest for heirloom midwestern and southern recipes, we didn't even make it out of Indiana. We got sidetracked by goats—lots of goats.

I've enjoyed the delicate, slightly lemony award-winning goat cheese from Capriole, manufactured in the southern part of the state, for years. This was the perfect opportunity to meet Judy and Larry Schad who create this marvelous delicacy at their country house, actually a restored stagecoach stop, deep in the woods.

The Schads are not at all your typical farmers; she has her doctorate in English and Larry is an attorney. She met us in the driveway, holding two birth-wet baby kids in her arms. "These babies were just born," she apologized. "You'll have to excuse us so we can get them on bottles right away. They have to learn how to suck immediately or we lose them."

Later, we toured their immaculate small dairy building where they process the milk from the 125-member goat herd they have built up from a pair of goats that were originally part of their children's 4-H project. "Going into the cheese business was not part of even our wildest dreams. But the goats had babies and were producing all this milk," laughs Judy. "Out of desperation, we learned to make cheese." Today, Capriole sends its cheese to restaurants and gourmet shops all over the United States, including Dean and DeLuca in New York, and by mail (page 299). The quality is impressive, and we enthusiastically sampled an herb-covered fresh fromage log;

chèvre pyramids in several flavors, including ash, pepper, shiitake, and parsley; plus one of their best-sellers, Festiva, a colorful jack, marbled with basil, garlic pesto, and sun-dried tomatoes.

Outside, Dick set up his camera tripod for pictures and was immediatley surrounded by a group of goats; one began munching his jacket with as much enthusiasm as we had given the cheese. "They are rather curious," apologizes Judy. Dick snaps away.

We drive on to Newburgh, a small quaint Kentucky River town but still in Indiana. The river is wide and placid at Newburgh, and on this summer day, we see small fishing boats and an occasional barge moving quietly upstream. Staying overnight at the Phelps Mansion Inn, we met our friends, the Klugers, at Clarinda's Cottage Tea Room for dinner. Marilyn Kluger has published several cookbooks and also writes for Gourmet magazine; Kurt owns and operates the Country Store, a real old-timey emporium that also reflects his wife's interest in fine cookery and herbs. The evening ended with our exchanging recipes, as it always does when two cooks get together.

The next morning we are served an excellent breakfast, then make time to visit all the town's antiques shops. Miraculously I find some gold-rimmed footed juice glasses that match the ones I use for sorbets and syllabub, a real find. Dick sighs and packs them away under the sofa in the van. He doesn't understand why cooks feel they need more than just one set of dishes and glassware.

We finally get out of Indiana into Illinois by noon. Whenever we are driving through the seemingly endless prairies of Illinois I marvel that this land was ever settled. Our country is so big! Yet from the beginning we were a restless folk and have always been on the move, as early as the late 1700s, looking for something better.

AMISH ESCALLOPED TOMATOES

SERVES 6

I stay in touch with the Amish community and had been told about an Amish woman who was making very nice faceless Amish dolls to sell. I had only the vaguest of directions for finding her house, and ended up going from farm to farm, asking for Esther Yoder. A lot of dogs barked at me. After several stops, I pulled into her yard about suppertime. However, she graciously showed me her dolls. As always when I am with an Amish cook, I enquired about her favorite recipes. "Oh, I like everything and so do the family. Tonight, though, I'm making scalloped tomatoes. It's nothing fancy," she said, "but it sure is good." I have added basil to this dish; it is quite optional.

One 1-pound 12-ounce can peeled tomatoes or 6 medium-sized ripe tomatoes, peeled and cored	½ teaspoon salt
	¼ teaspoon grated nutmeg
	Dash of pepper
2 tablespoons packed light brown sugar	1½ cups soft bread crumbs
2 teaspoons dried basil or 1½ tablespoons fresh minced	½ cup soda cracker crumbs
	3 tablespoons butter, divided

Preheat the oven to 375° F.

In a food processor, briefly process the tomatoes, brown sugar, basil, salt, nutmeg, and pepper together until the tomatoes are coarsely chopped. In a greased 3-inch-deep, 7½-inch-diameter soufflé dish, layer half of the bread crumbs, then half of the tomato mixture, then all of the cracker crumbs. Dot with half of the butter. Add the remaining tomatoes, top with the remaining bread crumbs, and dot with the remaining butter. Bake for 35 to 40 minutes, or until the top is golden and bubbly. Serve immediately.

SWEET POTATO HASH BROWNS WITH BACON AND ONIONS

SERVES 4 TO 6

In some parts of the country, hash brown potatoes are considered a breakfast dish, yet in the Midwest and the South, we find them served with grilled meats and even hamburgers. This recipe from Louisiana uses sweet potatoes instead of white potatoes, a tasty change. Using turkey bacon cuts down on bad fats, but if you prefer, you can substitute regular bacon.

4 medium sweet potatoes, peeled and quartered (about 2 pounds)	¼ teaspoon grated nutmeg
	Salt and freshly ground pepper to taste
1 tablespoon cider vinegar	
¼ cup peanut oil, divided	
6 slices of turkey bacon, cut into ½-inch pieces	Garnish: 3 to 4 tablespoons chopped parsley
½ cup chopped onion	

Place the potatoes in a medium saucepan and cover with cold water; add the vinegar. Bring to a boil and cook until tender, about 15 minutes. Drain and cover with cold water until cooled to room temperature, then cut into ¾-inch chunks.

In a large sauté pan, heat 1 tablespoon oil over medium heat. Add the bacon pieces and sauté until they are nearly done and beginning to crisp up, about 5 minutes. Add the onions and cook until they are golden to brown in color, about 5 minutes. Remove both from the pan with a slotted spoon and reserve.

Return the sauté pan to the stove, add the remaining oil, and heat until hot but not smoking. Add the potato chunks, sprinkle with the nutmeg, and cook without stirring until they are golden brown on the bottom, about 10 minutes. Turn the potatoes and cook 5 minutes longer. Remove from the heat, stir in the bacon and onions, season with salt and pepper, and sprinkle with the parsley. Serve immediately.

Sautéed Squash Salad with Basil and Mint

SERVES 6

This attractive and different summer salad was served to me by Nick De Gamo, a bachelor cook in Chicago, who regularly prepares his Italian grandmother's recipes when he entertains "because they taste the best." Rounds of yellow and green summer squash are sautéed in olive oil, then seasoned with basil, mint, and garlic, with a touch of balsamic vinegar added for piquancy. The dish can be made in advance and kept at room temperature until serving time.
Use tender young squash—ones about 8 inches long are just right.

4 medium zucchini	½ cup small fresh basil leaves
4 medium yellow squash	¼ cup small fresh mint leaves
About ½ cup olive oil	3 garlic cloves, finely minced
1 small onion, peeled, sliced,	Freshly ground pepper
and separated into rings	3 tablespoons basalmic vinegar

Wash the squash and trim the ends, but do not peel. Slice into ¼-inch rounds. Heat 3 tablespoons oil in an electric skillet to 350° F. Add the squash in batches (do not crowd) and cook until golden brown, about 3 minutes on each side, adding more oil as necessary. Transfer the cooked squash with a slotted spoon to a 9 × 12-inch serving platter, alternating green and yellow slices. They should overlap but still remain in one layer. Tuck in the onion rings and basil and mint leaves alternately with the squash. In a small bowl, combine the garlic, pepper, and vinegar and sprinkle it on the squash with a teaspoon. Cover tightly with plastic wrap and allow to stand for at least 1 hour. The longer it stands, the better it gets. If refrigerated, allow the dish to come to room temperature before serving.

Praline Ice Cream

MAKES 2 QUARTS

Pralines, those beloved southern confections (page 233), give this very special ice cream its delicate flavor.
Although it needs no topping, you could drizzle on a bit of chocolate sauce, and it is nice
to pass a tray of cookies when you serve this dessert. Let the ice cream soften slightly before serving.

3 cups whole milk	**1 tablespoon vanilla extract**
4 large egg yolks	**1½ cups whipping cream**
¾ cup sugar	**1½ cups pralines, broken into**
Dash of salt	**coarse ¼- to ½-inch pieces**

In the top of a double boiler over medium heat, scald the milk until bubbles form around the edge of the pan, about 10 minutes. In a medium mixing bowl, beat the egg yolks well. Pour about ½ cup of the hot milk over the egg yolks and blend. Add the egg mixture to the remaining hot milk, stirring with a wooden spoon; do not use a whisk. Place the double boiler top over simmering water; stir in the sugar and salt and cook until the mixture coats the back of a spoon. This will take 20 to 25 minutes. Remove from the heat, lay a piece of plastic wrap directly on the mixture, and chill thoroughly, about 1½ hours or overnight.

In a mixer bowl, whip the cream until it is not quite stiff enough to hold its shape. Fold the whipped cream into the chilled egg-milk mixture with the vanilla. Pour into the freezer can of an ice cream maker and process according to the manufacturer's instructions. (See Note on page 97 if using an old-fashioned freezer.) Just before the ice cream is done, fold in the crumbled pralines.

Really Good Chocolate Sauce

MAKES 2 CUPS

A friend of mine whose children eat lots of ice cream with chocolate sauce tried this recipe and
declared she'd never buy chocolate sauce in the grocery again—this homemade sauce was so good and
so easy and so economical. That is just the kind of recipe I like to have in my cookbooks.

1 cup light corn syrup	**⅛ teaspoon salt**
¾ cup sugar	**2 tablespoons (¼ stick) butter**
½ cup Hershey's cocoa powder	**½ teaspoon vanilla extract**
½ cup hot water	

In a medium saucepan, whisk the corn syrup, sugar, cocoa, water, and salt together. Cook over medium-low heat, stirring occasionally, until the mixture comes to a boil. Reduce the heat and slowly simmer for 10 to 12 minutes without stirring. Remove from the heat and add the butter and vanilla. Transfer the mixture to a mixer bowl and beat for 3 minutes; this is to assure a uniform texture without graininess. Pour into a container with a tight-fitting lid (I use an old pickle jar) and store in the refrigerator for up to 2 weeks. But need I tell you? It won't last that long.

This hand-cranked ice cream freezer has had plenty of use

BLACKBERRY COBBLER WITH LEMON CURD SAUCE

SERVES 12

Blackberries used to grow wild here in the Midwest, and my mother and I would pick them every summer along the roadside, clambering through sassafras thickets and patches of wild orange daylilies to reach them. Blackberries grow on thorny bushes, and though it was always hot weather, my mother insisted I protect my arms with long black stockings with the feet cut out to expose my fingers so I could pick the berries. We fastened small pails to our belts and picked and picked— all day, so it seemed. She always brought lemonade along, though, and sometimes cookies, which lifted both our spirits considerably.

Today most of the berries sold commercially come from Washington state, and there are nearly 450 named varieties. One of the most famous is the Marionberry, which has a fine, complex winey flavor. They are worth looking for, and buying them at a farmer's market is a lot easier than picking your own—believe me!

BLACKBERRY COBBLER
½ cup (1 stick) unsalted butter
1 cup all-purpose flour
2 cups sugar
1 teaspoon baking powder
½ teaspoon grated nutmeg
½ cup half-and-half
1 teaspoon vanilla extract
2 cups fresh or frozen blackberries

LEMON CURD SAUCE
6 large egg yolks, beaten
1 cup sugar
1 cup freshly squeezed lemon juice
¾ to 1 cup (1½ to 2 sticks)
   unsalted butter,
   cut into small pieces
1 tablespoon grated lemon zest

Prepare the Blackberry Cobbler: Preheat the oven to 350° F. Melt the butter in a square 9-inch baking dish in the preheating oven.

In a medium mixing bowl, whisk together the flour, 1 cup sugar, the baking powder, and nutmeg. Combine the half-and-half and vanilla in a measuring cup, then add to the flour mixture, blending until crumbly. Press the dough into the baking dish on top of the butter. (Some butter will spill over onto the dough.) In a medium saucepan, stir together the blackberries with the remaining 1 cup sugar over low heat until just warmed through. Pour over the dough and bake for 50 to 55 minutes, or until the crust is golden brown. The crust will rise to the surface. Serve warm or cold.

While the cobbler bakes (or cools), prepare the Lemon Curd Sauce: Strain the egg yolks through a sieve into a medium saucepan. Add the sugar and lemon juice, stir to combine, and cook over low heat until the mixture thickens and coats the back of a wooden spoon, about 5 minutes. Stir in the butter, 1 pat at a time, until it is fully incorporated and the mixture is smooth. Fold in the lemon zest.

To serve, place a large spoonful of lemon curd sauce on a plate and top with a slice of cobbler.

NOTE: *This recipe would taste equally good made with raspberries or other wild berries.*

CHERRY-PECAN CRUMBLE

SERVES 8 TO 10

Right after the strawberries are finished, it's cherry time! The cherry trees in our orchard were special to my brother and me; we peeled off the oozing sticky sap that appeared on the trunk of the tree and used it as chewing gum. We weren't depraved; chewing gum was not available during World War II and cherry gum was, well, a pretty fair substitute. The cherry trees were special to my mother as well; she forced boughs every spring into arching pink bouquets, and, in July, we could count on her deep-dish cherry pies and crumbles. I especially like the topping on this one; it has 2 cups of pecans among its ingredients. Serve it with heavy cream, whipped cream, or ice cream. I have made this with frozen cherries and it turns out just fine.

CHERRY FILLING
⅔ cup packed light brown sugar
2 tablespoons Minute Tapioca
¼ teaspoon grated nutmeg
   (or more to taste)
½ teaspoon almond extract
6 cups pitted tart red cherries
Red food coloring (optional)

TOPPING
1½ cups all-purpose flour
1½ cups granulated sugar
Speck of salt
¾ cup (1½ sticks) butter, cut into 1-inch slices
2 cups coarsely chopped pecans

Heavy cream, whipped cream, or ice cream

Preheat the oven to 350° F.

In a large bowl, mix together the brown sugar, tapioca, and nutmeg. Add the almond extract, cherries, and red food coloring if using, and combine thoroughly. Allow the mixture to stand for 10 minutes, then pour into a 9 × 13-inch greased baking dish.

Make the topping: In a bowl, combine the flour, sugar, salt, and butter with a pastry blender until it resembles coarse crumbs. (This can also be done in a food processor.) Mix in the chopped pecans and spoon the topping over the cherry mixture, spreading it out evenly. Bake the crumble for 1 hour, or until it is bubbling and the top is golden.

Serve slightly warm with heavy cream, whipped cream, or ice cream.

Church SOCIALS

*S*INCE I WRITE so frequently about rural America, I am often asked if the small towns are dying out as farms get larger and more men leave the land to work in the cities. I would have to answer "yes" and "no." We are losing small family farmers, for many reasons, all of them regrettable, and I deplore their passing. The small towns that service these rural communities, in some cases, do grow smaller, and it is hard for those merchants to compete with the malls in the nearby cities.

Yet as Dick and I drive all over the country, we see, to our relief, that small towns are not fading from view. In some instances, aggressive chambers of commerce have coaxed small industries (and sometimes, large ones) to settle in their communities, which keeps them flourishing. At the same time, there is also a decided movement of city residents to smaller communities, where life is more humanistic, the pace less grueling.

As long as a town can sustain a church, a fire department, and a tavern that serves decent food, the town will survive. And the most important of these three institutions is the church. A church is a reason for people to congregate, united by shared beliefs and goals and those church members will work their fingers to the bone finding ways to provide a Sunday school for their children. Church socials are one of the most common and best-loved ways to make money to support these programs.

A social has many guises—it can be a noodle supper (and the noodles are homemade, of course), a spaghetti supper, a homemade dough-nut day, a cake walk, a salad bar, a box social, a mincemeat stir-up day, or a holiday bazaar where you can buy anything from a quilt to a dried apple wreath. All of these bring the women, and a lot of the men, into the church to work, or to come and eat or buy. And they are unified in their goal—to keep those church doors open.

I love church socials. And I love their food.

*B*aked Chicken and Noodles *O*ld-Fashioned Chicken Loaf with Mushroom Sauce *A*ltenberg Chicken Potpie *B*risket and Sauerkraut with Dumplings *M*eat Loaf Roll Stuffed with Sauerkraut and Tomatoes *U*pside-Down Ham Loaf *S*paghetti and Meatball Dinner *K*entucky Burgoo *M*ethodist Church Potato Doughnuts *C*hurch Social Peach Ice Cream *C*hurch Cake Walk Fudge Cake *C*oconut-Pecan Filling and Frosting *A*pple Brown Betty

BAKED CHICKEN AND NOODLES

MAKES TWO 3-QUART DISHES TO SERVE 16 TO 20

For a successful church meal, the foods served must be hearty, economical to prepare, and preferably something that can be prepared in advance. This recipe is the one my mother most frequently took to the Flint Methodist Church for carry-in suppers; it is very old-fashioned, but one of the best of its genre. This kind of dish is still served at potlucks and carry-in meals all over the country. It makes a very large amount and could be halved, but since it freezes well, why not make the full recipe and freeze part for another time?

One 6-pound stewing hen	1 pound medium-wide noodles
2 large carrots, halved	3 hard-cooked eggs, coarsely chopped
2 celery stalks, halved	½ cup chopped parsley
2 medium onions, quartered	1 cup all-purpose flour
8 black peppercorns	Salt and white pepper to taste
Approximately 4 quarts water	4 cups finely crushed
2 cups (1 pound) plus 3 tablespoons butter	round buttery crackers
1 pound fresh mushrooms, coarsely chopped	

Place the hen, including the neck and the giblets (but not the liver), in a large stockpot. Add the carrots, celery, onions, peppercorns, and water. (The water should liberally cover the chicken—you need lots of broth for this recipe.) Cover and bring to a boil over high heat, skimming off any froth that forms on top of the stock. Reduce the heat and simmer, covered, for 2 hours, or until the chicken is very tender.

Meanwhile, over medium-low heat, melt 3 tablespoons butter in a large skillet. Add the mushrooms and sauté until golden brown, about 10 minutes; set aside.

When the chicken is done, remove it from the broth with tongs, transfer it to a shallow pan, and allow to cool a bit, then cut up the meat in fairly large pieces, discarding the bones and skin; set aside.

Strain the broth and degrease. Remove 7 cups of the broth from the stockpot and set aside. Bring the remaining broth, adding additional water if necessary, to a boil and add the noodles. Cook according to package directions until tender, then drain and set aside.

Preheat the oven to 375° F. Grease two 3-quart 9 × 13-inch flat casseroles and in each dish, layer the noodles, chicken, mushrooms, eggs, and parsley, beginning and ending with the noodles.

In a large saucepan, melt 1 cup of the butter over medium high heat. Whisk in the flour, cooking and stirring until it bubbles and becomes a smooth paste. Whisk in the reserved 7 cups of broth and continue cooking and stirring until the mixture thickens into gravy, about 10 minutes. Add salt and pepper to taste. Pour the gravy over the layers of chicken and noodles, making sure it gets down into the bottom of each dish.

In a small saucepan, melt the remaining cup of butter, then toss with the crushed crackers. Top each pan evenly with the crumbs. Bake the casseroles for 1 hour, or until they are heated through and the crumbs are golden brown.

NOTE: *You may freeze this dish before baking, but do not top with the crumbs until you are ready to bake it.*

OLD-FASHIONED CHICKEN LOAF WITH MUSHROOM SAUCE

SERVES 6

This soft savory chicken loaf, with its bread crumbs and rice, appeared at many church suppers across the Midwest at the turn of the century. The sauce is important to the success of this dish; don't omit it.

One 3- to 4-pound chicken or mixed
   meaty pieces
3 large eggs
1 cup cooked white rice
1 cup fresh bread crumbs
3 tablespoons butter, melted
1¼ cups chicken broth
1 cup milk

2 teaspoons powdered chicken stock base
   (optional, but it does add richness)
¼ teaspoon ground pepper
¼ cup chopped parsley
1 teaspoon hot red pepper sauce
½ teaspoon dried marjoram or
   2 teaspoons minced fresh
Mushroom Sauce (recipe follows)

In a large stockpot, simmer the chicken until tender, about 1 hour, depending on the age of the bird. (Chicken pieces will take less time.) Remove the meat from the bones, discard the skin and fat, and cut into small pieces. While boning the chicken, preheat the oven to 350° F. (You may cook and debone the chicken several days ahead.)

In a large bowl, beat the eggs lightly and stir in the rice, bread crumbs, butter, broth, milk, stock base if using, seasonings, and shredded chicken. Spoon into a greased 1½-quart casserole and bake for 50 minutes or until golden brown and puffy. Top with the Mushroom Sauce, and serve hot.

MUSHROOM SAUCE

3 tablespoons butter
¼ cup sliced fresh mushrooms
1 tablespoon all-purpose flour
1 cup chicken broth
3 tablespoons heavy cream

1 teaspoon minced parsley
1 tablespoon fresh lemon juice
¼ teaspoon paprika
Salt and pepper to taste

Melt the butter in a saucepan over medium heat. Add the mushrooms and sauté for 2 to 3 minutes, then stir in the flour. Cook and stir over medium-low heat until the mixture bubbles up in the center of the pan. Pour in the chicken broth and cream. Cook slowly until thickened, about 3 minutes, stirring constantly. Stir in the parsley, lemon juice, paprika, and salt and pepper. Keep warm until serving time.

ALTENBERG CHICKEN POTPIE

SERVES **6** GENEROUSLY

*I often say that I couldn't write my cookbooks without the help of scores of librarians and
that is absolutely sincere. It is so reassuring to find really comprehensive cookbook collections scattered
around the country, and they are not all in large cities. Many of these collections have been
carefully and lovingly amassed by thoughtful librarians making sure their own regional cookbooks have
been kept for the future. Madeleine Fisher of the Bell Memorial Library in Mentone, Indiana,
a town of a few hundred people, but the egg capital of America, shared with me this old, old recipe, which
would have been common at church socials. You won't be surprised that it is a chicken dish.
It has Pennsylvania Dutch antecedents, so this potpie is prepared not in a crust,
but rather simmered with large square noodles made of pastry dough. We both like it with saffron
but that is optional. And she cooks hers on top of the stove; I bake mine. It is certainly
plain country cooking, but I serve it to company, and they love it!*

1 recipe pie pastry (page 284)	1 large carrot, thinly sliced
8 large chicken breast halves, skin on, bone in	Salt and pepper to taste
6 chicken thighs, skin on	⅓ cup coarsely chopped parsley
6 chicken legs, skin on	4 cups chicken broth
4 large potatoes, peeled and	¼ teaspoon saffron threads
sliced ½ inch thick	or powdered saffron (optional)
3 medium onions, peeled	
and sliced ½ inch thick	Garnish: minced parsley

Roll out the pie pastry ¼ inch thick, and cut into 2-inch squares. You will need approximately 28 squares.
Set aside. Preheat the oven to 425° F.

In a heavy Dutch oven or roaster (mine is oval, 14 × 12 inches), arrange half of the chicken pieces,
potatoes, onions, carrots, seasonings, and the pastry squares in layers. Repeat, ending with a layer of pastry squares.

Heat the broth and add the saffron if using (it will tint the broth a nice rich yellow color). Pour the broth
over the chicken, cover, and bake for 30 minutes. Lower the heat to 325° F. and bake 2½ hours longer.
The chicken should be very tender. With a spatula and tongs, arrange the chicken and vegetables on dinner plates, and ladle some of the broth over all. Garnish with parsley. There will be enough for seconds,
and you will have requests!

BRISKET AND SAUERKRAUT WITH DUMPLINGS

SERVES 6

The Dutch, the Shakers, and the Germans all prepared beef brisket with sauerkraut,
a nice change from pork and sauerkraut. Many times the dish would be topped with dumplings, potpie
noodles, or served with spatzle. To ensure that the dumplings cook properly, use a large baking
pan that can also be used on top of the stove; I suggest a deep sauté pan, which is just about my favorite
pan anyway. If you don't want to bother with dumplings, boiled potatoes, dressed with butter
and chives, would also be a good accompaniment.
I broil the onion and meat the day before, wrap it in foil, and refrigerate it until I am ready to put it in
the oven with the kraut. This dish travels well; take it to your next church dinner.

3 pounds fresh beef brisket	**Pepper to taste**
1 large onion, chopped	**5 cups hot chicken broth or water**
2 teaspoons vegetable oil	**1 bay leaf**
1 pound sauerkraut, well drained	**Butter Dumplings (page 283)**
¼ teaspoon or more caraway seed	
2 teaspoons all-purpose flour	**Butter and horseradish**
1 tablespoon sugar	

Preheat the oven to broil. Line a 12 × 17-inch flat pan with foil and place the pan on it. Arrange the onions in a clump beside the meat and drizzle the oil over the onions. Broil the meat 6 inches from the heat, about 5 to 7 minutes on each side, and stir the onions with a fork so they too brown evenly.

Lower the oven temperature to 325° F. Place the kraut in an ovenproof 12-inch sauté pan and sprinkle it with the caraway seed, flour, sugar, and pepper. Transfer the brisket to the pan and work the onions into the kraut. Pour the hot chicken broth or water over all (there should be enough liquid to cover the meat; if not, add a bit more water) and add the bay leaf. Cover and bake for 1½ hours. Turn the brisket over and bake 1½ hours longer.

In the meantime, prepare the dumplings up to the point of adding the liquid. Remove the pan from the oven and place on top of the stove over low heat. Finish making the dumplings according to the recipe and drop onto the meat and kraut. Cover and simmer 25 minutes. To serve, remove the brisket from the pan, slice thinly, and arrange on a platter or in flat soup bowls. The kraut will be quite liquidy, so remove it with a slotted spoon. Add the dumplings to the soup bowls along with the meat and kraut. Pass butter to eat with the dumplings and horseradish for the meat.

MEAT LOAF ROLL STUFFED WITH SAUERKRAUT AND TOMATOES

SERVES 8 TO 10

In the 1930s, when our economy was much different, penny suppers were another way that churches made money, modest amounts to be sure. The women all contributed the food, which was "carried in," and at the door dollar bills were converted into pennies. And the food was sold for pennies—ten pennies for meat loaf, five pennies for escalloped tomatoes, five pennies for a piece of pie, one penny for a slice of bread and butter. Of course, people flocked in for these reasonably priced home-cooked meals.
Meat loaf always has been a great carry-in dish. And it doesn't have to be dull. In fact, this recipe is a very sprightly version, with a filling of sauerkraut and tomatoes.

2 teaspoons vegetable oil
¼ cup finely chopped
   green bell pepper
¼ cup finely chopped onion
2 large eggs
⅓ cup packed dark brown sugar
½ teaspoon ground mustard
¼ teaspoon ground pepper

¾ cup catsup
½ cup day-old bread crumbs
2 pounds ground beef
One 8-ounce can sauerkraut,
   drained, juice reserved
One 16-ounce can tomatoes,
   drained and diced

In a small saucepan, heat the oil over medium heat. Add the green bell pepper and onions and cook until the vegetables are softened, about 5 minutes. Set aside.

Preheat the oven to 350° F.

Meanwhile, in a large bowl, beat the eggs lightly with a whisk. Add the sugar, green bell pepper mixture, mustard, ground pepper, ½ cup catsup, and the bread crumbs and blend. Add the ground beef and combine the mixture thoroughly—you may have to use your hands.

Place the meat loaf mixture on a 15-inch length of foil and pat it out to a 10 × 12-inch rectangle. Sprinkle the sauerkraut, then the tomatoes evenly over the top of the meat. Place the meat patty on a large flat greased baking pan. Starting with the 10-inch side of the rectangle, lift the foil and start rolling the meat up like a jelly roll, patting it into a roll as you go. Flip the roll onto the pan, seam side down, and press the ends to seal the loaf. Pour the reserved sauerkraut juice over the roll, then drizzle on the remaining ¼ cup catsup (use a little more if you wish).

Bake the roll for 1 hour, or until golden brown. Cut into slices and serve hot. Any leftovers make very tasty sandwiches!

UPSIDE-DOWN HAM LOAF

SERVES 9

Ham loaves are often taken to church socials; there are many versions. Some use equal parts of veal with the ham, others are quite spicy, and some are glazed with a brown sugar and vinegar sauce. All are eaten with sighs of pleasure. This version, with its touch of ginger and curry, is inverted onto a platter after baking, and lo, there is a top layer of caramelized pineapple. "This is not your ordinary ham loaf," said Ada Carey of Clayton, Missouri, who gave me the recipe.

2 tablespoons butter, melted
¼ cup packed dark brown sugar
One 20-ounce can crushed
    unsweetened pineapple,
    drained well, juice reserved
Vegetable oil cooking spray
3 large eggs
6 cups coarsely ground cooked ham
    (I do this in the food processor)

1½ cups dry bread crumbs
½ cup chopped parsley
⅓ cup chopped onion
1½ teaspoons ground mustard
1½ teaspoons ground ginger
1½ teaspoons curry powder
¼ teaspoon black pepper

Preheat the oven to 375° F.

In a small bowl, mix together the butter, brown sugar, and drained pineapple. Coat a 10 × 10-inch baking pan with vegetable oil cooking spray; pour in the pineapple mixture and pat it out smoothly on the bottom of the pan.

In a large mixing bowl, beat the eggs with a fork. Stir in the ham, pineapple juice, bread crumbs, parsley, onions, mustard, ginger, curry powder, and pepper; mix well. Spread the ham mixture over the pineapple, patting it firmly over the pineapple. Bake for 45 minutes. Remove from the oven and allow to stand for 10 minutes. To serve, invert onto a serving platter. If any of the pineapple mixture remains in the bottom of the pan, pat it onto the loaf. Serve immediately.

A primitive herb mincer

SPAGHETTI AND MEATBALL DINNER

SERVES 12 TO 16

*Spaghetti dinners are a very popular fund-raiser at some churches. The men of the church really
get into this project—is serving spaghetti macho or something? No matter; this recipe is better than average.
Two pork chops are added to the sauce, which gives it real depth of flavor. Served cafeteria style,
with huge bowls of green salad and baskets of garlic bread, these dinners bring in the people in droves.
This would be equally good for a large buffet supper at home.*

MEATBALLS	SPAGHETTI SAUCE
1 pound lean ground beef	1 to 2 teaspoons olive oil
¼ teaspoon coarsely ground pepper	Two 1-inch-thick rib end pork chops
1 teaspoon salt	Four 6-ounce cans tomato paste
1 garlic clove, finely minced	8 cups defatted chicken broth
2 tablespoons finely minced parsley	1 teaspoon salt (or more to taste)
¾ cup packed freshly grated	½ teaspoon freshly ground pepper
Parmesan cheese	1 tablespoon dried basil or
1½ cups dry bread crumbs	½ cup chopped fresh
4 large eggs	A bit of sugar to taste
2 tablespoons olive oil	2 pounds thin spaghetti (spaghettini)

Make the meatballs: Combine the meat, pepper, salt, garlic, and parsley in a large bowl. Add the cheese, bread crumbs, and eggs and blend. Mix well and form into large marble sized balls. In a large skillet, heat the oil and brown the meatballs on all sides. Drain on paper towels.

Make the sauce: Heat the oil in a medium skillet and brown the chops on both sides; set aside. In a large deep kettle, combine the tomato paste, broth, salt, and pepper with a whisk. Add the chops and the pan drippings to the sauce.

Bring the mixture to a boil, reduce the heat, and simmer, partially covered, for 1½ hours, stirring frequently. Add the meatballs and basil and continue cooking for 30 minutes, or until the sauce reaches the consistency you want. Add more broth, if necessary. Taste and sprinkle in a bit of sugar to soften the sharp tomato flavor, if desired. Remove the chops and either discard or mince the meat finely and return to the sauce.

Cook the spaghetti according to package directions, adding 2 tablespoons of oil to the cooking water, which will prevent the spaghetti from clumping together. Drain well and serve the hot sauce and meatballs over the hot spaghetti.

KENTUCKY BURGOO

SERVES 10 TO 12

In the beginning, wild game, such as squirrel and duck, was always a component of this dish (in that way it is similar to the Brunswick stew of North Carolina). Today, we find it mostly in Kentucky, where it is served at political events, county fairs, some Derby parties, and at regional restaurants. In Owensboro, mutton is one of the ingredients; early Catholic immigrants raised sheep in this area, and the meat ended up in the burgoo. This is certainly the ideal church social soup, for it can be made in large quantities: Regional cookbooks offer recipes for serving up to a thousand people. The bony pieces of meat are important for the soup's flavor; I have substituted lamb for the mutton. This recipe is from an old Owensboro church cookbook and makes a superb one-dish meal.

1 pound pork shank or hocks	½ green bell pepper, diced
1 pound beef shank	½ red bell pepper, diced
1 pound breast of lamb	1½ cups fresh shelled lima beans or
One 4-pound stewing hen, cut up	One 10-ounce package frozen
2 medium onions, peeled,	1 cup fresh corn kernels or
plus ½ cup chopped onion	one 10-ounce package frozen
2 bay leaves	1 dried hot red chili pepper
6 coarsely chopped celery stalks	Salt and freshly ground
plus 1 cup chopped celery	pepper to taste
Handful of parsley sprigs	Hot red pepper sauce to taste
2 large potatoes, peeled and diced	Worcestershire sauce to taste
3 large carrots, peeled and diced	¾ cup finely minced parsley
One 28-ounce can tomatoes, with juice	1 tablespoon minced fresh
One 16-ounce can tomatoes, with juice	thyme or 1 teaspoon dried

In a very large stockpot, combine the pork, beef, lamb, hen, 2 medium onions, bay leaves, 6 chopped celery stalks, and parsley. Cover with water (approximately 6 to 7 quarts) and bring to a boil, skimming often, then reduce the heat to medium-low and simmer for 1½ hours. Remove the chicken with tongs, to a shallow-lipped pan to cool. Continue cooking the meats until they are tender and the meat begins to fall off the bones, approximately 2 to 3 hours longer. Meanwhile, strip the chicken off the bones, discarding the skin and bones. Cover and refrigerate.

When the meats are tender, remove them with tongs to a pan. Allow them to cool slightly and remove the meat from the bones. Cover and refrigerate. Strain the stock and refrigerate overnight to allow the fat to rise to the top and harden. Discard this fat the next day.

To the defatted stock, add the potatoes, carrots, tomatoes, green and red bell peppers, lima beans, corn, dried chili pepper, 1 cup chopped celery, and ½ cup chopped onion. Bring to a simmer and cook for 1 hour, or until the vegetables are very tender and the mixture has reduced somewhat and become thick. When the burgoo has reached the right consistency, add the reserved chicken and seasonings to taste. Simmer a few minutes longer, then remove the dried chili pepper. Transfer to a large soup tureen or individual bowls and serve with Mormon Corn Bread (page 120).

travel Notes
FROM THE SOUTH

It was with real pleasure that we headed South. In Kentucky, we spent our first night at Pleasant Hill, a former Shaker settlement outside of Harrodsburg. Our room in one of the restored dormitories was furnished with Shaker reproduction furniture and hand-loomed rugs. We had dinner and breakfast at the restored trustee's office, and the food lived up to the Shakers' reputation for presenting bounteous, well-seasoned meals. Driving on through rolling countryside, we were quite dazzled by the horse farms; the importance of the Derby was apparent. This is the land of Lincoln, bourbon, Stephen Foster, Daniel Boone and the Cumberland Gap, and Harriet Beecher Stowe, who wrote <u>Uncle Tom's Cabin</u>. Shelbyville is an antiques heaven, and as usual, Dick hurried me through the shops. And there is an outstanding place to eat here, the Science Hill Inn, known for Kentucky specialties, where we kept the waiter busy refilling the roll basket with southern biscuits and hot water corn bread.

At a friend's recommendation, we stopped in Owensboro for burgoo and barbecue. Kenneth Bosley, who operates the Moonlite Bar-B-Q Inn, specializes in both burgoo and barbecued mutton, ham, ribs, and chicken. In this big informal restaurant, the fragrance of smoky barbecue assails your senses as soon as you walk in, and you tend to overorder. "We serve 10,000 pounds of mutton barbecue a week," says Kenneth, "and another 10,000 pounds of beef, pork, and chicken combined." The locals are enthusiastic about this barbecue, make no mistake. And so were we.

We were too late for the dogwood and azaleas that line the streets of Paducah every spring, but the Museum of the American Quilter's Society had just opened and the display of contemporary, historical, and regional quilts quite took my breath away. The museum also offers quilting classes and seminars; quilters come in from all over the country to attend.

The landscape changes in Tennessee—pines cling stubbornly to the sides of the limestone shales that line the roads. The soil is a deep red, and as we drive in the mountains around Nashville, we can see small valleys below, dotted with small farmhouses. Morning fog fills these valleys like snow; it is rather mystical and difficult driving. I'm glad when we cross the line into North Carolina, in search of crab, cornmeal dumplings, shrimp, and scuppernong wine.

OWENSBORO, KENTUCKY

After having driven through the Cumberland Gap on a six-lane highway, I am in awe of Daniel Boone and his thirty men who first hacked through virgin forest to make the "Wilderness Road." We stop regularly to admire the views and talk to the locals about recipes. Burgoo seems to be on everybody's mind; at the Moonlite Bar-B-Q Inn the burgoo is as authentic and hearty as you'd wish, and the pit barbecue sandwiches are winners, too!

M

METHODIST CHURCH POTATO DOUGHNUTS

MAKES 3 ½ DOZEN

*At the small Methodist church in Flint, Indiana, I attended as a girl, one of the favored fund-raisers
was a doughnut fry. When the word went out "the women are making doughnuts this week," the orders flew
in; there was no need to advertise. These doughnuts, soft and cakelike, were famous. The batter
was mixed up at home a day in advance by the ambitious cooks, who then congregated at the church the next
morning at 5 A.M. to begin frying. The fried doughnuts were dipped in sugar and cinnamon
or glazed and then sold to devoted customers, who poured into the church all day long to pick up their
doughnuts. Held several times a year, the profits from the doughnut fries paid for updating the
church kitchen, carpeting the vestry, or painting the sanctuary.
After my mother died, I was sent a videotape of her and her friends in the church kitchen, frying
doughnuts—hundreds of doughnuts. The tape is one of my most treasured possessions.*

1 cup buttermilk, at room temperature	5½ cups all-purpose flour
½ teaspoon baking soda	2 teaspoons grated nutmeg
1 cup cool unseasoned mashed potatoes	4 rounded teaspoons baking powder
1 tablespoon butter,	2 teaspoons salt
at room temperature	6 cups vegetable oil for frying
1 tablespoon vanilla extract	2 tablespoons cider vinegar
3 large eggs	
2 cups granulated sugar	Confectioners' sugar for dusting

In a bowl, stir the buttermilk and soda together; set aside until the mixture puffs a bit, about 10 minutes. In a large mixer bowl, mix together the potatoes, butter, and vanilla; add the buttermilk mixture and beat. In a small mixing bowl, beat the eggs and sugar together until well combined; add to the potato mixture and blend, then set aside.

In a large mixing bowl, whisk together the flour, nutmeg, baking powder, and salt. Add the flour mixture all at once to the potato mixture and blend until just mixed. Divide the dough in 2 balls and refrigerate until thoroughly chilled or even overnight.

In a deep heavy pan or an electric deep fryer, heat the oil and vinegar to 360° F. On a floured surface, roll out half the dough to a ¾-inch thickness. Using a well-floured doughnut cutter, cut each doughnut cleanly with a straight up-and-down motion; don't twist the cutter in a circular fashion.

Using a metal spatula, slide each doughnut into the hot fat, frying 3 doughnuts at a time, no more. When the doughnuts come to the top of the fat, use tongs and turn them over and fry until brown, then turn over again and fry the other side until brown. Drain doughnuts on paper toweling and dust with confectioners' sugar. Also fry the doughnut holes—need I tell you? Store the doughnuts in airtight containers. They don't freeze particularly well, so eat them all up immediately. That will not be a problem!

CHURCH SOCIAL PEACH ICE CREAM

SERVES 8 TO 10

*Ice cream socials are one of the most popular church events. Each summer, the churches will
post announcements all over their area, giving the dates and times of the social. The women come early to the
church kitchen to stir up the custard base, and the men arrive later with the ice and the ice cream mixers.
It is not uncommon for the church to use several five-gallon electric mixers, which are impressively big. The days
of turning the ice cream crank by hand are over, thank goodness. That was hard work!
Some ice cream makers think that refrigerating the ice cream mixture overnight before churning it results
in a greater volume. I tend to agree, so if you have the time, allow for this extra step.
This is a hauntingly smooth and exquisite ice cream; when I make it at home, I like to drizzle a bit of orange-flavored
liqueur over the top, though I assure you they don't do that at the church socials I have attended!*

2 cups peeled and crushed ripe peaches	**1½ cups half-and-half**
1 tablespoon fresh lemon juice	**2 cups heavy cream**
1½ cups sugar, divided	**½ teaspoon almond extract**
¼ teaspoon salt	**2 teaspoons vanilla extract**
3 large eggs, lightly beaten	

In a large bowl, combine the peach pulp with the lemon juice and ½ cup sugar; set aside. In a medium
saucepan, whisk together the remaining 1 cup sugar, the salt, eggs, and half-and-half. Cook over medium
heat, stirring constantly, until the mixture thickens and just coats a metal spoon, approximately 18 to 20
minutes. Remove the custard from the heat and cool completely. Whisk in the heavy cream, almond and
vanilla extracts, and the peach pulp until thoroughly blended. Pour into the freezer can of an ice cream
maker and process according to the manufacturer's instructions.

NOTE: *If you are using an old-fashioned freezer, pack the outer container with 5 parts crushed ice to 1 part
rock salt. Freeze the custard until the mixture is thick but still soft. You can tell if it is done by the grinding sound
of the electric motor. Remove the paddles (this is the time when everyone gathers around with spoons to test
your recipe), drain off the excess water, and repack the freezer, using 8 parts ice to 2 parts rock salt. Cover all
with a thick terry cloth towel. Allow the ice cream to stand in the freshly packed ice for at least 1 hour and up to 4
hours. Dip into deep bowls and serve immediately.*

Ice cream accouterments

CHURCH CAKE WALK FUDGE CAKE

MAKES TWO 8-INCH LAYERS

Small country churches were the center of social activities during the late 1800s and early 1900s, and the church members were clever about planning parties that would bring people together as well as make money for the treasury. Cake walks were popular and the ladies of the church would bring in their fanciest cakes, which were then lined up on a table and numbered; a large circle, with corresponding cake numbers, would be outlined with chalk on the church basement floor or in the grass (with powdered chalk), and then the church pianist would play some appropriate tunes—nothing too fast—well, maybe "Yankee Doodle." Men would buy tickets for a dollar or two, depending on the times, and walk around the circle to the music, stopping when the music stopped. And if they were lucky, they were on a number and were able to claim the cake with the corresponding number. Generally the baker and the walker would meet for refreshments—the cake, now cut into pieces, and homemade ice cream. Of course, you had to pay ten cents for the ice cream. This was a money-making proposition! The evening would end with hymn singing. Such innocent days those were . . . This recipe is from the Fort Wayne, Indiana, Simpson United Methodist Church cookbook.

2 ounces unsweetened chocolate	**1 teaspoon baking soda**
1½ cups water	**1 teaspoon cream of tartar**
½ cup vegetable shortening	**¼ teaspoon salt**
1 cup packed light brown sugar	**1 teaspoon vanilla extract**
1 cup granulated sugar	
2 large eggs	**Coconut-Pecan Filling and**
2½ cups cake flour	**Frosting (recipe follows)**

Preheat the oven to 350° F. Grease and flour 2 8-inch round cake pans.

Over medium heat in a medium saucepan, melt the chocolate in the water; stir together, then boil for 2 minutes and set aside to cool. In a large mixer bowl, cream the shortening and sugars for 7 minutes, then add the eggs one at a time, beating well after each addition.

In a mixing bowl, whisk together the flour, soda, cream of tartar, and salt. Add the flour mixture alternately with the chocolate to the egg mixture, beginning and ending with the flour, then stir in the vanilla. Pour into the pans and bake for 30 minutes, or until the cake is just beginning to shrink away from the sides of the pan and the center of the cake springs back when lightly touched with your finger. Cool completely before removing from the pans. Frost with Coconut-Pecan Filling and Frosting.

COCONUT-PECAN FILLING AND FROSTING

1 cup evaporated milk	**1 teaspoon vanilla extract**
1 cup sugar	**1⅓ cups sweetened, shredded coconut**
3 large egg yolks, lightly beaten	**1 cup coarsely chopped pecans**
½ cup (1 stick) butter	

Over medium heat in a small saucepan, combine the milk, sugar, egg yolks, butter, and vanilla. Cook, stirring constantly, until the mixture thickens, approximately 20 to 25 minutes. Remove from the heat and stir in the coconut and pecans. Beat with a spoon until the filling has cooled and is of spreading consistency. Use one-third of the mixture for the filling, then frost the cake (top and sides) with the remaining mixture. Store the frosted cake in the refrigerator and bring to room temperature before serving.

SERVES 8

At church socials, we often encounter some old-time desserts whose recipes are rarely recorded in cookbooks anymore. Apple Brown Betty is a natural for church socials, for many cooks would have the ingredients readily at hand. No one seems to know why a Betty is a Betty and not, say, a Bonnie— apple brown Bonnie—it does have a nice ring. One thing I can tell you about Bettys, though—they always feature layers of apples and bread crumbs, which act as a very subtle thickener—you are not even aware they are there. Hard sauce to dollop on top is a must, though some misguided folks like ice cream or milk.

¼ cup (½ stick) butter
2 cups fresh bread crumbs
6 cups cored, peeled, and
    thinly sliced cooking apples
½ cup packed light brown sugar
1 tablespoon fresh lemon juice

1 teaspoon ground cinnamon
½ teaspoon ground allspice
½ teaspoon grated nutmeg
⅓ cup apple cider or juice

Hard Sauce (page 285)

Preheat the oven to 375° F.

Melt the butter in a saucepan, add the crumbs, and toss to combine; set aside. Grease a deep (that is important—don't use a shallow dish) 2-quart baking dish.

Sprinkle a few bread crumbs in the bottom of the dish—just a small handful. Arrange half of the apples over the bread crumbs, sprinkle with half the sugar, half of the lemon juice, half of the spices, then add half of the remaining bread crumbs. Repeat with the remaining apples, sugar, lemon juice, and spices. Pour the cider over the apples, then top with the remaining crumbs. Cover and bake for 45 minutes; remove the cover and test with a skewer or knife to see if the apples are cooked. The time on this will vary with the apple variety and their age. You may need to cook it a bit longer, uncovered. If you cook it too long, it will collapse. This doesn't hurt its flavor, but it's not quite as attractive. Actually, it's not too gorgeous anyway, but it has a superb flavor. Serve warm with Hard Sauce.

Farmer's MARKET

As WE DRIVE from state to state, it is so reassuring to see how numerous farmer's markets have become. Popping up around the country they confirm my sense that consumers are becoming more aware of what is "good" food, and want it fresh and unadulterated. And interacting with the farmer or the person who raised the produce gives us a sense of community, of rightness.

Many of the markets have evolved into famous, not-to-be-missed places to visit: the Lexington Market in Baltimore; New York City's Union Square Greenmarket; the West Side Market in Cleveland; the Central Market in Lancaster, Pennsylvania; the Reading Market in Philadelphia; the Dane County Market on Capitol Square in Madison, Wisconsin; and of course, the mother of them all, Pike Place Market in Seattle.

While I was raised in the country, I started going to the Fort Wayne Barr Street Market with my mother when I was just a tot. She didn't buy produce—goodness, we had enough of that at home—but she would buy dahlias, the most enormous dinner plate-sized dahlias I have ever seen, even to this day. Occasionally, she might break down and buy some sugar cookies or a loaf of homemade bread, if it looked unusually good, and I do remember a woman who sold open-faced peach pies.

These markets have also enabled some farmers to preserve the family farm—by providing a growing clientele that appreciates and will seek out locally raised foodstuffs. This healthy trend is coinciding with a renewed interest in heritage seeds and older fruit varieties. We seem to be discovering simultaneously that old can be good—and, in some cases, better. And how ideal to take these special foods and prepare them in traditional ways. The older, simpler recipes allow the sincere, true flavor of pristine produce to shine through. It would be hard to improve on Onions Baked in Milk when the onions are just hours out of the ground or Hot Herbed Tomatoes made with sun-warmed, vine-ripened fruit.

Hot Herbed Tomatoes Tomatoes with Sage Onion Pie Upside-Down Sweet Potato Cake with Maple Syrup Candied Carrots Sweet-and-Sour Caramelized Onions Polish Baked Cabbage Colache Cold Tomatillo Soup Acorn Squash with Spicy Butter-Honey Sauce Cleveland Ratatouille Pearl Buck's Sweet Potato Balls Stuffed Zucchini Yellow Summer Squash Rings Red Bell Pepper–Chive Dressing Barr Street Market Peach Cream Pie with Nutmeg Apples Stuffed with Mincemeat

ℋOT HERBED TOMATOES

SERVES 4 TO 5

Green markets are often showcases for farmers who grow small crops of exotic new produce. At New York's Union Square Greenmarket I first saw white tomatoes, as well as oddly shaped yellow ones, resembling gourds more than tomatoes. It is pretty hard to improve on the conventional Better Boy, though, and I recommend that fragrant red variety for this recipe. The tomatoes are served whole, so the presentation has quite a bit of style—it is not your ordinary stewed tomato.

¼ cup (½ stick) butter
1 teaspoon packed light brown sugar
½ teaspoon salt
Freshly ground pepper
4 or 5 firm-ripe medium tomatoes, peeled

¼ cup finely chopped celery
3 tablespoons minced fresh basil
2 tablespoons chopped parsley
2 tablespoons chopped chives

In a deep sauté pan, melt the butter and add the brown sugar, salt, and pepper. Add the tomatoes, cored side down. Cover and cook on low heat for 5 minutes. With a metal spatula, carefully turn the tomatoes right side up and spoon the butter mixture over them. Add the remaining ingredients to the pan juices and cook, uncovered, 5 minutes longer. Transfer the tomatoes to a platter or individual sauce dishes, spoon the pan juices and vegetables over them, and serve immediately.

𝒯OMATOES WITH SAGE

SERVES 4 TO 6

Tomatoes are so popular that they have developed into big business. Consequently, most supermarket tomatoes, which are planted and harvested by machine, tend to be grown for transportability rather than flavor. Most of the tomatoes found in farmer's markets are still planted and harvested by hand, though. I hope you will try this version of sautéed tomatoes—it's a winner. The cornmeal-sage crust is perfect for a juicy red tomato.

4 ripe medium tomatoes, cored
½ cup yellow cornmeal
½ cup grated Parmesan cheese
1 tablespoon finely minced fresh
   sage leaves or 1 ½ teaspoons powdered
1 teaspoon sugar

Salt and pepper to taste
¼ cup (½ stick) butter, melted
2 tablespoons olive oil or more as needed
2 garlic cloves, finely minced

Garnish: fresh parsley

Slice the tomatoes in ½-inch-thick slices. In a shallow dish, combine the cornmeal, cheese, sage, sugar, and salt and pepper. Dip each tomato slice first in the melted butter, then in the cornmeal mixture to coat and place on wax paper. Over medium heat in a large sauté pan, heat 1 tablespoon olive oil. Add the garlic and sauté until golden. Add half of the tomato slices to the pan and sauté until golden brown, about 3 to 4 minutes. Turn carefully and sauté the other side, about 3 minutes more. Transfer to a heated platter. Repeat with the remainder of the oil, garlic, and tomato slices. Serve immediately, garnished with parsley.

ONION PIE

SERVES 6 TO 8

*This is quaintly titled, for it is not really a pie, but rather a casserole of onions and cheese with
egg custard poured over the top. It is not at all quichelike. However, it is very good, and one of those cozy
nostalgic dishes that ought to be prepared more often.*

*Any large sweet onion can be used for this, but the Walla Wallas from Washington are super—
they contain 12 percent sugar, compared to the 8 percent sugar in other onions. Originally from Italy, seeds
for these onions were first planted in the Walla Walla Valley by an unknown Frenchman, and
Italian immigrants further developed the onion through years of selective breeding. You'll find lots of Walla Wallas
at the Pike Place Market in Seattle, but they also show up in supermarkets across the country.*

CRUST
⅓ cup butter
30 saltine crackers, finely crushed

FILLING
¼ cup (½ stick) butter
3 cups onions, sliced ½ inch thick
½ teaspoon grated nutmeg

½ pound extra-sharp cheddar cheese, grated
3 large eggs
1½ cups whole milk
½ teaspoon ground mustard
1½ teaspoons salt
¼ teaspoon coarsely ground pepper

Garnish: paprika and minced parsley

Prepare the crust: In a medium saucepan, melt the butter over low heat. Remove from the heat and add the crushed crackers. Toss together with a fork, then pour into an 8 × 8 × 2-inch square pan; press firmly onto the bottom of the pan and set aside.

In a 12-inch skillet, melt the butter over medium heat. Add the onions and sauté until golden brown, approximately 20 to 25 minutes. Drain off the excess fat and discard. Add the nutmeg, then spoon the onion mixture onto the top of the crumb crust. Sprinkle on the cheese.

In a small bowl, beat the eggs and add the milk, mustard, salt, and pepper. Pour over the onions and sprinkle the top with paprika. Bake for 30 minutes, or until the custard is set and the top is a golden brown. Garnish with parsley and serve hot.

Wrought-iron flatiron trivet

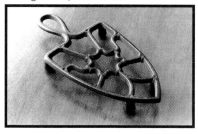

UPSIDE-DOWN SWEET POTATO CAKE WITH MAPLE SYRUP

SERVES 8 TO 10

At the French Market in New Orleans, you'll find great mounds of deep orange-colored sweet potatoes, for this is a favorite vegetable in the South. Louisiana is the country's leading producer of sweet potatoes; they flourish well in this particular soil and climate. Southern cooks serve them in a variety of ways—mashed, candied, in salads (page 143), and as a base for the smoothest, most divine pies I've ever eaten (page 192).
Although this spiffy side dish recipe adds a midwestern ingredient, maple syrup, it is not a dessert; seasoned mashed sweet potatoes are baked on top of a mixture of brown sugar, pecans, and maple syrup. After baking, the "cake" is inverted, and lo, the bottom is on the top and the dish is absolutely gorgeous. Serve it with your Thanksgiving turkey.

2½ pounds raw unpeeled sweet potatoes	½ cup pecan halves
2 large eggs	1 cup packed dark brown sugar
¼ teaspoon salt	3 tablespoons butter
¼ teaspoon white pepper	2 tablespoons maple syrup
½ teaspoon grated nutmeg	¼ teaspoon maple extract
1 teaspoon ground cinnamon	
1 teaspoon Angostura bitters (available at liquor stores)	

Cook the sweet potatoes in boiling water until tender. Drain and peel. Place the warm potatoes in a large mixer bowl and mash slightly. In another mixer bowl, combine the eggs, salt, pepper, nutmeg, cinnamon, and bitters, beating until light and fluffy. Add to the mashed potatoes and blend.

Preheat the oven to 350° F.

Generously grease the bottom and sides of a 9-inch round metal cake pan. Arrange the pecans over the bottom of the pan. Spread the brown sugar over the pecans, packing it lightly on top of the nuts. In a small pan, melt the butter. Add the maple syrup and extract, and pour it over the brown sugar layer—do not stir. Pack the mashed potatoes carefully but firmly over the brown sugar-pecan layer. Cover the dish with foil and bake for 1 hour; the potatoes should be firm and a knife inserted in the center should come out clean. When done, remove from the oven, remove the foil, and invert immediately onto a large serving plate, which should be several inches larger than the pan to allow for the melted brown sugar to run down the sides. Serve hot.

NOTE: *This dish may be prepared up to the point of baking 24 hours in advance and refrigerated. Allow about 20 minutes extra baking time if the dish is cold from being refrigerated.*

EN ROUTE TO NEW ORLEANS

travel Notes

I tend to forget that the Pilgrims, who landed at Plymouth Rock in 1620, weren't the first English group to settle in America; they've just had better press through the years due to Thanksgiving.

Of course the first English settlement was in Jamestown, Virginia. The year was 1607 and unlike the Pilgrims, this group was pro-English crown. It is easy to see evidence of England's influence in southern cookery, with numerous recipes for meat pies, trifles, and puddings.

The Virginia settlers experienced many of the same difficulties as the Pilgrims would thirteen years later—low food supplies; inadequate equipment for farming, hunting, and fishing; and no knowledge thereof anyway. Here too, the settlers survived only because of help from the Indians. Ultimately, tobacco made the colony wealthy, and the plantations flourished. Plantation life was deeply influenced by lifestyles of the British landed gentry; however, the elaborate and lavish meals and parties and upkeep of the elegant houses were made possible because of the African-American slaves, who also contributed their own African foodways to southern vittles, including rice and vegetable dishes and the undeniably wonderful sweet potato pie.

French cookery also had a strong influence on southern food. Because of the French Revolution, French chefs, including Louis XVI's own cook, immigrated to England, where rich Americans (including Thomas Jefferson) were influenced by their recipes and service. In some cases, when returning to America, they brought French cooks back with them to work in their own kitchens. Hannah Glasse, a well-known English cookbook writer, had watched this turn of affairs with great irritation and in a snit, wrote "the blind folly of this age, that would rather be imposed upon by a French booby, than give encouragement to a good English cook!" Astonishing how nothing changes, isn't it?

This trend was especially apparent in New Orleans, founded by the French, followed by a period of Spanish occupation. French chefs, fresh from Paris in the mid-1800s, began improvising with the fish from the Gulf of Mexico, adding to their classic recipes the indigenous ingredients of the region.

We stayed in the French Quarter, a National Historic District. Our courtyard, where we had breakfast every morning, was fragrant with sweet olive trees, bougainvillea, and Confederate jasmine. The coffee was dark and strong and the calas, a rice drop doughnut, light and tender. Walking through the Quarter, we marveled at the Spanish architecture with its interior courtyards and patios, tile roofs, and wrought-iron balconies. This is the city made familiar to us by Tennessee Williams, Truman Capote, Lillian Hellman, and William Faulkner. "Let's find the praline place," suggests Dick. He always knows how to set priorities.

CANDIED CARROTS

SERVES 6 TO 8

*During long cold winters, country cooks stored carrots in crocks and kept them in cold pantries
or in root cellars. The carrots stayed moist and fresh, and were used in a number of ways, including stews,
soups, puddings, cakes, cookies—it is quite a versatile vegetable.*

12 carrots, peeled and **sliced ⅛ inch thick**	**¼ cup (½ stick) butter**
1 bay leaf	**½ teaspoon ground allspice**
1 cup packed light brown sugar	**Salt and pepper to taste**

Place the carrots and the bay leaf in a medium saucepan and nearly cover with water. Cover the pan, bring
to a boil, then lower the heat and simmer until just tender, about 20 minutes. Drain, reserving ¼ cup of
the cooking liquid, and transfer the carrots to a flat 1-quart glass casserole.

Preheat the oven to 350° F.

In a small saucepan, combine the ¼ cup cooking liquid, brown sugar, butter, allspice, and salt and pepper. Bring to a boil and cook until the butter melts and the sugar has dissolved, whisking to combine. Pour
over the carrots and bake uncovered until the carrots are beginning to brown and appear candied, any-
where from 30 to 45 minutes. Serve immediately.

SWEET-AND-SOUR CARAMELIZED ONIONS

SERVES 6 TO 8

*Good vegetable dishes are hard to come upon, I think. And this one, which its name so well describes,
is a snap to make. Serve it with broiled meats or roasts and be prepared to share the recipe.
If you have a lot of onions to peel or if they are very small, to hasten the step, pour boiling water over the
onions and let stand 1 minute. Drain, cover with cold water, and then peel.*

4 very large sweet onions, peeled	**Salt and pepper to taste**
¼ cup cider vinegar	**Paprika**
½ cup (1 stick) butter, melted	
½ cup boiling water	**Garnish: chopped chervil or parsley**
½ cup packed dark brown sugar	

Preheat the oven to 300° F.

Slice the onions ¼ inch thick. Arrange in a 1-quart baking dish in a thin layer, no more than 2 or 3 slices
thick. In a small bowl, mix the vinegar, melted butter, water, and brown sugar; pour over the onions.
Sprinkle the top with salt, pepper, and paprika and bake for 1 hour. Check for doneness with a fork; the
onions should be tender, brown, and caramelized slightly. Remove from the oven and sprinkle with
chervil or parsley. Serve immediately.

POLISH BAKED CABBAGE

SERVES 10

*Cabbage is one of our most versatile vegetables and I know from experience that if I have a head
of cabbage on hand, I can create any number of interesting dishes. This one has Polish antecedents and was
given to me by a Winona Lake neighbor, Carol Piecuch, who, when her daughter married, prepared
Polish food for the reception of several hundred people. What a labor of love!
This version of baked cabbage is creamy on the inside, with a deep golden brown crust on the outside,
rather like hash browns. The dill is my addition—it adds a lilt to cabbage anytime.*

4 cups shredded cabbage
¼ cup minced fresh dill (optional)
1½ teaspoons salt
½ teaspoon pepper
1 tablespoon sugar

1 large egg
½ cup all-purpose flour
1 quart milk
1 tablespoon butter, melted

Preheat the oven to 350° F.

In a large mixing bowl, combine the cabbage, dill, salt, pepper, and sugar. Transfer to a well-greased
9 × 13-inch baking pan. In a medium bowl, beat the egg, then whisk in the flour and milk until smooth.

Slowly pour the milk mixture over the cabbage. Drizzle the melted butter over the top. Bake for 1
hour, uncovered, checking after 45 minutes to see if it is browning nicely. If the top is a deep golden brown
(like hash brown potatoes), cover with foil and continue baking 15 minutes longer. Cool for 10 minutes
before serving. It can be cut into squares or spooned out.

COLACHE

SERVES 6

*If you are in Santa Fe, you must be sure to go to the farmer's market at the Sanbusto Center.
(It is open on Tuesday and Saturday mornings, June through October.) You will find
southwestern baked goods, such as Sopaipillas (page 227) and fry bread, but also different types of tortillas,
blue corn, and an unbelievable array of chilies. Of course, you will want to bring home a ristra, that
decorative practical string of dried red chilies to hang in your kitchen.
This southwestern vegetable combination gets added zip from chili powder
and cumin, and it's a quick and colorful dish.*

¼ to ½ cup olive oil
1 garlic clove, minced
1 medium onion, chopped
1 small green bell pepper,
    seeded and chopped

1½ pounds yellow squash or zucchini,
    unpeeled and chopped
    into ¼-inch pieces
1½ cups peeled, seeded,
    and chopped tomatoes

**2 cups fresh corn kernels
or drained canned corn
1½ teaspoons chili powder**

**½ teaspoon ground cumin
1 teaspoon sugar
Salt and pepper to taste**

In a large sauté pan, heat the oil. Add the garlic and onions and sauté until transparent, about 3 minutes. Add the green bell pepper and squash and sauté about 3 to 5 minutes over medium heat. Stir in the remaining ingredients and cook until the mixture is heated through and the tomato juice is reduced a bit. Transfer to individual serving dishes, for it is a tad juicy.

COLD TOMATILLO SOUP

SERVES 6

Another fascinating foodstuff you will find at the Santa Fe market is tomatillos. They are pretty things, resembling tiny green tomatoes with straw-colored husks; they are a close relative of the ground cherry, which they resemble. I use tomatillos often for Green Tomatilla Salsa (page 288) and in this attractive subtle soup, which comes from the private recipe file of an early Spanish family that settled in Santa Fe.

**2 tablespoons vegetable oil
1 large onion, finely chopped
2 pounds tomatillos, husked,
   washed, and quartered
2 medium garlic cloves, minced
4 cups chicken stock
2 tablespoons finely chopped cilantro**

**1 teaspoon salt
1 teaspoon ground cumin
¼ teaspoon white pepper**

**Garnish: ½ cup sour cream and
   ½ cup ripe avocado, cut into ¼-inch dice
Warmed Tortilla Fingers (page 180)**

In a large saucepan, heat the oil over medium heat. Add the onions and sauté until softened, about 3 minutes. Add the tomatillos and stir until coated with onions. Add the garlic and stock and bring to a boil. Lower the heat to simmer and cook, partially covered, until the tomatillos are tender, about 7 minutes. Cool slightly.

Place the soup in a blender or food processor and puree. Pass the puree through a strainer into a bowl, pressing the solids with a wooden spoon. Stir in the cilantro, salt, cumin, and pepper and chill at least 4 hours.

To serve, ladle into bowls. Combine the sour cream and avocado and place a dollop on top. Serve with the warmed Tortilla Fingers.

NOTE: *This soup does not keep particularly well, so make it no more than one day in advance. It can also be served hot, though I do prefer it chilled.*

Butternut squashes, all in a row

Acorn Squash with Spicy Butter-Honey Sauce

SERVES 8

Squash is the third member of the culinary triumvirate (corn, beans, and squash) that dominated the New World's food supply until Columbus arrived. Those early Indians wouldn't have had this recipe, more's the pity. It is a happy combination of spices and honey that thoroughly enhance the already sweet squash. This is especially good with pork, I think.

4 acorn squash, cut in half, seeds removed	2 teaspoons grated orange rind
3 tablespoons butter	1 teaspoon ground cinnamon
⅔ cup honey	1 teaspoon grated nutmeg
2 tablespoons fresh lemon juice	½ teaspoon ground cardamom

Preheat the oven to 425° F.

Line a shallow 13 × 9-inch pan with foil and place the squash on it, cut side down. Add about ½ inch warm water to the pan and bake the squash for 30 minutes.

Meantime, in a small saucepan, melt the butter and blend in the remaining the ingredients with a whisk. Remove the squash from the oven, drain off the water, and turn the squash cavity side up. Divide the sauce equally among the 4 squash halves and baste the top of the squash as well. Bake the squash another 30 to 40 minutes, basting occasionally, or until the squash is very tender when pierced with a knife.

PHOTO POST CARD

AMERICA 25

THE SEED SAVER'S EXCHANGE, DECORAH, IOWA

This is a fascinating place. The 140-acre Heritage Hill Farm is devoted to preserving old vegetable seed varieties, 4,000 of them! These seeds are called "heirloom seeds" and any seed originating before 1940 falls into this classification. The farm also operates a Seed Saver's Exchange that has more than 6,000 members. Many gardeners save seed from year to year, from generation to generation and are able to share them through the exchange. Large seeded vegetables such as peas, beans, and squash are especially easy to harvest and dry. *M*

CLEVELAND RATATOUILLE

SERVES 4 TO 6

The West Side Market in Cleveland is partly in a landmark building complete with bell tower, tall arched ceilings with handsome tiled murals at one end; other vendors, wanting to share the precious space, are in spacious tents outside. You walk through aisles of flowers and cunningly stacked fruits and vegetables, and always overbuy because everything is so beautiful.
There is a large Italian community in Cleveland, and one of the purveyors at the market gave me his special recipe for ratatouille, that fantastic mélange of eggplant, bell peppers, tomatoes, and zucchini. Prepare several batches and freeze it; it may be necessary to drain off a bit of excess liquid after thawing, but the taste and texture will not be affected.

1 large eggplant, cut into ½-inch slices	1 bay leaf
Salt	1 teaspoon dried oregano or
4 to 6 tablespoons olive oil	3 tablespoons minced fresh
2 medium onions, seeded	½ teaspoon dried basil or
and coarsely chopped	1½ tablespoons minced fresh
1 large green bell pepper, coarsely chopped	½ teaspoon salt
2 garlic cloves, minced	¼ teaspoon ground pepper
¼ cup chopped parsley	2 medium zucchini, sliced ½ inch thick
5 large fresh tomatoes or	Salt and pepper to taste
one 1-pound can Italian tomatoes	
1 teaspoon sugar	

An hour before preparing the ratatouille, sprinkle the sliced eggplant on both sides with salt and stack in a colander to "weep" for 1 hour; this removes the bitter taste. Rinse and pat dry.

Meanwhile, in an 11-inch sauté pan, heat 2 tablespoons oil and add the onions, green bell pepper, and garlic; cook over medium heat until the onions are transparent, about 10 minutes. Add the parsley, tomatoes, sugar, bay leaf, oregano, basil, salt, and pepper; reduce the heat to low and simmer for 10 minutes.

Cut the drained eggplant into 1-inch cubes. Heat 2 more tablespoons of the oil in another sauté pan and sauté the eggplant over medium heat until tender, about 6 to 8 minutes. You may have to add a bit more oil—eggplant really absorbs it. Scatter the eggplant over the tomato mixture.

Add the sliced zucchini to the sauté pan in which the eggplant was cooked and sauté until it is barely done; scatter over the eggplant. Pat the vegetables gently down into the tomatoes, but don't stir them in—you don't want the vegetables to be mushy. Partially cover and simmer over low heat for 45 minutes; the liquid will cook away. Add salt and pepper to taste. Cool and serve at room temperature.

NOTE: *Sometimes I broil the eggplant and zucchini rather than sauté them—it takes less time.*

 PEARL BUCK'S SWEET POTATO BALLS

SERVES 6

Pearl S. Buck lived and traveled abroad for many years, and collected recipes, including this one for sweet potato balls, along the way. I have changed it slightly; you'll find it is an interesting vegetable accompaniment, with its hint of cinnamon and orange.

**2 cups mashed cooked sweet
potatoes (3 large potatoes)**
3 tablespoons all-purpose flour
2 tablespoons sugar
2 eggs, slightly beaten
1 teaspoon vanilla extract
1½ teaspoons ground cinnamon

1 teaspoon grated orange zest
Salt and white pepper to taste
**Approximately 1 quart
peanut oil for frying**

Garnish: confectioners' sugar (optional)

In a large bowl, combine the potatoes, flour, and sugar. Stir in the eggs, vanilla, cinnamon, orange zest, and salt and pepper. Form into 1-inch balls about the size of a walnut—a small ice cream scoop is ideal for this.

Meanwhile, pour enough oil in an electric skillet so it is ¾ inch deep. Heat the oil to 410° F. Drop in the balls 6 at a time, cook them 15 seconds, and with a slotted spoon, turn them over and cook them 30 seconds longer. They will puff slightly and be dark brown. Drain on paper towels and repeat until all the balls are cooked. Keep the cooked balls warm in the oven; sift a bit of confectioners' sugar over them, if desired. Serve warm.

PHOTO POST CARD

AMERICA 25

**PEARL S. BUCK HOUSE,
BUCKS COUNTY, PENNSYLVANIA**

We took a guided tour through Buck's 1835 farmhouse today—it is such an attractive place. She was the daughter of American missionaries and raised in China, later taught there, and moved here after her second marriage. She wrote eighty-five books, with *The Good Earth* winning the Pulitzer Prize in 1932. I did so enjoy her books when I was growing up, and look forward to testing her recipes.

M

STUFFED ZUCCHINI

SERVES 8

The market that surrounds the state capital building in Madison, Wisconsin, every Saturday morning is something to see. There are 200 vendors, making it the largest open-air market in the Midwest. In midsummer, the stalls are heaped high with fruits and vegetables of every description. There are also fine Wisconsin cheeses, breads, nuts, and locally raised wild rice. This time of year, the zucchini are tiny and the eggplants small and glossy. It is a perfect time to prepare this recipe combining those two vegetables. A handsome presentation, this dish can be made early in the day and refrigerated until it is time to be baked.

1 eggplant	1 red bell pepper, chopped
Salt	1 pound tomatoes, blanched,
8 medium zucchini	skinned, and seeded
Olive oil	1 tablespoon chopped fresh basil
1 onion, chopped	1 teaspoon chopped fresh thyme
2 garlic cloves, crushed	Salt and pepper to taste

Peel the eggplant and cut into ½-inch-thick slices. Place the slices in a colander and sprinkle with salt. Allow the eggplant to "weep" for approximately 20 minutes, then rinse off the salt and pat the slices dry with a paper towel. Chop into large pieces and set aside.

Preheat the oven to 400° F.

In a large saucepan of boiling water, blanch the whole zucchini for 1 minute. Cut each zucchini in half lengthwise and scoop out the seeds, using a small knife and teaspoon; set aside.

Heat 1 tablespoon oil in a medium sauté pan over medium-high heat. Add the onions and sauté until transparent, about 4 to 5 minutes, then add the garlic and cook for 5 minutes. Add the red bell pepper and eggplant, adding more oil as needed, and cook until all the liquid is evaporated. Add the tomatoes and cook for 5 minutes more; stir in the basil, thyme, and salt and pepper to taste. Place the zucchini, cut side up, in a 10 × 10-inch greased casserole and fill each one with the eggplant mixture. Bake for 20 minutes, or until the zucchini is heated through. Serve hot or at room temperature.

YELLOW SUMMER SQUASH RINGS

SERVES 4

New Jersey isn't just called the "garden state" because it needed a moniker. It provides nearby New York and Philadelphia with fresh foodstuffs— vegetables, fruit, and poultry. In the late 1800s, there was even a special train running from New Jersey's agricultural centers to New York City; it was known as the "Pea Line." Come summer, the markets are flooded with the bounty of New Jersey, including all sorts of squash—pattypans, zucchini, crooknecks, and long thin yellow summer squash. If you're not a squash lover, try this rather unorthodox preparation—bake them in bourbon and brown sugar.

2 yellow summer squash
   (approximately 8 inches long),
   cut into ½-inch rings
¼ cup bourbon
¼ cup (½ stick) butter, melted

2 tablespoons packed brown sugar
¼ teaspoon ground cinnamon
Salt and pepper to taste

Garnish: minced chervil

Preheat the oven to 375° F.

Line a jelly roll pan with aluminum foil. Arrange the squash rings in a single layer on the foil and prick them with a fork. Drizzle the bourbon over the squash and let stand for 5 minutes to absorb the liquor. Brush evenly with the melted butter, then sprinkle with brown sugar, cinnamon, and salt and pepper. Bake, uncovered, until tender, about 20 minutes. Garnish with the chervil and serve immediately, allowing at least 4 slices per person.

RED BELL PEPPER–CHIVE DRESSING

MAKES ABOUT 1 2/3 CUPS DRESSING

In season, I like to prepare this subtle but distinctive dressing, which is perfect for a salad of very delicate mixed greens or to drizzle over light cooked broccoli or asparagus.

2 very large red bell peppers
1 large garlic clove, peeled
   and roughly chopped
1 shallot, peeled and thinly sliced
2 cups chicken stock
3 tablespoons seasoned
   rice wine vinegar

½ cup canola or
   vegetable oil (not olive)
6 tablespoons chopped fresh chives
1½ teaspoons ground mustard
1½ teaspoons salt
½ teaspoon freshly ground black pepper
⅛ teaspoon ground red pepper

Cut the red bell peppers in half lengthwise; remove the seed core. Cut each in half again and remove all the white membranes. Place the red bell peppers, garlic, and shallot in a 2-quart saucepan and add the chicken stock. Bring to a boil, then lower the heat and simmer, uncovered, until the peppers are very soft, about 1 hour. Drain, reserving the broth for soup, and transfer the vegetables to a food processor bowl. Puree until smooth. Force the puree through a fine sieve into a medium bowl. Add the rice vinegar and slowly add the oil, whisking it in. Stir in the remaining ingredients. Serve at room temperature. It can be stored in the refrigerator for up to 1 week.

$\mathcal{B}$ARR STREET MARKET PEACH CREAM PIE WITH NUTMEG

SERVES 8

During peach season, I make up this pie filling in large amounts and pour the filling into pans lined with foil, not crusts, and freeze them. Once frozen, I transfer the foiled peach patties to large plastic bags and store until needed. It is then a simple matter to pop a peach filling, without the foil, into a pastry-lined pan, top with the cream, and bake. This is a generous pie, so be sure to use your deepest 9-inch pan or even a shallow 10-inch one. This pie should cool completely at room temperature before cutting; allow 5 hours for this. It will be hard to wait that long, but you can do it.

One 9-inch unbaked	Speck of salt
pastry shell (page 284)	¼ teaspoon grated nutmeg
3 cups peeled and sliced peaches	½ teaspoon almond extract
¾ cup granulated sugar	1 cup heavy cream
¼ cup packed light brown sugar	
¼ cup minute tapioca	Garnish: grated nutmeg

In a large bowl, combine the peaches, sugars, tapioca, salt, nutmeg, and almond extract. Allow the mixture to stand for 10 minutes, stirring occasionally.

Preheat the oven to 400° F.

Transfer the mixture to the pie shell and pour the cream over the top; do not mix in. Sprinkle some additional nutmeg on top. Bake the pie for 10 minutes, lower the heat to 350° F., and bake 50 minutes longer, or until the pie is bubbling up in the center. Remove to a rack and allow to cool for 5 hours before cutting.

An array of fresh peaches

APPLES STUFFED WITH MINCEMEAT

SERVES 6 TO 8

One of the pleasures of farmer's markets for me is the astonishing array of apple varieties.
This is the place to buy real apples, including antique apple varieties that assure you of getting an apple with
flavor and a decent texture. Once you've cooked with these special apples, you'll be spoiled forever.
Look for Black Gilliflower, Cox's Orange Pippin, Wolf River, Matzu's Japanese Golden,
Sheep Nose, Winter Banana, Strawberry, York Imperials, or my very own favorite, Northern Spy.
If your apple person doesn't have any of these varieties any of the time, well, shame on him.
Consider mail order from the Doud Orchards (page 298).
One of the simplest ways to prepare apples is to bake them. Stuff the cavity first with some
mincemeat,and you have a first-rate dessert. I frequently serve these
for brunch, accompanied by a pitcher of cream.

6 or 8 cooking apples,　　　　　　**1 tablespoon butter**
depending on the size
¾ cup mincemeat (page 211)　　　**Garnish: cream or ice cream**
Brown Sugar Sauce (page 287)

Preheat the oven to 350° F.

Wash and core the apples, paring away 1 inch of apple skin from the top of the apple—this will keep it from puffing out of its skin. Place the apples in a greased 10 × 7-inch flat baking dish. Stuff each apple with about 2 tablespoons of mincemeat.

Prepare the Brown Sugar Sauce and add 1 tablespoon butter. Pour over the apples and bake them for 1 hour, or until tender, basting occasionally. Serve in compotes with the sauce on top. A bit of ice cream is a nice touch, if you are serving the apples as a dessert.

Baking
DAY

IN THE EARLY years of our country's history, one or two days a week were set aside for baking; old journals indicate this was generally Wednesday and Saturdays (steamed breads and puddings were made on the alternate days, one reason we find so many old recipes for them).

Preparation for baking day actually began the day before, since the bread had to rise, and pies and cakes were readied in order to be baked at the same time. First the bread was slipped into the back of the oven on a peel (a long wooden paddle), then the chicken, meat, and fruit pies went in next. The beans, cakes, and Indian pudding were put in last, in front, where they could be removed earlier than the bread. Sometimes, depending on the size of the oven, cakes and puddings were baked after the bread came out and the heat was diminishing.

Inside ovens, built into the fireplace, were also primitive and threw off a lot of heat, and while that was not a problem during the winter, it certainly was during the summer. For some, this is still a fac-

tor to consider. When I was interviewing Amish women, I was struck by the number of them who had two stoves in their kitchens, one a bottled gas stove they used for cooking year-round, the other, a black iron stove fueled by wood or coal. The black iron stove is only used during cold weather.

All of the women worked on baking day, passing the skills from mother to daughter. Ingredients were seldom measured, and much of it was done by "feel" and by "eye." I realize how fortunate I am that my mother encouraged my being with her in the kitchen when I was just a tot. From the beginning, baking, for me, was always a pleasurable activity. Doubtless this was because I had my mother's undivided attention, playing with the flour was fun, and I received a great deal of approval for those early primitive attempts. Today we would call the time we spent together "quality time." It was a precious gift and one I appreciate anew each time I tie on my apron and pull out the flour and mixing bowls.

Funnel Cakes Cheese Biscuits Southern Rice Popovers Science Hill Buttermilk Biscuits
Onion-Herb Batter Bread Mormon Corn Bread Sunny Corn Muffins Finnish Cardamom Bread
Briarpatch Herb Bread Classic Herb Crescents Sourdough Starter Sourdough Biscuits
Sourdough Bread Indian Pudding Woodford Pudding Banana Bread
Cottage Cheese Fruit Bread Apple-Date Cake

FUNNEL CAKES
(DRECHTER KUCHA)
MAKES 6 LARGE CAKES

*These flaky pastries are still found in Amish markets across the country. It is fun to watch
them being made. Thin batter is drizzled through a funnel in a snail-like pattern into hot fat, fried until golden,
then sprinkled with confectioners' sugar. They are sometimes called plowlines, but I've never met a
farmer who plowed this way. Or at least he wouldn't ever admit it!
Don't be discouraged if your first cakes aren't perfect—it takes a bit of practice to get perfect ones.
In fact, you might want to plan on making a double recipe.*

1 cup all-purpose flour	**¾ cup milk**
1 teaspoon sugar	
1 teaspoon baking powder	**Corn oil for frying**
¼ teaspoon salt	**Confectioners' sugar for sprinkling**
1 large egg	**Molasses or maple syrup**

In a large bowl, whisk together the flour, sugar, baking powder, and salt. In a small bowl, beat the egg well;
add the milk and combine. Make a well in the flour mixture and pour in the egg mixture. Mix together with
a large spoon, then whisk to remove any lumps. Let the batter stand for 15 minutes and whisk again just
before frying so it is absolutely lump-free.

Heat ⅓ inch corn oil in an electric skillet to 390° F. When the oil is hot, place your finger under the bottom of a funnel opening and pour about ¼ cup of the batter into the funnel. Position the funnel over the
center of the skillet, remove your finger, and allow the batter to come out, drizzling a thin stream into the
hot oil in a circular path, working from the center of the skillet toward the sides as if forming a snail. Do
not stop pouring until the cake is complete. Fry for approximately 30 seconds, until golden brown, then
carefully turn the cake with tongs and fry an additional 15 to 20 seconds until done. Remove carefully with
a large metal spatula and tongs—they are very tender. Drain on paper towels. Sprinkle with confectioners' sugar or serve with molasses or maple syrup for a breakfast dish.

Handmade tin scoops

CHEESE BISCUITS

MAKES TWENTY-FOUR 2-INCH BISCUITS

Biscuits were common fare among early American cooks, especially on the wagon trains and the ranches. "Cookies," who worked the chuck wagons, ruled the roost; good cooks were harder to find than good cowboys. Frequently the cookies would stir up biscuit batter right in the self-rising flour bag, scooping it out and baking the biscuits in Dutch ovens over a campfire.
These are much fancier biscuits than those eaten on the range, but any cowboy would have relished them.

2 cups all-purpose flour	¼ teaspoon red pepper
4 teaspoons baking powder	¼ cup (½ stick) cold butter
1½ tablespoons minced onion	1 cup grated extra sharp cheddar cheese
1 teaspoon salt	¼ cup grated Parmesan cheese
1 teaspoon dried thyme	1 cup heavy cream
½ teaspoon crushed dried rosemary	

In a large mixing bowl, combine the flour, baking powder, onion, salt, thyme, rosemary, and red pepper; mix. Add the butter and cut in with a pastry blender until fine crumbs are formed. Add the cheeses and cream and stir until just mixed. Turn out on a floured surface and lightly knead 8 turns. Roll out, and using a 2-inch cutter, cut out 24 biscuits. Transfer to a greased baking sheet (do not crowd) and bake for 10 to 12 minutes, or until golden brown.

SOUTHERN RICE POPOVERS

MAKES 12

There is something so lavish and welcoming about a basket of homemade hot breads. One we should make often is popovers, for the ingredients are always on hand—flour, eggs, and milk.
Southerners make popovers with a bit of mashed rice added, creating a popover that has a creamy texture.
They do not rise quite as dramatically high, but no matter, they are divine.

1½ cups milk, at room temperature	¾ cup all-purpose flour
¾ cup mashed cooked rice, whirled for 20 seconds in a blender or food processor or mashed by hand	1 teaspoon vanilla extract
	½ teaspoon salt
	3 jumbo eggs, at room temperature

Place a 12-cup muffin or popover tin in the oven and preheat the oven and the tin to 450° F.

Pour the milk into a large mixing bowl, add the mashed rice, flour, vanilla, and salt. With a rotary beater or whisk, beat until well blended. Add the eggs one at time, beating in completely before adding the next.

Remove the hot pan from the oven and grease the cups. Fill the cups two-thirds full. Bake for 15 minutes, then reduce the oven heat to 350° F. and continue baking 20 minutes longer, or until the popovers are deeply golden and puffed. Do not open the oven during baking. Serve hot.

SCIENCE HILL BUTTERMILK BISCUITS

SERVES 8

Like all good southern cooks, Science Hill's chef Donna Gill has recipes for southern breads that are unsurpassed. The roll basket at the restaurant is always full of goodies, among them these buttermilk biscuits. She uses a soft wheat flour—you might want to order some, for it does make a difference (page 299).

1 cup buttermilk
½ teaspoon baking soda
2½ cups soft wheat white flour
2 teaspoons baking powder

1 teaspoon salt
½ cup plus 2 tablespoons
   vegetable shortening

Preheat the oven to 375° F.

In a small bowl, combine the buttermilk and soda and set aside. In a large mixing bowl, whisk together the flour, baking powder, and salt. Cut in the shortening with a pastry blender or 2 knives until the mixture resembles coarse crumbs. Stir in the buttermilk, about ¾ cup at first, adding more if necessary to make a stiff but workable dough. The batter will be quite springy.

Turn out onto a lightly floured surface and knead 10 times. Roll out lightly to ½-inch thickness and using a 2½-inch cutter, cut out biscuits, using a straight up-and-down motion. Don't twist the cutter or the edges of the biscuit will stick together and you will have lopsided biscuits. Bake for 15 minutes, or until the biscuits are pale yellow. Serve hot.

PHOTO POST CARD

AMERICA 25

SHELBYVILLE, KENTUCKY

One of the most delightful places to visit in Kentucky is the Science Hill Inn in Shelbyville. Originally a private girls' school built in 1824, Science Hill drew students from all over the wilderness. Now it houses a group of excellent antiques and gift shops and a fine restaurant that brings people in from several states.

M

ONION-HERB BATTER BREAD

SERVES 12

*A hot yeast bread adds panache to any meal, and this herb-flavored bread is
no exception. Because it requires no kneading it is quick to prepare. It calls for unbleached flour, which
is more like our old flours, when grains were ground at local grist mills.*

¼ cup (½ stick) butter	½ teaspoon rubbed sage
1 cup finely chopped onion	½ teaspoon dried basil
3¼ cups unbleached flour	¼ teaspoon dried rosemary, crumbled
2 packages active dry yeast	¼ teaspoon dried thyme
2 tablespoons packed light brown sugar	1 large egg
1 teaspoon salt	1¼ cups warm water

Melt the butter in a small skillet and sauté the onions over medium-low heat for 10 minutes; cool. In a large mixer bowl, combine 1½ cups of the flour with the yeast, sugar, salt, and herbs; combine thoroughly. Add the reserved onions and mix. Add the egg and water and blend at low speed for 3 minutes.

Stir in the remaining flour by hand. Transfer to a greased 2-quart round casserole or a 9 × 13-inch pan, cover loosely with plastic wrap, and let rise in a warm place until doubled in bulk, about 45 minutes to an hour. Meanwhile, preheat the oven to 375° F.

Bake the bread for 35 to 40 minutes, or until the top is golden brown. An instant-reading thermometer can be inserted into the side of the loaf; if it registers 200° F., the bread is done. Remove from the oven, tip out on a rack to cool, or slice and serve warm.

MORMON CORN BREAD

SERVES 12

*Even though Utah has become more urban and industrial, the conservative and stable
Mormon influence remains. Many Mormon cooks bake traditional breads, including corn bread. This sturdy
and firm version is sweetened with honey, a flavoring used often in Mormon cuisine.
In fact, Brigham Young had a cupola shaped like a beehive built on top of his house as a symbol of the
Mormon virtue of unremitting industry.*

1½ cups yellow cornmeal	1 ¾ cups buttermilk
1 cup all-purpose flour	3 tablespoons honey
1 teaspoon baking powder	5 tablespoons corn oil
1½ teaspoons baking soda	
1 teaspoon salt	Butter
1 large egg	Sorghum or honey

Preheat the oven to 350° F. Grease a 9-inch square pan and dust with a couple of handfuls of cornmeal; set aside.

In a large bowl, whisk together the cornmeal, flour, baking powder, soda, and salt. In a small bowl, beat the egg and add the remaining ingredients; blend.

Make a well in the dry ingredients and pour in the buttermilk mixture. Gently combine the two with a spoon, being careful not to overbeat. Transfer the batter to the prepared pan. Bake for 35 minutes, or until the top of the corn bread is firm and golden. Cut into squares and serve hot with butter and sorghum or honey.

Sunny CORN MUFFINS

MAKES 12 CORN MUFFINS

This is a very cakelike textured corn muffin with the added richness of brown sugar. The New England cook who gave me this recipe was quite emphatic about greasing the muffin tins heavily with bacon fat—"gives 'em real good flavor," she said, "then sprinkle the cups with more cornmeal." The bacon fat is a tasty idea, but you can certainly use vegetable shortening or spray.

½ cup (1 stick) butter	1 cup all-purpose flour
½ cup packed light brown sugar	3 teaspoons baking powder
1 large egg	1 teaspoon salt
1 cup yellow cornmeal	1 cup milk

Preheat the oven to 375° F. Grease a 12-cup muffin tin with bacon fat or vegetable shortening and then sprinkle with cornmeal; set aside.

In a mixer bowl, cream the butter and brown sugar for 5 minutes. Add the egg and blend well. In a small bowl, whisk together the cornmeal, flour, baking powder, and salt. With a rubber spatula, add the flour mixture to the egg mixture, alternating with the milk. Do not overmix or the muffins will have tunnels. Pour ¼ cup of batter into each muffin cup and bake for 20 to 25 minutes, or until the muffins are golden brown. Serve hot.

Iron corn stick pans

FINNISH CARDAMOM BREAD

MAKES 2 LOAVES

*The Europeans who helped settle America brought many of their old recipes along and,
using the ingredients found here, were sometimes able to duplicate what they had eaten at home—
real comfort food and that included bread recipes from the home country. This savory bread
glazed with a confectioners' sugar icing is a slow riser, so give it plenty of time.*

¼ cup (½ stick) butter	1 teaspoon ground cardamom
1½ cups milk	
1 package active dry yeast	GLAZE
6½ cups all-purpose flour	½ cup confectioners' sugar
2 large eggs, beaten	¼ cup half-and-half, milk, or
¾ cup granulated sugar	strong coffee
1 teaspoon salt	

Combine the butter and milk in a medium saucepan and heat until the butter is melted. Cool to luke-warm, then whisk in the yeast. Add 2½ cups of the flour and beat until the batter is smooth. Let the mixture stand ½ hour, or until a bubbling action starts. Beat in the eggs, sugar, salt, and cardamom. Blend in approximately 3½ cups flour, adding more if necessary. Knead thoroughly for 10 minutes. Place the dough in a large buttered bowl, turning it in the bowl so the dough is buttered on all sides. Cover with a towel or plastic wrap and let rise until doubled, about 1½ hours.

Divide the dough in half and cut each half in thirds to form 2 braided loaves (or shape into 2 conventional loaves). Place the shaped dough on greased cookie sheets and let rise until tripled in bulk, about 1½ hours.

Meanwhile, preheat the oven to 350° F. Bake the bread for 45 minutes, or until golden brown and the internal temperature is 200° F. (You can check this with an instant-reading thermometer.) Transfer to wire racks set over wax paper.

In a small bowl, combine the glaze ingredients, stirring until smooth. Pour the glaze over the breads while still warm. Cool completely.

NOTE: *This dough is also a good base for cinnamon rolls.*

BRIARPATCH HERB BREAD

MAKES 3 LOAVES

This light whole wheat bread a specialty of Clarinda's Cottage Tea Room, is enhanced by
herbs and nutmeg and makes a large quantity.

2 cups bread flour
1 package active dry yeast
2 tablespoons sugar
⅓ cup nonfat dry milk powder
1¾ cups hot water (120° F. to 130° F.)
1 large egg
¼ cup finely chopped parsley
1½ tablespoons chopped chives
    or ½ tablespoon dried

½ tablespoon chopped fresh basil
    or 1 teaspoon dried
1 teaspoon chopped fresh oregano
    or ⅓ teaspoon dried
½ teaspoon grated nutmeg
2 tablespoons vegetable oil
2 teaspoons salt
3 cups whole wheat flour, approximately
1 tablespoon butter, melted

Measure 1½ cups bread flour into a large bowl. Stir in the yeast, sugar, and dry milk. Pour in the hot water and blend to make a thin batter. Add the egg, parsley, chives, basil, oregano, and nutmeg; beat briskly by hand for 2 minutes. Allow this to proof and become bubbly, approximately 15 minutes.

In a large mixer bowl, combine the oil, salt, and 2 cups whole wheat flour. Using the flat paddle if your mixer has one, beat for 2 minutes. Allow to rest for 3 minutes, then add the yeast and herb batter slowly, using a dough hook. Knead for 8 minutes, adding more whole wheat flour if necessary. After kneading, place the dough in a very large greased bowl. Let rise until double in size, about 40 minutes. Punch the dough down and form into 3 loaves. Transfer each loaf to a 9 × 5 × 3-inch pan. Let rise to the top of the pan.

Meanwhile, preheat the oven to 350° F. and then bake for 35 to 40 minutes, or until the loaves sound hollow when tapped and the inner temperature registers 200° F. on an instant-reading thermometer. Remove from the oven and tip the loaves out to cool on a rack. Immediately brush with the melted butter. Allow to cool completely before slicing.

PHOTO POST CARD

AMERICA 25

NEWBURGH HERB FESTIVAL,
NEWBURGH, INDIANA

The Newburgh Herb Festival is held every weekend during May. This is a pretty, old, river town just across the river from Kentucky. Clarinda's Cottage Tea Room is just across from the Country Store, which is the center of activity for the festival. They serve lots of delicious recipes featuring the aromatic herbs being feted outside. Both the festival and Clarinda's are well worth a visit.

No matter how many times we've made the trip, I still get excited whenever we cross over the Mississippi River. And I feel the same about St. Louis; Saarinen's steel arch spans the horizon, emphasizing this city was the gateway to the West. Though it is now a sophisticated metropolis, its roots are early American. Those first people who came here to go on westward were mostly unlettered folk, hunters, disappointed farmers from the Atlantic seaboard and Europe, trappers, and old army scouts, as well as the adventurous. But they all agreed with Daniel Boone about the three essentials for travel at that time: "A good gun, a good horse, and a good wife." At this stage of civilization, one does not quarrel with their priorities. Most of those early settlers hoped to achieve what the small farmers of the East had, with a grain crop and a patch of ground where they could raise their own vegetables and have an orchard and a cow or two. Later they planned on having their own schoolhouses and envisioned a doctor and lawyer would occasionally pass through on horseback. Those seem like modest goals, but they paid dearly to achieve them.

The rivers were a most important link in the settlement of this region—the Missouri, the Illinois, the Wabash, and the Ohio all flowed into the vast current of the Mississippi, down through the South into the port of New Orleans.

Canals were built by immigrant labor, who came overland or up the rivers by keel boats or barges with partially covered decks, not the most luxurious mode of travel. Then railroads, also built with immigrant labor, began crisscrossing the country, providing transportation to what was to be the Great Plains granary, later a gigantic supermarket for the whole country.

The freedom to worship as they pleased brought in many religious groups, such as the Shakers, Amish, and Mennonites. They were a positive force in the settlement of the Midwest, with their farming skills and work ethic, obvious to all. Industrious Germans, bringing their brewmeister and bratwurst skills, were the second most influential group to arrive in America, and they scattered all over the West, adding their love of order and organization, as well as music and Lutheran churches, to communities wherever they settled.

The Scandinavians arrived and settled in the north, where the cold climate and deep forests reminded them of their homeland. Then the Irish, eager to escape the famine in their home country, came to help build the canals, as well as the Scotch, Dutch, and Poles. They set up housekeeping and made their sausages, their breads and pastries, their cheeses, and their wines. And the women began exchanging recipes at church, at the Grange meetings, and at market days. The overlapping of food styles began, and from that time on, in the prairies, the food style was frequently eclectic, and to the purist, sometimes confusing, but always generous.

The homesteaders were the first true inhabitants of the plains. They introduced a new and stable element—the family. It was a raw life with raw materials—with no trees on the prairie, their houses were made of sod, or "prairie marble," and the fuel was dried buffalo dung.

Three things helped their survival—the windmill, which provided them with water, and, second, a special iron plow developed by John Deere, a Vermonter who had moved to Illinois. The third thing, simple to our eyes, was barbed wire. No longer would the homesteader's crops be overrun by herds of cattle driven through by cowboys; but the barbed wire began to define boundaries and private property. It signaled the beginning of the stability of the farmer and his productive land in the Midwest.

CLASSIC HERB CRESCENTS

MAKES 16 ROLLS

Some of the most enticing food in Indiana is being served at The Classic Kitchen in Noblesville,
a small town close to Indianapolis. Owner-chef Steven Kneipp serves uncommonly delicious food in a sprightly blue
and white French country dining room. But the menus are unabashedly American. "This is a 'destination'
restaurant," says Steve. "People drive quite a way to come here to eat." You'll understand why when you get there.
All the breads at the restaurant are homemade, and each day's roll basket is a surprise.
These crescents are buttery, light, and very easy to make.

¼ cup warm water

1 tablespoon sugar

1 package active dry yeast

1 cup small curd cottage cheese,
   slightly warmed in the microwave

1 tablespoon dried fines herbes

2 tablespoons snipped chives or
   finely chopped green onion tops

¼ teaspoon baking soda

1 teaspoon salt

1 large egg

2½ to 2¾ cups unbleached white flour

½ cup (1 stick) unsalted butter, melted

Unsalted butter

In a small bowl, stir the warm water, sugar, and yeast together with a fork; set in a warm place to proof, about 10 minutes. In a mixer bowl, combine the cottage cheese, fines herbes, chives, soda, salt, and egg until well blended. When the yeast is bubbly, stir it into the cheese mixture. Mix in approximately 2½ cups flour until a stiff dough forms. If the dough is too soft, add the remaining flour as you knead it. Turn the dough out onto a floured surface and knead until elastic, about 10 minutes. Place in a buttered bowl and cover with plastic wrap. Let rise in a warm place until doubled in size, about 1 hour.

Meanwhile, preheat the oven to 350° F. Punch down the dough and transfer to a floured surface; roll out into a 13- to 14-inch circle. Spread the circle with half the melted butter, then cut into 16 triangles, like pie wedges. Starting from the bigger end, roll each wedge into a crescent. Transfer the crescents to a greased baking sheet and brush with the remaining melted butter. Let the crescents rise, uncovered, about 45 minutes, or until doubled. Bake for 12 to 15 minutes. Serve warm with unsalted butter.

OURDOUGH STARTER

*Baking bread without commercial yeast is quite interesting, for each batch of starter
will be different. Here are some hints to help you along: Always use unbleached flour. Do not use metal bowls.
If the starter develops a watery liquid on top, just whisk it back in. (The old-timers called this
"hooch" and sometimes drank it—I suggest you skip that.) A healthy starter will resemble cottage cheese with
unbroken bubbles. The older the starter, the stronger the ferment and sour flavor becomes.
Always add 1 teaspoon soda per cup of flour to your final bread-roll or pancake mixture
to neutralize the acid of the sourdough and give sweetness to and lighten the batter.
Bring the sourdough starter to room temperature before using; I remove mine
from the refrigerator and allow it to set out overnight before I begin baking in the morning. Feed the
sourdough right after you use it, or every two weeks, dipping out extra to give to
friends if you are not baking with it. And I do notice I get better results in the summer.*

2 cups whole milk   **½ cup sugar**
2 teaspoons red wine vinegar   **2 cups unbleached white flour**

In a medium ceramic or plastic bowl, combine the milk and the vinegar; allow to stand for 30 minutes. Whisk in the sugar and the flour. Cover with a square of cheesecloth and set aside in a draft-free place for 48 hours. Whisk the mixture every day to recombine the ingredients. When the mixture is bubbly and smells of yeast, you are ready to begin baking. If no bubbling occurs by the fifth day, or if mold appears on the top of the starter, discard the whole thing and start over.

Dip out the amount you need for the recipe, then feed the starter by whisking in 1 cup milk that has been soured with 1 teaspoon red wine vinegar, ¼ cup sugar, and 1 cup unbleached flour. Cover the mixture with cheesecloth and allow to stand overnight, or until the mixture is bubbly again. Cover loosely (plastic wrap is fine) and refrigerate. Do not bake with the sourdough the same day you feed it.

Sourdough can be frozen, but it should be thawed, fed, and kept in a warm place until it revives. You are dealing with a living thing here! If you have an unusually good starter going and don't want to lose it, it can be dried. Drop teaspoons of sourdough on wax paper and allow the wafers to dry for 2 days, turning them frequently. Pack in airtight jars. To reactivate, drop 3 wafers in ½ cup of warm water and allow the mixture, covered with cheesecloth, to stand overnight. This can be added to your recipe for starter and assures a well-flavored beginning.

OURDOUGH BISCUITS
MAKES **8** BISCUITS

*These quick biscuits are crusty on the outside and
tender and melting on the inside, rather like mini round loaves of bread.*

1 cup Sourdough Starter,   **1 cup unbleached white flour**
at room temperature   **¼ teaspoon baking soda**

½ teaspoon salt
½ cup vegetable oil (I use corn oil)

Butter and jam

Preheat the oven to 375° F.

In a large mixer bowl, combine all of the ingredients and beat until smooth. Place a heaping tablespoon of batter into 8 paper-lined muffin cups, smoothing out the top of the biscuit with your fingertips. Bake for 25 minutes, or until the muffins are golden brown and crusty looking. Remove from the oven and eat while warm with butter and jam.

Sourdough Bread

MAKES 1 LOAF

Long-time Alaskans call themselves "sourdoughs" after the early miners who came to settle that part of the country. But sourdough isn't exclusively Alaskan; American pioneers carried sourdough starters with them as they pushed the frontiers West. The "cookies" depended on it to feed the cowboys on the range, and the Forty-niners gave it as a precious gift to San Francisco. With a single pot of starter, a cook in the wilderness could leaven endless loaves of breads, dozens of biscuits, and stacks of flapjacks. This bread calls for the addition of quick-rise commercial yeast; this way you do not have to make a sponge. It does have two risings, so plan accordingly.

½ cup warm water
1 package active dry yeast
1 cup Sourdough Starter,
    at room temperature
¼ cup (½ stick) butter, melted
1 teaspoon baking soda

1 teaspoon salt
1 large egg, lightly beaten
2¾ to 3 cups unbleached white flour
Butter
Kosher salt

Place the warm water in a small warmed bowl and sprinkle on the yeast; whisk in and allow the mixture to proof for 10 minutes. In a deep mixer bowl, combine the sourdough starter, butter, soda, salt, egg, and proofed yeast mixture. Blend for 30 seconds. Gradually add 2 cups flour and beat well. Gradually add the remaining ¾ cup flour and knead for 6 minutes (by hand or with a dough hook attachment on your mixer), or until the dough is smooth and elastic. Add a bit more flour if needed. Place in a large greased bowl, greasing the top of the dough and covering loosely with plastic wrap or a tea towel, and let rise 1½ hours or more, until doubled. (The dough will be soft and puffy.) Punch down, then knead a few times until the dough is satiny and smooth again. Form the dough into a loaf and place in a greased 10 × 5-inch bread pan. Cover again and allow to rise a final hour.

Meanwhile, preheat the oven to 375° F. for at least 10 minutes. Bake the bread for 40 minutes, covering with a piece of foil if the bread begins to get too brown. The inner temperature of the bread should register 200° F. on an instant-reading thermometer. Remove from the oven and tip the bread out immediately onto a rack to cool. Brush the top of the loaf with soft butter and sprinkle with salt. Cool completely before cutting.

INDIAN PUDDING

SERVES 8

Boston's Durgin-Park goes back to Revolutionary days; now, as then, it is a successful restaurant, serving a thousand people each Saturday night. Though short on amenities, it is the place to enjoy the sturdy flavorsome food of New England—creamy fish chowders, Boston baked beans, johnnycake, boiled dinners, and most of all, Durgin-Park's famous Indian pudding. This is the standard against which all other Indian puddings are graded. To achieve that dulcet smoothness is not all that easy.

This recipe is adapted from the original, which was baked in stone crocks and made a much larger quantity. Scalding the milk first keeps the pudding from separating, as it is wont to do otherwise (though Fanny Farmer said that was what Indian puddings do). I bake mine in a 1½-quart bean pot without the lid; I do believe a clay or ceramic dish, deep rather than flat, works best. Be sure to eat it warm from the oven and top it with a scoop of ice cream, if you are so inclined.

3 cups whole milk	⅛ teaspoon grated nutmeg
½ cup yellow cornmeal	⅛ teaspoon ground cloves
¼ cup light molasses	⅛ teaspoon baking soda
2 tablespoons dark brown sugar	Speck of salt
2 tablespoons (¼ stick) butter at room temperature	1 large egg
1 teaspoon ground cinnamon	Ice cream (optional)
1 teaspoon ground ginger	

Preheat the oven to 275° F. Grease the inside of a 1½-quart bean pot or a 1- to 1½-quart deep baking dish—don't use a metal one.

In a heavy 2-quart saucepan, scald 2½ cups milk—little bubbles will form around the edges. Place the remaining ½ cup milk in a small bowl and gradually whisk in the cornmeal. Whisk the cornmeal mixture into the scalded milk very slowly and bring to a boil. Lower the heat and cook over low heat for 15 minutes, whisking often. The cornmeal will be very thick.

Meanwhile, in a small bowl, combine the molasses, brown sugar, butter, spices, soda, and salt. Break the egg into a small bowl and beat slightly; set aside. When the cornmeal is cooked, remove from the heat and whisk in the molasses mixture. Stir ½ cup of the hot cornmeal mixture into the beaten egg, then add it back into the cornmeal-molasses mixture and whisk well. Pour into the prepared dish and bake for 1½ hours. A skin will form on top of the pudding and it will be shaky when you remove it, but that is just the way it is supposed to be. Serve while it is very warm and top with a scoop of ice cream, if desired.

WOODFORD PUDDING

SERVES 9

This old, old Kentucky recipe is really a cake, but Sadie Caruthers of rural Bardstown, who gave me the recipe, insists it has always been called a pudding. I suspect it is actually an old English recipe transplanted to the New World. No matter; it is very moist, dark, a bit fruity, and finely grained. The sauce is excellent.

½ cup (1 stick) butter,
    at room temperature
1 cup granulated sugar
3 large eggs, at room temperature
1 cup blackberry jam
1 teaspoon baking soda
3 teaspoons sour milk (see Note)
1½ cups all-purpose flour
¾ teaspoon ground cinnamon
½ teaspoon grated nutmeg
½ teaspoon salt

CARAMEL SAUCE
½ cup (1 stick) butter
½ cup packed dark brown sugar
½ cup granulated sugar
½ cup heavy cream
1 teaspoon vanilla extract
Speck of salt

Preheat the oven to 325° F.

In a mixer bowl, cream the butter and sugar for 7 minutes. Add the eggs one at a time, blending well after each addition, then blend in the jam. Add the soda to the sour milk and stir, then add to the egg mixture and blend well. In a small bowl, whisk together the flour, cinnamon, nutmeg, and salt. Add the flour mixture to the egg mixture and combine until the ingredients are just blended. Pour the batter into a greased 8 × 8-inch pan and bake for 45 minutes, or until the top of the cake is golden brown and springs back when touched with your finger. Remove from the oven and cool.

Prepare the sauce: In a medium saucepan, melt the butter over medium heat. Add the sugars and cream and bring to a boil, stirring frequently. Boil and stir for 1 minute. Cool slightly, then stir in the vanilla and salt. To serve, cut the pudding into squares and serve topped with the hot sauce.

NOTE: *To make sour milk, place the milk in a small cup and add a drop or two of vinegar or lemon juice, stir, and allow to stand about 10 minutes, or until the milk looks curdled.*

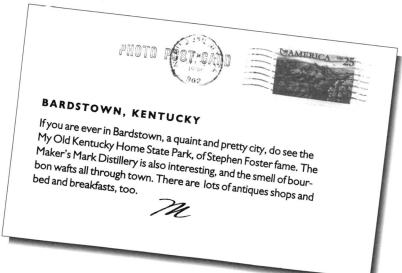

BARDSTOWN, KENTUCKY

If you are ever in Bardstown, a quaint and pretty city, do see the My Old Kentucky Home State Park, of Stephen Foster fame. The Maker's Mark Distillery is also interesting, and the smell of bourbon wafts all through town. There are lots of antiques shops and bed and breakfasts, too.

BANANA BREAD

MAKES 1 LOAF

*We always keep bananas on hand in the fruit bowl, and whenever some of them get overripe
I have an excuse to make this well-flavored, brown-speckled bread. Serve it plain or with butter or cream cheese;
it is also good toasted. Like all fruit breads, it gets better as it ages. It freezes well, too.*

⅓ cup vegetable shortening
⅔ cup sugar
2 large eggs
1 teaspoon vanilla extract
1¾ cups all-purpose flour

2¾ teaspoons baking powder
½ teaspoon salt
1 cup mashed very ripe bananas
  (about 3 medium bananas)

Preheat the oven to 350° F.

In a large mixer bowl, beat the shortening for 2 minutes until creamy. Gradually add the sugar, beating until light and fluffy after each addition. Add the eggs and vanilla; beat until thick and pale lemon in color. In a large mixing bowl, whisk together the flour, baking powder, and salt. Slowly begin adding the flour mixture to the sugar mixture, alternating with the mashed bananas and combining well after each addition.

Grease *only* the bottom of a 4½ × 8½-inch loaf or bread pan. Transfer the batter to the loaf pan and bake for 50 to 60 minutes. Test with a cake tester for doneness; it should come out clean when inserted into the middle of the loaf. Cool at least 10 minutes before removing from the pan. Cool completely on a wire rack.

COTTAGE CHEESE FRUIT BREAD

MAKES 1 LOAF

*Many farmers who bring in produce to market also bring homemade goodies, often
prepared by their wives. Homemade noodles, breads, pies, cookies, plus jams and jellies all appear on the
stands next to tomatoes, onions, and carrots. I sampled this cottage cheese fruit bread at the
stand of an Amish lady at the Lancaster Market; later I found the recipe for it in one of my Mennonite cookbooks.
An unusually memorable quick bread, it is moist with currants and cottage cheese and
brightened with lemon and orange zest. It keeps well in the refrigerator; serve it with butter or cream cheese.*

½ cup (1 stick) butter, at
  room temperature
⅔ cup packed light brown sugar
4 teaspoons grated lemon zest
4 teaspoons grated orange zest
2 cups small curd cottage cheese,
  at room temperature

2 large eggs, slightly beaten
2 cups all-purpose flour
1 tablespoon baking powder
1 teaspoon baking soda
1 teaspoon salt
2 cups dried currants

Preheat the oven to 350° F.

In a large mixer bowl, cream the butter and brown sugar together for about 1 minute on high speed, reduce the speed to medium, and beat 3 minutes. Mix in the grated lemon and orange zest, then add the cottage cheese and beaten eggs and beat well.

In a small bowl, whisk together the flour, baking powder, soda, and salt. Add the currants to the dry ingredients and stir well. Slowly add the dry ingredients to the egg mixture; mix until well blended. The batter will be quite stiff.

Grease a 5¼ × 9¼ × 3-inch loaf pan and gently spoon in the batter, lightly smoothing the top with a spoon. Bake for 1 hour and 15 minutes, then check with a skewer for doneness; it should come out clean when inserted in the middle. Return to the oven for 5 or 10 minutes, if necessary. Allow the bread to stand in the pan for 10 minutes, then tip out on a rack to cool completely.

APPLE-DATE CAKE

MAKES ONE 9-INCH CAKE

*The pioneer apple growers discovered the apples grown on the eastern slope of the
Cascade Mountains in Washington State were better tasting than those on the western slope—the long lasting
sunshine and fertile soil have made the Wenatachee Valley into the country's prime apple-producing region.
This unrepentantly good cake is tall and moist and keeps very well.
I like to serve it with an orange sauce (page 287).*

½ cup (1 stick) butter	½ teaspoon grated nutmeg
1 cup granulated sugar	¼ teaspoon ground cloves
1 large egg	¼ teaspoon salt
2 cups unsweetened applesauce	1½ cups chopped California dates
2¼ cups all-purpose flour	½ cup chopped nuts (pecans or
2 teaspoons baking soda	English walnuts)
1 teaspoon ground cinnamon	Sifted confectioners' sugar

Preheat the oven to 350° F.

In a large mixing bowl, cream together the butter and granulated sugar until light and fluffy, about 7 minutes. Beat in the egg and applesauce (the batter may look curdled) and blend. In a medium mixing bowl, whisk together the flour, soda, cinnamon, nutmeg, cloves, and salt. Stir the flour mixture into the creamed mixture; add the dates and nuts and stir well. Spoon the batter into a greased 9-inch springform pan. Bake for about 1 hour, or until a wooden pick inserted into the center comes out clean. Remove from the oven and cool in the pan for 15 minutes; remove the ring and transfer to a serving plate. When cool, dust with sifted confectioners' sugar.

The Glories
of
AUTUMN

THERE IS A SWEETLY melancholy feel to this season; there is a seldom used word for it—<u>plangent</u>. It comes with the diminishing light of October. The trees turn to fire, then yellow, and on one special day, as if by divine signal, the leaves fall quickly to the ground, leaving golden pools on the grass. The flower borders give us one last glorious hurrah, blooming with cheerful enthusiasm, unaware they are about to be blackened by frost.

These days in the kitchen, I work against time and the frost that will finish off the tomatoes. The fragrance of vinegar and spices fills the house and jars of chili sauce, tomato butter, and chutney line the kitchen counters. The first pot of chili of the season simmers on the back of the stove and I make a pumpkin pie for dessert—fall traditions all.

As I stir up my favorite condiments, I muse over the research we've done for our next leg of the journey. I have been fascinated by the journals of the women who were on the Oregon Trail, how they coped with feeding their families en route and all the hardships they endured. This country owes so much to those unsung, unknown women who followed their men into the wilderness. We will be partially going the same route and making a stop in Salt Lake City, where we've not been before.

We take the cats out for a brisk walk around the garden; we can smell winter in the air. And in the morning we waken to frost. Every leaf, every blade of grass is delicately painted with white crystal prisms. The sun comes out; there is a brief glitter, then it is gone. Summer is over and we're off to the mountains. Salt Lake City should be very beautiful.

Tailgate PARTIES

From the beginning, athletic competitions have brought together large groups of people that needed to be fed. Whether the sustenance took the form of hot dogs and popcorn at the ballpark, or the elegant picnics eaten by the patrons in their box at the races, food both plain and elegant has played an important role at these sporting events. And now, as then, a tailgating party with all the frills elevates the marriage of sports and food to a most delicious plane.

The early equivalent of today's tailgate would have been the back of a buggy, but even then, the emphasis was on foods that were as delicious as they are practical. In early American rural areas, traveling to a meeting spot and carrying food along was a common way for people to get together. These events were sometimes called "frolics," a term still used in Amish communities today. And we've long been a nation of picnic people. As a result, our early cookbooks record a delicious tradition of portable food. Meat pies were served fre-quently because they traveled well and both fruit pies and cakes were stacked to save space.

Early picnickers toted soup in stone jars to keep them cool on warm days and a chilled soup is still a lovely option for an Indian summer repast; fill the empty thermos with ice water and some ice pieces to chill it down, empty it out, then add the cold soup. This assures you of an icy cold soup when you are ready to serve it. I pack my old antique punch cups, wrapped individually in newspaper, for cold soups, but you can use plastic highball glasses instead. In cooler weather, pureed red bean soup seasoned with ham is a warming way to begin the meal—and served in mugs no spoons are necessary.

To round out the meal, add a home-baked bread of some kind and keep dessert simple and preferably not requiring the use of utensils—a basket of fresh fruit and homemade cookies will be just right. Finish off with hot coffee or a thermos of rich cocoa and you are ready for the entertainment, be it the NFL or the Babe Ruth league.

My Own Paté Red Bean Soup with Ham Roasted Tomato Soup with Rosemary
Purple Plum Soup Picnic Pie with Cheese and Ham Cheshire Pork Pie New England Lobster Rolls
Perfect Roast Beef (for Sandwiches or Dinner) Curried Sweet Potato Salad
Lemon Rice with Grapes Cheddar Bundt Bread Oatmeal-Raisin Scones Harwich Hermits
Ozark Walnut Bars Fruity Sangria Royal Hot Chocolate

# MY OWN PATÉ

SERVES 10 TO 12

Pâtés were certainly popular during the Victorian era and frequently were elaborately wrapped in pastry. After baking, they were filled with a brandied aspic, which was poured into a decorated opening of the top crust. These are very handsome and I have made them, but they are very time consuming to do, so I devised this recipe, which is more of a country loaf (in France, it would be called pâté de campagne). It is a most agreeable way to begin a meal as a first course, to serve on a buffet, or to use in sandwiches for a picnic. When the pâté is cut, there is a slice of brandied prune in the center of each slice.

¼ cup brandy

8 moist pitted prunes

1 pound lean bacon

1 large onion, quartered

1 garlic clove, peeled and cut
   into quarters

4 tablespoons coarsely chopped parsley

⅓ cup dry vermouth or white wine

1 teaspoon dried mixed herbs
   (thyme, savory, and oregano)

½ teaspoon salt

½ teaspoon grated nutmeg

½ teaspoon coarsely ground black pepper

½ teaspoon powdered sage

1 ½ pounds lean ground pork

1 pound ground veal

Dijon mustard, chutney,
   or seasoned mayonnaise

Preheat the oven to 375° F.

In a small saucepan over low heat, heat the brandy. Place the prunes in a small bowl and pour the hot brandy over them; steep for ½ hour. Set aside 7 strips of the bacon and cut the rest into chunks. Place the chopped bacon in a food processor bowl with the onion, garlic, and parsley and process together until smooth. Add the vermouth or white wine, herbs, salt, nutmeg, pepper, and sage, plus the brandy from the prunes, reserving the prunes. Blend well. In a large bowl, combine the pork and veal, then pour in the bacon mixture. Mix well, using your hands if necessary.

Line a 9 × 5-inch loaf pan crosswise with the reserved bacon, letting the ends hang over the edges. Place half of the meat mixture in the pan, patting it firmly into the corners. Lay the prunes end to end in a row down the middle of the loaf. Add the remaining meat, pressing it firmly on top of the prunes. Fold the bacon up over the top of the loaf. Cover with foil (or you may freeze it at this point), place in a pan of hot water, and bake for 1¾ hours.

Remove from the oven, drain off the juices, and cool the loaf on a rack. Tip out of the pan onto a large piece of foil, wrap it, and refrigerate overnight. For full flavor, wait 2 days before serving. The pâté will keep for 1 week, covered tightly, in the refrigerator. Slice thinly and serve with Dijon mustard, chutney, or a seasoned mayonnaise.

NOTE: *You may want to remove the bacon slices before slicing; they don't look particularly appetizing.*

RED BEAN SOUP WITH HAM

SERVES 8

*A pureed soup is the best choice for picnics. It transfers easily to thermos bottles or jugs
and you don't need spoons or bowls—just serve the soup in a mug or heavy paper cup. This red bean soup, flavored
with smoky ham, is an ideal cool weather picnic soup. I have adapted this recipe from Corrine Dunbar's
in New Orleans. The place no longer exists, which is a shame, for it was a pleasure to eat authentic southern food in
the old antebellum house that served as the restaurant. Soak the beans overnight before you begin the soup.*

1⅓ cups dried red kidney beans,
   rinsed and picked over
4 tablespoons (½ stick) butter
½ cup minced onion
1½ cups ground cooked ham
1 ham bone
2 celery stalks, coarsely chopped
1 teaspoon minced fresh thyme
   or ¼ teaspoon dried

1 bay leaf
1 garlic clove, finely minced
1 teaspoon salt
½ teaspoon coarsely ground pepper
½ cup dry sherry

Garnish: 4 hard-cooked eggs
   and 8 lemon slices

Soak the beans overnight in water to cover. The next day, rinse and set aside.

In a small saucepan, melt the butter. Add the minced onion and sauté over medium heat for 3 minutes, or until softened. In a large stockpot, combine the drained beans, sautéed onion, ground ham, ham bone, celery, thyme, bay leaf, garlic, salt, and pepper with 4 quarts of water. Bring to a boil, then reduce the heat and simmer, partially covered, for 1½ hours, or until the beans are tender. Remove the ham bone, cool the mixture, and puree in a food processor or blender until the mixture is smooth, dividing it into batches if necessary.

At this point, the soup can be refrigerated until needed. Transfer the soup to a large saucepan and reheat over medium heat until it is hot; add salt and pepper to taste. At serving time, put 1 tablespoon of sherry into each of 8 heated bowls and ladle the soup into the bowls. Garnish each serving with ½ chopped hard-cooked egg and a lemon slice.

An assortment of pioneer containers

ROASTED TOMATO SOUP WITH ROSEMARY

SERVES 6

*The Spanish brought tomatoes to California from Mexico, and eventually took the seeds back to
Europe with them. The Italians adored the new fruit with a passion, although Northern Europeans viewed the tomato
with suspicion, believing it was poisonous. Jefferson scoffed at that notion, and raised tomatoes for salads
at Monticello. In southwestern cookery, tomatoes combine perfectly with chilies, and this cold tomato soup, with
its hint of olive oil and rosemary, is a perfectly grand starter. Roasting the tomatoes first in the
oven gives the soup a real depth of flavor. And because it can be served hot or cold, it is a good year-round dish.*

8 to 10 medium to large tomatoes, cored	1 cup defatted chicken broth
Two 6-inch mild chilies, halved and seeded	½ to 1 cup half-and-half
½ cup olive oil	Salt and pepper to taste
1 large onion, peeled and sliced	2 dashes of hot red pepper sauce
2 large garlic cloves, halved	
2 teaspoons fresh rosemary	Garnish: toasted pumpkin seeds

Preheat the oven to 350° F.

Line a large shallow baking pan (12 × 17 inches) with foil and place the tomatoes and chilies in it. Drizzle about ¼ cup oil over the top of the vegetables. Bake for 30 minutes, then turn. Add the onion, garlic, and rosemary and drizzle the remaining oil over all. Bake ½ hour longer. Remove from the oven and cool.

Transfer the tomato mixture in batches to the food processor and whiz until smooth. Pour into a saucepan if serving hot or a large mixing bowl. Add the chicken broth, half-and-half, salt and pepper, and hot red pepper sauce, and whisk to mix. Either heat the soup and serve or chill in the refrigerator until ready to serve. Garnish each serving with some toasted pumpkin seeds.

PURPLE PLUM SOUP

SERVES 6

*This delightful plum soup is so flavorful and dramatic in color that you will be absolutely charmed.
It is ideal for tailgating since it can be sipped from cups or glasses; no spoons are needed. Serve it in old cut glass
tumblers or punch cups before dinner. This may sound like a very contemporary recipe, but in fact
fruit soups like this one were popular in Europe during medieval times.*

1 cup sour cream	1 tablespoon sugar
One 1-pound 14-ounce can purple plums	¼ teaspoon almond extract
with juice, pits removed	¼ teaspoon ground cinnamon

In a blender or food processor, blend the sour cream and gradually add the plums, then the sugar, almond extract, and cinnamon. Process for 1 minute, or until the mixture is smooth and creamy. Transfer to a glass container and chill. If the mixture separates, simply whisk it back together right in the container.

A pewter pitcher on homespun

PICNIC PIE WITH CHEESE AND HAM

MAKES ONE 9-INCH PIE

*I admit to an inordinate fondness for meat pies. They are so comforting, so sturdy, so practical.
This adaption of an old English recipe is a perfect picnic dish, or buffet entrée dish, for it is quite hearty
and certainly attractive. It is a good recipe to carry about; just leave the springform rim on the pie until you reach your
destination, then cut and serve. Ham and three kinds of cheese give the filling a lot of flavor.*

2 cups diced cooked ham	¼ cup minced onion
One 15-ounce container ricotta cheese	1 teaspoon Italian seasoning
One 15-ounce container small curd	Salt and pepper to taste
cottage cheese, drained	Dash of hot red pepper sauce
⅔ cup grated Parmesan cheese	
3 large eggs, lightly beaten	1 recipe Perfect Pie Pastry (page 284)
½ cup dry bread crumbs	1 egg yolk, beaten
½ cup minced fresh parsley	

Preheat the oven to 375° F.

In a large mixing bowl, combine the ham, cheeses, eggs, bread crumbs, parsley, onion, Italian season-ing, salt and pepper, and hot red pepper sauce; stir until well blended. Set aside.

On a floured surface, roll two-thirds of the pastry out to an ⅛-inch thickness. Line a 9-inch springform pan with the pastry, pressing the dough onto the bottom and up the sides of the pan; trim and reserve any overhanging pastry. Spoon in the cheese mixture and fold the pastry that extends above the filling toward the center of the pan. Roll the remaining chilled pastry to ⅛-inch thickness and place over the filling. Moisten the edges with water and seal the top with the bottom pastry. Brush the surface of the pie with the beaten egg yolk. Using any pastry scraps, decorate the top crust with small pastry cutouts and brush again with the yolk. Bake for 1 hour, cool to room temperature, then chill.

To serve, remove the sides of the springform pan and cut into wedges. Serve at room temperature.

A wooden lemon juicer

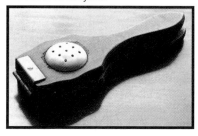

CHESHIRE PORK PIE

SERVES 6

Meat pies and poultry pies are part of our English heritage; as early as the fourteenth century,
London cookshops were making deep-dish meat pies encased in heavy crusts called "coffins" and prepared
in deep black iron kettles. Here in America Colonial cooks adapted the dish, finding it easier to bake the pies in their
brick ovens in shallow dishes rather than in deep pots. This keeps and travels well; no doubt many
pioneers left home with such pies among their trail provisions, prepared by loved ones left behind.
This is a beautiful pie, thick and golden and filled with pork, a few apples (which gives
it a certain lilt), and a generous amount of sage. Serve it with a salad and you have a complete meal.

1 recipe Perfect Pie Pastry (page 284)
2 pounds pork loin, all fat removed
    and cut into ¾-inch cubes
2 teaspoons ground sage
1 teaspoon salt
½ teaspoon pepper

4 firm cooking apples, such as
    Granny Smith, peeled, cored, and sliced
2 tablespoons sugar
¾ to 1 cup cider
1 tablespoon butter, cut into small pieces
1 large egg, beaten

Preheat the oven to 350° F.

Roll out half of the pastry thickly. Line your deepest pie plate (either a 9- or 10-inch will do) with pastry and set aside. Place half of the pork in the bottom of the shell, sprinkle with half the sage, salt, and pepper. Top with half of the apples and half of the sugar. Repeat with the remaining ingredients. Add the cider almost to the top of the apples and dot with the butter.

Roll out the top crust and place it on top of the pie, crimping the edges. Slash the top so the steam can escape and brush the crust with the egg. Bake the pie for 1½ hours, or until the top is a deep golden brown and juices are bubbling up in the center of the pie. Remove from the oven, allow to stand for 15 minutes, then cut into 6 wedges and serve warm.

INDEPENDENCE, MISSOURI

The starting place for the Oregon Trail was Independence, Missouri. Today we visited the spot where so many arduous journeys began, and it was very moving. On the smooth surfaces of "newspaper rocks" you can still read the poignant messages carved there by the people traveling with the wagon trains. I found many early cookbooks in the library here.

FROM THE MOUNTAIN STATES

We left Indiana in dense fog; with fall just around the corner, goldenrod and purple asters line the roadsides, and the leaves are beginning to turn. We are eager to see Colorado's yellow aspens, a first-time experience for us. Three days later, we arrived at the Rockies.

Civilization bypassed this region for centuries, ignoring the precious silence, the deep-shadowed red rock canyons, the azure sky banked with clouds. Finally, the Spanish came, determined to find gold, then Lewis and Clark, who were determined to find the Pacific coast, and the fur traders, who were determined to get back to St. Louis and Detroit as fast as they could to sell their pelts. In 1849, the Gold Rush brought wagon trains by the score down into California via the Oregon Trail, but no one stopped and stayed in this inhospitable land.

It wasn't until 1843 that the first large immigration to this area started—200 families and 120 wagons going to "Oregon country," heaped with belongings, setting out from Independence, Missouri. Ultimately the Oregon Trail led an estimated 350,000 to 550,000 westward during the next quarter of a century. It wasn't a cheap journey; the wagon itself cost at least $100 and the total outlay for provisions came to $1,000, a huge amount in those days.

The cooking equipment was quite simple and sturdy—black iron spiders and Dutch ovens, a churn and water keg. From the simplest ingredients and in the most primitive cooking conditions—the sky as the roof and the ground as the floor, and over a fire made of sagebrush, or twigs, or buffalo chips—the pioneer woman cooked the meals that sustained the wagon trains west on the long and arduous trip over the mountains.

In the 1840s, German immigrants arrived from Europe to escape one of the potato famines and headed west, many of them stopping in Ohio. Others pushed onto the Dakotas, to Montana and Wyoming, and some, on down to Texas.

Then came the Scandinavians, Austrians, and Swiss, all with recipes from home, which they tried to duplicate as soon as they were settled, using the foods they found on hand. We can thank these people for beer and brats, dumplings and cheese, kraut and rice puddings.

When gold was later discovered in Colorado and Nevada in 1859, another wave of immigration began from the east. "Pike's Peak or bust" was the rallying cry. The miners, looking always for more gold lodes and silver as well, moved into Idaho, Wyoming, and Montana.

Many English settled in Montana, where they marveled that the cattle could survive the harsh winters, enabling them to enjoy beef roasts as they never had in England. These settlers brought their recipes for breads, pies, puddings, and beans. Mrs. I. R. Randall wrote frequently back to England in the 1880s, and in one letter she says, "We went to Bozeman today on the train. It is a nice little town of about 3,000. The main street, which is generally six inches deep in either dust, mud or snow, has some good buildings and boasts two villainous hotels, but in the stores you can get any conceivable thing you want, except, perhaps, a Paris bonnet. I felt exactly as if we had been to London and back for a day."

SERVES 4

*One of the most memorable treats of traveling along the Maine coast is picking up a
lobster roll at a lobster shack. A lobster roll is a simple lobster salad served in a hot dog-type roll (cut open on
the top rather than on the side). Accompanied by a cold drink and blueberry pie for dessert, this is
typical New England fare. Natives have strong feelings about lobster rolls; some old-timers maintain they should
contain nothing more than lobster meat, a touch of onion, and mayonnaise. Others add a bit of celery.
But the most important thing is to have lots of sweet lobster meat. This makes the ultimate tailgate sandwich.*

2 live Maine lobsters	**½ cup mayonnaise**
(1¼ to 1½ pounds each)	**Salt and white pepper to taste**
2 celery stalks, finely chopped	**Butter, at room temperature**
1 tablespoon finely minced onion	**4 hot dog or lobster rolls**

Bring a large pot of salted water to a boil. Plunge the lobsters into the water headfirst. Partially cover the
pot and when the water returns to a boil, cover and boil the lobsters for 10 minutes. Remove with tongs
and allow to cool. Split the lobsters lengthwise and crack the claws, allowing the water to drain off.
Remove the meat from the shells, roughly chop into ½-inch pieces, and transfer to a large bowl. Add the
celery, onion, mayonnaise, and salt and pepper and combine lightly with the lobster; set aside.

Preheat the broiler. Butter the insides of the rolls and place on a shallow pan, buttered side up. Broil
about 6 inches from the heat until the rolls are golden and crispy, about 3 minutes. Fill with the lobster
salad and serve immediately.

ERFECT ROAST BEEF (FOR SANDWICHES OR DINNER)

SERVES 12

*Thinly sliced roast beef, pinkish in the middle, lightly herbed with garlic and thyme, makes a mouth-watering sandwich
when placed between slices of homemade bread or hard rolls. Small wonder it's
a perennial picnic favorite. Add a jar of Salsa Mayonnaise (page 288) to the picnic basket, and you'll have a hit.
This rolled rib is nonfail, and believe me, it turns out perfectly every
time if you follow the baking instructions to the letter. To give yourself peace of mind, though, do use a meat thermometer.*

One 6-pound boneless beef rib roast, tied	**½ teaspoon dried thyme or**
4 teaspoons finely minced onion	**1½ teaspoons fresh minced**
4 teaspoons finely minced garlic	**Salt and coarsely ground pepper to taste**
4 teaspoons minced parsley	**Paprika**

Before placing the beef in the oven to roast, let it come to room temperature outside of the refrigerator.
Allow approximately 2½ hours for this.

Preheat the oven to 500° F.

Place the roast, fat side up, on a rack in a shallow roasting pan. With a knife, make slashes of different depths approximately 2 inches apart over the top of the roast. In a small bowl, combine the onion, garlic, parsley, and thyme. Stuff each slash in the roast, using approximately $\frac{1}{3}$ to $\frac{1}{2}$ teaspoon of the seasoning mixture until all of it is used. Sprinkle salt and pepper and paprika liberally over the roast. Insert a meat thermometer (*not* instant-reading) into the center of the roast.

Place the roast in the oven and cook 5 minutes per pound for medium rare, 7 minutes per pound for medium. Then turn the oven *off and do not open the oven door* until the total cooking time equals 2 hours. (For a 6-pound roast, cook for 30 minutes at 500° F., then allow the roast to remain in the turned-off oven an additional 90 minutes, for a total of 2 hours in the oven.) Remove from the oven and allow to stand for 10 minutes before carving. Cut into slices and place on a heated platter or chill and slice as needed for sandwiches.

CURRIED SWEET POTATO SALAD

SERVES 6

*In the South, where sweet potatoes are common and very popular, we found many novel recipes
for preparing this vegetable, quite beyond the variations on candied and mashed versions. Sweet potato salad
is a most intriguing dish and the green crunch of the broccoli with the added zip of chutney
and curry makes this salad very different. Make it a day in advance and keep it chilled until serving time.*

2 large peeled sweet potatoes	**$\frac{1}{2}$ cup Major Grey's chutney**
1 tablespoon cider vinegar	**1 tablespoon curry powder**
1$\frac{1}{2}$ cups small broccoli florets	**(or more to taste)**
$\frac{1}{2}$ cup minced celery	**1 tablespoon minced parsley**
$\frac{1}{4}$ cup dried currants or raisins	**1 teaspoon ground cumin**
3 tablespoons finely minced onion	**$\frac{1}{2}$ teaspoon turmeric**
$\frac{1}{2}$ cup mayonnaise	**$\frac{1}{4}$ teaspoon white pepper**
$\frac{1}{2}$ cup sour cream	

Place the potatoes in a deep pan with the vinegar and water to cover. Bring to a boil, lower the heat to medium, and simmer for 35 minutes, or until the potatoes are easily pierced by a fork but are not mushy. Drain and cool under cold running water. Peel the potatoes and set aside.

Blanch the broccoli florets in boiling water for 2 minutes and drain well.

In another medium bowl, combine the celery, currants, onion, mayonnaise, sour cream, chutney, curry powder, parsley, cumin, turmeric, and pepper. Chop the sweet potatoes into $\frac{3}{4}$-inch cubes and place in a large bowl. Pat the broccoli dry with a towel and add to the potatoes along with the combined dressing ingredients. Toss lightly and chill.

EMON RICE WITH GRAPES

SERVES 12

*Sturdy salads, such as this rice dish with its hint of lemon and quite a few green grapes,
make good tailgate food, for they hold up well.*

4 tablespoons (½ stick) butter
2 cups uncooked white rice
4 cups boiling water
Juice of 2 to 3 large lemons
   (to yield ½ cup juice)
2 cups seedless green grapes,
   sliced in half lengthwise

Grated zest of 2 lemons
⅛ teaspoon white pepper
Scant ¼ teaspoon hot red pepper sauce
2 teaspoons finely snipped fresh
   or freeze-dried chives
½ cup finely chopped fresh coriander

Melt the butter in a heavy 3-quart saucepan. Add the rice and cook, stirring, about 3 minutes, or until it turns opaque. Stir in the boiling water, cover the pot with 3 layers of paper toweling (it absorbs the steam), then put on the lid (the paper will hang out, but that's okay). Simmer over medium low heat for 20 minutes. Do not remove the lid during cooking. Remove from the heat, fluff with a fork, cover with fresh toweling, and let the rice stand for 30 minutes.

    Meanwhile, combine half the lemon juice with the halved grapes and let stand for 30 minutes. Place the rice in a large bowl, add the remaining lemon juice and zest, pepper, hot red pepper sauce, chives, and coriander, and combine well. Add the grapes with lemon juice and toss again. Serve at room temperature.

NEW IBERIA, LOUISIANA

Rice is a big crop in the South; Konriko, the oldest rice mill in the country, has been producing rice for all those gumbos and jamba-layas for the last seventy-five years. Next to the old mill is a company store, which is also on the National Register of Historic Places. Patterned after the old company stores of Louisiana sugar cane plantations of past years, it offers all sorts of rices, native foods, cooking utensils, and Cajun crafts.

CHEDDAR BUNDT BREAD

MAKES 1 BUNDT LOAF

An herb-flavored cheese layer in the middle of this easy-to-prepare batter bread makes this an outstanding addition to any picnic meal. Serve it sliced or presented on a footed cake stand, for it is very attractive. It can be made in advance and frozen. This recipe came to me from the librarian in Nauvoo, Illinois.

FILLING
½ cup (1 stick) butter,
    at room temperature
¼ teaspoon dried marjoram
¼ teaspoon dried thyme
2 tablespoons finely minced onion
1 tablespoon finely minced parsley
1 cup grated extra-sharp
    cheddar cheese

BREAD
2½ cups all-purpose flour
2 tablespoons sugar
1 teaspoon salt
2 packages active dry yeast
½ cup milk
½ cup water
¼ cup (½ stick) butter,
    at room temperature
1 large egg, slightly beaten
1 tablespoon poppy seed

Butter

Prepare the filling: In a small bowl, combine the butter, marjoram, thyme, onion, and parsley; mix well. Stir in the cheese and set aside.

Prepare the bread: In a large mixer bowl, combine 1½ cups flour with the sugar, salt, and yeast. Mix well and set aside. In a small saucepan, combine the milk, water, and butter and heat over medium-low heat until the butter is melted and the milk is warm. Add the milk to the flour mixture along with the beaten egg. Blend at low speed until moistened, then beat at medium speed for 3 minutes. By hand, gradually add the remaining flour to make a stiff batter.

Generously grease a 9- or 10-inch tube or bundt pan. Sprinkle the sides and bottom of the pan with the poppy seeds. Spoon half of the batter into the pan, spreading evenly. Spread the filling over the dough, top with the remaining batter, and pat it on firmly. Cover with a slightly dampened cloth and place in a warm area to rise until doubled in size (about 1 hour).

Meanwhile, preheat the oven to 375° F. Bake the bread for 35 to 40 minutes, until golden brown. Remove from the oven and immediately tip the bread out onto a rack to cool. Serve with butter.

OATMEAL-RAISIN SCONES

MAKES 12 SCONES

*Fresh baked goods bring an air of elegance to a picnic or tailgate party. The morning of the
picnic, stir up these very nice scones, and after they are baked, split and butter them, place them in a
napkin-lined basket, and take them along on the picnic with a jar of preserves.*

¼ cup plus 1 tablespoon sugar
2 cups all-purpose flour
2 cups quick-cooking oatmeal
1 tablespoon baking powder
1½ teaspoons baking soda
½ teaspoon grated nutmeg
½ teaspoon salt

¾ cup (1½ sticks) butter, chilled
 and cut into ½-inch pieces
1⅓ cups buttermilk
1 teaspoon vanilla extract
1 cup raisins
1 large egg
3 tablespoons milk

In a large bowl, whisk together ¼ cup sugar, flour, oatmeal, baking powder, soda, nutmeg, and salt. With
a pastry blender, cut the butter into the flour mixture until it resembles coarse meal. Make a well in the
flour mixture and pour in the buttermilk and vanilla; combine with a spoon rather gently until the dough
just holds together. Stir in the raisins. Set the mixture aside for 1 hour.

   Preheat the oven to 400° F.

   On a lightly floured surface, divide the dough in half. Roll each half into a circle 1 inch thick and about 6
inches in diameter; cut into 6 wedges like pie. Transfer the scones to a baking sheet. In a small bowl, beat
the egg and milk together; brush on the tops of the dough, then sprinkle with the remaining 1 tablespoon
sugar. Bake on the middle oven rack for 20 minutes, or until golden brown. Serve hot.

Hot beverage servers

HARWICH HERMITS

MAKES EIGHTEEN 2¼ × 2-INCH SQUARES

This moist bar cookie, heavy with raisins, currants, nuts, and a bit of citron, gets its distinctive flavor from spices originally brought from the Indies. The recipe comes from the days of the clipper ships and is named for a Cape Cod port. In those days the cookies were packed in tole canisters and sent on voyages around the Horn; I doubt they made it that far, but they are good keepers. You might want to dab these with a bit of orange frosting (page 285), though that is not authentic.

½ cup (1 stick) butter	½ teaspoon ground cloves
½ cup sugar	¼ teaspoon ground mace
2 large eggs, well beaten	¼ teaspoon grated nutmeg
½ cup light molasses	⅛ teaspoon allspice
2 cups all-purpose flour	3 tablespoons chopped citron
½ teaspoon salt	¼ cup chopped raisins
⅔ teaspoon baking soda	½ cup chopped currants
⅔ teaspoon cream of tartar	¼ cup chopped English walnuts
1 teaspoon ground cinnamon	

Preheat the oven to 350° F.

In a large mixer bowl, beat the butter and sugar for 4 minutes until light. Add the beaten eggs and molasses; beat well. In a large mixing bowl, whisk together the flour, salt, soda, cream of tartar, cinnamon, cloves, mace, nutmeg, and allspice; set aside. In a small bowl, toss the chopped fruits with ¼ cup of the flour and spice mixture until well coated (this keeps them from sticking). Add the remaining flour mixture to the batter and beat well. Stir in the fruits and walnuts. Pour into a greased 9 × 13-inch glass baking dish, spreading the batter out evenly. Bake for 30 minutes, or until the center springs back when touched with your finger. Cut into squares while warm.

N O T E : *Raise the oven temperature to 375° F. if using a metal pan.*

OZARK WALNUT BARS

MAKES 32 SMALL BARS

The Ozark Mountains (some might call them a range of hills) extend from southern
Illinois, across Missouri, and into Arkansas and Oklahoma. The hills are covered with timber, including
walnut trees, so in this region you find many good recipes using these nuts. This cookie is triple
layered, filled with apricot preserves as well as walnuts, and also has some chocolate in it—a very good
combination. Like most bar cookies, these are rather quick to prepare.

½ cup (1 stick) butter,
    at room temperature
1 cup packed light brown sugar
1¼ cups all-purpose flour
⅓ cup apricot preserves
2 large eggs
¼ teaspoon salt
1 teaspoon vanilla extract
2 tablespoons cocoa powder
1½ cups finely chopped walnuts

ICING
6 ounces semisweet chocolate
2 tablespoons light corn syrup
2 teaspoons orange juice
2 teaspoons boiling water

½ cup chopped walnuts

Preheat the oven to 375° F.

In a large mixer bowl, cream the butter and ¼ cup brown sugar for 3 minutes. Gradually add the flour and beat only until the mixture holds together. Pat the dough evenly over the bottom of an unbuttered 9-inch square cake pan with your fingertips. Bake for 10 minutes.

Meanwhile, stir the preserves to soften and set aside while you prepare the filling. Beat the eggs in a mixer bowl at high speed for 2 or 3 minutes, then beat in the salt and vanilla. On low speed, add the remaining ¾ cup brown sugar and the cocoa. Increase the speed to high and beat 2 to 3 minutes more. Fold in the nuts by hand.

Remove the hot crust from the oven and spread with the preserves. Pour the filling over the preserves and tilt the pan to level the filling. Bake the cookies for 25 minutes longer, then allow to cool completely.

Make the icing: Melt the chocolate in a double boiler over simmering water. Add the corn syrup, orange juice, and boiling water; stir until smooth. Spread the icing evenly over the cooled cookies and sprinkle with the chopped nuts. With a wide spatula, press the nuts slightly into the icing. Let stand a few hours before cutting.

FRUITY SANGRIA

SERVES 6 TO 8

Sangria fits the bill for so many occasions; take it along on tailgate picnics, or serve it on the patio or to start a warm weather brunch. We can thank the Spanish for sangria; it is an old, old recipe. It can be made with either red or white wine, but I tend to prefer this lighter version, garnished with woodruff. Woodruff, sometimes called sweet woodruff, is a bright green herb with tiny white flowers that is often used as a ground cover. It is the traditional garnish for May bowls, but it is also nice for sangria.

2 bottles fruity dry white wine
1 cup Grand Marnier or other
   orange-flavored liqueur
¼ cup sugar
¼ cup halved seedless red grapes
¼ cup halved seedless green grapes

6 orange slices, halved and seeded
½ red apple, unpeeled, cored,
   and sliced thin

Garnish: fresh mint or woodruff

In a pitcher, with a wooden spoon, combine the white wine, Grand Marnier, and sugar. Add the grapes, orange slices, and apple slices. Chill the sangria, stirring occasionally, for 2 hours. The sangria may be made up to 24 hours in advance and kept covered and chilled. Serve the sangria over ice, garnished with mint or woodruff.

ROYAL HOT CHOCOLATE

SERVES 6

There is nothing more comforting than a cup of hot chocolate, and we take thermos bottles of it along on fall and winter picnics. This version is both delicious and practical; you can make it even if you happen to be out of milk, not too unusual a happening for lots of us, no matter how well we plan. The secret of this rich drink is sweetened condensed milk; if you have a can on hand plus some baking chocolate, you will have a wonderful beverage in no time.

Two 1-ounce squares Hershey's
   unsweetened baking chocolate
One 14-ounce can sweetened
   condensed milk
4 cups boiling water

1 teaspoon vanilla extract
Speck of salt

Garnish: whipped cream and
   ground cinnamon (optional)

In the top of a double boiler over hot, not boiling, water, melt the chocolate. Whisk in the condensed milk. Gradually add the boiling water, stirring until well blended, then add the vanilla and salt. Transfer to a thermos bottle or drink immediately. You can garnish this with whipped cream and a bit of cinnamon, if you like, though I don't bother with that on picnics.

Country
COOKING

As DICK AND I traveled from hamlet to hamlet, we discovered that small-town roadhouses, mom-and-pop cafés with just a handful of tables, and country bars were repositories of authentic American cookery. Most often found in pockets of the country where trendy food has yet to make inroads, these homely spots continue to pack 'em in year in and year out. It was not uncommon to see lines of enthusiastic patrons queueing up outside for the Wednesday night special of fried chicken and biscuits, or believe it or not, liver and onions.

These plain eating spots with their Formica tables adorned with ketchup bottles and napkin dispensers share a valuable secret that brings in appreciative diners from miles around—local cooks who prepare food in simple, uncontrived ways that are rarely duplicated in home kitchens.

All over the United States the same recipes show up: thick vegetable soups, spicy chili, fried chicken, mashed potatoes, coleslaw, and always an assortment of pies. Combined with the regional specialties of the area, these country dishes are the foundation of American cookery, and we can thank these cooks, mostly untrained, who have kept these important food traditions alive.

In South Carolina we savored a grits-based spoon bread. In an Iowa main street café we sampled succulent and moist fried chicken that had been marinated in buttermilk. The accompanying biscuits were sautéed in the same skillet the chicken was fried in—this was superb eating.

Though these might all be considered provincial country dishes, all lend themselves well for entertaining menus. My grandfather had an expression he used when he saw people pretending to be something they weren't; he would frown and say reprovingly, "They're putting on the dog." It is no longer necessary to "put on the dog" when you entertain. Use these recipes next time you invite friends for dinner, and enjoy sincerely good food.

Chicken-Fried Steak with Gravy Meat Loaf with Sage Shrimp, Chicken, and Sausage Jambalaya Fried Chicken with Chicken-Fried Biscuits Stuffed Pork Chops Shakertown Corn Pudding Escalloped Onions with Marjoram Country Cheese Pudding Owendaw Spoon Bread Apple Salad with Pecans Bacon Salad Dressing from the Biltmore Estate Mormon Steamed Carrot Pudding Cinnamon-Apple Compote Caramel Dumplings Peach-Orange Cobbler with Cardamom and Nutmeg

CHICKEN-FRIED STEAK WITH GRAVY

SERVES 6

*There were few tender cuts of beef out on the range; even steak was tough and chewy.
Using a mallet, the cook would hammer the steak pieces thin, then prepare the steaks as he did fried chicken;
there weren't many recipes in his repertoire. This dish is still being prepared from memory in farm kitchens
and country cafés around the country. For those who might not have the recipe, here 'tis. It's a lusty dish that should
be accompanied by a big bowl of mashed potatoes. Filet mignon pales in comparison.*

1¾ to 2 pounds round steak, cut
    about ½ inch thick and tenderized
    by the butcher (the pieces should
    be quite thin—ask to see the
    meat before it is wrapped)
Salt and pepper
2 large eggs
4 dashes of hot red pepper sauce
½ cup all-purpose flour
3 ounces saltine crackers,
    finely crushed (about 2 cups)
¼ cup corn oil (or more if needed)

GRAVY
¼ cup all-purpose flour
2 cups milk
2 teaspoons Worcestershire sauce
Salt and pepper to taste

Garnish: 2 tablespoons minced parley

Season each steak on both sides with salt and pepper, rubbing it into the meat. In a shallow dish, beat the eggs together with the hot red pepper sauce. Place the flour and crumbs on 2 separate sheets of wax paper. One at a time, dredge the steaks in the flour, then dip in the egg mixture, then coat with the cracker crumbs.

In a large heavy skillet, heat the oil over low heat. Add the steaks and cook slowly, turning them carefully once or twice. It will take about 20 or 30 minutes until the meat is fully cooked through and the crumb coating is brown and crisp. Transfer the meat to a heated platter, cover, and keep warm.

Make the gravy: Pour the oil remaining in the skillet through a sieve; save 4 tablespoons and discard the rest. Return any cracklings from the sieve to the skillet along with the 4 tablespoons oil and set over low heat. Whisk the flour into the oil and cook, constantly stirring and scraping, for 2 minutes, or until the mixture bubbles up in the center. Gradually whisk in the milk and Worcestershire and raise the heat slightly to bring the gravy to a simmer. Cook, stirring often, scraping the browned deposits from the bottom of the skillet, 5 to 6 minutes, or until the gravy has thickened. Season to taste with salt and pepper.

Arrange the steaks on a platter and present the gravy in a gravy boat. Serve immediately, garnished with minced parsley.

Meat Loaf with Sage

SERVES 6

I am just delighted that meat loaf has become respectable again, and it is amusing to see it appearing on menus of very posh places. It is even more amusing to note how many people order it—especially men. Hurrah for meat loaf! If you only just like the flavor of sage, reduce the amount in this recipe to ¾ teaspoon. If you love the flavor of sage, use the whole teaspoon. Either way, it is a nicely flavored loaf and the leftovers make great sandwiches.

⅔ cup dry bread crumbs
¾ cup milk
2 large eggs, beaten
¼ cup finely chopped onion
2 tablespoons Worcestershire sauce
¾ to 1 teaspoon dried rubbed sage
1 teaspoon salt
½ teaspoon pepper
¼ teaspoon grated nutmeg

1 pound ground round steak
½ pound lean ground pork

SAUCE
3 tablespoons light brown sugar
1 teaspoon powdered mustard
⅓ teaspoon grated nutmeg
⅓ cup ketchup

Preheat the oven to 350° F.

In a medium bowl, soak the bread crumbs in the milk for about 5 minutes. Add the beaten eggs, onions, Worcestershire, sage, salt, pepper, and nutmeg; mix well. Add the meats and combine all together lightly but thoroughly. Transfer the mixture to a greased 9 × 5 × 3-inch loaf pan. Set aside.

In a small bowl, combine all of the sauce ingredients and mix well. Pour the sauce over the loaf and bake for 1½ hours, or until it has shrunk slightly away from the sides of the pan. Cut into slices and serve.

Mallet for tenderizing meat

SHRIMP, CHICKEN, AND SAUSAGE JAMBALAYA

SERVES 4 TO 6

*First, you pronounce it jum-buh-lie-ya. This beloved Acadian or Cajun dish is highly
seasoned with any combination of beef, pork, ham, poultry, smoked sausage, or seafood, and it most
frequently includes tomatoes. In Louisiana, the sausage would be andouille (hard to find,
most places) and the ham would be tasso, but you can substitute your own local products. It is a more
complex dish than many country offerings, but very typical in that part of the country and not
considered fancy fare at all. This is a one-dish meal—add some corn muffins and you'll have a feast.*

½ cup vegetable oil

½ pound boneless, skinless
   chicken breast, cubed

1 pound smoked sausage,
   sliced ½ inch thick

2 garlic cloves, minced

1 cup chopped onion

½ cup chopped celery

½ cup chopped green bell pepper

One 16-ounce can tomatoes with juice,
   coarsely chopped

2 teaspoons dried thyme

3 medium bay leaves

⅛ teaspoon ground allspice

¼ teaspoon cayenne pepper

½ teaspoon coarsely ground pepper

½ teaspoon ground cumin

1 teaspoon salt

2 cups raw long-grain white rice

4 cups chicken stock

1 pound medium shrimp,
   shelled and deveined

In a Dutch oven, heat the oil. Add the chicken and brown lightly, then remove with a slotted spoon and set aside. Add the sausage and lightly brown; remove with a slotted spoon and set aside with the chicken. Add the garlic, onions, celery, and green pepper to the Dutch oven and sauté over medium heat until the vegetables are tender and translucent. Do not brown. Return the sausage and chicken to the pot and add the tomatoes, thyme, bay leaves, allspice, peppers, cumin, and salt. Simmer for 10 minutes. Add the rice and stock; stir thoroughly and bring to a boil, then simmer over low heat, covered, for 15 minutes. Gently fold in the shrimp. (Avoid excessive stirring to prevent the rice from becoming mushy.) Tightly cover and continue to simmer for 15 minutes, or until the liquid is absorbed and the rice is tender. Transfer to a large tureen or deep plates and serve hot.

FRIED CHICKEN WITH CHICKEN-FRIED BISCUITS

SERVES 6

This is real down-home food, and though the custom of frying the chicken, then frying the biscuits in the same skillet is thought of as southern, actually it was a cooking technique used by lots of cooks on the wagon trails who used as few pots and pans as possible, given the scarcity of water.
The chicken is beautifully dark and crispy and the biscuits, though not fine-grained, are a bit chewy and chicken-flavored, and lightly pink from the paprika. You will notice there is no fat in the biscuit dough; they absorb what they need from the drippings.

6 chicken breast halves and 6 thighs	BISCUITS
2 cups buttermilk	2 cups all-purpose flour
Vegetable oil	1 tablespoon baking powder
1 cup all-purpose flour	1 tablespoon sugar
2 teaspoons paprika	½ teaspoon salt
1 teaspoon pepper	1¼ cups milk
Salt	

Wash and dry the chicken pieces. In a shallow pan, marinate the chicken pieces in the buttermilk for 4 hours, turning 2 or 3 times. Drain, discarding the buttermilk.

In an electric skillet or fry pan, heat ½ inch of vegetable oil to 375° F. Place the flour, paprika, pepper, and salt in a plastic bag; add the chicken 2 or 3 pieces at a time and shake until well coated. Place the chicken pieces in the heated oil and fry. (Leave the skillet uncovered for crispy chicken.) Fry on each side for approximately 20 minutes, or until browned and crispy. Remove the chicken to an ovenproof platter and keep warm in the oven while you prepare the biscuits.

In a medium bowl, whisk together the flour, baking powder, sugar, and salt. Stir in the milk with a fork and mix well—the mixture will be gooey. Heat the remaining oil in the skillet to 375° F. Drop the mixture by teaspoonfuls into the oil. Cook, turning once, until golden brown on each side, about 4 minutes on each side. Drain on paper towels.

Stuffed Pork Chops
SERVES 6

This is an old country recipe, with the stuffing seasoned with rosemary, celery, and onions.
It is a specialty in both restaurants and homes in Pella, Iowa.

6 double thick loin pork chops
¾ cup all-purpose flour
1½ teaspoons salt
4 to 6 tablespoons vegetable oil
Pepper to taste

STUFFING
1½ cups dry bread crumbs

½ cup finely chopped celery
¼ cup finely chopped onion
3 tablespoons butter, melted
1 tablespoon chopped parsley
1 teaspoon dried rosemary, crushed
Enough chicken broth to moisten the
    stuffing plus 1 to 1½ cups
Salt and pepper to taste

Preheat the oven to 300° F.

Make a pocket in each pork chop with a sharp knife or have your butcher do it. In a pie pan, combine the flour and salt and dredge the pork chops in it.

In a large skillet, heat the oil over medium-low to low heat. Add the pork chops and brown on both sides very slowly until golden, about 20 minutes; they will still be pink inside. Set aside.

Prepare the stuffing: Brown the bread crumbs in a skillet over medium heat for a few minutes. Transfer to a medium bowl and add the celery, onions, butter, parsley, and rosemary. Moisten the stuffing mixture with the chicken broth just enough to hold the crumbs together. Season with the salt and pepper.

Fill the pockets of the pork chops and close each one with a toothpick. (They will only close partially and some of the stuffing will spill out, but that's all right.)

Place the pork chops in a 9 × 13 × 2-inch baking pan and add 1 cup chicken broth. Cover tightly with a lid or foil and bake for 3 hours, basting the chops every 45 minutes. Add more broth if the pan juices start to dry up—this will depend on the amount of fat in the chops.

PELLA, IOWA

Pella is a thriving Dutch community in eastern Iowa, settled in 1847 by immigrants looking for religious freedom. Their food styles have remained with the Old Country; fruit soups, casserole-type dishes such as pig hocks with cabbage, stewed chicken and rice, plus all sorts of steamed puddings are still made by the descendants of the original 800 settlers. During their Tulip Festival in May local restaurants feature these homey specialties.

HAKERTOWN CORN PUDDING

SERVES 4 TO 6

One of the great treats at Pleasant Hill's Shaker Village is eating at the Trustee's House; the curving stairways will take your breath away. The dining room serves Shaker specialties and their vegetables are raised in a splendid garden right outside the Trustee's House windows—now those are fresh ingredients! The corn pudding is brought steaming hot to every table in a freshly baked white oval casserole and, blissfully, seconds are offered.
This corn pudding is a bit like a flan—soft, quivery, with a custard layer—and an absolute delight.

3 tablespoons butter, softened	3 whole eggs, slightly beaten
2 tablespoons sugar	2 cups corn kernels, fresh or frozen
2 tablespoons all-purpose flour	1¾ cups milk
1 teaspoon salt	

In a large bowl, blend the butter, sugar, flour, and salt. Add the eggs and beat well with a rotary beater or mixer on low. Stir in the corn and milk. (If using frozen corn, chop it up a little first to release the milky juices.) Pour the ingredients into a buttered, flat, 10 × 6-inch casserole and bake at 325° F. for 45 minutes, stirring once halfway through the baking period.

When done, the pudding will be golden brown on top and a knife inserted in the middle will come out clean.

NOTE: *The mixture can be prepared ahead of time and kept in the refrigerator. Stir well, then pour into a baking dish and bake as instructed.*

PHOTO POST CARD

AMERICA 25

SHAKER VILLAGE OF PLEASANT HILL, KENTUCKY

This is the third largest Shaker community in the United States and was settled in 1805. The village is most picturesque with handsome architecture, gardens, and lots of demonstrations going on, depicting Shaker crafts. The Shaker dances were thrilling to see. The food is outstanding, and we are able to stay in the modernized Shaker dormitories—what fun! Shaker cookery is as marvelous today as it was in the 1800s. I was delighted to find the recipe for Kentucky Stack Pie I'd been seeking in one of their cookbooks.

M

Dried gourds were common containers in pioneer kitchens

ℰSCALLOPED ONIONS WITH MARJORAM

SERVES 4

*This dish, an old New England recipe, can be made with any mild onion. Sweet and creamy, it
is simplicity itself and a delectable accompaniment to grilled meats or broiled fish.
I found the recipe in an old cookbook from Newburyport, Massachusetts, a quaint New England town
that is practically a museum of American Federalist architecture.*

5 to 6 medium white onions	3 tablespoons butter or margarine,
1 tablespoon all-purpose flour	cut into little pieces
2 teaspoons sugar	1 cup whole milk
Salt and pepper to taste	
Dried or fresh marjoram	Garnish: paprika
Finely chopped parsley	

Preheat the oven to 450° F.

Peel and slice the onions thinly—you will need 3 cups. In a small bowl, combine the flour and sugar; set aside. Grease a 2-quart casserole and place one-third of the onions in the bottom of the dish. Sprinkle a little of the flour mixture over the onions, some salt and pepper, a tiny bit of marjoram, and some parsley. Make 2 more layers in the same manner. Lift the onions lightly with fork tines to make sure the flour is distributed evenly. Scatter the butter pieces over the top and pour the milk over all; do not mix in. Sprinkle with paprika. Bake for 45 minutes, or until the top is golden brown. Serve hot.

travel Notes FROM CALIFORNIA

En route to California, we drove first through the Badlands and then Death Valley; when we arrived in Barstow, the first big town beyond the valley, it looked like a green oasis after all those hours in the barren desert. Barstow was a desert junction for overland wagon trains and after our long trip, Dick and I could identify a bit with the earlier settlers. But our journey, in an air-conditioned van complete with television and computer, was a far cry from the sixteenth-century Spanish wagon trains.

Instead of the golden cities, the Spanish explorers found scorched deserts dotted with forbidding rock formation and thorny cactus, sheltered green valleys, snow-topped mountains guarding uninterrupted horizons, and a coastline pounded by violent waves. This land became known as the Golden State, so perhaps the Spanish were more successful than they knew.

We must credit the Spanish for introducing the horse and the cow to this landscape; these developed into two indispensable elements for civilizing life in western America. However, the most important legacy of those early Spaniards were the twenty-one Franciscan missions the

COUNTRY CHEESE PUDDING

SERVES 6

Cracker crumbs, milk, cheese, and eggs—plain cooking materials, to be sure. Yet combined and baked what you have is a nicely textured cheese soufflé without the risk. I like it with roast beef (page 142). This recipe is from a collection of old family recipes given to me by Jenny and Harry Bryan from Indianapolis—they thought I would appreciate having a copy of his mother's collection of old recipes, and they were right.

1 cup coarsely crushed soda crackers

2 cups whole milk

1½ cups grated extra-sharp
    cheddar cheese

3 large eggs, beaten

½ cup minced parsley

1 tablespoon Worcestershire sauce

½ teaspoon ground mustard

¼ teaspoon salt

⅛ teaspoon baking soda dissolved in
    1 teaspoon hot water

Garnish: paprika

Preheat the oven to 350° F.

In a large bowl, combine the cracker crumbs and milk. Let the mixture stand for approximately 2 to 3 minutes, or until the crumbs are soft and have lost their crispness. Add the cheese, eggs, parsley, Worcestershire, mustard, salt, soda, and pepper; blend well.

Pour into a buttered 1½-quart ovenproof soufflé dish, and sprinkle paprika over the top. Bake for 1 hour, until the pudding is puffed and golden brown. Serve immediately.

Spanish Catholic Church began building in 1769. Each mission was about a day's walk from the next; the El Camino Real, the winding worn footpath that connected them, eventually became California's first highway.

The friars converted many of the Indians to Christianity and also taught them European farming techniques, including how to plant the cherished olive, fig, and grape cuttings brought from Spain. By 1830 the missionaries, remembering the good wines of home, were producing 50,000 gallons a year, stamped by local Indians and fermented in barrels or cowhide bags.

The Spanish influence on American agriculture is impressive: olives, oranges, oats, barley, and wheat, plus their Andalusian cattle. The missionaries, mindful of what they might need on their own tables, planted tomatoes, cumin, and coriander seeds from Mexico. And there were always orchards at the missions—peaches, apricots, plums, and apples. Avocados flourished, as did juicy figs.

We drove on up the coast on Route 101 to Santa Barbara, one of the prettiest cities in California. It looks very Spanish with its Mediterranean-style architecture, with the slopes of the Santa Ynez Mountains at its back and the Pacific Ocean lapping at its feet. Onward to the North.

WENDAW SPOON BREAD

SERVES 12

*This grits-style country spoon bread from South Carolina is sometimes
spelled "awendaw." No matter how you spell it, though, it is most certainly an "attic receipt." Typically, it
has no flour, so it does not rise as high as conventional spoon breads. The texture is as delicate
as the flavor. It is very moist and custardlike, so serve it on individual bread and butter plates with lots of butter.*

2 tablespoons (¼ stick) butter,	**2 cups milk**
at room temperature	**1 cup white cornmeal**
2 cups hot cooked hominy grits (see Note)	**1 teaspoon salt**
4 large eggs	

Preheat the oven to 350° F.

Stir the butter into the hot grits and let it melt. In a large mixing bowl, beat the eggs well. Add about ¾ cup of the hot grits to the beaten eggs and whisk smooth; gradually add the rest of the grits. Slowly add the milk, then the cornmeal and salt. The batter should look like a thick custard. Transfer to a greased 10-inch square pan and bake 35 to 45 minutes, or until the top is golden brown. Serve immediately.

N O T E : *Cook the grits according to package directions. Proceed with the rest of the recipe while the grits are still hot.*

PPLE SALAD WITH PECANS

SERVES 10

*Every fall, we drive to a nearby orchard in Denver, Indiana, and buy all sorts of wonderful
antique apple varieties to bring home to enjoy over the next few months. The Doud Orchard, a family operation,
is thoughtfully maintained by Stephen Doud, who knows just about everything there is to know
about apples. This is also the place to buy blended cider, caramel apples, and apple butter, plus pumpkins
and gourds; no wonder it is one of our traditions to visit there annually.
Since apple salad is a favorite of my husband's, I set right to work to prepare this recipe when we arrive home.
The sour cream dressing with its touch of brown sugar makes a most fetching fruit salad.*

10 small red-skinned apples, such as	**¼ cup plus 1 tablespoon mayonnaise**
Jonathan or red Romes, cored and diced	**⅓ cup dark seedless raisins**
3 celery stalks, chopped	**½ cup heavy cream**
½ cup chopped pecans	
¼ cup packed light brown sugar	**Garnish: Boston lettuce**
½ cup sour cream	

Prepare the apples and cut them into a large bowl. Add the celery and pecans; toss until combined and set aside. In a small mixing bowl, stir together the brown sugar, sour cream, and mayonnaise. Fold in the raisins. In a chilled mixer bowl, whip the cream until just stiff, then fold it into the sour cream mixture, combining gently but well. Pour over the apples and toss lightly until the apples are coated. Serve in a large bowl lined with the lettuce or on lettuce-lined individual salad plates.

$\mathscr{B}$ACON SALAD DRESSING FROM THE BILTMORE ESTATE

MAKES 1 QUART

You might not associate the Biltmore Estate outside of Asheville, North Carolina, with country cooking, but believe it or not, this is a Biltmore recipe.
This makes a generous amount of dressing, but it keeps indefinitely in the refrigerator.

1 pound bacon, cut into julienne strips
2½ cups diced celery
1 medium onion, diced
¾ cup cider vinegar
¼ cup Dijon mustard
1 teaspoon salad herb seasoning
½ teaspoon ground mustard

¼ teaspoon white pepper
2 cups sugar
¼ teaspoon browning and seasoning
  sauce, such as Kitchen Bouquet
2 tablespoons cornstarch mixed with
  2 tablespoons cold water

In a large sauté pan over medium-high heat, brown the bacon and cook until crisp. Drain off two-thirds of the fat. Add the celery and onions to the bacon and sauté until lightly browned, approximately 9 minutes. Add the vinegar and cook, uncovered, until the mixture has been reduced by half, about 3 minutes. While cooking, stir in the Dijon mustard and seasonings. When the mixture has been reduced by half, add the sugar and cook until dissolved. Stir in the browning and seasoning sauce. Slowly pour in the cornstarch mixture, stirring until the dressing is thickened. Cool, then transfer to a storage container and refrigerate. To serve, dip out the amount of dressing you need (I allow 2 tablespoons per person) and reheat the dressing in the microwave until it is very hot but not boiling. Drizzle over the greens, toss, and serve.

PHOTO POST-CARD

AMERICA 25

THE BILTMORE ESTATE, ASHEVILLE, NORTH CAROLINA
Part of the fun of visiting this magnificent residence is eating there. The dining room is in the old stable and appropriately called the Stable Café. The former resident horses had a good life, as you will see. The space has been left intact, including the roomy stalls. The food is excellent and it is a good place to lunch.

MORMON STEAMED CARROT PUDDING
SERVES 6

*Carrot puddings appear in many old cookbooks and many of them had grated potatoes among
their ingredients as well as carrots, for these would have been the provender available in the root cellar. This is not
too unusual a dessert when you think of it, since it is rather like a carrot cake, only steamed.
This delightful dessert is from an old Mormon cookbook. It is very moist and spicy.
It can be served with Hard Sauce or Brown Sugar Sauce, flavored with lemon and cinnamon.
The original recipe called for ground suet, which you can use if you like, but the oil works very well.*

½ cup grated carrots
½ cup fresh white bread crumbs
½ cup all-purpose flour
1 cup dark raisins
½ cup currants
⅓ cup buttermilk
½ cup vegetable oil
2 large eggs, well beaten
1½ teaspoons baking powder

1 teaspoon vanilla extract
½ teaspoon baking soda
½ teaspoon ground cinnamon
¼ teaspoon ground cloves
⅛ teaspoon grated nutmeg
¼ teaspoon salt

Hard Sauce (page 285) or
    Brown Sugar Sauce (page 287)

Fill a large kettle or steamer fitted with a rack with water and bring the water to a boil. Meanwhile, in a large mixer bowl, combine all of the ingredients. Transfer the batter to a well-greased 6-cup pudding mold. Remove the steamer basket and place the pudding on it, then lower it into the kettle. Steam the pudding over low heat for 1½ hours, checking regularly to make sure the water does not boil dry.

Remove the pudding mold and allow it to stand for 10 minutes; loosen the edges with a knife and tip out onto a serving plate. Cut into wedges and serve hot, with Hard Sauce or Brown Sugar Sauce.

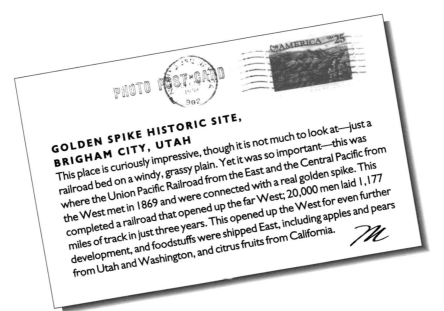

GOLDEN SPIKE HISTORIC SITE, BRIGHAM CITY, UTAH
This place is curiously impressive, though it is not much to look at—just a railroad bed on a windy, grassy plain. Yet it was so important—this was where the Union Pacific Railroad from the East and the Central Pacific from the West met in 1869 and were connected with a real golden spike. This completed a railroad that opened up the far West; 20,000 men laid 1,177 miles of track in just three years. This opened up the West for even further development, and foodstuffs were shipped East, including apples and pears from Utah and Washington, and citrus fruits from California.

English ironstone dessert molds

CINNAMON-APPLE COMPOTE

SERVES 6

*This is rather misnamed, but the country cook who gave me this recipe told me she always
served these apples in individual footed compote dishes. So to her, and she emphasized this—"This is an
apple compote." Call it what you will, in its simplicity, it is a lovely, easy dessert made from readily
available ingredients. I must admit, I serve this in footed compote dishes too.*

6 cups firm baking apples, such as
Cortland, Northern Spy, or
yellow Delicious, cored, pared,
and cut into ½-inch-thick slices
1½ cups packed dark brown sugar

1½ teaspoons ground cinnamon
¼ cup plus 1 tablespoon butter

Garnish: sweet or sour cream

Preheat the oven to 375° F.

Arrange the apples in a flat 11 × 17-inch glass dish. Cover the apples with the sugar and sprinkle with
cinnamon. Toss the mixture together and dot the top generously with the butter. Cover and bake for 30
minutes, then uncover and continue baking approximately 15 minutes longer—the time will depend on
the type of apple.

The apples will puff up when done. They should be removed from the oven right at that point before
they collapse. Transfer to individual serving dishes, and serve warm with either sweet or sour cream.

CARAMEL DUMPLINGS

SERVES 8

*This dish was originally made in a Dutch oven, the all-purpose pan of the settlers
and pioneers—the equivalent of the sauté pan! These kinds of recipes using just pantry basics—flour, milk,
sugar, and spices—that these early cooks devised still cause me to marvel. They are so good, they
are so easy, and there is so much variation that I have to admire their ingenuity.
Maple syrup, molasses, and brown sugar were the earliest sweeteners, for white sugar was very
expensive in Colonial days. It came from England in tall cones and was very compact and hard. The mistress of
the house (this was too costly an item to have been entrusted to anyone else) had a special set of
shears that she would use to cut off the needed amount.*

CARAMEL SAUCE
1½ cups packed dark brown sugar
⅛ teaspoon salt
1 teaspoon ground cinnamon
1½ cups hot water
2 tablespoon (¼ stick) butter
1 teaspoon vanilla extract

DUMPLINGS
1¼ cups all-purpose flour
1½ teaspoons baking powder
⅓ cup granulated sugar
¼ teaspoon salt
2 tablespoons (¼ stick) butter
⅓ cup milk
½ teaspoon vanilla extract

Make the Caramel Sauce: In a heavy, small saucepan, combine the brown sugar, salt, and cinnamon with the hot water; add the butter and vanilla and bring to a boil, stirring constantly. Reduce the heat and simmer for 5 minutes.

Make the Dumplings: In a medium mixing bowl, whisk together the flour, baking powder, sugar, and salt. Cut in the butter with a pastry blender or 2 knives until it has the texture of coarse oatmeal. Add the milk and vanilla and blend well. On a lightly floured surface, gently knead the dough into a smooth ball. Divide it into 4 equal parts, then divide each part in half to make 8 dumplings. Roll each into a ball and drop onto the hot syrup. Immediately cover the saucepan tightly and simmer for 20 minutes without lifting the lid. No peeking. Serve warm.

PEACH-ORANGE COBBLER WITH CARDAMOM AND NUTMEG

SERVES 6

Old-fashioned? Yes. Delicious? Yes! Yes! Cobblers have been popular desserts since the Pilgrims landed. However, we have the Spanish to thank for bringing the delectable peach to the New World, when they opened the mission at St. Augustine, Florida. The peach seedlings, however, flourished best in Georgia, and by the 1900s, peaches were being shipped from Georgia by newfangled refrigerated cars to such faraway places as Montana and New York.
This cobbler recipe has a touch of orange, cardamom, mace, and nutmeg—it is not at all puritanical.

4 cups sliced fresh peaches or one 20-ounce bag frozen	¼ teaspoon grated nutmeg
½ cup fresh orange juice	⅓ cup cold butter
2½ tablespoons Minute Tapioca	1 large egg
1½ cups all-purpose flour	⅓ cup milk
1 tablespoon grated orange zest	½ cup granulated sugar
2 teaspoons baking powder	½ cup packed brown sugar
¼ teaspoon salt	3 tablespoons butter, softened
¼ teaspoon ground cardamom	1 cup hot water
¼ teaspoon ground mace	Garnish: heavy cream

Preheat the oven to 375° F.

Place the peaches in a buttered flat 2-quart 12 × 7 inch dish and add the orange juice and tapioca; combine and set aside. In a large mixer bowl, mix the flour, zest, baking powder, salt, and spices. Cut in the cold butter until the mixture resembles coarse crumbs. In a small bowl, beat the egg and add the milk. Pour over the flour mixture and stir until just moistened; the batter will be quite stiff.

Drop the dough onto the peaches by scant tablespoons—6 rows of 4 is a good arrangement. In a small bowl, combine the sugars and softened butter. Add the hot water to the sugar-butter mixture and whisk until combined. Pour this over the peach-dough mixture; do not mix it in. Bake 30 minutes if using fresh peaches or 40 minutes if using frozen peaches. The cobbler should bubble up in the center and be golden brown when done. Serve warm with cream.

Satisfying
SOUPS

AMERICANS HAVE ALWAYS relied on soups to provide hearty nourishment, dating back to Colonial days and iron pot cookery. For convenience and economy, early housewives prepared soups as a way to use up leftovers, to extend costly ingredients, and as a convenience; they could leave a kettle of soup unattended, simmering for hours over a low fire, while they worked in the garden or the fields.

These heirloom soups remain among our favorites today and many older recipes fit in beautifully with contemporary menus either as a starter, a lunch entrée, or the centerpiece of a supper buffet. Main-dish soups are a sensible way to entertain casually. Now that there is an emphasis on eating simpler meals, hearty old soups such as Basque Lamb and Bean Soup will make a sturdy, one-dish offering. And certainly nothing could be more enticing than Chicken and Smoked Sausage Gumbo

served with Southern Rice Popovers (page 118).

As a first course, a light soup is a festive way to start a meal. I adore cold soups, for there is no last minute heating up and no pot to wash. Pureed cold soups can be served in punch cups or antique water glasses in the living room before the meal, allowing the hostess to be in the kitchen and dining room looking after the main course.

I double most soup recipes so half can be frozen for those days when I need a meal in a hurry. The soup containers are labeled and dated on the front of the container, not the lid.

It is also nice to take pots of soup to people as gifts: when new neighbors move in, if a friend has a new baby or is under the weather, if there is a funeral in the family—these are all times when stopping by with a nourishing soup is a very thoughtful and tangible way of giving support to someone who needs a little extra help.

Chilled Spiced Peach and Cantaloupe Soup Chilled Blueberry-Orange Soup Cream of Peanut Soup Green Pea Soup with Savory Cape Cod Fish Chowder Chicken and Smoked Sausage Gumbo Basque Lamb and Bean Soup Savory Lentil Soup with Kielbasa Mulligatawny Pumpkin Soup with Spicy Dumplings Succotash Soup New England Oyster Stew Ruby Red Beet Soup Orange-Butternut Soup with Ginger Parsnip Chowder Tortilla Fingers Creamy Broiled Garlic Toast

CHILLED SPICED PEACH AND CANTALOUPE SOUP

MAKES 12 PUNCH CUPS

Steeping whole spice seeds in a hot liquid, then combining the liquid with other ingredients is an old country way of adding more flavor to recipes. This technique appears often in German and Scandinavian dishes, and certainly both groups of these early immigrants loved cold fruit soups, which have been common in the Midwest since the mid-1800s.
I like serving this in antique punch cups, pouring the soup from an antique pitcher. Packed into a vacuum flask, it is also very nice for an alfresco lunch.

½ cup orange juice
1 teaspoon dried anise seed
4 whole allspice berries
2 large ripe peaches, peeled,
  pitted, and diced
1 medium cantaloupe, peeled and cubed

½ cup medium-dry sherry
  (I like Meier's from Ohio)
3 tablespoons grated orange rind
3 tablespoons honey
1 teaspoon ascorbic acid (see Note)

In a small saucepan, combine the orange juice, anise seed, and allspice berries. Cover and bring to a boil. Remove the pan from the stove and allow to stand for 1 hour. Strain the liquid through a fine sieve and reserve; discard the seeds.

In a food processor, puree half at a time of the peaches, cantaloupe, sherry, orange rind, and honey together and transfer to a large juice pitcher. Repeat with the remaining half. Stir in the orange juice mixture and ascorbic acid; refrigerate overnight.

NOTE: *The ascorbic acid (Fruit Fresh is one widely available brand) will keep the peaches from darkening and adds tartness. It is found in the canning section of many supermarkets. If unavailable, substitute 1 tablespoon fresh lemon juice.*

Ohio stoneware bowl

CHILLED BLUEBERRY-ORANGE SOUP

MAKES 2 QUARTS

*During the summer, we go to a local blueberry farm to pick berries; this is easy,
rather pleasant work, for you stand upright while you do it. We make pies and muffins, then squirrel
away the rest in the freezer for use the rest of the year.
One of the prettiest and most enchanting ways to use blueberries is in this intensely
colored soup. I serve it in blue glass compotes placed on top of green majolica plates and top the soup
with fresh mint. It is almost too pretty to eat—but not quite!*

2 envelopes unflavored gelatin	2 teaspoons ground cinnamon
1 cup sugar	2 cups half-and-half
5 ½ cups orange juice	
4 cups fresh or frozen blueberries	Garnish: fresh blueberries and mint sprigs

In a medium saucepan, mix the gelatin with the sugar and then stir in 1 cup orange juice. Cook over low heat until the gelatin is completely dissolved, about 5 minutes. Stir in the remaining orange juice, blueberries, and cinnamon. Simmer, stirring frequently and crushing the berries slightly with the back of a spoon, for about 15 minutes, or until the berries are tender. Cool completely. Stir in the half-and half and refrigerate until ready to serve. Top each serving with 5 fresh berries and a sprig of mint. Serve ice cold.

CREAM OF PEANUT SOUP

SERVES 6

*This is a marvelously rich soup, and anyone who likes peanuts will be absolutely enamored. It is as
smooth as silk and as good cold as hot. Peanut soups are popular all over the South, a testament to George
Washington Carver (1859–1943), the African-American agriculturalist who developed products from peanuts, sweet
potatoes, and pecans, hoping to produce new sources of income for southern farmers.*

2 tablespoons (¼ stick) butter	1 quart rich chicken stock
½ medium onion, chopped	1 cup smooth peanut butter
1 celery stalk, chopped	
2 tablespoons all-purpose flour	Garnish: parsley sprigs or chopped peanuts

Melt the butter in a deep saucepan. Add the onions and celery and sauté over medium heat until softened but not brown, 4 or 5 minutes. Stir in the flour and cook until a roux forms, bubbling up in the center, but don't allow it to brown. Add the chicken stock, whisking constantly, and bring the mixture to a boil. Remove from the heat and strain into a large saucepan, discarding the solids; set aside and allow to cool slightly.

Place the peanut butter in a food processor or blender. Add about 2 cups of the chicken stock mixture to the peanut butter and blend until smooth. Slowly pour this into the saucepan of remaining broth, mixing well with a whisk. Reheat, but *do not boil*. Serve immediately, garnishing with parsley sprigs or chopped peanuts or both.

GREEN PEA SOUP WITH SAVORY

SERVES 6 TO 8

*As soon as early peas were ready to pick in our garden, the first dish we had (since there weren't
a lot of them the first picking) was creamed peas and new potatoes. Later, when the peas really began to bear,
we would freeze a lot of them, and then if any were left, we had pea soup, accompanied by hot corn bread
and a pitcher of our own honey. I remember sitting on the front porch at the farm, faced with a bushel
of unshelled peas and thinking with self-pity, "This has to be the most boring job in the whole world." Nonetheless,
this pea soup with its touch of onions and savory is an aristocratic soup, worth the effort of shelling a few peas.*

6 tablespoons (¾ stick) butter	Salt and white pepper to taste
1½ cups coarsely chopped onions	Few shakes of hot red pepper sauce
3 cups chicken broth	1 tablespoon finely minced fresh savory
7 cups fresh peas (frozen can be	or ¾ teaspoon dried
substituted in a pinch)	
2 teaspoons sugar	Garnish: sour cream and grated nutmeg

Melt the butter in a medium stockpot. Add the onions and cook slowly until they are soft and clear, about 15 minutes. Add the chicken broth, peas, sugar, and salt and pepper, and hot red pepper sauce; simmer for 15 minutes, then add the savory and cook 5 minutes longer. Cool slightly.

Transfer the mixture to a food processor and puree until smooth. Strain the soup to remove the pea skins. (At this point, the soup can be refrigerated overnight.) Before serving, return the soup to a saucepan and reheat slowly. Transfer to soup bowls, garnish with the sour cream, and sprinkle a bit of nutmeg on top of the cream. Serve immediately.

Spoons from coin silver

CAPE COD FISH CHOWDER

SERVES 12

Fish chowder has many versions, some with tomatoes and some with odd vegetables, like green beans, but the original New England version was just potatoes and milk. At this time, the chowder kettle, rightfully called a chaudière, was an important part of a young girl's dowry.
This recipe makes a large amount—it is very good rewarmed, but if it sounds like too much to you, simply halve it.

¼ pound salt pork, finely diced
4 medium onions, chopped
   into ¼- to ½-inch pieces
6 cups potatoes, peeled
   and cut in ½-inch dice
Two 8-ounce bottles clam juice
One 2-ounce jar red pimientos,
   diced (optional)

3 to 4 pounds fish fillets (use a firm, skinless
   white fish, such as cod or haddock)
1½ quarts half-and-half or milk
½ cup (1 stick) butter
½ teaspoon dried thyme
Salt and pepper

Garnish: chopped parsley and paprika

In a large stockpot, cook the salt pork slowly over medium heat until it is totally crisp. Remove from the pot with a slotted spoon to paper towel to drain; set aside. Add the onions to the pot and sauté until soft and translucent, without browning, about 10 to 12 minutes. Add the potatoes, clam juice, and enough water to barely cover the potatoes and onions. Bring to a boil, cover, and simmer until the potatoes are almost tender, about 25 minutes. Add the pimientos. Layer the fish fillets over the potatoes, then add the half-and-half, butter, thyme, and salt and pepper to taste. Bring just to a simmer over low heat and poach the fish, uncovered and without boiling, until it is flaky, about 15 minutes. (Try to keep the fillets intact—they will break up naturally during serving.) Ladle into soup bowls and garnish with the chopped parsley and paprika. Pass the reserved salt pork to sprinkle on top.

Ironstone soup tureen with tray

CHICKEN AND SMOKED SAUSAGE GUMBO

SERVES 10 TO 12

*There are those who consider gumbo the soup du jour of Louisiana and I won't quarrel
with that. There is much disagreement over whether it is a soup or stew, but it is most certainly Cajun, not Creole.
The gumbo can be thickened with okra or with filé powder, which is made from dried sassafras leaves.
Some cooks, myself included, add the filé at the table, for if you happen to boil the gumbo with the filé in it, the
gumbo gets stringy and green-looking, a poor state of affairs. This tastes best if made a day
or two before, and it should always be served over rice.
There are as many versions of this dish as there are cooks, and who is to say which one is best—
that is, if you don't live in New Orleans. Leah Chase sums it all up rather nicely: "Cooking a good gumbo is just
like religion. Rules don't make a cook any more than a sermon does a saint." Amen. No matter what
your religion is, this is a great dish for entertaining; I recommend it highly.*

1 pound smoked sausage (preferably andouille), cut into ½-inch slices	1 to 2 garlic cloves, minced
½ cup all-purpose flour	One 28-ounce can tomatoes, chopped
½ teaspoon salt	2 bay leaves
½ pound chicken, cut into bite-size pieces	1 teaspoon dried thyme
½ cup vegetable oil	1 teaspoon salt
½ cup vegetable oil	¼ teaspoon red pepper
½ cup all-purpose flour	½ teaspoon ground black pepper
1 cup chopped onions	7 cups chicken stock
½ cup chopped celery	5 to 6 cups cooked rice
½ cup chopped green bell pepper	
	Garnish: parsley and chopped green onion
	Filé powder

In a large sauté pan, brown the sausage over medium-high heat, remove, and set aside. Combine the flour and salt on a piece of wax paper and lightly dredge the chicken pieces in it. Add the oil to the sauté pan and fry the chicken until golden brown, about 7 minutes, remove, and add to the sausage.

Make a roux: In a large stockpot over medium-high heat, heat ½ cup oil until very hot. Add the ½ cup of flour all at once, stirring constantly. Lower the heat to medium and cook the roux until it is medium brown in color. Immediately stir in the onions, celery, and green bell peppers and turn off the heat. (The hot roux will begin to cook the vegetables, while the cold vegetables will stop the roux from overcooking. The vegetables need to cook until tender and translucent but should not brown.) Adjust the heat back to medium and add the garlic and browned sausage and chicken, then the tomatoes, remaining spices, and chicken stock. Bring to a simmer, cover, and cook for 1½ hours. Place about ½ cup cooked rice in the bottom of each shallow soup bowl; top with the gumbo. Garnish with parsley and chopped green onions. Pass the filé powder for individual seasoning.

Perforated spoons for skimming stock

BASQUE LAMB AND BEAN SOUP

MAKES 3 QUARTS

The mark of real Basque food in the early days of sheepherding was that it was hearty yet flavorful. With just a black iron pot, some garlic, and imagination seasoned with memory, the Basques left their stamp on regional food in the mountain states as well as some regions in California. Since lamb was always available and dried beans were a staple, this dish was bound to come into being.

1 pound dried Great Northern beans	1 bay leaf
2 tablespoons vegetable oil or bacon fat	Scant handful parsley
1 cup chopped onion	½ teaspoon dried thyme or 2 teaspoons fresh
2 lamb shanks (1 pound each)	2 whole cloves
2 garlic cloves, minced	20 whole black peppercorns
10 cups water	Salt to taste
2 cups peeled and diced tomatoes or one 1-pound can, undrained	Garnish: chopped parsley

Soak the beans for 4 hours or overnight in water to cover; drain and set aside. Heat the oil in a large stock-pot, then add the onions and lamb shanks and sauté for 10 minutes over low heat, or until the shanks are nicely browned on all sides. Add the garlic for the last minute or so of browning.

Add the drained beans, water, tomatoes, bay leaf, parsley, thyme, cloves, and peppercorns; bring to a boil. Reduce the heat and simmer, covered, for 2½ hours.

Remove the shanks from the soup; trim the meat from the bones and return it to the soup. Add salt to taste. Serve with chopped parsley.

PHOTO POST CARD

AMERICA 25

BOISE MOUNTAINS, IDAHO

The country here is spectacular—mountain ranges, lots of forests (timber is a big industry), and we had a chance to interview some Basques, who came here from France and Spain to herd sheep. Their language and foodways hold them together, and we have eaten some really good Basque food—quite a few lamb dishes, as you might guess, and all very well seasoned.

M

$\mathscr{S}$AVORY LENTIL SOUP WITH KIELBASA

MAKES ABOUT 3 ¹/₂ QUARTS

Lentils are an important crop in California and cooks there use them in a lot of clever ways. Still, it is hard to improve on lentil soup, and since lentils don't have to be soaked overnight, this soup is a rather quick main dish. It is quite thick, so you can add up to 2 additional cups of broth after the cooking is completed if you prefer.

2 cups lentils, washed and picked over	2 celery stalks, chopped
7 cups chicken broth	1 medium onion, chopped
1 bay leaf	½ medium bell pepper, chopped
1 tablespoon vegetable oil	One 28-ounce can tomatoes,
1 pound pork or turkey kielbasa,	coarsely chopped
cut into thin slices	1 teaspoon dried summer savory
2 carrots, chopped	or 1½ tablespoons fresh

Place the lentils in a deep stockpot and add the chicken broth and the bay leaf. Cover and bring to a boil, then lower the heat and simmer, covered, for 35 minutes.

In the meantime, heat the oil in a large skillet. Add the sausage, carrots, celery, onions, and bell pepper and sauté until the sausage is browned, about 10 to 12 minutes.

Add the sausage and vegetables to the cooked lentils along with the tomatoes and savory. Bring to a boil and simmer 10 minutes longer to combine the flavors. Add more chicken broth, if desired.

travel $\mathscr{N}otes$ FROM NORTHERN CALIFORNIA

"Sourdough territory," says Dick as we approach San Francisco. That's just part of the story. Food was and always has been an important element of the city's culture; its early name was Yerba Buena (which means "good herb"), after the spicy wild herb that rambled over the hills around the bay and was used by local cooks to import a tangy flavor to soups and stews. After 1849 and the discovery of gold at Sutter's Creek, the town became a wild ramshackle place of tents and hastily constructed lean-tos along muddy streets. We can thank those early prospectors for making sourdough bread a San Francisco specialty. Later waves of immigrants arrived in the 1880s and after, providing the town with a degree of order and a mix of nationalities that has enriched its foodways to this day.

Eventually Italian immigrants would settle in California's valleys and raise their favored foods from the old country—artichokes, zucchini, bell peppers, tomatoes, and broccoli, beginning the California obsession with vegetables that has never ended.

MULLIGATAWNY

SERVES 6 TO 8

There are versions of this soup in recipe files across America, but common to all of them are curry powder, rice, and some sort of meat broth. The name is derived from the Tamil, a people who inhabit southern India and Ceylon. The word actually means pepper and water, and the soup is generally quite spicy. The British are credited for popularizing Mulligatawny around the world, and the recipe came to America via English sea captains. This recipe is from Steven Kneipp.

4 tablespoons (½ stick) butter	8 cups defatted chicken stock
2 medium onions, chopped	1 tablespoon curry powder
1 green bell pepper, chopped	½ teaspoon ground cardamom
1 red bell pepper, chopped	3 tablespoons tomato paste
2 cups peeled and chopped apple,	¼ cup honey
(use a firm cooking apple,	2 cups chopped cooked chicken breast
such as Granny Smith or Rome)	Salt and white pepper to taste
2 cups chopped celery	
¼ cup all-purpose flour	Garnish: plain yogurt and chutney

In a large stockpot, heat the butter over medium heat. Add the onions, bell peppers, apples, and celery and sauté 10 minutes. Sprinkle in the flour and continue cooking for another 3 to 4 minutes. Add the 8 cups chicken stock all at once, stirring to combine, then add the curry powder, cardamom, tomato paste, and honey. Simmer 30 to 40 minutes, partially covered. Add the cooked chicken and cook just a minute or two longer, or until the chicken is just heated through. Do not overcook. Add salt and pepper to taste. Ladle into bowls and garnish with the yogurt and chutney.

While San Francisco has a quaint European feeling with its meandering steep streets lined with the Victorian houses nicknamed "painted ladies," in contrast, Los Angeles has a sprawling restless energy. It is a young city with very old roots. Freeways connect the city's modern architecture to older neighborhoods with Spanish serenity. Founded in 1781, it was a sleepy pueblo until 1846 when it was seized from Spain by the United States and became a vigorous frontier town. With the discovery of gold in 1849, Los Angeles was on its way to becoming an important metropolis, with waves of people moving in daily in quest of a better life. Drawn by the climate, the entertainment industry, and real estate, the city's citizens have many faces. Hispanics, Chinese, Italian, Japanese, and Korean communities added their recipes to the health food buff's, and now we see and taste a cuisine that is exceedingly eclectic. With an abundance of fresh fruits, vegetables, and seafood, plus creative chefs, Los Angeles' foodways influence the rest of the country. Any new trend in the food world starts here, from tofu to Thai. And grilling is the only acceptable way to prepare anything and everything—or so we are led to believe.

PUMPKIN SOUP WITH SPICY DUMPLINGS

SERVES 6

Pumpkin was on the menu at just about every meal in the early days at
Plymouth Plantation. A popular Pilgrim ballad declared:

We have pumpkin at morning and
pumpkin at noon;
If it were not for pumpkin, we
should soon be undone.

I wish I could have given them the recipe for this savory pumpkin soup topped with
soft dumplings. It is a most satisfying lunch dish for the fall or winter.

2 tablespoons vegetable oil	**DUMPLINGS**
½ cup chopped onion	**1¼ cups all-purpose flour**
Two 1-pound cans unseasoned pumpkin	**2 teaspoons baking powder**
5 cups chicken broth	**½ teaspoon salt**
1 cup milk	**½ teaspoon ground cumin**
3½ tablespoons chili powder	**1 large egg**
¾ teaspoon ground cumin	**⅓ to ½ cup milk**
½ teaspoon salt	**2 tablespoons vegetable oil**
¼ teaspoon ground black pepper	
	Garnish: butter and finely minced parsley or chives

Heat the oil in a large deep saucepan. Add the onions and sauté until soft, 4 or 5 minutes. Add the pumpkin, then blend in the chicken broth and milk with a whisk. Add the chili powder, cumin, salt, and pepper and bring to a simmer.

Meanwhile, prepare the dumplings: In a large bowl, whisk together the flour, baking powder, salt, and cumin. In a small bowl, beat the egg until fluffy, then add ⅓ cup milk and the oil. Add the liquid all at once to the flour mixture, stirring only until the flour is moistened. If necessary, add more milk to make a manageable but stiff dough.

Check the thickness of the soup; if too thick (and it will be thicker after the dumplings cook in it), add some more broth or milk. Drop the dumpling mixture by rounded tablespoonfuls (10 ought to do it) onto the simmering soup. Cover and cook over medium-low heat for 20 minutes; *do not lift the lid* during the cooking time or the dumplings will fall. Ladle the dumplings and soup into deep bowls, top with a bit of butter and the parsley or chives and serve immediately.

SUCCOTASH SOUP

SERVES 4 TO 6

Succotash comes from the Indian word, m'sickquatash, *which means "maize not crushed or ground."
However, the Indians and early settlers learned that a mixture of corn (maize) and beans was a tasty and nourishing
combination. But they never could have envisioned this suave soup made of the same ingredients, all
dressed up with butter, herbs, and cream. I can suggest you serve it at Thanksgiving time, but it is really good year-round.*

¼ cup (½ stick) butter
⅔ cup finely chopped onion
⅓ cup finely chopped celery
One 10-ounce package frozen lima
   beans, thawed, or 2 cups fresh
One 10-ounce package frozen corn,
   thawed, or 2 cups fresh
2 cups chicken stock

¼ teaspoon dried marjoram
¼ teaspoon ground nutmeg
2 dashes of hot red pepper sauce
1 cup half-and-half
Salt and white pepper to taste

Garnish: finely minced fresh parsley or savory

Melt the butter in a stockpot over medium heat. Add the onions and celery and simmer for 5 to 7 minutes, or until the vegetables are golden. Add the lima beans and cook another 5 minutes. Add the corn and cook 2 minutes longer. Remove half the vegetable mixture and puree it in a food processor. Return the pureed mixture to the stockpot. Add the chicken stock, marjoram, nutmeg, and hot red pepper sauce and simmer for 10 minutes. Lower the heat and add the half and-half, then salt and pepper to taste. Cook over low heat without boiling for 5 minutes. Transfer to a soup tureen or ladle into individual bowls and garnish with the parsley. Serve immediately.

Sweet corn ready for the pot

NEW ENGLAND OYSTER STEW

SERVES 4

The favored oyster dish among the watermen, the old English word for the men who made their living on the water as a fisherman, trader, or even smuggler, was oyster stew. It is always made without any frills, just oysters, butter, and milk.

¼ cup (½ stick) butter
One 8-ounce container oysters with liquid
2 cups half-and-half or whole milk
Liberal dash of hot red pepper
  sauce to taste

Salt to taste
Crushed saltines or oyster crackers
  to thicken, if desired

Garnish: butter, paprika, or parsley

In a medium saucepan, melt the butter over medium heat. Add the oysters and liquid and poach gently just until the oysters' edges curl. *Do not overcook.* Stir in the half-and-half or milk and hot red pepper sauce. Do not boil. Taste before seasoning; shellfish is often salty enough by itself. Some cooks add crushed crackers to thicken the stew at the stove, other cooks let each diner add their own crackers at the table. Serve in bowls with a dollop of butter and a sprinkling of paprika or chopped parsley on top.

RUBY RED BEET SOUP

SERVES 6 TO 8

This is a beautiful way to begin a meal. The soup is surprisingly substantial, so serve small portions if using as an appetizer. Baking beets is a good way to prepare them for any recipe—much less messy than simmering them in water on top of the stove, and the beets can be baked, peeled, and chopped ahead of time.

4 medium beets
3 tablespoons butter
¾ cup coarsely chopped onion
3 medium potatoes, peeled
  and coarsely chopped
2 cups chicken broth

2 teaspoons lemon juice
Salt and pepper to taste
1½ cups half-and-half

Garnish: minced chives

Preheat the oven to 400° F.

Wash the beets and trim off all but 1 inch of the tops but leave the root intact. Wrap the beets loosely in a foil packet, place on a foil-lined cookie sheet, and bake until tender, about 1 hour. Open the packet and cool the beets under cold running water. Slip off the skins and discard. Chop the beets coarsely and set aside.

Melt the butter in a heavy saucepan and add the onions; cook until the onions are transparent. Add the potatoes and the chicken broth. Cover and bring to a boil, lower the heat, and simmer until the potatoes are tender, about 25 minutes. Cool slightly.

Meanwhile, puree the beets until smooth in a food processor; transfer to another bowl. Place the cooled potato mixture in the food processor bowl and puree until smooth. Add to the pureed beets and combine well. Stir in the lemon juice and salt and pepper. (At this point, the soup can be refrigerated overnight.)

Before serving, return the soup to a saucepan and add the half-and-half. Heat slowly but do not boil. Ladle into bowls, garnish with chives, and serve.

ORANGE-BUTTERNUT SOUP WITH GINGER

SERVES 8 TO 10

This is one of those practical picnic soups that can be served cold in warm weather or hot in cold weather. Butternut squash is now available year-round, but I make this soup in the fall, reducing it, but not adding the cream, then freezing it. As I need it, I thaw it, add the cream, and serve it either hot or cold. Its golden orange color makes it a handsome way to start a meal.

⅓ to ½ cup vegetable oil
2 cups chopped onion
2 butternut squash, peeled
   and cubed (about 3 pounds)
¼ cup snipped fresh dill
½ teaspoon ground ginger
½ cup dry white wine

1 cup fresh orange juice
   or ½ cup orange marmalade
2 quarts chicken stock,
   preferably homemade
1 cup heavy cream
Salt and white pepper to taste

Heat the oil in a heavy stockpot over medium heat. Add the onions and squash and sauté until the onions are golden, about 5 to 6 minutes. Add the dill and ginger and continue cooking. Just before the mixture is ready to brown, add the white wine and continue cooking until the wine is reduced a bit, 3 to 4 minutes. Add the orange juice or marmalade and chicken stock and bring the mixture to a full boil for about 4 to 5 minutes. Lower the heat and simmer, partially covered, for 20 to 25 minutes, or until the squash is completely tender.

Cool a bit, then puree the mixture in a food processor. Return to the stockpot and reduce the soup by about one-fourth over moderately high heat, 15 to 20 minutes. Stir in the cream, add salt and pepper to taste, bring just to a boil, and serve immediately or refrigerate until needed and serve cold.

PARSNIP CHOWDER

SERVES 8

Parsnips give this wonderfully hearty winter soup a touch of natural sweetness that is nicely offset by the salty bacon. It is quite a different soup and a very satisfying one. The parsnips and onion can be cleaned, chopped, and then refrigerated the day before the soup is prepared. If the parsnips have a woody, yellow core, cut it out and discard.

6 strips of pork or turkey bacon,
    cut into 1-inch pieces
1 large onion, chopped
1½ pounds parsnips, peeled
    and cut into ½-inch cubes
1½ pounds potatoes, peeled
    and cut into ½-inch cubes
2½ cups chicken broth (or a bit more)

1 bay leaf
2 cups half-and-half
¼ teaspoon coarse pepper
2½ tablespoons butter,
    at room temperature
2½ tablespoons all-purpose flour

Garnish: minced parsley

In a deep pan, sauté the bacon and onions together until the bacon is cooked; transfer the mixture to a small bowl and reserve. To the pan, add the parsnips, potatoes, chicken broth (it should cover the vegetables), and the bay leaf. Cover and simmer for about 25 minutes, or until the vegetables are tender. Add the half-and-half and pepper and bring the mixture to a boil.

Meanwhile, in a small bowl, mix the butter and flour together into a paste. Gently stir the paste into the soup a half teaspoon at a time, taking care not to break up the vegetables. Let the soup cook until thick, about 10 minutes, then add the reserved bacon and onions. Ladle into bowls and garnish with parsley.

TORTILLA FINGERS

MAKES 48 FINGERS

I like to serve these as an accompaniment to soups and salads—they are a nice change from crackers or mini biscuits. They are very crispy, and nicely seasoned with chili powder and cumin.

Twelve 6-inch corn tortillas
3 tablespoons corn oil
¾ tablespoon ground cumin

¾ tablespoon chili powder
Coarse salt

Place the tortillas on 2 foil-lined jelly roll pans; let them stand, uncovered, for 1 hour. Preheat the oven to 425° F.

In a measuring cup, whisk together the oil, cumin, and chili powder. With a teaspoon, sparingly drizzle a bit of the oil mixture on each tortilla, then with the back of the spoon, spread the oil over the entire surface of the tortilla. Turn the tortillas over and repeat. With scissors, cut each tortilla into 4 strips or "fingers." Bake for 4 minutes, and using a spatula, turn the fingers over and bake 3 minutes longer. Don't let them overbrown. The fingers closest to the outside of the pan will get done first—remove those early if you see this happening.

Sprinkle the fingers immediately with the salt and transfer them to paper towels to cool. They may be made a day in advance and stored in an airtight container.

CREAMY BROILED GARLIC TOAST

SERVES 8

Many soups, such as the Savory Lentil Soup with Kielbasa, or the Cincinnati Chili, or Mulligatawny, are hearty enough to be one-dish meals. Add some crudités and a hot bread, and you've rounded out the menu very nicely. One very quick bread I serve with soups (and main-dish salads) that is always very popular is broiled cheese toast. The cheese mixture can be made in advance and stored indefinitely in the refrigerator. And in a pinch, I've served this as a cocktail accompaniment. It is a good topping to have on hand.

1¼ cups mayonnaise
6 garlic cloves, finely minced
1 cup grated Parmesan cheese
¾ cup grated extra-sharp cheddar cheese

1½ tablespoons milk or cream
½ teaspoon paprika
¼ cup finely minced parsley
One 20-inch loaf French bread

Preheat the broiler, with the rack 6 inches from the heat.

In a small bowl, mix the mayonnaise, garlic, and Parmesan cheese. Combine the cheddar cheese and milk or cream in a small saucepan and heat over medium-low heat, stirring constantly so it doesn't scorch, until melted. Remove from the heat and whisk the mayonnaise mixture into the cheese mixture. Stir in the paprika and parsley.

Cut the loaf in half lengthwise as for a hero sandwich or cut it into individual slices. Arrange the bread on a baking sheet and toast lightly under the broiler until just golden. Spread the toasts generously with the cheese mixture, return to the oven, and broil 2 to 3 minutes, or until the cheese is bubbly and deep golden brown. Cut into serving pieces if the loaf was left whole and serve hot.

An Embarrassment of
PIES

*P*IES ARE A uniquely **American** dessert. They are still regularly made for family meals and you find them at many social outings—county fairs, church suppers, and at the fish fries sponsored by the local fire departments and PTAs. Fruit pies are the most common, with apple being the number one favorite, especially when served warm with a slice of mild longhorn cheese or a scoop of ice cream.

Actually I am not too embarrassed about the number of pie recipes I've collected here, for I consider pie to be the ultimate dessert. When I end a meal with several different dessert offerings I have discovered that the pie always disappears first.

Yet for all that, pie baking has nearly become a lost art. Partly, I think, it is because we've been made to feel guilty about eating pie, which is unfortunate, and partly because a lot of cooks are intimidated by the thought of making piecrust, which is tragic. The piecrust recipe on page 284 is foolproof and very forgiving. I do urge you to try it. And if this piecrust business still sounds too overwhelming, just go buy some ready-made ones and pat them into a metal or glass pie pan, and fill them according to these recipes.

I have not included recipes for basic fruit and cream pies other than the apple pie; you can find those in other cookbooks. The ones offered here are those I fell in love with and found to be very distinctive. Frequently the ingredients reflect the part of the country where I found the recipe, such as the Pear-Apple Pie with Spicy Crumb Streusel from Utah, where pears are an important fruit crop, and the extraordinary Macadamia Nut Cream Pie from Hawaii.

There are two things to bear in mind in order to make good pies: 1. Use good-quality deep pans, preferably metal (not flimsy aluminum). 2. Wait until you see the filling bubbling up in the middle of the pie before you remove it from the oven. The bubbles indicate that the bottom crust is done.

Pear-Apple Pie with Spicy Crumb Streusel Perfect Apple Pie Apple Butter–Pumpkin Pie with Streusel Topping Kentucky Pie Amish Coconut-Oatmeal Pie Sauerkraut Cream Pie Country Sorghum Pie Winner's Circle Pie Kentucky Stack Pie Southern Peanut Butter Pie Sweet Potato Pie German Sweet Chocolate Pie Jeff Davis Pie Macadamia Nut Cream Pie Date-Pecan Pie Honey-Raisin Pie Sunny Lemon Pie

PEAR-APPLE PIE WITH SPICY CRUMB STREUSEL

MAKES ONE 9-INCH PIE

Fruit pies are the quintessence of country American desserts and this version from Utah, which combines pears with the more expected apples, creates a very different and subtly flavored pie. The crisp topping, with its hint of lemon and mace, is a nice contrast with the juicy filling. Do try this pie—it's wonderful.

TOPPING
½ cup light brown sugar,
    loosely packed
½ cup (1 stick) butter, softened
Finely grated zest of 1 lemon
    (2 teaspoons)
¼ teaspoon ground mace
1 cup all-purpose flour

FILLING
⅔ cup granulated sugar
1 tablespoon Minute Tapioca
½ teaspoon ground cinnamon
¼ teaspoon freshly grated nutmeg
⅛ teaspoon ground mace
2 tablespoons fresh lemon juice
2 pounds green apples (about 4 large)
1 pound fully ripened pears (2 large)

Pastry for a deep 9-inch pie shell (page 284)
2 tablespoons (¼ stick) butter

Preheat oven to 350° F.

Place all of the topping ingredients in a food processor bowl and process until crumbly. Set aside.

Make the filling: Combine the sugar, tapioca, cinnamon, nutmeg, and mace in a medium bowl; whisk in the lemon juice and set aside.

Peel, core, and cut the apples into thin slices and place in a large bowl. Peel, core, and cut the pears into thin slices and add to the apples. Add the sugar-tapioca mixture; toss well and transfer to the pie shell. Dot the top with the butter, then sprinkle the topping mixture evenly over the pie. Place the pie on a foil-lined baking sheet and bake until golden brown, about 1 hour. Cover lightly with foil and bake 30 minutes longer, or until the apples are tender and the juices are bubbling out of the pie.

Church social pie carrier

PERFECT APPLE PIE
MAKES ONE 9-INCH PIE

Early New Englanders frequently ate apple pie for breakfast, and though the custom began in
New England, it spread across the country. In a heated discussion about apple pie for breakfast, an exasperated
Ralph Waldo Emerson settled the matter by exclaiming, "What is pie for?" But it was a fixture at
other meals in New England as well; Yale University served apple pie at supper for more than 100 years.

Pastry for a 2-crust pie (page 284)

7 cups tart apples, pared, cored,
   and sliced
1 tablespoon fresh lemon juice
   (optional)
1 cup granulated sugar
¼ cup packed dark brown sugar

Speck of salt
2 tablespoons all-purpose flour
1 teaspoon ground cinnamon
¼ teaspoon grated nutmeg
¼ teaspoon ground cardamom
2 tablespoons (¼ stick) butter,
   cut into small pieces

Preheat the oven to 375° F.

Roll out half the pastry thinly on a floured surface and line a 9-inch pan, patting it in firmly.

Place the sliced apples in a bowl and sprinkle with lemon juice if they lack tartness. In a small mixing bowl, whisk together the sugars, salt, flour, cinnamon, nutmeg, and cardamom; sprinkle over the apples and stir gently to mix. Place the apple mixture in the pastry-lined pie pan and dot with butter. Roll out a top crust, roll onto the top of the apples, and seal the edges; slash to let the steam escape. Sprinkle the pie with a little granulated sugar and bake for 40 minutes, then place a square of aluminum foil over the pie and bake for an additional 10 to 15 minutes longer. The juices in the pie should be bubbling up through the slash in the middle of the pie. Cool on a rack and serve warm or at room temperature.

Whole nutmegs and graters

Apple Butter–Pumpkin Pie with Streusel Topping

MAKES ONE 9-INCH PIE

My mouth just watered when I read through this recipe for the first time. Pumpkin pie with a touch of apple butter? Plus a streusel topping? Marvelous! This is a firm dark pie that is at its best served slightly warm (it can be reheated in the microwave) with a bit of whipped cream on top. The recipe yields a very generous amount of filling, so do not use a foil pan. (I actually don't think you should use foil pans anyway.)

Pastry for a deep 9-inch pie shell (page 284)

FILLING
3 large eggs
1 cup pumpkin puree
1 cup apple butter
½ cup packed dark brown sugar
2 teaspoons Angostura bitters (available at liquor stores)
½ teaspoon ground cinnamon
½ teaspoon ground ginger

½ teaspoon grated nutmeg
¼ teaspoon salt
1 cup evaporated milk

STREUSEL TOPPING
½ cup all-purpose flour
⅓ cup packed dark brown sugar
⅓ cup coarsely chopped pecans
3 tablespoons butter, softened

Garnish: whipped cream or ice cream

Preheat the oven to 375° F. Prepare the pie shell and set aside.

Make the filling: In a mixer bowl, beat the eggs slightly, then blend in the pumpkin puree, apple butter, sugar, bitters, spices, and salt until the spices are thoroughly incorporated into the mixture. Add the milk and beat until it is well combined. Pour the filling into the unbaked shell and bake the pie for 50 or 60 minutes, or until a knife or skewer inserted in the middle comes out clean.

While the pie bakes, make the Streusel Topping: In a small bowl, combine the flour, brown sugar, and pecans. Work in the butter with a whisk.

Sprinkle the streusel over the top of the pie and bake 15 minutes longer. Cool slightly, then serve warm with a dollop of whipped cream or a scoop of ice cream.

KENTUCKY PIE

MAKES ONE 9-INCH PIE

*This recipe came out of the "milk pie" or "poor man's pie" tradition in which common
ingredients found in every cook's kitchen are combined to create an economical but toothsome sweet. Kentucky
pie is very similar to Amish brown sugar pie, but the texture is different due to the addition of eggs.
When the pie is first removed from the oven, it is still a bit quivery and shaky—this kind of a pie was called a
"nervous" pie. Perhaps that better describes the cook?
The pie puffs up in the center and falls when it cools so it is a very thin pie too, but that's all right—it is very rich.*

Pastry for a 1-crust 9-inch pie
(page 284)

½ cup (1 stick) butter
3 cups packed light brown sugar

3 large eggs
½ cup half-and-half
1 teaspoon vanilla extract
Cinnamon

Preheat the oven to 450° F. Roll out the pastry thinly and pat firmly into the pan.

In a large mixer bowl, cream the butter and brown sugar together until light, about 3 minutes. Beat in the eggs one at a time, blending well after each addition. Add the half-and-half and vanilla and mix well, but do not overbeat. Pour into the pie shell and lightly sprinkle with cinnamon. Bake for 10 minutes, then reduce the heat to 350° F. and continue to bake for 30 minutes longer, or until a knife inserted in the center comes out clean. Cool completely before cutting.

AMISH COCONUT-OATMEAL PIE

MAKES ONE 9-INCH PIE

*This Amish pie is frequently served at Mennonite restaurants, as well as at their large
quilt auctions across the country, and many people have written me for the recipe. The original recipe did not
call for coconut, but there is no question that it jazzes this country dish up a bit. I like it topped with
a bit of Crème Fraîche (page 285), though that is certainly not Amish.*

Pastry for a 1-crust 9-inch pie
(page 284)

¾ cup packed light brown sugar
¼ cup granulated sugar
2 tablespoons (¼ stick) butter
3 large eggs, lightly beaten

½ cup light corn syrup
½ cup water
1 teaspoon vanilla extract
¼ teaspoon salt
¼ teaspoon grated nutmeg
½ cup shredded coconut
½ cup quick-cooking oatmeal

Preheat the oven to 350° F. Roll out the pastry and line the pie pan.

In a large mixing bowl, blend the sugars and butter until well mixed. Add the eggs one at a time, blending well after each addition. Mix in the corn syrup, water, vanilla, salt, and nutmeg and combine. Stir in the coconut and oatmeal.

Pour into the pastry shell and bake for 35 to 40 minutes, or until the top is golden brown. Cool thoroughly before cutting.

SAUERKRAUT CREAM PIE

MAKES TWO 9-INCH PIES

*I know you must think this is a dotty sort of recipe. Trust me—this is a delicious pie.
The recipe was developed by the Harveysburg Community Historical Society in Harveysburg, Ohio, for the
Ohio Sauerkraut Festival. It is a variation of chess pie, an American heirloom recipe. Each year,
hundreds of pieces of this pie are sold at the Ohio Sauerkraut Festival in Waynesville, Ohio (page 292) to raise
funds for the Society's Black School Museum project. When you taste this, you'll see why.*

Pastry for two 9-inch single-crust pies (page 284)	**5 large eggs, well beaten**
	1 cup milk
	1 teaspoon vanilla extract
½ cup sauerkraut	**2 tablespoons fresh lemon juice**
½ cup (1 stick) butter, softened	**2 tablespoons yellow cornmeal**
2 cups sugar	**2 tablespoons all-purpose flour**

Preheat the oven to 350° F. Roll out the piecrust on a floured surface and line 2 pie pans; set aside.

Drain the kraut and rinse with cold water, then squeeze dry and set aside. In a mixer bowl, cream the butter and sugar thoroughly, about a minute. Add the eggs, milk, vanilla, and lemon juice and blend. In a small mixing bowl, whisk together the flour and cornmeal. Add the flour mixture to the egg mixture and blend; fold into the kraut. Pour into the unbaked pie shells. Bake for 55 to 60 minutes, or until a knife inserted in the center comes out clean. Cool completely before cutting and serving.

COUNTRY SORGHUM PIE

MAKES ONE 9-INCH PIE

*Sorghum is a cereal grass that resembles corn, and even though it is the third leading
cereal crop of the United States, most of it is used for animal fodder. But one of its by-products is the sweet juice
extracted from the stalks, which is boiled down to produce a thick dark syrup called sorghum molasses.
Sorghum is much milder in flavor than regular molasses and is used as a table syrup, especially in the South, but you
can find it in the Midwest and the mountain states too. It can be ordered by mail (page 300). This is a
unique sort of pie, touched with a bit of sugar and pecans on top, and very delectable.*

Pastry for a 1-crust 9-inch pie (page 284)	**¾ cup packed light brown sugar**
	1 tablespoon all-purpose flour
	1 tablespoon cornstarch
3 large eggs, at room temperature, separated	**½ teaspoon ground cinnamon**
	½ teaspoon grated nutmeg
1½ cups sorghum	**¼ teaspoon salt**
2 tablespoons (¼ stick) butter, melted	**⅓ to ½ cup coarsely chopped pecans**
1 teaspoon vanilla extract	**1 to 2 tablespoons granulated sugar**

Preheat the oven to 425° F. Roll out the pastry and line the pie pan.

In a mixer bowl, beat the egg yolks until thick for at least 3 minutes. Add the sorghum, melted butter, and vanilla; mix well. In a small bowl, whisk together the brown sugar, flour, cornstarch, cinnamon, nutmeg, and salt. Slowly add the dry ingredients to the sorghum mixture; mix well.

In a separate bowl beat the egg whites until stiff peaks are formed. Gradually fold the egg whites into the batter. Pour into the unbaked pastry shell and bake for 15 minutes. Remove from the oven and sprinkle with the pecans and granulated sugar. Lower the heat to 375° F. and bake for 20 to 25 minutes longer, covering with a piece of foil if the top of the pie begins to overbrown. The filling will still be a bit shaky but will firm up as it cools. Remove to a rack and cool completely.

*W*INNER'S CIRCLE PIE

MAKES ONE 9-INCH PIE

*In the late 1950s Walter and Leaudra Kern created a dessert for their restaurant in
Melrose, Kentucky, they dubbed Derby Pie®. Wisely, they copyrighted the name and the original
recipe remains a closely guarded secret.
However, we do know the pie is a winning combination of light corn syrup, chocolate chips,
walnuts, and Kentucky bourbon and has become that state's signature pie under such names as Thoroughbred
Pie, Bluegrass Pie, and so on. When baked, the pie is quite firm, so it travels well; consider it for a
carry-in supper when you have been assigned to bring dessert.*

Pastry for a 1-crust 9-inch pie (page 284)	**1 teaspoon vanilla extract**
	Speck of salt
	2 tablespoons bourbon
3 large eggs	**½ cup chocolate chips**
1 cup sugar	**½ cup chopped walnuts**
¾ cup light corn syrup	**(I like half English, half black)**
¼ cup (½ stick) butter, melted	

Preheat the oven to 350° F. Roll out the pastry and set aside.

In a mixer bowl, beat the eggs slightly. Add the sugar and mix until well blended, about 3 minutes. Add the corn syrup, melted butter, vanilla, and salt and blend well. Stir in the bourbon, then fold in the chocolate chips and nuts. Pour into the pastry shell and bake for 1 hour. Remove from the oven and cool completely on a rack before cutting.

MELROSE, KENTUCKY

Driving through Kentucky is such a treat! The horse farms, with their white-pillared porches fronting brick mansions, the land surrounded by white fencing, seem to be from another era. I expect to see Rhett and Scarlett coming around the corner in a buggy anytime. Kentucky also signals the beginning of regional Southern cookery, and one of the favorite local desserts is the rightfully famous Derby Pie. It has a mystique all it's own, and I hope to find a good recipe to take home with me.

M

KENTUCKY STACK PIE

MAKES 16 SMALL PIECES

According to my research, this pie recipe dates back to pre–Civil War days, when the all-day picnic or barbecue was the way many plantation hostesses entertained. Each invited family would bring something to the picnic and sometimes that was pie. Since it was so difficult to travel with several pies separately, someone devised the idea of stacking them. The recipe evolved into a stack of chess pies held together with caramel frosting, with the remaining frosting covering the top and sides of the pie.
The pie filling was similar to a sugar or chess pie, but the pies were made quite thin and the filling was firmer. After reading about this pie in several old cookbooks, I knew I had to try it and so I set to work. What I discovered is that stack pie is not difficult to make. It should be made the day of serving, and because it is so rich, it serves a great many folk. Need I add it is a fabulous dessert? And I never use the word fabulous. *Well, hardly ever. This recipe is adapted from the cookbook* We Make You Kindly Welcome *by Elizabeth Kremmer from the Shaker Village of Pleasant Hill.*

1 recipe pie pastry (page 284)

FILLING
10 egg yolks (use jumbo eggs,
** large ones if not available)**
3 cups sugar
1 cup evaporated milk
1½ cups (3 sticks) butter, melted
** and cooled**
1 tablespoon vanilla extract
1 tablespoon grated orange zest
Speck of salt

FROSTING
¾ cup (1½ sticks) butter
1½ cups packed dark brown sugar
¼ cup plus 2 tablespoons evaporated milk
1½ teaspoons vanilla extract
Speck of salt
3 to 4 cups confectioners' sugar

You will need four 9-inch pie pans. Do not use foil pans. Divide the pastry into fourths, roll out one piece very thinly, and place it in the pan. Trim the crust to the edge of the pan but do not crimp the edges; allow the top edge of the pastry to lie flat on the rim. Set aside.

The next 3 crusts should be more shallow. Roll out 3 more pastries, transferring them to the pans, but do not bring the crust up over the top of the pan lip. Trim off the excess pastry with a knife. Don't worry about it slipping down during baking; the filling will hold it in place. Preheat the oven to 350° F.

Place the egg yolks in a large mixer bowl and beat for 3 minutes. Add the sugar gradually, then add the milk and melted butter gradually. When blended, add the vanilla, orange zest, and salt and mix in.

Fill the first pie shell to the top, then divide the remaining filling evenly between the 3 remaining shallow pastry shells. Bake the pies for 10 minutes, then with a toothpick, prick out any air bubbles that appear on top of the pies. Continue baking the pies for another 15 to 18 minutes, or until they are golden, checking them regularly and pricking the bubbles. Remove the 3 thinner pies to a rack. Immediately cut away any excess top pastry with a sharp knife and discard. Leave the thicker pie in the oven an additional 5 minutes, or until golden. Remove that pie, leaving the crust intact, and allow all the pies to cool completely.

Meanwhile, start the frosting: Melt the butter in a small saucepan. Whisk in the brown sugar and bring the mixture to a boil over medium-high heat, whisking all the time. Reduce the heat and simmer the mix-ture for 2 minutes, whisking now and then. Add the milk and bring again to a boil. Remove from the heat, transfer the mixture to a large mixer bowl, and allow to cool.

When cool, add the vanilla and salt, then gradually beat in the confectioners' sugar. Beat until the frost-ing is the right consistency for spreading.

Assemble the pie(s): Leave the thicker pie in its pan; it will be the bottom layer. Cover it with a light coating of frosting. Run a spatula around the crust of one of the pies and ease it out of the pan onto the frosted pie; with your hands, gently pat it down onto the first pie. Frost the top lightly. Repeat with the remaining pies. If one should break or crumble a bit, carefully lay the pieces into place; the frosting will cover up all mistakes. Actually, I didn't have much of a problem with this and you probably won't either; the shallow pies slip very easily out of their pans. When all 4 pies are atop of one another frost the whole thing, just like you would a cake. Be sparing with the frosting, though, for this is already a very sweet dessert. If you have frosting left over, put it between graham crackers for the children.

Do not refrigerate the pie; cover it lightly with plastic wrap until serving time. Cut it into 16 very thin wedges and serve. You won't believe the adulation you will receive for this dessert. You earned it!

SOUTHERN PEANUT BUTTER PIE

MAKES ONE 9-INCH PIE

Peanut butter pies are one of those southern delights that have been embraced by anyone who likes peanut butter; our numbers are legion.
Try this topped with a bit of Crème Fraîche. Let me assure you this is stiff competition for pecan pie.
The pie shell is to be chilled before filling, so plan accordingly.

Pastry for a 9-inch pie shell,
    chilled (page 284)

3 large eggs
1 cup dark corn syrup
½ cup sugar
½ cup smooth peanut butter

1 teaspoon vanilla extract
1 teaspoon grated orange zest
1 cup salted peanuts without skins,
    coarsely chopped

Garnish: Crème Fraîche (page 285)

Preheat the oven to 400° F. Roll out the pastry in advance, line the pie pan, and chill in the refrigerator for at least an hour.

In a mixer bowl, beat the eggs just until frothy. Add the corn syrup, sugar, peanut butter, vanilla, and orange zest; beat until smooth. Stir in the peanuts, then pour into the chilled pastry shell. Bake for 15 min-utes, then reduce the oven temperature to 350° F. and continue baking for 30 minutes more. The filling will be firm and dark brown in color. Cool thoroughly before cutting and serving. Serve with Crème Fraîche.

SWEET POTATO PIE

SERVES 6 TO 8

Sweet potato pie, a traditional southern dessert, is often likened to pumpkin pie, but I personally find them quite different. This pie is much more velvety and silky than pumpkin pie, more subtle in flavor—need I add it is superb? A friend of mine adds a splash of Grand Marnier, and though not traditional, it is a very nice touch.

Vegetable oil

3 medium to large sweet potatoes

Pastry for a 1-crust 9-inch pie
  (page 284)

4 tablespoons butter
  (½ stick), at room temperature

½ cup granulated sugar

¼ cup packed dark brown sugar

1 teaspoon grated orange zest

½ teaspoon ground cinnamon

½ teaspoon grated nutmeg

⅛ teaspoon salt

3 large eggs

One 5-ounce can evaporated milk

2 tablespoons Grand Marnier or
  other orange-flavored liqueur (optional)

Garnish: Whipped Cream Topping (page 286)

Preheat the oven to 425° F. Scrub, dry, and oil the potatoes and wrap individually in foil. Bake for 1 hour, or until they are tender. Meanwhile, roll out the pastry and line a 9-inch pie pan.

When the potatoes are done, open the foil, slash the skin of each potato, and allow them to cool. Lift away the peel and scoop out the flesh into a large mixer bowl. Add the butter and mash the potatoes until they are smooth. Add the sugars, orange zest, spices, and salt; blend. In a medium bowl, beat the eggs and blend in the milk and liqueur. Add to the potato mixture and beat in by hand. Pour the mixture into the pie shell and bake for 10 minutes, then lower the heat to 300° F. and bake 45 to 55 minutes longer. The pie will puff up and the center should feel smooth but not sticky when you touch it lightly with your finger. Remove the pie to a rack and cool completely. Serve with the Whipped Cream Topping.

GERMAN SWEET CHOCOLATE PIE

MAKES ONE 9-INCH PIE

If you like pies and chocolate, make this one right away! This is one of the best recipes in the book! Intensely chocolaty, a bit soft like fudge topping, and with the added texture of coconut and nuts playing off the smooth filling, well, this is a pie to crow about. It can be refrigerated, but bring it to room temperature before serving.

Pastry for a 1-crust 9-inch pie
  (page 284)

4 ounces German sweet chocolate

¼ cup (½ stick) butter

One 15-ounce can evaporated milk

1½ cups sugar

3 tablespoons cornstarch

⅛ teaspoon salt

2 large eggs, slightly beaten

1 teaspoon vanilla extract

1⅓ cups sweetened, flaked coconut

½ cup chopped pecans

Preheat the oven to 375° F. Roll out the pastry and line a 9-inch pie pan; set aside.

In a small saucepan over low heat, melt the chocolate and butter, stirring until combined. Remove from the heat and stir in the milk; set aside. In a large mixer bowl, combine the sugar, cornstarch, and salt. Beat in the eggs one at a time. Add the vanilla and mix thoroughly, then gradually blend in the chocolate mixture. Pour into the unbaked pastry shell. In a small bowl, combine the coconut and pecans, then sprinkle them evenly over the pie filling. Bake for 45 minutes, until the edges of the crust are golden brown and the filling is partly set. Remove from the oven and cool at least 4 hours before cutting. The filling will become firm as it cools. Cut into wedges and serve.

JEFF DAVIS PIE
MAKES ONE 9-INCH PIE

When I served this luscious pie to a friend, I told her it was called Jeff Davis Pie after the president of the Confederacy during the Civil War. She said, "Oh, that Jeff Davis." We're talking about American history and Jefferson Davis here, and a pie that is well known in the South, for very good reason. It is unforgettably good. Dark with spices and with dates, raisins, and nuts suspended in a creamy custard, this recipe was sent to me by a viewer in Mississippi, where Davis spent time as a cotton planter. Before the Civil War, he had been the secretary of war and was considered innovative: He even imported camels for army use in the desert; it didn't catch on.

Pastry for a 1-crust 9-inch pie
  (page 284)

½ cup (1 stick) butter
2 cups packed light brown sugar
4 large egg yolks
2 tablespoons all-purpose flour
1 teaspoon ground cinnamon
1 teaspoon grated nutmeg

Speck of salt
1 cup heavy cream
1 teaspoon vanilla extract
½ cup chopped dates
½ cup dark raisins
½ cup chopped pecans

Garnish: Whipped Cream Topping (page 286)

Preheat the oven to 425° F. Roll out the pastry and line a 9-inch pie pan; set aside.

In a large mixer bowl, cream the butter and sugar until smooth, about 3 minutes. Beat in the egg yolks one at a time, blending well after each addition. In a small bowl, whisk together the flour, cinnamon, nutmeg, and salt; blend into the egg mixture until smooth. Gradually blend in the cream and vanilla. Stir in the dates, raisins, and pecans by hand and blend well.

Prick the bottom of the pastry shell all over with a fork and bake for 6 minutes, checking frequently to prick air bubbles and to pat the sides up with a fork if they slip. Lower the oven heat to 300° F. Fill the pastry shell and bake for 40 minutes; cool completely. Serve with Whipped Cream Topping.

MACADAMIA NUT CREAM PIE

MAKES ONE 9-INCH PIE

*Macadamia nuts are also called "Queensland nuts" for they originated in Australia. The plant
was brought to Hawaii in 1890 and was first used as an ornamental shrub. It wasn't until the 1930s that
the nut began to be used as a food.
And what a food! A round, white, innocent-looking little nut, the
macadamia's sweet delicate flavor is perfect with cocktails or used in cookies or salads. Another way
to showcase this Hawaiian specialty (now the state's third largest food crop) is in this alluring cream pie with a
custard base. It will create a few extra dishes to wash, but that's okay; this pie is worth it.*

Pastry for a 1-crust 9-inch pie (page 284)	3 tablespoons cornstarch
	¼ teaspoon salt
	2 large eggs, separated
One 3-ounce package cream cheese, at room temperature	1 cup or a 3½-ounce jar chopped unsalted macadamia nuts (if using salted nuts,
⅓ cup sour cream	roll in paper toweling to remove as
1¾ cups milk	much salt as possible)
½ cup plus 1 tablespoon sugar	1 cup heavy cream
1 envelope unflavored gelatin	1 teaspoon vanilla extract

Preheat the oven to 425° F. Roll out the pastry and line a deep 9-inch pan. Prick the pastry all over with a
fork and bake for 6 to 8 minutes, checking frequently to prick air bubbles and to pat the sides up with a
fork if the pastry begins to slip down. Remove from the oven and cool completely.

In a small mixing bowl, blend the cream cheese with the sour cream until smooth. Gradually stir in the
milk and then set aside. In the top of a double boiler, mix the sugar with the gelatin, cornstarch, and salt
(omit if using salted nuts).

Slowly stir the cream cheese mixture into the sugar mixture. Cook over boiling water, stirring frequently with a rubber spatula, until the mixture is very thick and smooth and the consistency of cream
sauce, about 10 to 15 minutes.

In a small bowl, beat the egg yolks with a fork. Add a small amount of hot filling to the egg yolks and
blend well, then return all to the double boiler. Cook, stirring constantly, for about 2 minutes. Remove
the top pan with the filling from the double boiler and set aside until lukewarm. In a mixer bowl, whip the
egg whites until they hold a stiff peak, then fold into the warm filling. Chill until the filling is cool but not set.

Meanwhile, preheat the oven to 350° F. Spread the nuts in a single layer on a baking sheet. Toast in the
oven for about 5 minutes, stirring once.

In a mixer bowl, whip the cream until stiff. Fold the whipped cream, the vanilla, and half of the nuts into
the cooled filling; pour into the baked pastry. Chill for 2 to 3 hours or overnight. Before serving, sprinkle
with the remaining nuts.

DATE-PECAN PIE

If you like pecan pie, you will be euphoric about this pie, for the addition of dates further embellishes an already superb desert. Store dates in an airtight container in the refrigerator; refrigerated dates will retain their moisture and flavor up to 8 months, frozen dates, for up to a year.

Pastry for a 9-inch pie shell	**¼ cup sugar**
(page 284)	**¼ cup (½ stick) butter, melted**
	1 teaspoon grated orange zest
3 large eggs	**¾ cup chopped dates**
1 cup dark corn syrup	**¾ cup pecan halves**

Preheat the oven to 425° F. Roll out the pastry and line a 9-inch pie pan; set aside.

In a large mixer bowl, beat the eggs until well blended. Add the corn syrup, sugar, butter, and orange zest and mix well. Stir in the dates and pecans. Pour into the pastry shell and bake for 15 minutes. Lower the heat to 375° F. and bake for another 20 to 25 minutes, or until the center is slightly firm. Remove from the oven and allow to cool completely before cutting.

travel Notes FROM HAWAII

The Hawaiian Islands are famous for their sensual landscapes, deep-blue seas, and brilliant oversized flowers that make mainland gardeners groan with envy—the lush, colorful vegetation never ends. As gardeners from the Midwest, we reel with pleasure, and yes, desire, when we view the islander's flower borders.

It is a long flight from Los Angeles to Hawaii; 2,400 miles west from California, out in the Pacific. The Polynesians were the original settlers of the 122 islands, though they are a mélange of many races and nationalities. Hawaii's population includes Chinese, Filipino, and Japanese, and all have contributed customs and foodways to the multifaceted life of the state.

The largest source of income comes from military bases, with agriculture being the second source. It won't surprise anyone to find out that one-third of the world's supply of pineapple comes from Hawaii. Of course, tourism also brings dollars to these islands.

The world didn't know of Hawaii until 1788, when Captain Cook of the British Navy discovered it. The islands were important immediately as a base for whaling and as a trading link to the Orient. Local chiefs ruled the islands until 1800, when the area was finally united under a Hawaiian king. The islands became a possession of the United States in 1898, after most of the islands came under control of American sugar planters. Today, as in earlier days, rice, fresh fruits such as bananas, papayas, mangoes, and coconut, along with pork are mainstays in the islander's diet and the indigenous macadamia nut is prized around the world.

HONEY-RAISIN PIE

I found this pie so interesting; it is much lighter in flavor and texture than most raisin pies, and it has a golden hue because orange juice is the liquid. Honey is the sweetener, which gives it a slightly different flavor as well. Honeybees were originally brought from England by the early colonists. Until that time, with the exception of an inferior type of honey produced by wasplike insects in Mexico and what is now California, honey was unknown in North America. For the eastern American Indians, its arrival was a mixed blessing. The honeybee was often a harbinger of white encroachment; when bees were sighted, it meant the white man was less than seventy-five miles away and the Indians knew to move westward to safer territory.

Pastry for a 2-crust pie (page 284)

1 cup fresh orange juice (2 large oranges)
3 tablespoons fresh lemon juice
⅔ cup cold water
½ cup honey
1 teaspoon vanilla extract

¼ teaspoon mace
¼ teaspoon salt
Grated zest of ½ orange
3 tablespoons cornstarch
¼ cup water
1⅔ cups seedless raisins
1 tablespoon all-purpose flour
1 tablespoon butter, cut into small pieces

Preheat the oven to 425° F. Roll out the pastry and line a 9-inch pan with half of it, and set aside.

In a medium saucepan, combine the orange juice, lemon juice, water, honey, vanilla, mace, salt, and orange zest and bring to a boil over high heat. Stir together the cornstarch and water in a small bowl, then gradually add to the hot mixture, whisking constantly until thickened. Stir in the raisins, then remove from the heat. Sprinkle the flour over the bottom of the pie shell, then pour in the filling. Dot with the butter. Roll out the top crust, cover the filling, crimp the edges to seal, and slash the top so the steam can escape. Bake for 35 to 40 minutes. Cool slightly and serve warm.

The Spanish people have given our American culinary world so much. As the missionaries and soldiers moved up from Mexico, they carefully brought seeds and slips of plants they had found there. In spite of their warlike zeal, there were those among them who recognized the importance of the new plant foods they were discovering along the way. And one of those was the lemon. Lemon juice enhances the flavors of everything from drinks to dessert, and one of the most classic lemon desserts is lemon pie. I like this tart and citrusy recipe, for it is rather like a chess pie, though not quite as dense in texture.

**Pastry for two 1-crust 9-inch pies
   (page 284)**

**6 large eggs plus 2 egg yolks
1 cup fresh lemon juice (5 to 6 lemons)
½ cup fresh orange juice (1 large orange)**

**1½ cups sugar
1 cup heavy cream
1 teaspoon vanilla extract
½ teaspoon grated lemon zest
Speck of salt**

Preheat the oven to 425° F. Roll out the pastry and line two 9-inch pie pans. Prick the pie shells all over with a fork. Bake for 3 minutes. Prick again and pat the pastry up the sides of the pan with the back of a fork if it is slipping (it probably will be). Bake 2 minutes longer, then remove from the oven to cool.

Meanwhile, prepare the filling. Slowly beat together the eggs, lemon juice, orange juice, sugar, cream, vanilla, lemon zest, and salt until the mixture is combined but no bubbles or froth has formed. Pour the mixture into the baked shells and bake 30 to 35 minutes, or until the filling is deep golden on top. Cool thoroughly on a rack before serving.

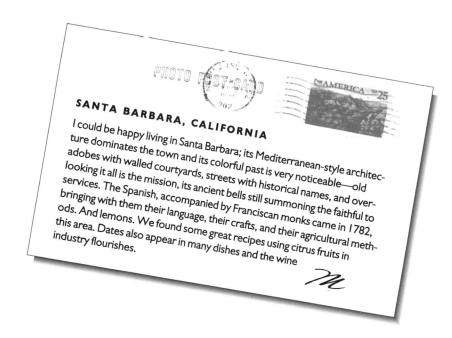

PHOTO POST CARD

SANTA BARBARA, CALIFORNIA

I could be happy living in Santa Barbara; its Mediterranean-style architecture dominates the town and its colorful past is very noticeable—old adobes with walled courtyards, streets with historical names, and overlooking it all is the mission, its ancient bells still summoning the faithful to services. The Spanish, accompanied by Franciscan monks came in 1782, bringing with them their language, their crafts, and their agricultural methods. And lemons. We found some great recipes using citrus fruits in this area. Dates also appear in many dishes and the wine industry flourishes.

M

Putting
THINGS BY

*B*EFORE THE CIVIL WAR, most of a woman's year was spent preserving food for her family. Drying and salting was an early way to keep fish, meat, fruit, and vegetables for a long period, and salt cod was a prized commodity on the East Coast, as were dried apples and cured smoked pork cuts.

Foods immersed in a brine, such as corned beef and kraut, were also popular. Preserving with vinegar and sugar was another way to plan for winter's barrenness. Stone or glassware jars were in use by 1820 and Mason jars appeared in 1858. The War Between the States accelerated the need for tin can goods, in their infancy in the 1840s, with the cans made by hand by tinsmiths. By 1870, we were consuming thirty million cans of food annually.

I grew up during a period when housewives found it an absolute necessity to preserve the food they raised. During World War II market shelves were often bare and when something rare, like canned peaches, came in they were rationed. Canned corned beef, smoked oysters, caviar, and anchovies—well, they were luxuries almost beyond my young girl's comprehension. If any of us groused about having to forgo pineapple or some such frivolous thing, my father would frown and say, "Just remember the poor boys down there in those submarines; they need the food worse than we do." He was right, but part of me childishly envied those diners at the bottom of the Pacific.

To make up for what was unavailable in the stores, everybody "put food by." From wild pheasant to ground cherries, women canned their hearts out. Preserving food was a skill that we all possessed, just as we knew how to iron a shirt—everyone's mother did it, we watched, we did it.

After I was married and doing my own preserving, I discovered I loved doing it and I was so proud of the results. Rows of shining canned tomatoes, applesauce, strawberry jam, preserves, and vegetables of all kinds lined the shelves; I almost hated to eat any of it since it was so pretty.

Even today I still do the special things, such as soups, fruit butters, special jellies, chutneys, and a favorite pickle or two.

*B*lueberry Butter *A*pple Ketchup *S*trawberry Sun Preserves *E*lderberry Jelly
*R*ose Geranium Jelly *Q*ueen Anne's Lace Jelly *B*lueberry Syrup *A*pple Chutney *T*omato Chutney
*P*ennsylvania Dutch Dried Corn *B*read-and-Butter Pickles for Threshing Day
*P*reserved Apple Pie Filling and Crumb Topping *A*mish Mincemeat

BLUEBERRY BUTTER

MAKES 8 PINTS

*Fruit butters are almost a thing of the past; you will still find them in some specialty food shops,
but they are rather costly to buy. Butters are a type of preserve, made with less sugar than jams or jellies and cooked
down very slowly. The mixture is thick and needs watching so it won't burn. If you have a Flame Tamer
(this is a perforated metal pad, available at cookware specialty stores), place it on the top of the burner and cook the
butter on low. You certainly can make this butter without the tamer, but be vigilant; the spicy deep
blue butter, slathered on hot biscuits (page 119), will be worth it.*

8 cups fresh blueberries	**1 teaspoon ground allspice**
8 large cooking apples, such	**1 teaspoon ground mace**
as Granny Smith, Summer	**1 teaspoon grated nutmeg**
Transparent, or Lodi (see Note)	**Fresh lemon juice to taste**
8 cups sugar	

In a large deep pan over medium-high heat, combine the blueberries, apples, sugar, allspice, mace, and nutmeg. Bring to a boil, then lower the heat and simmer, uncovered, for 1 hour, stirring occasionally. Cook until the mixture becomes thick; this time varies. Let the mixture cool slightly, taste, and add a bit of lemon juice for tartness, if needed. Transfer to the bowl of a food processor and puree until smooth. (You may need to do this in batches.)

To freeze, transfer the blueberry mixture to eight 1-pint freezing containers. Cool completely, cover, and freeze.

To can, return the blueberry mixture to the cooking pot and bring to a boil over medium-low heat, watching it carefully so it doesn't burn. Ladle into hot sterilized pint jars, wipe the top of the jars with a damp paper towel, and top with hot sterilized lids and rings and screw closed. Process in a hot water bath for 15 minutes, counting the time after the water has returned to a rolling boil.

Remove the jars from the hot water and cool on a towel-lined rack. Be sure the top seal has taken—it will be sunken in. Store in a dark place.

NOTE: *Summer Transparent apples (sometimes called Yellow Transparent) will be in season the same time as the blueberries. This is a very old Russian apple, brought here in 1870. It is pale green, with a tender skin, and makes the very best apple pie and applesauce—it is a favorite with the Amish here in the Midwest. If you can't find this apple, ask for Lodi—one of its parents was the Transparent, and while larger, it is similar in flavor, color, and form. These are not eating apples, nor do they keep well, but they are quite wonderful for cooking.*

APPLE KETCHUP

MAKES 1 PINT

*Well, do we spell it catsup or ketchup? Food historians speculate it derives from the Chinese
word "kôe-chiap" and meant the brine of pickled fish or shellfish. But in England in 1711, the word appeared in
print and was spelled "ketchup." The British took these exotic names and used them for their own pickled
condiments of anchovies or oysters that were popular at that time.
Cookbooks of the last century abound with unusual ketchup recipes—mussel ketchup, walnut ketchup, oyster
ketchup, and so on. So this apple ketchup really sounds pretty conventional after all.
Only it isn't. It resembles a thick chunky dark applesauce and should be served as a relish with roasts—
pork roast or ham springs immediately to mind. Seasoned with cloves, cinnamon, allspice, plus horseradish, it has a
lot more dash than ketchup. But I don't think it would be good with French fries.*

6 large firm tart unpeeled cooking apples, cored and cut into eighths	½ teaspoon dry mustard
	½ teaspoon ground cinnamon
1 medium onion, finely minced	½ teaspoon ground allspice
1 cup distilled white vinegar	½ teaspoon salt
½ cup sugar	¼ cup prepared vinegar-based
½ teaspoon freshly ground black pepper	(not creamy) horseradish
½ teaspoon ground cloves	

Place the apples in a large heavy pot and add about 2 cups water to cover. Bring to a boil, then lower the heat and simmer, uncovered, until the apples are soft and the water has mostly evaporated, about 15 minutes.

Let the mixture cool slightly, drain off any excess water, and puree the apples in a food processor until fairly smooth—the peel will be finely textured, which is what you want. Return the puree to the cooking pot. Add the remaining ingredients to the puree, heat to a boil, then reduce the heat to low and simmer, uncovered, for 1 hour longer. Cool and refrigerate.

travel Notes FROM THE FAR WEST

Driving up the coast toward Oregon and Washington, a wild naturalness prevails. This time of the year, the beaches are empty and gray whales swim by on their way to Mexico. The ocean has left dramatic inroads in the rocks where oysters and crabs flourish in icy isolation. We feasted on chinook salmon and panfried Yaquina oysters whenever we saw them listed on the menu, which, fortunately for us, was quite often.

When the first trappers from Canada arrived here, they found Indians who lived quite well, since the land, unlike arid California, provided wild fruits, berries, and nuts in abundance, and the streams were so filled with salmon that during migration all the Indians had to do was stand at any rise in the river and club them as they leaped up the rapids.

Fashion and fur were the big motivation to come to this part of the country. Beaver, mink,

STRAWBERRY SUN PRESERVES

MAKES 2 ½ TO 3 CUPS

My mother occasionally made strawberry preserves this way, more for the experience than practicality, I think. However, during the years when women had to use wood and coal stoves in the summer, letting the sun provide the cooking heat was good thinking.
One thing I especially like about this recipe is that the berries remain whole. It is an especially good jam to use for strawberry trifle. You will note that no pectin is used; Mother Nature does all the work. Because of the variation in the sun's temperature, the humidity, and even the wind, the length of time this process takes is not precise. I find two days in the sun generally assures the texture of jam I prefer. You will need two ¼-inch-thick pieces of glass or plastic.

**4 cups whole strawberries,
cleaned and hulled
2½ cups sugar**

**2 teaspoons fresh lemon juice
Speck of salt**

Gently combine all of the ingredients in a heavy 2-quart saucepan. Cover and bring to a boil over medium-high heat. Lower the heat to medium and cook 8 minutes, stirring occasionally. Wipe down the sides of the pan twice with a damp paper towel wrapped around the blade of a long knife. This removes any undissolved sugar crystals that might cause the jam to "sugar" later on. Skim off the foam and discard. Pour the jam into 2 deep platters approximately 9 × 14 inches. Refrigerate overnight.

The next morning (it should be a hot and sunny day; if not, keep the berries refrigerated until the weather changes), cover each platter with a piece of glass or plastic, propping it open on one end with a wedge of paper to allow the moisture to evaporate. Loosely cover the platters with a layer of cheesecloth to keep out insects. Place in a location that remains sunny all day. Allow the berries to remain outside until sunset. Refrigerate them overnight.

The next day, set the platters outside again as above. Allow the jam to stay in the sun all day, then check for thickness. If it is too thin for your taste, refrigerate overnight and set outside for a third day. When the jam is thickened, it is ready to eat. This recipe makes such a small amount, I recommend you not bother to process it, but transfer the preserves to a jar and store them in the refrigerator for immediate use.

NOTE: *Plastic wrap will not work in place of the glass; the covering must be rigid enough to prop open.*

muskrat, and weasels that turned into ermine in the winter provided the pelts that were in such demand in American and European cities. Lewis and Clark had mapped out the Oregon Trail in 1805, and John Jacob Astor began white settlement of the region when he opened a fur trading post at Astoria, Oregon, in 1811. Homesteaders from all over traveled the Oregon Trail, lured by the promise of free land—many were from the Midwest, of English, German, Swedish, and Scottish ancestry, and good farmers, too. After the Civil War ended in 1865, even more settlers arrived, hoping to find a better life than they had left in the war-torn South. The West has always been bright with promise. Russians migrated across the Bering Strait and Chinese, Japanese, and Mexicans emigrated north out of California—it is no wonder we see such a conglomeration of foodstuffs at the Pike Place Market in Seattle—it is a mini West Coast United Nations.

ELDERBERRY JELLY

MAKES APPROXIMATELY 7 CUPS

*If you are lucky enough to find some elderberries before the birds have their happy feast, take the
opportunity to make this most elegant of jellies. I have recently planted my own elderberries at the end of our garden,
so I will not have to drive around the countryside looking for wild ones. The bushes have fragrant trusses
of blooms and are very decorative, as well as providing the tiny purple fruits that are so prized for pies and jellies.
To remove the berries from the stems, use a wide-toothed comb. And be very gentle.*

3 pounds elderberries	**½ cup lemon juice**
7 cups sugar	**2 packages powdered pectin**

Remove the stems from the elderberries. In a large heavy kettle, crush the fruit with a potato masher one
layer at a time and gently heat until juices start to form. Cover and simmer 15 minutes, stirring occasionally.

Transfer the cooked fruit to a dampened jelly bag or a large colander or sieve that has been lined with
several thicknesses of dampened cheesecloth. Let drip into a large bowl or measuring cup that will hold at
least 3 cups. When the dripping has almost stopped, gently press or squeeze the bag. Measure the juice; if
you have slightly less than 3 cups of juice, add a bit more water (or apple juice) to the pulp in the bag and
squeeze again.

Pour the juice into a 6- or 8-quart saucepan. Stir in the sugar (be sure to use the full amount!) and
lemon juice. Bring to a full boil over high heat, stirring constantly. Stir in the pectin all at once and bring the
mixture back to a full rolling boil (a boil that cannot be stirred down), stirring constantly. Boil hard for 1
minute, continuing to stir constantly. Remove from the heat and skim off the foam with a large spoon.
Immediately ladle into hot glasses or jars, leaving ½-inch headspace at the top of the glass or ⅛-inch space
at the top of jars. With a damp cloth, remove any spills from the inner sides, rims, and threads of the jars.
Process 15 minutes in a hot water bath, counting the time after the water has again come to a rolling boil
after the jars are immersed. Remove to a towel-lined rack. Store in a cool place.

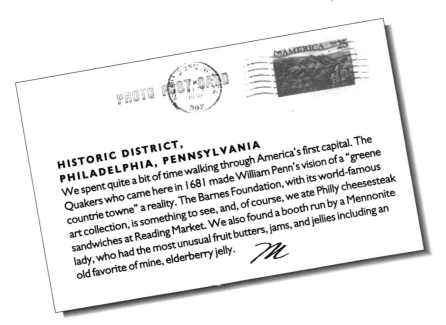

**HISTORIC DISTRICT,
PHILADELPHIA, PENNSYLVANIA**
We spent quite a bit of time walking through America's first capital. The
Quakers who came here in 1681 made William Penn's vision of a "greene
countrie towne" a reality. The Barnes Foundation, with its world-famous
art collection, is something to see, and, of course, we ate Philly cheesesteak
sandwiches at Reading Market. We also found a booth run by a Mennonite
lady, who had the most unusual fruit butters, jams, and jellies including an
old favorite of mine, elderberry jelly.

ROSE GERANIUM JELLY

MAKES APPROXIMATELY EIGHT 8-OUNCE JARS

*Scented geraniums were favorite houseplants at the turn of the century, and in many old
recipes their leaves were used to flavor foods such as angel food cake and cream-based puddings.
This jelly is very attractive, with an intriguing flavor.*

4 cups bottled apple juice
½ cup fresh lemon juice
10 cups sugar
8 large fresh rose geranium leaves

½ teaspoon butter
1 package powdered pectin
Few drops of red food coloring

In a large kettle, combine the apple juice, lemon juice, sugar, and rose geranium leaves. Bring to a full boil over high heat, stirring constantly. Boil 1 minute. Add the pectin all at once and continue to stir and boil hard for an additional minute. Remove from the heat.

Skim off the foam and remove the geranium leaves with tongs and discard. Tint the jelly a pale pink with food coloring. Ladle into hot sterilized jelly glasses, leaving a ¼-inch space at the top of the jars. Seal with sterilized rings and caps and process 5 minutes in a boiling water bath, counting the time after the water again comes to a boil after the jars are immersed. Remove to a towel-lined rack. Store in a cool place.

QUEEN ANNE'S LACE JELLY

MAKES FIVE 8-OUNCE JARS

*This wasn't an uncommon recipe 100 years ago and the English still use elderberry and Queen Anne's
lace flowers to flavor some of their desserts. Queen Anne's Lace has other names, including Lady's Needlework,
Devil's Oatmeal, and the charming Irish name of Gypsy's Umbrella, which is what my mother called it.*

4 cups water
18 large Queen Anne's lace flower heads
¼ cup fresh lemon juice

1 package powdered pectin
3½ cups plus 2 tablespoons sugar
Red food coloring (optional)

Bring the water to a boil and remove from the heat. Add the flower heads, pushing them down into the water; cover and steep for 30 minutes. Remove the lid and let the mixture cool slightly, about 15 minutes. Strain the liquid through a dampened cheesecloth, discarding the flower heads.

Measure out 3 cups of the liquid into a 4- to 6- quart pan. Add the lemon juice and the pectin and bring to a rolling boil, stirring constantly. (It is very important to keep stirring.) Add the sugar, stirring constantly, and cook until the mixture returns to a rolling boil. Boil 1 minute longer. Remove from the heat. Add enough red food coloring, if using, to tint the jelly pink, then skim off any foam. Pour into sterilized jars, leaving ¼-inch space at the top. With a damp cloth, remove any spills from the rims and threads of the jars. Process in a hot water bath for 5 minutes, counting the time after the water has returned to a rolling boil. Remove to a towel-lined rack. Store in a cool place.

205

BLUEBERRY SYRUP

MAKES 4 CUPS

My grandmother Manahan made fruit syrups all summer long, which she then used on waffles and pancakes until maple syrup was available again in the spring. I used to go blueberry picking with her; to make the time pass more quickly, she would insist we sing Methodist hymns as we stripped the large blueberries off the tall bushes. I never eat blueberries without thinking of "Mine Eyes Have Seen the Glory of the Coming of the Lord." I like this vividly colored syrup with Pavlova or over homemade ice cream.

4 cups blueberries, stemmed and washed	3 cups sugar
3 cups water	1½ tablespoons fresh lemon juice
1½ teaspoons grated orange rind	¼ teaspoon salt

Place the blueberries in a saucepan and mash well with a potato masher. Add 1 cup water and the orange rind. Bring to a boil and simmer for 5 minutes. Strain through a fine sieve, pressing the berries with a rubber spatula. You will have about 2½ cups of liquid.

Combine the remaining water with the sugar in a saucepan. Bring to a boil and boil until the mixture reaches about 260° F. on a candy thermometer. Add the blueberry liquid and boil 1 minute more. Skim if necessary. Cool. Stir in the lemon juice and salt. Freeze or pour into sterilized jars and place in a hot water bath for 30 minutes.

APPLE CHUTNEY

MAKES 4 PINTS

Chutneys, a fruity and spicy mélange or relish, are often served with Indian foods. The British adored chutneys and now they are used as a counterpoint with meat dishes from any country. I serve this aromatic mixture with poultry or pork in little ramekins right on the dinner plate.

2 pounds cooking apples, such as Wolf River or Cortland, peeled, cored, and coarsely chopped	1 quart cider vinegar
2 pounds ripe tomatoes, peeled, cored, and coarsely chopped	2 tablespoons mustard seed
2 cups (about 3 medium) onions, coarsely chopped	1 tablespoon curry powder
1 pound seedless raisins	2 teaspoons salt
2 pounds brown sugar	1 teaspoon ground allspice
	1 teaspoon ground coriander
	1 teaspoon ground cumin
	1 teaspoon ground ginger
	½ teaspoon ground cloves

In a large stockpot, combine all of the ingredients. Bring the mixture to a boil, lower the heat, and simmer uncovered for 1½ to 2 hours, or until the chutney is thick but is still a bit runny. Ladle into sterilized pint jars and freeze or process in a hot water bath for 10 minutes.

Tomato Chutney

MAKES 4 PINTS

*Chutneys, those spicy relishes that originated in India, are as diverse in flavor as the country
is in climate and customs. The word chutney is an anglicized version of the Hindi word chatni, or pickle, and
they first became popular during the British Colonial rule in India. The British sea captains spread this
delightful dish around the world, a fine contribution to society indeed!*
*Unlike syrupy dark commercial mixtures, this chunky apple-tomato–based version is an inviting
red color, dotted with golden raisins and sensitively spiced with garlic (typical of Sri Lanka), crystallized ginger,
and allspice. It makes a great gift, if you can bear to part with it.*

9 medium-size ripe tomatoes, seeded,
  peeled, and chopped
5 tart apples (Granny Smith), cored,
  peeled, and finely chopped
4 cups cider vinegar
1½ cups packed light brown sugar
1 cup chopped onions
1 cup seedless golden raisins
¼ cup chopped red bell pepper

¼ cup chopped green bell pepper
¼ cup finely minced crystallized ginger
2 large garlic cloves, minced
3 teaspoons curry powder
  (or more to taste)
2 teaspoons salt
½ teaspoon coarsely ground pepper
1 teaspoon ground allspice
1 teaspoon ground cinnamon

In a large kettle, combine all the ingredients. Bring to a boil, reduce the heat, and simmer, uncovered, over
low heat until the mixture thickens, about 2½ hours. Stir frequently to prevent scorching. Ladle the chutney into hot sterilized jars, leaving ½-inch headspace. Adjust the lids to seal. Process in boiling water bath
for 5 minutes, counting the time from when the water comes again to a rolling boil.

   NOTE: *The chutney can also be frozen if you prefer.*

Crockery conserve jar and dish

PENNSYLVANIA DUTCH DRIED CORN

MAKES 6 PINTS

This is one of those special old recipes that came out of a time when it was easier to dry food than to preserve it any other way. The drying seems to intensify the sweetness of the corn, and even today, this is a very appealing dish. The dried corn resembles pale brownish Grape-Nuts when it is finished; it is necessary to soak it in water to reconstitute it before cooking. This recipe came to me from Marjorie Meyer of the Teetor House, a very fine bed and breakfast in Hagerstown, Indiana.

2 dozen very large ears fresh sweet corn (you will need 16 cups corn, cut off the ear)
1½ cups sugar
2 cups half-and-half

¼ teaspoon coarse (not iodized) salt

Butter
Salt and pepper to taste

Husk the corn, remove the silk thoroughly, and cut it off the cob with a sharp knife, scraping the cobs with the back of the knife to remove all the corn and milk. Transfer the corn to a heavy large kettle and add the sugar, half-and-half, and salt. Stir to combine, bring the mixture to a boil, reduce the heat to low, and simmer, uncovered, for 20 minutes. If all the liquid has not been absorbed, raise the heat to medium-high, and watching it carefully, cook and stir until all the half-and-half has evaporated. You don't want the corn to brown; when it begins to sizzle, you should remove the pan from the heat.

Preheat the oven to 200° F.

Divide the corn between 2 jelly roll pans, spreading it out evenly on the pans. Bake it for 18 to 24 hours. Stir it occasionally, about every 3 to 4 hours, to keep it from sticking together and to the pan. (Remove from the oven during the night and start baking again the next day.) The length of time it takes to dry depends on the amount of rainfall, the age of the corn, and so on. Mine has never taken 24 hours to dry. The corn will be golden brown and rattle when it has dried completely.

Remove from the oven, cool completely, and transfer to coffee cans or plastic containers and freeze until needed.

To prepare the corn for a meal, allow ½ cup dried corn per person and place in a medium saucepan. Cover completely with water and allow to stand for 4 hours. Drain off any excess water and heat gently, adding butter and salt and pepper to taste.

$\mathcal{B}$READ-AND-BUTTER PICKLES FOR THRESHING DAY

MAKES 10 PINTS

As a little girl, I was always thrilled to be taken to my grandparents' farm for threshing day. The big threshing machine was moved into the barnyard, the horses brought in the sheaves of wheat, the wheat was separated out and stored in the granary, and the straw spewed out into a big pile. The straw stack was so much fun to slide down and into, but it was actually a forbidden thing to do, as our tracks would hold water, which caused the straw to rot. I am embarrassed (sort of) to admit my brother and I occasionally played in it anyway when we thought no one was watching.

But threshing day was also memorable because of the food that my grandmother had been preparing for perhaps a week in advance. There would be at least twelve men to feed for two meals, so it was a big project. I considered it a privilege to peel potatoes, cut the pies, and fill the water glasses. One thing she always served, and indeed prided herself on, were her bread-and-butter pickles, which she also gave as gifts to her special friends at church. We would hint about having them on other occasions, but she would shake her head regretfully and say, "No, those are for threshing day and to give away." I always wondered why she didn't make more of them. Her recipe would now be well more than 100 years old, for she'd gotten it from her mother.

25 slender medium cucumbers	1 cup water
3 medium onions, as big around as the cucumbers	2 teaspoons mustard seed
	1 tablespoon celery seed
2 medium red bell peppers	1 teaspoon coarsely ground pepper
1/2 cup coarse (not iodized) salt	1 teaspoon ground ginger
2 cups cider vinegar	1 teaspoon ground cinnamon
2 cups sugar	1/2 teaspoon ground turmeric

Scrub the cucumbers with a brush and slice them 1/8 to 1/4 inch thick. Peel and slice the onions. Halve the red bell peppers and remove the seeds and ribs, then slice into strips. Place the vegetables in deep pans in layers, sprinkling each layer with salt. Allow the vegetables to stand for 3 hours, then drain.

Combine the vinegar, sugar, water, mustard and celery seeds, pepper, ginger, cinnamon, and turmeric in a deep kettle and bring to a boil over high heat. Add the cucumbers, onions, and red bell peppers and bring again to a boil. Lower the heat to medium and cook the mixture for 5 minutes. Using tongs, pack the pickles tightly in 10 hot sterilized pint jars. Ladle in the hot brine, leaving 1/2-inch headspace. Wipe the rims of the jars, cover with the lids, screw tight, and process in a hot water bath for 10 minutes, counting the time from when the water comes to a boil again after the jars have been totally immersed. Remove from the water and cool on a towel-lined rack. Store in a dark place.

$\mathcal{P}$RESERVED APPLE PIE FILLING AND CRUMB TOPPING

MAKES 6 QUARTS

In late July, the Summer Transparent apples appear in the farmer's markets—
small and green, they make out-of-this-world applesauce and pies. The trees bear heavily and the apples do not
keep well—what to do? Preserve the rascals with a mixture of sugar, spice, and thickening and you
can have nearly instant apple pie all winter long. Line a pie pan with pastry, add one jar of filling, and top with a second
crust or the crumb topping. After canning, the fruit may settle a bit, leaving space at the
top of the jar. That is perfectly all right, and the apples are safe to use. Each quart will make one 9-inch pie.

FRUIT
6 pounds Summer Transparent apples,
  peeled, cored, and sliced
6 tablespoons Fruit Fresh (see Note)

SYRUP
4½ cups granulated sugar
1 cup cornstarch
3 tablespoons fresh lemon juice
1 tablespoon salt
4 teaspoons ground cinnamon
1½ teaspoons grated nutmeg
10 cups water

CRUMB TOPPING
1¼ cups all-purpose flour
1¼ cups regular or quick-cooking oatmeal
¾ cup packed light brown sugar
1 teaspoon ground cinnamon
¾ cup (1½ sticks) butter,
  at room temperature

In a large bowl, toss the prepared apples with the Fruit Fresh. Tightly pack sterilized quart jars with the apple slices to within ½ inch of the rim.

In a large saucepan, mix the sugar, cornstarch, lemon juice, salt, cinnamon, nutmeg, and water; bring to a boil. Immediately ladle the hot syrup into the filled jars, leaving ½-inch headspace. Wipe off the top of the jar with a clean damp cloth. Top with sterilized lids and rings and process the quarts for 25 minutes in a hot water bath, starting to count the time after the water has returned to a boil after the jars have been added.

Remove the jars from the water and place on a towel-covered rack in a draft-free place. Allow to cool completely. Check to make sure the seal has taken, then store in a dark, cool place.

For the topping: In a medium bowl, mix the flour, oatmeal, brown sugar, and cinnamon together. Cut in the butter with a pastry blender or 2 forks until the mixture resembles coarse crumbs. This can be made in advance and stored indefinitely in the refrigerator until needed.

To make a pie: Pour one quart of filling into an unbaked 9-inch pie shell, top with half the crumb topping and bake at 350° F. for 45 to 55 minutes, or until the juices bubble up in the middle. To make an apple crisp: Omit the crust and pour 2 quarts of the pie filling into a greased 9 × 13-inch dish. Sprinkle the topping over and bake at 350° F. for 35 to 45 minutes, or until the top is bubbling in the middle.

NOTE: *Fruit Fresh is a powdered ascorbic acid that prevents fresh fruit from darkening. It is available in the canning-preserving area of the supermarket.*

mish Mincemeat

MAKES 5 QUARTS

This recipe also appears in Cooking from Quilt Country, *and I use it again without apologies, for I haven't found one better. The cherries are a Michigan custom that makes it very special. One quart of mincemeat is enough for a 9-inch pie. You might want to serve it with Brandy Sauce (page 264) for an ultimate dessert experience or slightly warmed over ice cream or as a trifle or strudel filling (page 275). It can be canned or frozen and keeps indefinitely.*

3½ to 3¾ pounds beef shank,
    2-inch crosscut, trimmed
½ pound ground suet
    (have the butcher do this)
2½ quarts chopped cooking apples, such as
    Cortland, McIntosh, or Northern Spy
2 pounds seedless golden raisins
One 10- to 16-ounce box dried currants
¼ pound citron, diced
2 tablespoons diced candied orange peel
3 cups apple cider
2 cups sugar

2 cups light corn syrup
¾ cup cider vinegar
Grated zest and juice of 1 lemon
4 teaspoons ground cinnamon
2 teaspoons salt
2 teaspoons grated nutmeg
2 teaspoons ground allspice
2 teaspoons ground ginger
1½ teaspoons ground cloves
Two 1-pound cans pitted sour
    cherries, drained

In a large kettle or pressure cooker, cook the meat until tender (see note). While the meat is still warm, grind it coarsely or use a food processor to shred it. (A food processor can also be used for chopping the apples.) In a large, deep pot, combine all the ingredients except the cherries. Simmer, uncovered, until the mixture is juicy but not runny, about 1½ to 2 hours. Add the cherries for the last 15 minutes of cooking. Let cool. Mincemeat not used within 3 days can be frozen for up to 6 months.

NOTE: *The shank is a very flavorful cut, but it requires long cooking. A pressure cooker is ideal for this and should be used according to directions. An alternative method is to preheat the oven to 325°F., place the shanks in a large roaster, and add enough warm water to cover the meat completely. Bake for 3 hours, or until the meat is tender, making sure there is always plenty of liquid in the pan.*

Winter's
PLEASURES

RETURNING HOME FROM THE West in late fall, Dick immediately starts fall chores by removing the frost-tattered dahlias from the dining room window boxes and storing the roots. He replaces the window box pots with flowering kale and surrounds them with pine boughs. The cats follow him around, their fur fluffed out to forestall the chill.

I've been making Christmas cookies and candy since November. I like to start early in the morning and watch the rising sun's rays from my kitchen window, streaking the cold sky first blue, then purple, then with an explosion of pink. My mother said that whenever the sky was pink in the morning that meant that the angels were making Christmas cookies. And if there is a heaven where angels make cookies, my mother will be there, supervising.

At his study desk, Dick muses over the route and our appointment calendar and suggests this would be a good time to head for the Southwest since both Santa Fe and San Antonio are known for their Christmas activities. I am eager to experiment with southwestern chilies and my friends in Santa Fe make promises about the fantastic food, including heirloom recipes, we will enjoy there—I believe, I believe!

To decorate the house, we cut pine, juniper, and arborvitae branches in the garden; as we gather materials for the swags and wreaths, great flocks of geese move against the sky in formal unison. During the night, the snow comes silently, converting our garden into pale white shapes of spheres and cones. Going out to fill the bird feeders, the snow's purity and the garden's stillness feel like a benediction.

The gifts are wrapped and the house decorated for our return just before Christmas; I leave with a happy heart.

Warming Foods from the
SOUTHWEST

BEFORE I BEGAN my research and travels for this book I was well aware of the important contributions the English and Germans had made to our food heritage. But I must confess I was surprised to see how persuasive and wide-ranging the Spanish influence has been. Not only has the cuisine of an entire region been seasoned with the panoply of Spanish flavorings, but a host of now indispensable foods were originally introduced in this country by early Spanish settlers.

When the Spanish arrived, they found the Indian inhabitants eating corn, beans, squash, and game, including wild turkey and mountain sheep. These foods still form the backbone of southwestern food today. However, the additions of new foods, such as chilies, which were a Spanish contribution, carried from the Aztec and Mayan civilization in Mexico add intricate shades of flavor.

What we call Mexican food is everywhere from highway diners to fine restaurants. We ate our fill of chili con carne, [called a "bowl of red" in Texas], red salsa, and always for dessert smooth soothing flan. Since Mexican or southwestern food is now served in every state of the Union, including Hawaii, we mistakenly think of it is a new trendy cuisine. Ummm, 'fraid not. Most of these recipes have been around for centuries; Anasazi beans and tortillas are as much a part of our cooking heritage as Boston baked beans and Indian pudding.

When eating out, it is wise to ask which chili is hotter, and that is a good question to ask your grocer when you shop for ingredients for the sauces. Two hundred varieties of chilies are grown in New Mexico alone, but only about twenty-five of them are commonly used. Other popular seasonings are saffron, cilantro, anise, and pumpkin seeds, which fortunately are readily available across the country or via mail order. Pine nuts add great texture. These creamy subtle kernels grow on the piñon tree, which is also the state tree of New Mexico.

Here in the Southwest, four different cultures and foodways have come together in a marvelous symbiosis—Pueblo, Spanish, Mexican, and Anglo. All have contributed their own heirloom recipes.

Quesadillas Melon and Strawberry Compote with Ginger Chili Con Carne Cactus Stew
Mike Acosta's Red Chili Sauce Birria Brisket Chili Baked Pork Spareribs Anasazi Pot Beans
Tossed Greens with Guacamole Dressing Orange-Date Salad with Pumpkin Seeds
Fresh Tomato and Cucumber Salad Almond and Apricot Compote Southwest Flan Sopaipillas

QUESADILLAS

MAKES ABOUT 40 PIECES

This hors d'oeuvre is a favorite around San Antonio and is served in bars, restaurants, and at private parties. The filling can be made in advance, which is especially helpful. Be sure to use flour tortillas, not corn, which will taste too coarse and raw. This recipe appears in many local San Antonio cookbooks.

Five 10-inch or eight 7-inch flour tortillas
½ cup (1 stick) butter, softened
1 pound Monterey Jack cheese, grated
¼ cup finely minced onion
One 2-ounce jar red pimiento, drained
   and minced

One 4-ounce can mild green chilies, drained
   and minced
2 tablespoons minced cilantro
1 teaspoon ground cumin
½ teaspoon chili powder

Preheat the oven to 400° F.

Spread one side of each tortilla with the butter and place on an ungreased baking sheet, buttered side up. Bake 5 minutes, or until barely golden. (They may be toasted up to 2 hours ahead and kept covered.)

In a medium bowl, toss together the remaining ingredients. Sprinkle evenly over the toasted tortillas. Bake 5 to 8 minutes, or until the cheese is bubbly. Transfer the quesadillas to a cutting surface and cut into wedges. Serve hot.

MELON AND STRAWBERRY COMPOTE WITH GINGER

SERVES 6

Melons flourish in Texas and are shipped all over the country. Combined with fresh strawberries and topped with a mixture of sour cream, honey, and crystallized ginger, this compote can be served as a first course for brunch or as a dessert. Ginger appears frequently in Texas cookery, a legacy of the large group of Germans who settled there in the 1800s.

1 ripe melon (cantaloupe or honeydew or
   both), rind removed and cut into chunks or
   balls (approximately 4 cups)
2 cups hulled and halved fresh strawberries
½ cup orange juice
2 tablespoons packed light brown sugar

1 cup sour cream or vanilla yogurt
¼ cup honey
3 tablespoons finely chopped crystallized ginger

Garnish: fresh mint leaves

Place the melon chunks and strawberries in a 9 × 13-inch dish. In a measuring cup, combine the orange juice and brown sugar and pour over the fruit. Marinate the melon in the refrigerator for at least 2 hours, stirring occasionally. Combine the sour cream or vanilla yogurt, honey, and ginger in a small bowl and refrigerate for about 30 minutes. Spoon the fruit into individual serving bowls and top with the sour cream mixture. Garnish with fresh mint leaves.

TO SAVE TIME, we decided to fly to the Southwest instead of taking the van as we sought out our southwestern recipes. Looking down at the Grand Canyon, dramatically forbidding from the air, I wondered what those early explorers thought when they first encountered it. Did they wish they'd never left home?

Arriving in Albuquerque, New Mexico, we rented a car and drove to the Acoma Pueblo, a reservation of 2,500 Native Americans. A most commanding sight, the nearly 400-foot-high mesa rears out of the desert, monolithic and primitive. The Indians who lived on top (some say since the time of Christ) thought they were safe from invasion, but the Spanish soldiers ultimately wore them down and the missionaries converted them to Christianity. It's a haunting place.

We reached Santa Fe in the late afternoon, eager for a pitcher of margaritas. Stopping at the southeastern corner of the gaily decorated plaza before going on to our hotel, we found the marker that reads THE END OF THE SANTA FE TRAIL. "I thought we'd never make it," murmured Dick wryly. The winter sun felt good on our faces and looking around the colorful plaza and seeing the Palace of Governors and the Cathedral of St. Francis (which played an important role in Willa Cather's Death Comes for the Archbishop), I began to worry that the one week we had planned for the Santa Fe area would not be enough. We wanted to attend some of the winter dances held by the Indian Pueblos and many of the churches present concerts as well; December is a good time to be in this city where Indian, Spanish, and Anglo mingled traditions give Santa Fe its distinctive flavor.

We were dazzled by the regional landscape: golden desert stretching on for miles, with its army of stalwart cactus, then suddenly enfolding itself into deep mountain ranges. The hills are slashed with red-walled canyons and dotted with ancient pueblos; we are constantly reminded of long-gone civilizations.

Some of the early southwestern Indian tribes lived in permanent villages like those of Mexico and they even had an irrigation system to water their crops. These settled Indians' well-designed and sturdily built adobe apartments were several stories high and give us a glimpse of an organized orderly society.

The descendants of some of those early Spanish are still there and they have retained many Spanish ways; Santa Fe's cookery (as well as New Mexico's) still has Spanish elements that distinguish it from other types of Mexican cookery that we encounter in the Southwest. Blazing swags of red chili ristras are evident everywhere, and hot discussions about the merits of each variety of chili is a favorite local pastime. The combination of Santa Fe's high altitude, warm days, and cool nights, plus the intense light give the Santa Fe chilies their distinctive flavor. When combined with local corn tortillas in a myriad of ways, the food here is distinctly not Tex-Mex nor Mex-Cal. Santa Fe has a cuisine all its own. When we walk back to our hotel after dinner, the fragrance of burning piñon wood scents the night air and church bells toll in the night.

CHILI CON CARNE

SERVES 4 TO 6

In the Midwest, I grew up thinking chili was a ground meat and tomato soup, seasoned with chili powder. When I was first introduced to the authentic chili of the Southwest by a Texan friend, Pauline Watson from Ralls, it was a whole new taste sensation. The texture is so different—chunks of meat, no beans, and the sauce is rich, dark, and silky. This recipe calls for chili puree, and if you've not made it before, it is a technique you will enjoy learning. The puree can be stored, tightly covered, in the refrigerator for 3 days or frozen for a month. We are able to get the dried chili pods at our local supermarkets, but if they are not available in your area, look for a Mexican market.

¼ **pound large dry New Mexico, Big Jim, or California chilies (12 to 15)**
1½ **cups boiling water**
3 **tablespoons olive oil**
2 **cups finely chopped onions**
4 **garlic cloves, minced**
1¼ **pounds lean beef, cut into** ¾**-inch cubes**

1¼ **pounds lean pork shoulder, cut into** ¾**-inch cubes**
2 **teaspoons ground cumin**
1 **teaspoon dried oregano**
1 **teaspoon salt**
4 to 5 **cups chicken or beef stock**

With scissors, snip the stems off all the dried chili pods and slit them open. Shake out as many of the seeds as possible and rinse the chilies briefly under cold running water. Snip into 1-inch pieces. Transfer to a heatproof bowl and cover with the boiling water. Cover the bowl with a lid and let this stand until the water is cool, about 2 hours, stirring them once or twice.

With a slotted spoon, transfer the softened chili pieces to a blender jar or food processor bowl. Process briefly, scraping down the sides of the jar. Add some of the soaking water and process again. Continue adding water, blending, and then scraping down the sides until the water has all been used and the chili puree is smooth. Transfer the puree to a strainer set over a bowl. Add 2 tablespoons hot tap water to the blender and puree briefly to rinse the blades and the inside. Add this residue to the puree in the strainer. Force the pureed chilies through the strainer with a stiff rubber spatula, discarding any seeds and tough bits of peel remaining in the strainer. There should be about 1¼ cups puree. If there is more, use it all. If there is less, soak, simmer, and puree additional chilies.

Heat the oil in a large stockpot over low heat. Add the onions and garlic and cook, covered, for 10 minutes, stirring once or twice. Add the beef, pork, chili puree, cumin, oregano, and salt; cook for 5 minutes, tossing and stirring often. Stir in the chicken or beef stock, raise the heat, and bring to a boil. Lower the heat, partially cover the pan, and cook, stirring occasionally, until the meat is very tender and the dish has thickened, about 2 hours. Serve in shallow bowls, accompanied by black beans or Anasazi Pot Beans (page 222) and tortillas.

CACTUS STEW

SERVES 6 TO 8

*Mike Acosta of Santa Barbara is descended from one of Santa Barbara's earliest soldier-settlers who
came here when the Presidio was founded in 1782. Mr. Acosta is in his seventies now and is renowned as much for his
knowledge of early Santa Barbara history as he is for his authentic early Santa Barbara cookery. He has been
cooking since he was in his teens, learning to make Spanish dishes from his mother. The Cactus Stew is a family recipe,
and he picks the cactus leaves from a plant in his front yard. However, the pads, as they are called, are
available across the country at Mexican groceries and at some larger supermarkets, as is masa harina, a type of corn flour.
The stew is a mellow mélange of cactus (when cooked, it is very mild in flavor
and firm in texture, like a carrot), pork, red chili sauce, and herbs. Served with rice and beans, it is a real treat.
Mr. Acosta makes his own chili sauce, but recommends the Las Palmas brand if you want to save time.*

5 nopales (cactus pads)
3 garlic cloves
¼ cup coarsely chopped cilantro
Speck of salt
2 pounds lean pork shoulder roast, cut
    into bite-size chunks
2 cups water
2 tablespoons masa harina

One 16-ounce can Las Palmas red chili sauce or
    2 cups homemade (recipe follows)
1 teaspoon dried oregano leaves
¼ teaspoon ground cumin
Salt to taste

Garnish: chopped fresh cilantro

Remove the spines from the cactus (some markets will have this already done for you), but don't peel.
Chop coarsely and transfer to a 3-quart saucepan. Add 1 garlic clove, the cilantro, and salt, cover with
water, and bring to a boil. Lower the heat and simmer, covered, for 15 minutes. Set aside in the cooking
liquid.

Meanwhile, brown the meat in a large sauté pan in its own fat, about 15 minutes. Drain off the excess
fat and discard. In a medium bowl, whisk together the water and masa harina. Blend in the chili sauce and
add to the pork. Mince the remaining 2 garlic cloves and add to the pork, along with the oregano leaves,
cumin, and salt. Cover and simmer for 20 to 30 minutes.

Remove the cactus from the cooking liquid with a slotted spoon and add to the meat mixture. Cover
the stew and simmer another 20 to 25 minutes. Garnish with cilantro.

MIKE ACOSTA'S RED CHILI SAUCE

MAKES 1 SCANT QUART

7 long dry red California or New Mexico chilies
4 cups water
3 large garlic cloves, crushed
½ teaspoon dried oregano

1 teaspoon ground cumin
Salt to taste
2 tablespoons white wine vinegar
1 tablespoon olive oil

Cut open the chilies and remove the seeds. Cut or tear the chilies into 2-inch pieces and place in a 3-quart saucepan with the water. Bring to a boil, lower the heat, cover, and simmer for 20 minutes. Remove from the heat and let stand for 1 hour.

Transfer the chilies and cooking liquid to a blender with the remaining ingredients. Puree thoroughly and store in the refrigerator in a tightly covered container until needed.

BIRRIA BRISKET

SERVES 6 TO 8

Birria is a highly seasoned stew indigenous to the mountains of central Mexico and is traditionally made with lamb. Like all good recipes, it traveled; when it crossed the border to the nearby plains where cattle were raised instead of sheep, the beef brisket was substitued for the lamb. Now we find the dish all over the Southwest and the recipe changes a bit each time. This version is cooked slowly over low heat in a mixture of chilies, red wine, and spices. The cooked shredded meat is then served in tortillas, a most happy ending.
This recipe came to me from a friend who teaches art in Santa Fe. One of her students brought the birria to lunch one day, and the whole class wanted the recipe; you'll understand why when you taste it. You may want to order the beef in advance. Also, wear rubber gloves and do not touch your face or eyes when working with the chilies if you have sensitive skin; the inner membranes are responsible for the heat.

4 dried New Mexico or California chilies (these are the large dried red ones)

2 small dried hot red chilies

4 cups water

1½ cups dry red wine

¼ cup red wine vinegar

4 garlic cloves

1½ teaspoons ground cumin

1 teaspoon dried oregano leaves

¾ teaspoon ground cinnamon

One 3-pound beef brisket, center cut, all fat removed

4 very large onions, peeled and thinly sliced

Approximately 16 warm (flour or corn) tortillas

Garnish: chopped fresh cilantro, sour cream, and lime wedges

Remove and discard the stems and seeds from both kinds of chilies. Rinse them and place in a 2-quart saucepan with the 4 cups water. Bring to a boil, cover, and let stand until the chilies are softened, about 1 hour; drain. In a food processor or blender, combine the chilies with the wine, vinegar, garlic, cumin, oregano leaves, and cinnamon and chili puree. Press through a strainer to remove the skins.

Place the meat in a 12 × 15-inch roasting pan, top with the onions, and pour the chili mixture over all. Seal the pan with foil and marinate overnight in the refrigerator.

Preheat the oven to 350° F. Cover the brisket and bake for 4 hours, or until the meat is very tender. With 2 forks, shred the meat, mixing it in with the onions and pan juices. (At this point, the mixture can be refrigerated for up to 3 days.) To reheat, cover and bake in a 350° F. oven for about 35 to 40 minutes. Serve the meat with the warmed tortillas, plus the cilantro, sour cream, and lime wedges.

MARCIA ADAMS' HEIRLOOM RECIPES

CHILI BAKED PORK SPARERIBS

SERVES 4

Using chili powder to season ribs is a titillating way to prepare pork. If you lean toward milder seasonings, use just ⅓ cup chili powder; I use the entire ⅔ cup and do not find the ribs hot, just very well seasoned. The ribs must be marinated at least 24 hours and up to 48, so plan accordingly. This is not a red sweet-and-sour saucy rib, quite the opposite. They are very tender. Pass farmer's handkerchiefs, dipped in hot water and wrung out, after the meal for cleaning up hands and mouths.

⅓ to ⅔ cup chili powder

½ cup fresh orange juice

¼ cup olive oil

2 tablespoons fresh lemon juice

3 medium garlic cloves, peeled and minced

4 teaspoons ground cumin

1 tablespoon minced orange zest

1 tablespoon honey

One 6-ounce can tomato paste

2 teaspoons dried oregano

1 teaspoon salt

1 teaspoon pepper

6 pounds pork spareribs, chine bones cracked for easier serving

In a small bowl, stir together the chili powder, orange juice, oil, lemon juice, garlic, cumin, orange zest, honey, tomato paste, oregano, salt, and pepper.

With a sharp knife, slash a shallow crosshatch pattern into the meaty side of the ribs. Brush the chili mixture over both sides of the ribs, rubbing it well into the crosshatching. Place the ribs meaty side down in a large foil-lined pan and cover tightly. Refrigerate for at least 24 hours or up to 48 hours.

Preheat the oven to 350° F. Position the rack in the upper third of the oven. Uncover the ribs, place in the oven, and bake meaty side down for 30 minutes. Turn the ribs over and bake for another 35 to 45 minutes (covering them loosely with foil if the ribs get too brown), or until they are tender.

Transfer the ribs to a cutting board and let them rest, covered with foil, for 10 minutes. With a thin sharp knife, cut the ribs apart and serve immediately.

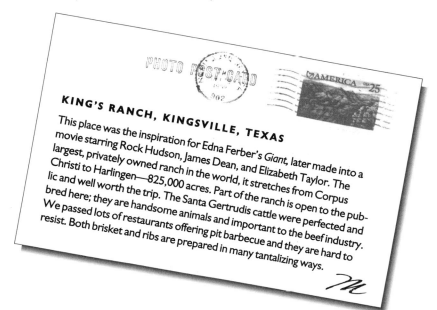

PHOTO POST CARD

AMERICA 25

KING'S RANCH, KINGSVILLE, TEXAS

This place was the inspiration for Edna Ferber's *Giant*, later made into a movie starring Rock Hudson, James Dean, and Elizabeth Taylor. The largest, privately owned ranch in the world, it stretches from Corpus Christi to Harlingen—825,000 acres. Part of the ranch is open to the public and well worth the trip. The Santa Gertrudis cattle were perfected and bred here; they are handsome animals and important to the beef industry. We passed lots of restaurants offering pit barbecue and they are hard to resist. Both brisket and ribs are prepared in many tantalizing ways.

NASAZI POT BEANS

SERVES 12

*Mettje Swift creates outdoor banners inspired by the ancient artifacts of the Anasazi people, who built
intricate communities in the cliffs and canyons of the Southwest from Colorado to Arizona. Her tall banners of primary
colors are like flags whipping in the brisk winds and harsh sunlight of the mountains—the landscape
is her inspiration and to see her banners is rather like seeing fiber totems; they are quite perfect in their setting.
At her studio in Durango, Colorado, she speaks of another subject—food.
"I've lived in Anasazi country ever since I was a child, and my idea of a good meal is having a pot of cooked
Anasazi beans on hand." These beans (pronounced A-na-saw-zee) are a mottled red and
white bean, very flavorful, and considered meatier and sweeter than other beans. I hope you will seek them out;
they are frequently available at health food stores and food co-ops.*

2 pounds dried Anasazi beans
3 quarts water
1 medium onion, coarsely chopped
3 dried red chili pods, rinsed, stemmed,
   seeded, and chopped
3 garlic cloves, minced

¼ pound very lean bacon, diced
4 teaspoons salt

Garnish: diced tomatoes, shredded cheese,
   chopped green bell peppers, sour cream, and
   minced fresh cilantro

Pick over and wash the beans under running water in a sieve. Transfer the beans to a tall 8-quart stockpot
and add the water, chopped onions, chilies, garlic, and bacon. Bring to a boil, then reduce the heat and
simmer for 2 hours, stirring occasionally. Stir in the salt and simmer for 1 hour longer, or until tender.
(The age of the beans, the altitude of your area, and the shape of the pot will all affect the cooking time.)

   Serve the beans and some of their liquid in big shallow bowls. Top each serving with diced tomatoes,
shredded cheese, chopped green bell peppers, sour cream, and a sprinkle of minced fresh cilantro.

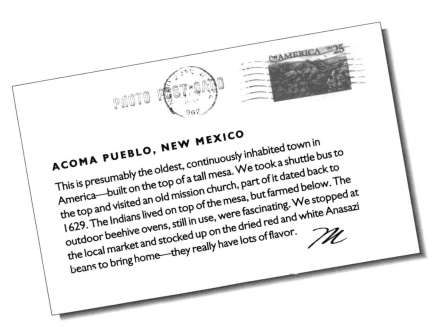

ACOMA PUEBLO, NEW MEXICO
This is presumably the oldest, continuously inhabited town in
America—built on the top of a tall mesa. We took a shuttle bus to
the top and visited an old mission church, part of it dated back to
1629. The Indians lived on top of the mesa, but farmed below. The
outdoor beehive ovens, still in use, were fascinating. We stopped at
the local market and stocked up on the dried red and white Anasazi
beans to bring home—they really have lots of flavor.

Tossed Greens with Guacamole Dressing

SERVES 6 TO 8

*When serving southwestern food, you might also like to serve this salad—the
smooth avocado dressing is very appropriate, and toasted green pumpkin seeds add a nice crunch.
I keep a jar of them in my refrigerator for salad garnishing.
Because the avocados discolor, this dressing does not keep well; don't make it more than 2 hours in advance.*

SALAD
**2½ to 3 quarts mixed greens,
 cleaned and chilled**
6 to 8 scallions, chopped

DRESSING
**1 medium avocado, peeled, pitted,
 and coarsely chopped**
1 small onion, peeled and quartered
1 garlic clove, peeled and quartered

2 teaspoons sugar
1 tablespoon fresh lemon juice
1 teaspoon Worcestershire sauce
½ teaspoon chili powder
Dash of hot red pepper sauce
1 cup mayonnaise
Green food coloring (optional)

Garnish: ½ cup toasted green pumpkin seeds

Clean and bag the lettuce early in the day. About an hour before serving, place the chopped scallions in the bottom of a chilled salad bowl and top with the greens, torn into bite-size pieces. Cover with plastic wrap and refrigerate.

Make the dressing: In a blender or food processor bowl, puree the avocado, onion, and garlic until nearly smooth. Add the sugar, lemon juice, Worcestershire, chili powder, and hot red pepper sauce. Blend until very smooth. Add the mayonnaise and a drop of green food coloring, if desired, and blend until the mixture is combined. Refrigrate until needed, then pour over the chilled greens and toss lightly. Garnish with the pumpkin seeds and serve immediately.

ORANGE-DATE SALAD WITH PUMPKIN SEEDS

SERVES 4

I find this salad a perfect complement to southwestern food. It combines all the specialties of the area—dates, oranges, and pumpkin seeds—with lettuce and some fresh mint. A very indigenous dish, it is a great mélange of texture, color, and flavor. The salad dressing includes a hint of allspice and cinnamon.

DRESSING
3 tablespoons olive oil
2 tablespoons orange juice
1 tablespoon rice wine vinegar (available at most groceries)
1 tablespoon water
¼ teaspoon ground allspice
¼ teaspoon ground cinnamon
Salt and pepper to taste

SALAD
2 heads Boston lettuce, separated into leaves and rinsed
4 small oranges, peeled, sliced, and seeded
⅓ cup coarsely sliced dates
2 tablespoons green pumpkin seeds (pepitas)
1 to 2 teaspoons finely chopped fresh mint

Garnish: 4 mint sprigs

Prepare the dressing in advance, if desired. Place all the ingredients in a glass jar and shake to combine. Reserve until needed.

To assemble the salad, arrange a generous amount of Boston lettuce on each of 4 chilled salad plates. Top with the orange slices and sprinkle with some of the dates, pumpkin seeds, and chopped mint, in that order. Drizzle the salad dressing over all and garnish with a mint sprig. Serve immediately.

FRESH TOMATO AND CUCUMBER SALAD

SERVES 4 TO 6

I love this salad because of the contrasting textures. And the seasonings are different; cilantro, that favorite from the Southwest, and mint, which grows nearly everywhere, give this country garden combination a real lilt. Though I like it with Mexican foods, it is also good with gumbos and to take to tailgate picnics. Try this also with Picnic Pie (page 139).

1 cup diced celery
⅓ cup chopped green bell pepper
⅓ cup chopped red bell pepper
⅓ cup chopped yellow bell pepper
1 cucumber, peeled, seeded, and cut into ½-inch cubes
4 medium tomatoes, seeded and chopped
4 scallions, green tops included, or 1 small sweet onion

½ cup chopped parsley
2 tablespoons chopped cilantro
1 tablespoon minced fresh mint
2 tablespoons fresh lemon juice
¼ cup olive or vegetable oil
½ teaspoon salt
1 teaspoon toasted cumin seed

In a large bowl, several hours before serving time, combine the celery, peppers, cucumbers, tomatoes, scallions, parsley, cilantro, and mint; chill well.

At least ½ hour before serving, combine the lemon juice, oil, salt, and cumin seed in a small bowl. Pour over the vegetables and toss lightly to combine. This has quite a bit of liquid, so serve it in bowls or cups.

ALMOND AND APRICOT COMPOTE

SERVES 10

*I can't think of a better dessert to end a spicy southwestern dinner and it can be made and refrigerated several days in advance. Apricots are also a popular fruit in this part of the country, with 90 percent of our entire country's output being raised in California, many which find their way to the Southwest.
I find the very best dried apricots at the health food stores;
they cost a little more, but it's worth it, and no sulphur dioxide has been used in the drying process.*

8 ounces dried apricots	**1 cup slivered almonds, toasted (see Note)**
4 cups apple juice	
¼ cup (½ stick) butter	**Crème Fraîche (page 285) or ice cream**
¼ cup sugar	

Combine the apricots and apple juice in a medium bowl, cover with plastic wrap, and let stand overnight in the refrigerator. Transfer the apricots and juice to a medium saucepan, partially cover, and bring to a boil over medium heat. Reduce the heat and simmer for 10 minutes, or until the apricots are tender. Remove the pan from the heat, gently stir in the butter and sugar, and let cool slightly. When cool, stir in the almonds. Transfer the compote to a serving bowl or individual dessert dishes and serve with Crème Fraîche or a small dip of ice cream.

NOTE: *Toast the almonds in a 350° F. oven for 10 minutes, stirring once or twice.*

A chopping device

$\mathscr{S}$OUTHWEST FLAN

SERVES 12

Flan, a baked custard coated with caramel, is a classic Spanish dessert. It is also a popular ending to Mexican and southwestern meals, and you will find it on nearly every restaurant menu as well as on dinner tables in southwestern homes. It is quick to prepare, and this recipe serves twelve, so I frequently have it on my dessert buffets. It can be made 2 days in advance—good news for the busy cook!

1 quart half-and-half	⅓ cup Kahlúa
2 cups sugar, divided	1 tablespoon vanilla extract
½ cup water	1 teaspoon ground cinnamon
Speck of cream of tartar	Speck of salt
8 jumbo or 9 large eggs	

Preheat the oven to 350° F.

Scald the half-and-half in a deep saucepan until bubbles form around the edges, about 4 minutes; remove from the heat and set aside. Place 1 cup sugar, the water, and cream of tartar in a heavy skillet and cook over medium heat for 15 to 25 minutes. Watch the caramel closely; it should turn a rich, golden brown, like tea. Pour immediately (and you have to hustle, or it will get too dark) into a large 12 × 6 × 3-inch loaf pan, spreading it evenly over the bottom of the pan. Place the pan in the refrigerator to harden the caramel, about 15 minutes.

In a large mixer bowl, beat the eggs just until frothy; don't overbeat. Add the scalded half-and-half, the remaining 1 cup sugar, Kahlúa, vanilla, cinnamon, and salt. Blend well on low speed, not allowing bubbles to form. Pour the custard into the loaf pan over the hardened sugar mixture. Set the loaf pan into a pan of hot water (the water should come up to halfway on the sides of the loaf pan) and bake for 1¼ hours.

Remove the flan from the hot water bath, allow to cool, then chill overnight or up to 2 days. To serve, loosen the edges of the flan with a knife and invert onto a lipped tray. Cut into slices and spoon some of the caramel sauce over each serving.

$\mathscr{S}$OPAIPILLAS
(SOFT PILLOWS)
SERVES 6

*These classic soft puffed fritters, a specialty of the Southwest, are a real treat. Serve
these light, golden brown puffs as you would hot biscuits or fresh bread, though they are quite unlike either of
those—they sort of resemble an ethereal pita. Honey is the traditional accompaniment, or
they are also served as a sandwich, pulled apart and filled with seasoned meats or chili and, of course, salsa.*

2 cups all-purpose flour	⅔ cup warm water
2½ teaspoons baking powder	Corn oil for deep-frying
½ teaspoon salt	
2 tablespoons solid vegetable shortening	Confectioners' sugar or honey

In a large bowl, whisk together 1¾ cups flour, the baking powder, and salt. Cut the shortening into the dry
ingredients until it resembles coarse crumbs. Gradually stir in the water until a loose dough is formed.
Sprinkle 2 tablespoons of the remaining flour onto a pastry cloth and knead the dough about 1 minute,
until it is smooth. Roll the dough out until it is ¼-inch thick, cover it with a kitchen towel, and let it stand
for at least 15 minutes but not more than 30 minutes.

In a deep skillet, heat 2 inches of oil to between 375° F. and 390° F. Trim the edges of the dough to
form a neat rectangle. Cut the rectangle into twelve 3-inch squares or triangles. Stretch each piece gently,
then lower it into the oil; keep turning with tongs until it browns and puffs evenly on both sides. Remove
from the oil to paper toweling to drain. Repeat with the remaining dough. Serve hot, sprinkled with confectioners' sugar or honey.

PHOTO POST CARD

AMERICA 25

THE PLAZA, SANTA FE, NEW MEXICO

The first thing we did when we arrived here was to find the stone
marker and plaque in the plaza that marks the end of the 1,000-
mile Santa Fe Trail. Weary travelers also called Santa Fe the "City
of Desire." I can see why. The picturesque, old plaza is shaded by
arching trees, and the flagstone walks are lined with comfortable
benches. We stopped in at a bakery for coffee and a snack and in
this case it was sopaipillas, those ethereal Mexican crullers.

$\mathcal{M}$

December
SWEETS

MAKING FUDGE CAN probably be credited for starting many a new cook on their way to bigger (I can't say better) things. Before television, cookie and candy making was a common family recreation, and there is no better time to reintroduce children to this pleasure than at holiday time, when giving tins or plates of confections to friends is a common tradition. During December we reinvoke those good times when we get out the candy pan and thermometer, the cinnamon and silver dragees.

Cookie and candy making are not difficult, but they do take a bit of practice. Here are some hints that will help a first-time confectioner: Make candy on sunny, cool, and dry days; if you <u>must</u> make candy on humid overcast days, cook the candy longer and to a temperature two degrees higher than the recipe suggests. Always make candy in a deep heavy-bottomed pan at least four times the volume of the ingredients; it will save you dreadful messes on the stove. Use a wooden spoon (it won't conduct heat) and do use a candy thermometer.

The biggest problem encountered in candy making is that it "sugars." This is frequently caused by sugar crystals on the sides of the pan getting down into the candy mixture in the pan, which is quite a different sort of sugar crystal by this time. To avoid this, bring the sugar and water to a boil, covered. The steam will wash down the crystals on the sides of the pan. Wrap a long knife with wet paper toweling and remove the residue from the sides of the pan after the lid-on step. Should the candy begin to sugar, add a small amount of water, about a tablespoon, and begin all over again.

Watch the candy temperature closely; it takes quite a while to reach 220° F., then, whoosh, it goes up rapidly. Experience has taught me to get down on eye level with the thermometer at this stage. Cool the mixture to around 110° F. before beating.

Now some cookie pointers: Bake your cookies on parchment paper. It prevents the cookies from sticking. The butter or fat should be at room temperature if they are to be creamed. Add the sugar gradually to the fat and don't rush the beating of the fat and sugar; this step incorporates air into the cookie dough. If you are storing soft or frosted cookies, layer them between sheets of wax paper.

Buttery Nut Caramels Black Walnut Fudge Haystacks Coconut Peaks
Pecan Penuchi Peanut Brittle Golden Peanut Butter Fudge Creole Pralines Christmas Pecan Bars
Railroad Cookies Mrs. Alcott's Gingersnaps Cocoa Sandies Joe Froggers Pumpkin Cookies
Dutch Almond Squares Black Walnut–Date Bars Potato Chip Cookies Caraway Comfets

BUTTERY NUT CARAMELS

MAKES ABOUT 80 PIECES

*Susan Raver, my assistant, is a whiz; not only can she make a computer hum at a red-hot pace, but she
is also an excellent cook. Frequently she brings me recipes from her church, and they are always good. This recipe
is from one of her friends, who got it from another friend in another church where these caramels are
made to sell at their Christmas bazaar. Could this be called an ecumenical recipe?*

1 cup (2 sticks) butter
2¼ cups packed light brown sugar
Dash of salt
1 cup light corn syrup

One 14-ounce can sweetened condensed milk
1½ teaspoons vanilla extract
½ cup coarsely chopped nuts

Evenly butter a 9 × 9 × 2-inch pan and set aside—do not overbutter or the caramels will be greasy.

In a heavy saucepan over medium heat, melt the butter and stir in the sugar and salt. Pour in the corn syrup, mixing thoroughly with a whisk. Slowly pour in the milk, stirring constantly until blended. Using a candy thermometer, cook to 245° F., stirring occasionally—the mixture will be very bubbly. Remove the saucepan from the heat and stir in the vanilla and nuts, then immediately pour into the prepared pan. Let the candy cool completely before cutting into 1-inch squares. Wrap each square in plastic wrap and store in an airtight container at room temperature.

BLACK WALNUT FUDGE

MAKES APPROXIMATELY 3 DOZEN PIECES

*I recall with great fondness those Sunday nights at home on the farm when my
brother Gordon and I made taffy, popcorn balls, and fudge. Black walnuts were always available, and as soon
as the fudge was cooked and stirred, we poured it into deep ironstone platters. This was more of a winter activity
than a summer, and sometimes we made it if we had friends in for overnight. Such innocent pleasures . . .
Do not stir this mixture while it is cooking or it will "sugar."*

2 cups packed light brown sugar
1 cup heavy cream
1 tablespoon butter
2 tablespoons light corn syrup

1 cup coarsely chopped black walnuts (English
walnuts may be substituted)
1 teaspoon vanilla extract
Dash of salt

In a heavy 3-quart saucepan, combine the brown sugar, cream, butter, and corn syrup. Stir well. Cook over medium heat *without stirring* to 234° F. on a candy thermometer. This may take 10 to 15 minutes. Remove from the heat and let cool for about 15 minutes. *Do not stir*. When cooled to 160° F., add the walnuts, vanilla, and salt. Beat with a wooden spoon until the mixture creams. Pour into a buttered 8-inch square pan. Allow to cool completely and cut into squares.

HAYSTACKS
MAKES ABOUT 3 DOZEN

*This is a most engaging confection, with a lot of personality—I mean, you'd notice how great
they look on a platter of a lot of other candies!*
*This recipe came via Florida, where we think of coconuts as being one of the native foods. Actually they arrived
there by mistake. The tough, hairy brown coconuts washed up on shore in 1879 after a ship from the West Indies was
wrecked off the coast. The buoyant nuts floated ashore and took root. And now we can enjoy such delights
as coconut cake, piña coladas, and these captivating candies.*

8 cups flaked sweetened coconut	**2 teaspoons vanilla extract**
1½ cups finely chopped walnuts	**13 large egg whites**
2 cups chopped dates	**2 cups sugar**
½ teaspoon salt	

In a large mixing bowl, combine the coconut, walnuts, dates, salt, and vanilla; stir well. In the top of a double boiler over simmering water, combine the egg whites and sugar; stir until the mixture is frothy and the temperature on a candy thermometer reaches 120° F., approximately 10 to 15 minutes. Meanwhile, preheat the oven to 350° F. Then pour the egg whites over the coconut mixture; stir well. Using a small ice cream scooper, form into balls and place on a lightly greased or parchment-lined baking sheet. Bake for 20 minutes, or until golden brown, allowing the candies to cool completely before removing them from the pan.

COCONUT PEAKS
MAKES 18 TO 20

*By tradition, Mormon families set aside one night a week (generally Monday) for the entire
family to spend time together. Candy making has always been a happy way for them to pass these evenings. Some
very pleasant memories and some very good recipes come from this tradition.*
*And if you like coconut candy bars, this candy is for you! The recipe is very easy too; no candy
thermometer is needed. However, you might find a candy-dipping fork helpful. They can be purchased for a little
more than a dollar at any candy-making supply store. (Check your Yellow Pages.) You can use the fork
also to dip small cookies in glaze-type frosting.*

½ cup (1 stick) butter (no substitutes)	**3 cups flaked sweetened coconut**
1 teaspoon vanilla extract	**2 cups confectioners' sugar**
Speck of salt	**6 ounces semisweet chocolate**

In a 4-quart pan, melt the butter over low heat. Remove from the heat and add the vanilla and salt. Blend in the coconut and confectioners' sugar, mixing well. Meanwhile, melt the chocolate in a double boiler over simmering water.

Mold the coconut mixture first into large marble-sized balls (when I played marbles in the schoolyard, we called these aggies) and then with your fingers, form a peak at the top. Pack the balls very firmly or they will fall apart when dipped in the chocolate.

Dip the bottom half of each ball into the melted chocolate and place on a wax paper–lined tray. Chill until firm and remove from the refrigerator just before serving. These can be made 5 days in advance and stored in airtight plastic containers in the refrigerator.

PECAN PENUCHI

MAKES 32

Sometimes this candy is spelled penuche, *but in this case, the yellowed old card bearing this recipe came to me with this spelling and we called it pen-OO-chee. It is a creamy near relative of fudge and made with brown sugar, milk, and butter. The name comes from* panocha *or* panucha, *a coarse brown sugar produced in Mexico. I found that so interesting, since this candy is very common in Indiana and has been since 1900. Did this recipe originate in Mexico? If so, when, and who brought it to the Midwest? I find these food mysteries so fascinating, and someday someone will doubtless enlighten me or I will come across the answer in some book I am browsing through. Anyway, this was one of the first candies we children were allowed to make by ourselves when we were growing up; it is a good one for beginning candy makers.*

3 cups packed light brown sugar	1½ teaspoons vanilla extract
1 cup whole milk	1½ cups pecan pieces
2 tablespoons (¼ stick) butter	Speck of salt

Combine the sugar and milk in a 4-quart heavy-bottomed pan and cook over medium heat, stirring constantly with a wooden spoon to avoid curdling. Cook until the soft-ball stage is reached: 234 to 240° F. (approximately 16 to 17 minutes). Remove the pan from the heat, add the butter, and set aside to cool *without stirring*. When lukewarm (110° F., approximately 1 hour, but keep checking), beat until thick and creamy, about 2 minutes by hand. Add the vanilla, pecans, and salt and mix thoroughly. Transfer immediately to a lightly buttered 8 × 8 × 2-inch pan. Cool completely and cut into 1 × 2-inch squares.

Peanut Brittle

MAKES ABOUT 2 ½ POUNDS

Across the country, many church circles make peanut brittle at holiday time as a fund-raising project. Orders are taken in advance for this special candy that is generally prepared in early December. This is my mother-in-law's recipe, and I can vouch for it firsthand, for it is an Adams family tradition to serve it at Christmas. It is a rather light-flavored brittle, and can also be made with pecans.

2 cups sugar

1 cup light corn syrup

½ cup water

1 pound shelled raw peanuts,
   without skins

1 teaspoon baking soda

3 tablespoons butter

Dash of salt

In a heavy 4-quart saucepan, combine the sugar, corn syrup, and water. With a damp paper towel, wipe down the sides of the pan. Without stirring, cook over medium-high heat until a candy thermometer registers 260° F. Butter a large cookie sheet and set aside. Add the peanuts and begin stirring frequently to prevent scorching; continue cooking until the temperature is 290° F. Remove from the heat and add the soda, butter, and salt. Stir vigorously. Pour out onto the prepared cookie sheet. Turn the mass over as it cools and pull and stretch it for a thin candy.

Allow to cool completely and break into pieces. Store in an airtight container; theoretically it will keep for up to a month, but in all probability, you are going to eat this up long before a month has passed!

Golden Peanut Butter Fudge

MAKES APPROXIMATELY 3 DOZEN PIECES

Peanut butter was developed by a St. Louis, Missouri, doctor and was one of the new foods sampled at the World's Fair in 1904. This popular spread has gone on to become an American classic. Adding it to fudge yields a creamy golden fudge that is popular with folks of all ages.

Be sure that you blend all of the ingredients thoroughly before you start to cook. Moving the sugar crystals around in the pan when they are changing from a granule to a liquid will cause the candy to "sugar" and become grainy. Don't stir candies while cooking unless otherwise instructed.

1 pound packed light brown sugar

3 cups granulated sugar

2 tablespoons light corn syrup

1½ cups half-and-half

2 tablespoons (¼ stick) butter

1 teaspoon cream of tartar

One 18-ounce jar chunky peanut butter

2 teaspoons vanilla extract

Measure the sugars, corn syrup, half-and-half, butter, and cream of tartar into a heavy 4-quart saucepan. Stir well. Bring to a boil over medium heat *without stirring*. Insert a candy thermometer, then reduce the heat to low and continue to cook to 240° F. *Do not stir the mixture while cooking or it will sugar.* Remove from the heat and drop the peanut butter and vanilla into the hot mixture. (*Still do not stir.*) Allow to sit approximately 10 minutes to cool slightly. When slightly cooled, beat with a wooden spoon until the fudge begins to firm up. Transfer to a buttered 8-inch square pan and allow to cool completely. Cut into squares to serve. The fudge will dry out after it is cut, so keep the candy well wrapped.

CREOLE PRALINES

MAKES APPROXIMATELY 40

First of all, this candy name is pronounced PRAH-leen, not PRAY-leen. It is an old, old French confection, named after a seventeenth-century diplomat César Duplessis-Praslin, who is said to have shared his cook's almond candy with Louis XIII, a rather high recommendation. At least there is no record of the king's refusing the candy. French pralines are still made with almonds or hazelnuts and they are brittle and shiny, while Creole or New Orleans pralines are opaque and a tad grainy, often made with pecans.
In the South, you'll find pralines presented alongside little pastries and cookies, and sometimes a dish of them will be passed with coffee after dessert. They are best eaten fresh, but will keep for a week in a tightly covered tin.

2 cups granulated sugar	**1 cup whole milk**
1 cup packed light brown sugar	**2 tablespoons dark corn syrup**
½ cup (1 stick) unsalted butter (no substitutes)	**4 cups pecan halves**

In a heavy 3-quart saucepan, combine the sugars, butter, milk, and corn syrup. Cook over medium heat for 15 minutes, stirring occasionally. Add the pecans and continue cooking until the mixture reaches 236°F. on a candy thermometer. Remove from the heat and allow to cool about 5 minutes. Then beat the praline mixture until the syrup becomes cloudy and the mixture thickens slightly. Immediately drop by spoonfuls onto parchment or a double layer of wax paper. Allow to cool, peel away the paper, and then store the pralines, with wax paper between the layers, in an airtight container.

PHOTO POST CARD

AMERICA 25

THE FRENCH QUARTER, NEW ORLEANS, LOUISIANA

Dick has really enjoyed the jazz here, and I really enjoyed the food. It is hard to choose which restaurants to go to, but we have done our best. This morning we took a short boat trip on the river and this afternoon, a literary walking tour around the French Quarter, which we enjoyed enormously. Sister Mary's pralines at St. Clare's Monastery were very good, and I also bought their cookbook, a collection of recipes.

M

Covered butter dish in the thistle pattern

CHRISTMAS PECAN BARS

MAKES 54 SMALL BARS

My mother was a fine cookie baker and at holiday time, she produced some unforgettable confections. The two of us would spend Saturdays in November baking our hearts out, and I remember those times with pleasure. We had a few favorites, which we made traditionally each year, such as Mexican wedding rings and these pecan bars. This is an adaptation of her recipe. When you are preparing the filling, watch it carefully, for it burns QUICKLY! Also, I think these taste better the second day after they have "ripened."

COOKIE CRUST
½ cup (1 stick) butter, at
   room temperature
¼ cup plus 2 tablespoons
   vegetable shortening
½ cup sugar
1 egg
Grated zest of 1 lemon
½ teaspoon vanilla extract
¾ cup cake flour

½ cup all-purpose flour
¼ teaspoon salt
⅛ teaspoon baking powder

PECAN FILLING
⅔ cup packed brown sugar
¼ cup granulated sugar
½ cup honey
1¾ cups coarsely chopped pecans
¼ cup heavy cream

Preheat the oven to 350° F.

Prepare the crust: In a large mixer bowl, cream the butter, shortening, and sugar together, then add the egg, lemon zest, and vanilla; mix well. In medium bowl, whisk together the flours, salt, and baking powder. Gradually add to the creamed mixture and mix until combined. Pat the dough firmly into an ungreased 13 × 9-inch pan and bake for 10 minutes. Remove from the oven and set aside.

Prepare the pecan filling: In a medium saucepan melt the butter, sugars, and honey together over medium heat. Insert a candy thermometer and slowly bring to a slow rolling boil, cooking and stirring constantly for 2½ minutes or until the candy thermometer reads no more than 235° F. Remove the pan from the heat and stir in the pecans and cream. Immediately pour over the crust, spreading the nuts out evenly. Lower the oven temperature to 325° F. and bake the cookies for 30 minutes longer. Cool and cut into 1 × 2-inch bars.

NOTE: *These freeze very well.*

RAILROAD COOKIES

MAKES 4 DOZEN

These cookies have lots of names: rolled date cookies, pinwheel cookies, date snails, and dilly-dallys.
The railroad name is presumably because people thought the dark trail of filling in the pale brown cookie dough
resembled railroad tracks winding up and around the valleys and hills. (This was from a time when
railroad tracks were thought glamorous.)
Whatever name they go by, these recipes are all based on a stiff butterscotch batter that is rolled out,
spread with a date-nut filling, then rolled up and sliced. The rolled cookie dough will keep
for a week in the refrigerator if tightly wrapped in plastic wrap. This is one of those cookies that
often prompts cries of "Oh, my grandmother made those."

1 cup vegetable shortening	**DATE-NUT FILLING**
2 cups granulated sugar	**2 cups finely chopped dates**
1 cup packed light brown sugar	**½ cup granulated sugar**
3 large eggs	**½ cup water**
1 teaspoon vanilla extract	**1 teaspoon vanilla extract**
4 cups all-purpose flour	**½ cup ground pecans**
1 teaspoon baking soda	
1 teaspoon ground cinnamon	
½ teaspoon cream of tartar	
½ teaspoon salt	

In a large mixer bowl, cream the shortening and the sugars thoroughly, then add the eggs and vanilla. In a medium bowl, whisk together 2 cups flour with the soda, cinnamon, cream of tartar, and salt and add to the creamed mixture; blend well. Gradually add the remaining 2 cups flour to make a firm dough, stiff enough to handle and roll easily. (You will have to mix this with your hands unless you have a heavy-duty electric mixer.) Divide the dough into 2 balls, wrap well, and chill for at least 2 hours or overnight.

Make the filling: In a medium saucepan, combine the dates, sugar, and water and cook over low heat until thick, stirring constantly to prevent scorching—this takes about 3 minutes. Add the vanilla; cool, then stir in the ground nuts.

Take out half the dough (leaving the other to chill), and on a lightly floured surface roll out into a 9 × 13-inch rectangle, ⅓ inch thick. Spread half of the filling over the entire rectangle, then roll up like a jelly roll, starting from one long edge. Cover the roll with plastic wrap and refrigerate for 2 hours. Repeat the procedure with the remaining dough and filling.

Preheat the oven to 350° F. When the dough is well chilled, slice each roll into ¼-inch-thick slices and place on a lightly greased or parchment-lined cookie sheet. Bake for 15 minutes, until lightly browned. Cool on racks and store in a tightly covered container.

MRS. ALCOTT'S GINGERSNAPS

MAKES 8 TO 9 DOZEN

It is nice to think that the Alcott/March girls had these as a treat, not to mention Ralph Waldo Emerson and Thoreau. They are a very crisp cookie, and taste of molasses and ginger. The dough handles very well. If you like gingersnaps, this version is really terrific. I think Jo March might have used that expression if she were around today.

½ cup (1 stick) butter, at room temperature	½ teaspoon ground ginger
½ cup sugar	½ teaspoon salt
½ teaspoon baking soda	3¾ cups all-purpose flour
	1 cup dark molasses

In a large mixer bowl, beat the butter until creamy, about 1 minute. Gradually add the sugar, beating 3 minutes longer. Add the soda, ginger, and salt and blend, then add the flour alternately with the molasses, beginning and ending with the flour; blend well. The dough will be quite stiff, and if you don't have a beater with a very strong motor, you may have to finish this step by hand. Refrigerate the dough for 1 hour.

Preheat the oven to 350° F.

Roll out the dough to about ⅜ inch thick on a lightly floured surface. Using a 1½-inch round cutter, cut out the cookies and transfer them to a parchment-covered cookie sheet. Bake for about 7 to 8 minutes, until firm. Remove to a rack to cool. Pack in tins or freeze. These cookies keep very well.

PHOTO POST CARD

AMERICA 25

LOUISA MAY ALCOTT HOUSE, CONCORD, MASSACHUSETTS

Concord, Massachusetts in the mid-1800s must have been like a conventional American Bloomsbury—Bronson, Alcott, Emerson, and Thoreau all lived here and were part of the Transcendental School of Philosophy. And visiting Louisa May Alcott's house is just like walking into the pages of Little Women. We found her recipe for apple slump as well as her mother's gingersnap recipe in the gift shop. What fun! Will try it as soon as we return home.

COCOA SANDIES

MAKES 2 DOZEN COOKIES

You will want to try this cookie developed in the Hershey kitchens. An intensely chocolate, buttery cookie, half of it is glazed with chocolate frosting, which gives it a most sophisticated look.

1 cup (2 sticks) butter, at room temperature	**GLAZE**
1¼ cups confectioners' sugar	3 tablespoons butter
1½ teaspoons vanilla extract	⅓ cup Hershey's Cocoa
½ cup Hershey's Cocoa	¼ cup plus 3 teaspoons water
¼ teaspoon salt	1 teaspoon vanilla extract
1¾ cups all-purpose flour	1 ½ cups confectioners' sugar
	Speck of salt

Preheat the oven to 350° F.

In a large mixer bowl, beat the butter, sugar, and vanilla until creamy, about 3 minutes. Add the cocoa and blend well. Add the salt, then gradually add the flour, blending until smooth.

On a lightly floured surface, roll the dough to about ½-inch thickness. Use a cookie cutter to cut out the cookies and transfer to an ungreased cookie sheet. The scraps can be gathered and rerolled.

Bake the cookies for 20 minutes, or until just firm. Cool slightly on the sheet, then transfer to a wire rack to cool.

Make the glaze: In a small saucepan, melt the butter over low heat. Stir in the cocoa and ¼ cup water. Cook over low heat, stirring constantly, until the mixture thickens and becomes smooth. Remove from the heat and stir in the vanilla. Gradually add the sugar and salt, stirring with a whisk until smooth. If needed add more water, 1 teaspoon at a time, to achieve a spreadable consistency.

To dip the cookies, tip the pan of chocolate toward you and dip about half of each cookie into the glaze. Place on a wax paper–covered rack until the glaze is set. Store the cookies in layers, separated by wax paper, in tightly covered tins in a cool but not cold place.

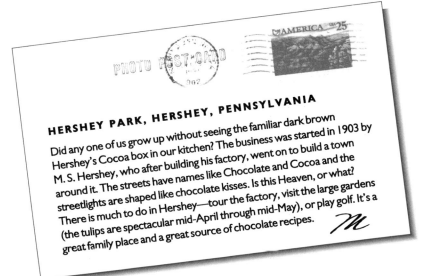

HERSHEY PARK, HERSHEY, PENNSYLVANIA

Did any one of us grow up without seeing the familiar dark brown Hershey's Cocoa box in our kitchen? The business was started in 1903 by M. S. Hershey, who after building his factory, went on to build a town around it. The streets have names like Chocolate and Cocoa and the streetlights are shaped like chocolate kisses. Is this Heaven, or what? There is much to do in Hershey—tour the factory, visit the large gardens (the tulips are spectacular mid-April through mid-May), or play golf. It's a great family place and a great source of chocolate recipes.

JOE FROGGERS

MAKES 18 TO 20

*This is one of those New England recipes that should be reprinted regularly so it never drops
from sight—and so the story isn't forgotten. There really was a Joe Frogger, and he lived in Marblehead,
Massachusetts, during the 1800s by a pond called Uncle Joe's Frog Pond. The local fishermen would give him rum, and
in exchange, he would make batches of very large chewy, spicy molasses cookies for them to take to sea.
He never gave out the recipe, but he did allow that it was the rum and
seawater that kept them soft. When he died, people feared that was the end of those famous cookies, but a
woman named Mammy Cressy, who claimed to be Joe's daughter, gave the recipe to just one
fisherman's wife. Soon every woman in Marblehead was making Joe Froggers, and they became the town's favorite
Sunday night supper, along with a pitcher of milk. (I said they were big cookies, didn't I?)*

3½ cups sifted all-purpose flour	1 cup dark molasses
2 teaspoons ground ginger	1 teaspoon baking soda
½ teaspoon ground cloves	½ cup (1 stick) butter, at room temperature
½ teaspoon ground nutmeg	1 cup sugar
½ teaspoon ground allspice	3 tablespoons dark rum combined with
1 teaspoon salt	5 tablespoons water or ½ cup water
	(the original recipe called for seawater)

In a large bowl, whisk together the flour, ginger, cloves, nutmeg, allspice, and salt. In a small bowl, combine the molasses and soda. The mixture will foam and double in volume. Set aside. Meanwhile, in a large mixer bowl, cream the butter and sugar until fluffy and light in color, about 5 minutes. Beat in the molasses mixture, then the rum and water (or just the water) and mix well. Stir in the flour mixture a cup at a time, beating well after each addition. Cover and chill the dough in the refrigerator at least 8 hours or preferably overnight.

Preheat the oven to 375° F.

On a floured surface, roll out the dough to a ⅓- to ½-inch thickness. Cut with a large (4-inch) round cutter. Place the cookies on a greased cookie sheet at least 3 inches apart and bake on the middle oven rack for 10 minutes, or until the tops feel firm to the touch. Remove from the oven and let cool for 1 to 2 minutes, then carefully transfer with a large spatula to wire racks. Allow the cookie sheets to cool completely between bakings. Store the cookies in a tightly covered container; they will keep for 2 or 3 weeks.

PUMPKIN COOKIES

MAKES 4 1/2 DOZEN

This is one of the best cookies I know! They are so moist and flavorful and the butterscotch frosting makes them even better. They are quick to make too. I like them for a snack with a glass of milk, though they are certainly fine enough for an afternoon tea.

1 cup (2 sticks) butter, at
   room temperature
1 cup sugar
1 cup canned pumpkin
1 large egg
1 teaspoon vanilla extract
1 teaspoon Angostura bitters
   (available at liquor stores)
2 cups all-purpose flour
2 teaspoons pumpkin pie spice
1 teaspoon baking powder
1 teaspoon baking soda
1 teaspoon ground cinnamon

1 teaspoon salt
½ teaspoon ground cloves
½ cup dark raisins
½ cup chopped pecans

FROSTING
1 cup packed dark brown sugar
6 tablespoons (¾ stick) butter
¼ cup milk
1 teaspoon vanilla extract
Speck of salt
2 cups confectioners' sugar

Preheat the oven to 325° F.

   In a large mixer bowl, cream the butter and sugar together for 3 minutes. Add the pumpkin, egg, vanilla, and bitters and mix well. In another bowl, whisk together the flour, pumpkin pie spice, baking powder, soda, cinnamon, salt, and cloves. Slowly add the flour mixture to the pumpkin mixture; mix until combined. By hand, stir in the raisins and pecans. Drop by heaping teaspoonfuls onto a greased cookie sheet. Bake for 10 to 15 minutes, or until the top of the cookie springs back when touched with your finger. Transfer to racks and cool completely before frosting.

   Meanwhile, make the frosting: In a small saucepan, melt the brown sugar and butter together, then stir in the milk. Bring to a boil over medium heat, lower the heat, and cook gently for 3 minutes, stirring now and then. Remove from the heat and cool. Stir in the vanilla, salt, and confectioners' sugar and beat until well combined.

DUTCH ALMOND SQUARES

MAKES 4 DOZEN

One of the cookies you might find in Solvang is this three-layered almond square.
Cakelike on the bottom, there is a fragrant marzipan-type filling in the middle and the top is a crisp
nut-topped meringue. All in all, it is a rich and unusual cookie.

½ cup (1 stick) butter, at
    room temperature
1½ cups plus 2 tablespoons sugar
1 large egg plus 1 egg yolk
1 cup all-purpose flour
1 teaspoon salt

1 cup almond paste (marzipan)
2 teaspoons fresh lemon juice
1 teaspoon vanilla extract
3 large egg whites
½ cup chopped almonds

Preheat the oven to 325° F.

In a large mixer bowl, cream the butter slightly, then gradually add ½ cup sugar and beat for 2 minutes. Beat in the egg and egg yolk. Stir in the flour and ¾ teaspoon of the salt by hand. Spread the mixture into an ungreased glass 9 × 13-inch pan, making a smooth layer. Bake the crust for 15 minutes, until it is set but not brown.

In a food processor bowl, mix together 1 cup sugar, the almond paste, lemon juice, vanilla, and the remaining ¼ teaspoon salt; reserve. In a large mixer bowl, beat the egg whites until frothy, then sprinkle the remaining 2 tablespoons sugar over the whites and continue beating until stiff peaks form. By hand, fold the almond paste mixture into the egg whites with a rubber spatula and spread over the baked crust. Sprinkle the almonds on top and bake the cookies for 25 minutes, or until golden brown. Cool partially and cut the cookies while still warm into 48 narrow bars. These freeze well.

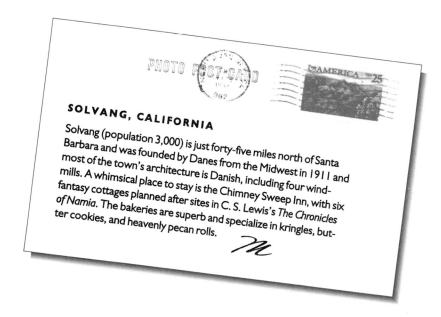

PHOTO POST CARD

AMERICA 25

SOLVANG, CALIFORNIA

Solvang (population 3,000) is just forty-five miles north of Santa Barbara and was founded by Danes from the Midwest in 1911 and most of the town's architecture is Danish, including four wind-mills. A whimsical place to stay is the Chimney Sweep Inn, with six fantasy cottages planned after sites in C. S. Lewis's *The Chronicles of Narnia*. The bakeries are superb and specialize in kringles, but-ter cookies, and heavenly pecan rolls.

BLACK WALNUT–DATE BARS

MAKES 40

This is a cakelike cookie, very moist and substantial, and if you like black walnuts and dates, you will become very fond of this cookie. It travels and stores well too. The recipe came from a 1940 Allen County, Indiana, home economics cookbook. Those ladies knew how to bake, no doubt about it. Dust with confectioners' sugar if you like.

3 large eggs	5 tablespoons all-purpose flour
1 cup sugar	1 teaspoon baking powder
2 teaspoons vanilla extract	½ teaspoon salt
2 tablespoons (¼ stick) butter, melted	1 cup chopped dates
2 tablespoons grated orange zest	1 cup chopped black walnuts

Preheat the oven to 350° F.

In a mixer bowl, beat the eggs and sugar together for 3 minutes. Add the vanilla, butter, and orange zest. In a small bowl, whisk together the flour, baking powder, and salt. Add it to the egg mixture and blend. Add the dates and walnuts and stir just to combine. Spread the dough in a greased 7 × 12-inch (2-quart) baking dish and bake for 25 minutes, or until the top is golden brown and springs back when touched with your fingertip. Allow the cookies to stand for 15 minutes, then cut into 1 × 1½-inch bars. Cool completely, then store in tins with wax paper between the layers.

POTATO CHIP COOKIES

MAKES ABOUT 40

Susan Raver, my secretary/assistant/super food tester/friend, arrived one day with a tale about a cookie her friend, Rosemary Noecker, serves. "They are made with potato chips," she said, "and they are really good." I was very skeptical, to say the least. The next day, she brought me a container of them and I had to eat my words—and the cookies. They are delicious—rich like shortbread, they remind me a bit of a cookie called pecan sandy. Will this be an heirloom recipe of tomorrow? There's a good chance.

1 cup (2 sticks) butter, at room temperature	1½ cups all-purpose flour
1 cup confectioners' sugar	¾ cup crushed fresh potato chips
1 large egg yolk	½ cup finely chopped pecans
1 teaspoon vanilla extract	Garnish: confectioners' sugar

Preheat the oven to 350° F.

In a large mixer bowl, combine the butter and sugar and beat for 3 minutes. Add the egg yolk and vanilla and mix well. Gradually add the flour. By hand, fold in the potato chips and pecans. Drop by teaspoonfuls onto a greased cookie sheet and bake for 15 minutes. Transfer to a cooling rack, and while still warm, sift confectioners' sugar over the tops of the cookies. Cool completely and pack in airtight containers.

CARAWAY COMFETS

MAKES 6 DOZEN

Comfets are little sweet confections that in Colonial days were often flavored with musk or bergamot. The most popular ones were always those flavored with caraway seeds. Comfets resemble a delicate shortbread; I recommend them highly and they are real conversation pieces.

1 cup (2 sticks) butter,	**¼ teaspoon baking powder**
at room temperature	**¼ teaspoon salt**
½ cup sugar	**1 teaspoon caraway seeds**
2 cups all-purpose flour	

In a mixer bowl, cream the butter and sugar together until light and fluffy, about 3 minutes. In another medium bowl, whisk together the flour, baking powder, and salt; add to the butter mixture. Blend well, then stir in the caraway seeds.

Spread a sheet of wax paper the size of your largest cookie sheet on the counter, dust with flour, and then use a floured rolling pin to roll out the dough ¼ inch thick on the paper. Using a rolling pin and the palm of your hand, form a rectangle approximately 12 × 15 inches—a uniform ¼-inch thickness rather than the size of the rectangle should be your guide. Transfer the dough and cookie sheet to the refrigerator to chill for at least an hour.

Preheat the oven to 375° F. Cut the cookies into small shapes, approximately 1½ inches in size (these can be squares, if you like) and prick 2 or 3 times with a fork. Transfer the cookies to the baking sheet and bake for approximately 7 minutes. Watch them, for they burn quickly. Remove from the oven when they are a pale yellow. Cool on racks and pack tightly in tins.

Some Rather Fancy
FOODS

T IS IN THE EARLY winter months, with its accompanying holidays, that we begin to make plans for what I call "serious entertaining." In keeping with the season, our plans may be more elaborate and it is an occasion for some seasonal dishes, such as steamed puddings.

Beef has traditionally been the meat of choice for entertaining. I think a stuffed beef tenderloin is an ideal main dish, for it is elegant, quite easy to prepare, and serves a group. The Victorians were known for their standing ribs of roast beef and other extravagant offerings as well as their lavish table settings and many-coursed meals. Mrs. Astor in New York set the tone for this Gilded Age, and the rest of the country did their best to keep up.

During this period, china manufacturers scrambled to provide sets of china with every conceivable dish, including butter pats and finger bowls. Dining accouterments included cheese scoops, angel food cake breakers, corn cob scrapers, and asparagus tongs, while towering tiered epergnes held fruit and flowers high above the table and the viewer's eye range.

Today, we have sensibly adandoned most of these extravagant practices (having neither the staff nor the time to bring them off), but happily the same is not true of these festive foods. The oysters, roasts, and steamed puddings have never gone out of style and these particular dishes have been with us from the beginning, when the first English settlers arrived in the New World. And the prospect of serving these gala meals to a large assembly of friends or family still sends us scooting off to our mother's china closet or to antiques shops and flea markets to seek out Haviland bouillon cups, pearl-handled silver, and heavily embroidered white napkins to give our contemporary tables style and panache.

Smoked Oyster Pâté Barbecued Pecans Creamy Cheese Soufflé Goat Cheese Pie
Sautéed Veal Chops with Thyme Mushroom and Walnut Stuffed Beef Tenderloin Cider Roast Pork
with Sweet Potatoes and Apples Classic Jonathan Chicken with Currants and Cream
Grilled Salmon Wild Rice with Oysters and Mushrooms Roast Turkey with Savory Gravy
Corn Bread–Apple Dressing with Sage Rosemary Potatoes Spicy Tomato Aspic Brussels Sprouts
with Almonds Green Salad with Pear Dressing Cranberry-Apple Rolled Spice Cake

SMOKED OYSTER PÂTÉ

SERVES 12

*Among the first foods to be canned commercially were lobster, oysters, and salmon, and
although they cannot replace the fresh versions, canned smoked oysters still bring a sense of luxury to a meal.
This old recipe from California is quick to prepare and very elegant; even the most discriminating
Victorian San Francisco hostess would have approved. This can be made 2 days in advance and kept refrigerated.
Serve with Bremner wafers or other plain crackers.*

½ cup finely chopped toasted
  pecans (see Note)
One 4-ounce can smoked oysters,
  drained and finely chopped
Dash of Worcestershire sauce

1 tablespoon minced parsley
One 8-ounce container soft
  cream cheese

Garnish: minced parsley

In a medium bowl or food processor, combine the pecans, oysters, Worcestershire, and parsley.
Transfer to a small serving dish (I use an antique butter dish, 5 inches in diameter, 2 inches deep) and pack
it in smoothly. Top with the cream cheese, smoothing it out on top. Sprinkle additional parsley on top and
refrigerate until serving time.

NOTE: *To toast pecans, sprinkle the chopped nuts with a bit of vegetable oil and salt and bake at 325° F. for
5 to 8 minutes, or until the nuts are golden. Stir once or twice during the baking period.*

BARBECUED PECANS

MAKES 1 POUND

*I prefer to serve nuts and nothing else during the cocktail hour so as not to spoil my guests' appetites. Barbecued
Pecans fill the bill nicely. The woman who gave me this recipe said in a southern Georgia drawl, "Why, ma
family has been making these for just yea-uhs." I can see why. I am going to make them for years to come myself. This
recipe can be doubled and frozen, which gives you a goodly supply to have on hand for unexpected company.*

1 pound whole fresh pecan halves
¼ cup vegetable oil
⅓ cup Worcestershire sauce

¾ teaspoon salt
8 dashes of hot red pepper sauce

Preheat the oven to 300° F. Place the pecans in a colander and rinse them with very hot water. Shake the
colander and drain the nuts well.

Cover a jelly roll pan with aluminum foil and transfer the nuts to the pan. In a small bowl, combine the
oil, Worcestershire, salt, and hot red pepper sauce with a whisk. Drizzle over the nuts and toss gently
with a wooden spoon to combine them with the seasonings. Bake the nuts for 30 minutes, stirring occasionally, or until they are browned. Cool and freeze until needed.

CREAMY CHEESE SOUFFLÉ

MAKES 4 TO 6 SERVINGS

*Soufflés have French antecedents and we tend to think of them as difficult dishes. However, adding
Minute Tapioca to the egg mixture eliminates the risk, and you can count on puffy soufflés that also have stability.
We can credit the Portuguese for bringing the tuberous roots of a tropical plant called cassava to Europe
from South America about 400 years ago. Used as a thickener and stabilizer, it has been a favorite with cooks
for centuries. Minute Tapioca was developed by Boston landlady, Susan Stavers, in 1894, when one of her boarders
complained about the lumpy tapioca pudding she served. He suggested she grind the tapioca in her coffee grinder.
She did and the result was a creamy, delightful pudding that everyone endorsed with enthusiasm.
She packed the ground tapioca in paper bags and sold it to other Bostonians until she was bought out by a newspaper
publisher, John Whitman, who organized a company to produce tapioca commercially.
Today, thanks to a critical sailor and Susan Stavers, I am able to serve this soufflé instead of potatoes with grilled steak
or chicken. It has a delightful texture and an intense cheese flavor.*

¼ cup Minute Tapioca	1 cup whole milk
⅛ teaspoon white pepper	4 eggs, room temperature
¼ teaspoon salt	1 cup shredded extra-sharp
¼ teaspoon ground mustard	cheddar cheese
2 teaspoons Worcestershire sauce	

Preheat the oven to 350° F.

Combine the tapioca, pepper, salt, mustard, Worcestershire sauce, and milk in a medium saucepan and let stand for 5 minutes. Meanwhile, separate the eggs, placing the yolks in a small bowl and the whites in a large mixer bowl.

Place the tapioca mixture over medium heat and cook, stirring constantly, until the mixture comes to a boil, about 4 to 5 minutes. Remove from the heat and add the shredded cheese, whisking until the cheese is completely melted. Set aside.

Beat the egg yolks until light and thick. Gradually beat in the warm tapioca-cheese mixture.

Beat the egg whites until stiff but not dry. Fold the egg yolk-cheese mixture into the whites. Don't overmix; some white streaks should remain in the batter. Pour into an ungreased 1½-quart round baking dish. Place the dish in a pan of hot water and bake for 50 to 55 minutes, or until the top of the soufflé is deeply browned and firm. Serve hot.

NOTE: *If you like spicy seasonings, this soufflé can be given a southwestern accent by adding a half to a whole chipotle chili in adobo sauce, finely chopped, to the soufflé mixture just before it is poured into the baking dish. Omit the white pepper and ground mustard.*

GOAT CHEESE PIE
MAKES TWO 9-INCH PIES

This recipe came to me from the Schads, talented Indiana goat cheese makers. Since I am enthusiastic about goat cheese, I fell in love with this creamy delicate pie, which is a splendid way to begin a meal. It could even be served as a luncheon dish. Each pie will make 10 to 12 appetizer servings or 8 entrée servings. This recipe is ideal for larger groups, as it makes two pies. Or you can halve the recipe if you prefer.

2 unbaked 9-inch pastry shells
  (page 284)
1 large onion, sliced
2 tablespoons (¼ stick) butter
12 ounces soft goat cheese, at
  room temperature
9 large eggs, at room temperature

3 cups half-and-half, at room temperature
3 tablespoons Dijon-style mustard
Salt and white pepper to taste
Paprika

Garnish: minced parsley

Preheat the oven to 425° F. Prick the bottoms of the pie shells and bake for 8 minutes, or until lightly browned, watching carefully that the sides do not slip down. If this happens, gently pat back up into place with the back of a fork. Set aside to cool.

Lower the oven temperature to 350° F. In a medium skillet, sauté the onion in the butter until soft; set aside. In a large mixing bowl, beat the goat cheese until smooth. Add the eggs one at time, beating in after each one (but don't overbeat), then add the half-and-half, blending well. Add the sautéed onion, mustard, and salt and pepper and blend. Pour into the prepared pie shells and sprinkle lightly with the paprika. Bake for 30 to 45 minutes, or until golden brown. The pie will be a bit shaky but will firm up as it cools. Garnish the tops of the pies with the minced parsley. Serve at room temperature.

Butter tool, pastry crimper and trimmer

$\mathscr{S}$AUTÉED VEAL CHOPS WITH THYME

SERVES 4

The farmer-owned, farmer-operated market Pike Place Market features Provimi veal, among zillions
of other foodstuffs and fish. This recipe was given out by the butcher behind the counter.
The sauce of olive oil, balsamic vinegar, and thyme is a marvel of flavor; it creates a dish so succulent that
it is hard to believe it can be prepared in a matter of minutes.
Balsamic vinegar, that aromatic import from Italy, has entered mainstream cookery here in the States; we are blessed.

4 center loin veal chops
   (about 10 ounces each)
Salt and freshly ground pepper
¼ cup all-purpose flour
3 tablespoons olive oil
2 tablespoons chopped parsley
1 tablespoon chopped onion
4 bay leaves

4 whole garlic cloves, peeled
4 sprigs of fresh thyme, leaves removed,
   or 1 teaspoon dried
2 tablespoons balsamic vinegar
¾ cup chicken stock

Garnish: minced parsley and fresh thyme sprigs

Sprinkle the chops with salt and pepper. Place the flour in a flat dish and dredge each chop, shaking off any excess. In a large heavy skillet, heat the oil over medium-high heat. Add the chops and brown them on both sides, approximately 5 minutes per side. Add the parsley, onions, bay leaves, garlic, and thyme and cook for 3 minutes, tossing the vegetables lightly now and then. Pour the vinegar around the chops and cook until reduced by half. Add the chicken stock, cover, and simmer for 15 to 20 minutes, or until the chops are tender. Remove and discard the bay leaves and garlic cloves. Serve the chops on a large platter with the sauce poured over them. Garnish with more parsley and sprigs of fresh thyme.

SEATTLE, WASHINGTON
We have come to Seattle at the right time—we've had sunshine every day! It's a great food city, with the Pike Place Market right downtown. Shopping there is like a moveable feast, and we sampled our way around the place with glee, picking up recipes from many food purveyors. Also visited Sur La Table, a fine cookware shop across the street—my cup runneth over. This was a boom town after the Yukon gold rush in 1897, and it still has a bit of an outpost feeling to it. Pioneer Square is the old part of town and where we found the wonderful Elliot Bay Book Company. Why don't we move here?

MUSHROOM AND WALNUT STUFFED BEEF TENDERLOIN

SERVES 8 TO 10

In some towns across the country, there are still frozen lockers used mostly by farm families to hold the extra meat that cannot be stored in home freezers—a side of beef takes up a lot of room. This generous amount of meat offers a great assortment of cuts, and certainly one of the most eagerly anticipated pieces of meat is the fillet. In some households, including ours, the fillet was reserved for grown-up company and stuffed with a savory filling. As a child, I remember envying the guests who were invited to enjoy this elegant dish and wishing I could join them at the table.

Make the stuffing a couple of days in advance and either serve the stuffed tenderloin hot with Rosemary Potatoes (page 258) or presented thinly sliced at room temperature for buffet service.

1 whole beef fillet, trimmed and butterflied, at room temperature (approximately 3 pounds)
3 tablespoons olive oil
2 tablespoons minced onion
1 garlic clove, minced
1 small red bell pepper, chopped
½ pound fresh mushrooms, finely chopped

⅓ cup coarsely chopped English walnuts
¼ cup minced parsley
1 large egg
¼ cup soft bread crumbs
½ teaspoon dried thyme or 1½ teaspoons minced fresh
½ cup dry red wine

Preheat the oven to 425° F. Flatten out the tenderloin on wax paper; cut eight to ten 12-inch lengths of butcher's twine and lay across a greased shallow roasting pan at 1-inch intervals (I use a 12 × 17 inch lipped cookie sheet).

To make the stuffing, heat 1 tablespoon oil in a heavy sauté pan and add the onion, garlic, and red bell peppers; sauté for 5 minutes over medium heat. Add the mushrooms and continue sautéing until the mushrooms begin to brown and all of their liquid has cooked off, about 7 minutes. Remove from the heat and cool. Stir in the walnuts and parsley.

In a small bowl, beat the egg slightly. Add the bread crumbs and thyme and combine. Add the egg mixture to the mushroom mixture. (This can be refrigerated up to 2 days at this point.) Arrange the filling in a 1-inch-wide strip down one side of the meat. Bring the other side of the meat up over the filling; if some of the filling oozes out, tuck as much of it back in as you can. Transfer the tenderloin to the prepared pan and tie the meat with the twine at about 1-inch intervals. Insert a meat thermometer into the meat only.

In a small bowl, combine the remaining 2 tablespoons oil and wine. Brush all over the meat and add the remainder to the pan. Roast the fillet for 10 minutes, reduce the heat to 350° F., and cook an additional 30 to 35 minutes for medium-rare meat (150° F. to 160° F.), basting occasionally with the pan juices. Remove from the oven and allow the meat to rest for 15 minutes before slicing it or allow it to cool completely, wrap it in foil, refrigerate, and serve it at room temperature within a day or two. I prefer this in thin slices, serving 2 slices per person.

CIDER ROAST PORK WITH SWEET POTATOES AND APPLES

SERVES 6 TO 8

This old recipe came from a regional San Antonio cookbook and reflects the melding of both the German and Southern settlers. It is most unusual. Pork was the most popular meat on the frontier; we can thank our friend the pig for sustaining civilization as it moved westward. To prepare this succulent roast with its spicy cider sauce, be sure your butcher understands that you do not want the roast suspended in one of those silly mesh bags.

3½-pound boneless pork loin roast
1½ cups apple cider or apple juice
2 cups packed dark brown sugar
¼ cup (½ stick) butter
3 tablespoons fresh lemon juice

2 teaspoons ground allspice
2 teaspoons grated lemon zest
6 medium sweet potatoes, peeled and cut
   into ½-inch slices
3 medium apples, cored and cut into ¾ -inch slices

Preheat the oven to 325° F. Place the roast in a large roasting pan, insert a meat thermometer, and bake for 1½ hours.

Meanwhile, combine the cider, sugar, butter, lemon juice, allspice, and lemon zest in a medium saucepan. Bring to a boil, then reduce the heat and simmer for 5 minutes, stirring frequently. Remove from the heat. (This can be done several days in advance and refrigerated.)

Remove the roast from the pan and skim off as much fat as possible from the pan juices. Return the roast to the pan and arrange the sweet potatoes and apples around the roast. Pour the Cider Sauce over the potatoes and apples. Return to the oven and roast for 1 to 1½ hours longer, basting the roast, potatoes, and apples frequently with the pan juices. When the roast registers 160° F. on the thermometer, remove from the oven, allow to rest for 10 minutes, then carve the meat into slices and serve immediately, accompanied by the potatoes and apples. Transfer the pan juices to a gravy boat and pass at the table.

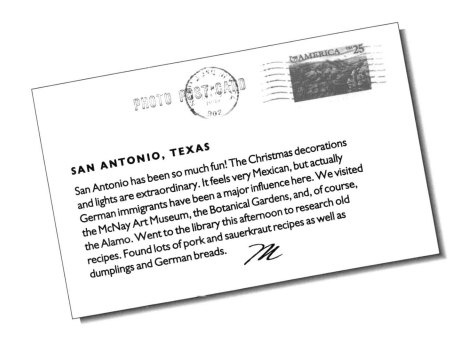

PHOTO POST CARD

AMERICA USA 25

SAN ANTONIO, TEXAS

San Antonio has been so much fun! The Christmas decorations and lights are extraordinary. It feels very Mexican, but actually German immigrants have been a major influence here. We visited the McNay Art Museum, the Botanical Gardens, and, of course, the Alamo. Went to the library this afternoon to research old recipes. Found lots of pork and sauerkraut recipes as well as dumplings and German breads.

M

WE LEFT SANTA FE with reluctance but San Antonio beckoned. It is a beautiful old city, especially at Christmas. Having been governed under six flags—France, Spain, Mexico, the Republic of Texas, the Confederate States of America, and finally the United States—it has a colorful, stormy past. Today it is a cosmopolitan city with a feel of Venice and Paris because of the San Antonio River Walk or the Paseo del Rio. The riverbanks are lined with flagstone and cobblestone paths, and at night, lights twinkle overhead and the dinner cruise launches float by. By day, the paths are filled with sightseers, shoppers, and mariachi bands playing Christmas carols. We stop in at a Mexican bakery for a treat—burnt milk bars and candied watermelon.

With over 55 percent of the population having a Spanish-language surname, this is the most Mexican city north of the Rio Grande and this is where chili began, or at least commercial chili. Cowboys had been eating it on the trail before the turn of the century. San Antonio chili was made from beef so tough that it had to be cut up to be chewable, and then it was combined with chili ancho, a coarse red pepper, and wild marjoram. A German from Braunfels found a way to extract pulp from the chili pods and, mixing this with spices, he created chili con carne, which he started canning and selling commercially in 1908.

The whole history of Texas is like a crazy quilt of unrelated squares and patches representing the numerous ethnic groups from its earliest days. Outside influences are apparent in the state's foodways. Butting up against Arkansas and Louisiana, east Texas is more southern and here we see an emphasis on rice dishes, recipes for crawfish and okra, and southern-style desserts. Central and southern Texas were settled by

ranchers who lived on sparse rations of beans, corn bread, and beef. To many of us, the idea of thousands of longhorn steers moving along a dusty trail, accompanied by cowboys on horseback, is an indelible image of this part of the country. Walt Whitman wrote: "Bright-eyed as hawks, always on horseback, with their swarthy complexions and their broad-brimmed hats, with loose arms raised and swinging as they rode." The cowboys headed the cattle to Abilene and markets beyond. Texas endures as the mythical heart of cattle country and beef is still one of the state's most popular foods.

The missionaries and later the settlers introduced other fruits and vegetables, including tomatoes, sweet potatoes, avocados, as well as oranges and lemons that had migrated around the world from China to Portugal and Spain.

The Gulf of Mexico provides ingredients for dishes that hint of Creole from neighboring Louisiana—shrimp, crayfish, and lobster are often served as gumbos on Texas tables. Germans arrived in large numbers and we find their influence in breads, cakes, and pastries, as well as the spices of Middle Europe—allspice, cinnamon, cloves, ginger, and nutmeg. They used them with beans, squash, and corn; and again, we have the "melting down" of the traditional foodways to combine regional food of astonishing variety.

We rented a car and drove to Kingsville, the site of the King Ranch, and then onto Corpus Christi; the bay provides a harbor with a shipping channel through the Gulf of Mexico. When the town was settled, it was considered a "small village of smugglers and lawless men, but with few women and no ladies." I am happy to report there are any number of ladies now living in Corpus Christi.

We take a late lunch of Gulf seafood down on the waterfront, knowing it will be our last meal in the sunshine for a while. It is time to fly back to Indiana for Christmas and the New Year.

CLASSIC JONATHAN CHICKEN WITH CURRANTS AND CREAM

SERVES 8

*This is not a particularly old recipe, but I do know that many cooks like to serve chicken when
they entertain and also want a recipe that is unique. You'll be impressed with this
sautéed chicken dish, which is accompanied by apples and currants and napped with cream and brandy.
It is quick to prepare and unforgettably good. The recipe is from Steven Kneipp.*

¼ cup (½ stick) butter
8 chicken breast halves, skinned, boned,
   and flattened with a meat mallet
4 small firm Jonathan apples, peeled,
   cored, and sliced
¼ cup dried currants

2 teaspoons dried tarragon
¼ cup applejack or calvados
2 cups heavy cream
Salt and white pepper to taste

Garnish: tarragon sprigs

Melt the butter in a large heavy skillet. Add the chicken breasts and sauté about 5 minutes on each side, or
until the chicken loses its opaqueness and is just cooked. Transfer to a heated platter and keep warm.
Drain the excess fat from the skillet, leaving about 1 tablespoon of the drippings. Add the apples, currants,
and tarragon to the skillet and sauté over low heat until the apples are just tender, about 5 to 8 minutes.

Pour the apple brandy into a 1-cup metal ladle. Heat the brandy in the ladle and light with a match.
Place the ladle in the skillet, with its bottom resting on the bottom of the pan, and *slowly* pour the flaming
brandy over the apple mixture. Cook for a few seconds until the flame dies; then increase the heat and
cook until the liquid in the pan is syruplike, about 2 to 4 minutes. Add the cream and, over high heat, boil
until the sauce reduces and will coat the back of the spoon, about 5 minutes. Season with salt and pepper.
Pour the sauce and apples over the chicken; garnish with sprigs of fresh tarragon.

GRILLED SALMON

SERVES 8

Salmon is one of the great special dishes of the Northwest, and we had it at almost every meal we were there, even for breakfast, scrambled with eggs. Many northwesterners like their salmon simply prepared, grilled with just a dash of lemon. The addition of brown sugar to this basting sauce gives the fish a bit of crustiness that is very pleasant. Serve with Potato Salad with Mustard Dressing (page 75).

⅓ cup butter

⅔ cup packed dark brown sugar

3 tablespoons lemon juice

2 tablespoons minced fresh tarragon
  or ½ teaspoon dried

Salt and pepper to taste

Eight 10- to 12-ounce salmon fillets

In a medium saucepan, melt the butter over medium heat. Add the brown sugar and stir until dissolved. Add the lemon juice, tarragon, and salt and pepper, stirring until heated through, about 3 minutes.

Place the fillets in a well-greased grill basket, brush with the sauce, and grill directly over medium coals for 4 to 6 minutes per ½-inch thickness, or until the fish flakes when tested with a fork. Turn once during cooking. Brush occasionally with the basting sauce and again just before serving.

PHOTO POST CARD

AMERICA 25

SALMON BAKE AT TILLICUM VILLAGE, SEATTLE, WASHINGTON

We took a boat over to Blake Island and Tillicum Village, a former Indian summer fishing camp in Puget Sound, for a salmon bake—it was loads of fun! When we got off the boat, we were given a cup of butter clams in broth, a very hospitable way to begin. Native Americans cook the fish on cedar stakes by hot-smoking it close to a fire burned down to embers. It was perfectly done. The rest of the meal is served buffet style, and the adventure ended with authentic Northwest coast Indian dancing. We enjoyed it all!

M

WILD RICE WITH OYSTERS AND MUSHROOMS

SERVES 6

As soon as the "R" months (September through December) arrive, it is time to think of oysters.
We have always attached importance to oysters in this country, and our enthusiasm for them doesn't abate.
Oyster stew and escalloped oysters are the classic ways to use them, but here is another
recipe you should consider. The recipe came from an old Minnesota cookbook, which explains the wild rice—it
is an important crop in that state. Mushrooms and oysters are combined in a cream sauce
with a touch of curry, then mixed with wild rice and baked. A most luxurious dish, it is unusual too.

One 6-ounce package long-grain
  wild rice and seasonings
2⅓ cups beef stock
5½ tablespoons butter
2 tablespoons chopped onion
1½ cups (½ pound) fresh mushrooms,
  cleaned and sliced

1½ tablespoons all-purpose flour
1 teaspoon curry powder
¼ teaspoon salt
¼ teaspoon coarsely ground pepper
1½ pints oysters, drained and
  liquid reserved
¼ cup heavy cream

Cook the rice according to package directions, using beef stock in place of water. When the rice is tender, about 45 minutes, stir in 2 tablespoons butter.

In a sauté pan, melt 1½ tablespoons butter and add the onions and mushrooms. Sauté over medium heat until the mushrooms are cooked and their liquid has cooked off, about 6 to 10 minutes. Add the flour, curry powder, salt, and pepper; stir and cook until the mixture is bubbling up in the center of the pan, about 3 to 4 minutes. Add ½ cup reserved oyster liquid, then the cream. Continue cooking and stirring until the mixture is creamy and thick, about 3 minutes.

Melt the remaining 2 tablespoons butter in a small saucepan. Add the oysters and cook gently over medium heat, just until the edges begin to curl, about 3 minutes; set aside.

Preheat the oven to 325° F. Spoon half the rice into a greased 1½ quart casserole. Arrange half the oysters on top. Cover with the remaining rice and oysters. Spoon the mushroom sauce over all. Cover and bake for 20 minutes, then uncover and bake another 20 minutes, or until the top is golden brown.

Sterling napkin rings with antique linens

ROAST TURKEY WITH SAVORY GRAVY

My mother always roasted her turkey with a butter-drenched cheesecloth on top. According to her, this method kept the otherwise dry breast very moist. In preparing this book, I decided I would duplicate her recipe, and sure enough, she was right, the breast meat stayed very moist (though I must tell you at one point during the roasting, I considered serving the cheesecloth and discarding the turkey! The cheesecloth looked pretty tasty). Roasting the neck and giblets with the turkey in the basting juices eliminates the need to make turkey stock. And to further speed up the meal, I didn't stuff the turkey but made an absolutely knockout corn bread dressing (page 257) to serve separately. All in all, this is quite an improved (read "speedier") way to cope with turkey and all the trimmings. The total cooking time will be about 3 hours. For your own peace of mind, use a meat thermometer to check its doneness.

One 12-pound turkey, preferably fresh, including the neck and giblets, except the liver
2 cups very coarsely chopped onions
3 large carrots, cut into 1-inch chunks
3 celery stalks, cut into 1-inch chunks
12 whole black peppercorns
6 whole cloves
1 bay leaf
Double thickness of cheesecloth, approximately 9 × 18 inches

¼ cup (½ stick) butter
1 cup defatted chicken broth

GRAVY
6 tablespoons (¾ stick) butter
9 tablespoons all-purpose flour
5 cups defatted chicken broth
Dash of Worcestershire sauce
Salt and pepper to taste

Position the oven rack to the lower third of the oven and preheat the oven to 325° F. Remove the giblets and neck from the bird's neck and body cavity, rinse, and set aside. Rinse the turkey inside and out and pat it dry with paper towels; cut off any visible fat and discard. Set the turkey in a large roasting pan and add the giblets and neck to the pan as well. Run a long piece of kitchen cord under the turkey, tying the legs close to the body so they won't roast too quickly.

Tuck a few of the vegetables in both the neck and body cavities and scatter the remaining vegetables, peppercorns, cloves, and the bay leaf around the turkey. Insert a meat thermometer into the meaty part of the thigh, close to the body. Dampen the cheesecloth in hot water and place over the turkey.

In a small saucepan, heat the butter and the chicken broth together until the butter melts. With a pastry brush, lavishly baste the turkey and cheesecloth. Place the turkey in the oven and roast for 30 minutes. Baste the turkey with the butter-broth mixture. Roast another 30 minutes and repeat. Roast for 1 hour and baste again, using up all the butter-broth mixture. Continue roasting until done, about 45 minutes longer, basting with the pan juices if you are close to the oven. When the meat thermometer registers 170° F. and the drumsticks move easily, remove the turkey from the oven and transfer to a cutting board. Tent with foil topped with newspapers (great insulators) and terrycloth towels if you are not quite ready to carve it; this will keep it warm.

Transfer the roasted vegetables, turkey neck, and giblets from the roasting pan along with the pan juices to a strainer set over a bowl. Press hard with the back of the spoon to extract all the juices. Discard the solids and degrease the pan juices—I use a degreasing pitcher, a very handy gadget.

Make the gravy: In a medium saucepan over low heat, melt the butter. Whisk in the flour and cook, stirring often without allowing the flour to brown, for about 3 minutes. The mixture should be very bubbly. Combine the pan juices with enough of the chicken broth to make 6 cups of liquid. Add all at once to the butter-flour mixture and whisk and cook until the gravy is thickened and bubbles up in the center of the pan, about 10 minutes. Season with the Worcestershire and salt and pepper. Carve the turkey and serve accompanied by the gravy and corn bread dressing.

CORN BREAD–APPLE DRESSING WITH SAGE

SERVES 12 GENEROUSLY

As long as I have been writing cookbooks, I have been getting regular requests for corn bread dressing. After experimenting, this is the one that I like best and I think you will too. It is crumbly, light, yet moist and the apple gives it special oomph. You will need one recipe of the Mormon Corn Bread as the base. Quite a few of the steps can be done in advance so you won't have much to do the day you bake the dressing. I have stuffed turkeys with this, but it is simpler to bake it separately and serve as a side dish with the turkey and gravy. This is also good with pork and beef.

1 recipe Mormon Corn Bread (page 120), baked at least a day in advance
3 tablespoons butter
1½ cups chopped onions
¾ teaspoons dried thyme
1½ tablespoons dried leaf sage, crumbled
1 large cooking apple, such as yellow Delicious or red Romes, peeled, cored, and chopped
½ teaspoon salt
½ teaspoon ground pepper
¼ cup minced parsley
1¼ cups defatted chicken broth

Crumble the corn bread coarsely; you will need 6 to 7 cups; set aside. Melt the butter in a large skillet. Add the onions, thyme, and sage and sauté for 5 minutes. Add the apples and sauté 5 minutes longer, stirring now and then; cool. *The dressing can be prepared to this point 2 days in advance.*

The day of serving, preheat the oven to 400° F. In a large mixing bowl, combine the corn bread crumbs, the onion mixture, salt, pepper, and parsley. Pour the chicken broth over the corn bread mixture and toss lightly to combine. Transfer to a greased deep 2-quart baking dish and bake the dressing, covered, for about 40 to 50 minutes, or until heated through.

ROSEMARY POTATOES

SERVES 8

*Originally, this country recipe was made with butter, but I have substituted olive oil with
what I think is great success. Roasting the potatoes in a shallow pan with herbs and garlic plus the oil gives them
a sweet flavor. It is one of those dishes you can put in the oven and ignore until serving time.*

2½ pounds baking potatoes	1½ tablespoons minced fresh rosemary or
⅔ cup olive oil	1 teaspoon dried
2 tablespoons minced parsley	2 large garlic cloves, minced
2 tablespoons minced fresh chives	Salt and freshly ground pepper to taste

Peel and slice the potatoes thinly, about ⅛ inch thick. Place them in a deep bowl and cover with water. Refrigerate until needed—this can be done several hours in advance.

Preheat the oven to 350° F.

In a large bowl, combine the oil, parsley, chives, rosemary, garlic, and salt and pepper.

Drain the water off the potatoes and dry them between 2 towels. Transfer the potatoes to the bowl with the oil mixture and stir to coat all the slices. Spread the potatoes out on a shallow 12 × 17-inch lipped cooking pan. Bake for 1¼ hours, or until the potatoes are tender and golden brown. It is not necessary to turn them. Serve immediately.

SPICY TOMATO ASPIC

SERVES 4 TO 6

*I am not at all fond of Jell-O salads, which is putting it mildly. Yet I do yearn, now and then, for tomato
aspic. There are certain dishes that seem to require that piquant, cold tomato
accompaniment and no other dish will do. For those of you who might have long ago tossed out
your recipe, here is a really well-seasoned version. The recipe is from Dave Lewis, an
interior designer from Indianapolis. He has assisted us with three different houses, and we're still good friends!*

2 envelopes gelatin	Salt and white pepper to taste
½ cup cold water	1 tablespoon finely chopped green bell pepper
2 cups vegetable juice cocktail	1 tablespoon finely chopped celery
½ cup white vinegar	1 tablespoon finely chopped onion
⅓ cup sugar	Bibb lettuce
½ teaspoon ground allspice	Mayonnaise (optional)
¼ teaspoon ground cloves	

In a medium saucepan, combine the gelatin and cold water and allow to stand for 1 minute. Whisk in the vegetable juice, vinegar, sugar, allspice, cloves, and salt and pepper. Bring to a boil over medium heat and stir now and then, making sure the gelatin is dissolved.

Chill the mixture until it is syrupy and the consistency of unbeaten egg whites, about 20 minutes. Stir in the green bell peppers, celery, and onions. Pour into an 8-inch square pan, cover, and refrigerate until set. Cut in squares and serve on Bibb lettuce, with a dab of mayonnaise, if desired.

$\mathscr{B}$RUSSELS SPROUTS WITH ALMONDS

SERVES 4

Brussels sprouts are one of my favorite vegetables to serve at winter dinner parties—their texture and flavor combine well with many meat dishes. It was not uncommon for the Victorians to add nuts to their vegetable dishes, but of course, they cooked most of their vegetables to death. This combination of lightly cooked sprouts, almonds, and a touch of garlic and lemon is a good company dish.

1 pound Brussels sprouts	**½ teaspoon salt**
2 tablespoons (¼ stick) butter	**½ teaspoon ground pepper**
¼ cup slivered or sliced almonds	
1 garlic clove, crushed	**Garnish: lemon twists and dill, savory,**
1 teaspoon grated lemon zest	**or parsley sprigs**
1 tablespoon fresh lemon juice	

Trim any browned leaves off the sprouts and cut an X into the stem end of each. In a medium saucepan, cook the sprouts in boiling salted water 4 to 5 minutes, or just until tender. Drain well and place in a warmed serving dish.

Meanwhile, melt the butter in a small skillet. Add the almonds and garlic and sauté over low heat until the almonds are golden brown, about 3 to 4 minutes. Stir in the lemon zest and juice, salt, and pepper and mix well.

Sprinkle the almonds over the sprouts; stir gently to mix. Garnish with lemon twists and herb sprigs.

Mother-of-pearl–handled flatware

GREEN SALAD WITH PEAR DRESSING

SERVES 8

What a festive salad this is! Assorted greens and radicchio are topped with slices
of green-skinned pears and green pumpkin seeds. The dressing has a touch of honey and celery seed.
Arrange this on a large platter, then toss just before serving. The dressing can be
made in advance and stored in the refrigerator.

SALAD DRESSING	SALAD
2 canned pears (4 halves)	3 to 4 heads Boston lettuce
½ cup fresh lemon juice	2 to 3 handfuls curly endive leaves
¼ to ½ cup honey (to taste)	1 small head radicchio
1 teaspoon grated lemon zest	2 green-skinned pears, cored and
½ teaspoon celery seed	thinly sliced
½ teaspoon salt	Toasted green pumpkin seeds
¼ teaspoon white pepper	(see Note)
1 cup vegetable oil (not olive)	

Make the Salad Dressing: Place all of the ingredients except the oil in a blender or food processor bowl. Process until well blended. Gradually add the oil. Transfer to a glass jar and refrigerate until needed. This dressing can be made several days in advance.

Assemble the salad: Arrange the Boston lettuce in an attractive pattern on a large platter, then arrange the endive, radicchio, and pears on top. Drizzle the dressing over all, then sprinkle at least ½ cup of the toasted pumpkin seeds over all.

NOTE: *To toast pumpkin seeds, place 8 ounces green pumpkin seeds in a shallow pan, drizzle 2 teaspoons vegetable oil and ¼ teaspoon salt over the top, and bake in a preheated 350° F. oven for 6 minutes, stirring twice. Cool. Store in the refrigerator in an airtight container.*

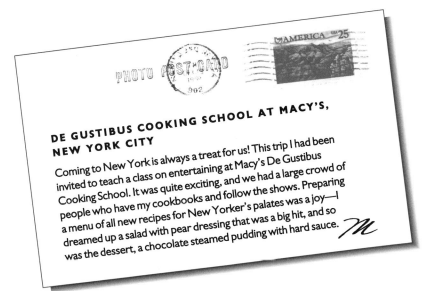

♥AMERICA USA 25

PHOTO POST-CARD
902

DE GUSTIBUS COOKING SCHOOL AT MACY'S, NEW YORK CITY

Coming to New York is always a treat for us! This trip I had been invited to teach a class on entertaining at Macy's De Gustibus Cooking School. It was quite exciting, and we had a large crowd of people who have my cookbooks and follow the shows. Preparing a menu of all new recipes for New Yorker's palates was a joy—I dreamed up a salad with pear dressing that was a big hit, and so was the dessert, a chocolate steamed pudding with hard sauce.

CRANBERRY-APPLE ROLLED SPICE CAKE

SERVES 6 TO 8

This is a most pleasant holiday cake—a spicy jelly roll–type cake filled with a mixture of cooked cranberries and apples. You'll have requests for the recipe when you serve it—it came to me from Clarinda's Cottage Tea Room in Newburgh, Indiana.

FILLING

2 large Granny Smith apples,
   peeled, cored, and quartered
1 cup fresh cranberries
½ cup sugar
2 cinnamon sticks
¼ cup water

CAKE

5 large egg whites, at room temperature
Speck of salt
Speck of cream of tartar
1 cup sugar, divided
5 large egg yolks
¼ cup sifted cake flour
¼ teaspoon ground allspice
2 teaspoons ground cinnamon

Garnish: confectioners' sugar

In a medium saucepan, combine the apples, cranberries, sugar, cinnamon sticks, and water. Simmer over medium heat for 20 to 30 minutes, stirring regularly. Remove from the heat and allow the mixture to cool, then discard the cinnamon sticks. Transfer the mixture to a food processor bowl and puree. Chill the filling until needed.

Preheat the oven to 350° F.

In a large mixer bowl, beat the egg whites with a speck of salt until frothy. Add the cream of tartar and beat until the egg whites hold soft peaks. Gradually add ½ cup sugar and continue beating the egg whites until they hold stiff, glossy peaks. In another large bowl, beat the egg yolks with the remaining ½ cup sugar until the mixture is thick and pale yellow, about 5 minutes. Add the flour, allspice, and cinnamon. Gently fold in the egg white mixture just until combined. Line a 10 × 15 × 1-inch jelly roll pan with aluminum foil and butter the foil. Pour in the batter, then spread it evenly with a rubber spatula. Rap the pan on the counter once or twice to eliminate air bubbles. Bake for 22 to 25 minutes, or until the cake is firm to the touch. Allow the cake to cool in the pan. Carefully remove the whole cake from the pan and transfer to wax paper.

Spread the cooled filling over the cake, spreading it to within ¼ inch of the edges of the cake. Roll the cake from the short end, slowly peeling away the paper as you roll the cake. Finish with the end on the bottom. Trim the 2 ends to even up the roll, if necessary. Wrap the cake in plastic wrap and chill for 4 hours. Dust with confectioners' sugar and slice with a serrated knife.

Dessert BUFFET

WE AMERICANS HAVE always appreciated desserts. From the earliest days when the Pilgrim cooks added maple syrup to Indian pudding, we have cherished a sweet ending to our meals.

When the pioneers moved west, they were careful to include molasses among their provisions and dried fruits, especially apples. Upon arriving in the Midwest, they discovered that an early hippie ecologist, John Chapman, had been way ahead of them and anticipated their needs for fruit. He had planted apple seeds in nurseries along the frontier, the apple whips free for the taking and planting.

When the Industrial Age brought income and upward mobility to America, simple country desserts like apple slump, pies, and stack cakes slipped out of sight, except in rural areas, and more elaborate concoctions such as baked Alaska, creme brûlée, and other French-influenced sweets became popular. Restaurants, such as Delmonico's, which at one repast had live swans swimming on a pond atop a table with a gold cage from Tiffany's to keep them from flying off, also influenced American hostesses. (Though I doubt if many attempted to duplicate the swan idea; they are notoriously bad-tempered birds, and the aforementioned waterfowl behaved rather badly at the dinner; it was mating season.)

Today the Victorian idea of a dessert buffet is still a very appealing way to entertain on a Sunday afternoon or after another occasion—the theater or concert, a graduation, a christening. Stay away from a conventional mealtime, set the table way in advance and cover with a sheet, and have all the desserts made and frozen (or at least most of them) so you won't feel harried the day of the party. I recommend at least five desserts, including a tray of fresh fruit and cheese, plus coffee and tea. When the guests arrive, pass among them with a tray of sherries, both dry and sweet, and champagne, if the budget allows. Skip the swans.

Apple Cake with Hot Sherry Sauce Holiday Orange Torte Steamed Chocolate Cake
Steamed Molasses Pudding Baked Pumpkin Custard Floating Island with
Spun Caramel Science Hill Biscuit Pudding with Warm Bourbon Sauce Honey Crust Cake
Kentucky Stack Cake Delicate Mincemeat Strudel Chocolate Velvet Cheesecake Golden Jelly Roll
with Orange Curd and Coconut Blueberry Gingerbread Date-Ginger Steamed Pudding

APPLE CAKE WITH HOT SHERRY SAUCE

SERVES 16

Apples are an important fruit crop in the Mid-Atlantic states and we find unusually fine recipes for using them in old cookbooks. This is from an old Baltimore church cookbook. One of the ingredients is sherry, which was a legitimate cooking ingredient before Prohibition. It certainly enhances this cake. Dark, moist, spicy, and rich, the sherry sauce is buttery and golden. The cake is very good without the sauce, too.

½ cup sweet sherry
4 cups baking apples, peeled, cored, and chopped (such as Granny Smith or Ida Red)
2 cups all-purpose flour
2 teaspoons baking soda
1 teaspoon salt
2 teaspoons ground cinnamon
1 teaspoon grated nutmeg
½ teaspoon ground allspice
2 cups sugar
2 large eggs

½ cup vegetable oil
2 teaspoons vanilla extract
1½ cups chopped pecans

HOT SHERRY SAUCE
½ cup (1 stick) butter
1 cup sugar
½ cup half-and-half
1 teaspoon vanilla extract
Speck of salt
2 tablespoons sherry

Preheat the oven to 350° F. (If you are using a glass dish, lower the oven temperature to 325° F.)

In a large mixing bowl, pour the sherry over the prepared apples; set aside. In another mixing bowl, whisk together the flour, soda, salt, cinnamon, nutmeg, and allspice; add to the apples and toss to mix.

In a large mixer bowl, beat together the sugar, eggs, oil, and vanilla for 2 minutes until creamy and light yellow in color. Add this mixture gradually to the apples, stirring well after each addition. Add the pecans and blend.

Pour into a greased and floured 9 × 13-inch pan or glass dish. Bake for 1 hour, or until done and the cake springs back when touched in the center with your finger.

Prepare the Hot Sherry Sauce: Melt the butter in a small saucepan, then stir in the sugar, half-and-half, vanilla, and salt; cook over low heat, whisking until smooth. Slowly add the sherry a tablespoon at a time, whisking it in. Ladle the warm sauce over each slice of warm cake.

HOLIDAY ORANGE TORTE

SERVES 8 TO 10

This very old recipe of my Grandmother Grabill's is one of our favorite holiday desserts. She used to prepare the orange in a hand grinder attached to her kitchen table, and though I still have the grinder, I now use the food processor for this step. The brandy sauce is truly fine, and she also served it on mincemeat pies and over fruitcake slices. The only time a bottle of liquor appeared in her house was when she made this sauce. She had such strong negative feelings about alcohol that she wouldn't permit my grandfather even to park his car in front of the local tavern, which he would never enter under any circumstances, and in a town of 500 people, everyone knew that anyway. But appearances mattered to my very proper grandmother, even if she did make brandy sauce. This torte is better a day after baking.

TORTE

2 tablespoons (¼ stick) butter, at
  room temperature
1¼ cups sugar
1 whole orange, cut into sixths,
  seeds removed
1 cup golden seedless raisins
2 cups all-purpose flour
1 teaspoon baking soda
½ teaspoon salt
1 cup buttermilk or sour milk
½ cup orange juice

BRANDY SAUCE

1 cup (2 sticks) butter
1 pound dark brown sugar
Juice and grated zest of 2 lemons
½ cup brandy
2 eggs, slightly beaten

Preheat the oven to 350° F. Line the bottom of a 9 × 5 × 3-inch loaf pan with wax paper, then coat with a vegetable oil cooking spray.

In a large mixer bowl, cream the butter and 1 cup of the sugar for 7 minutes. In a food grinder or food processor, grind the orange (rind and all) and the raisins. Add to the creamed mixture and mix well.

In a medium mixing bowl, whisk together the flour, soda, and salt. Begin adding the flour mixture to the butter mixture alternating with the buttermilk or sour milk, beginning and ending with the flour mixture, mixing until combined. Pour the batter into the prepared pan and bake for 1 hour. Remove the cake from the oven and while still hot, mix the remaining ¼ cup sugar with the orange juice and pour over the cake. When this juice has been entirely absorbed, turn the cake out onto a rack and remove the wax paper.

Prepare the Brandy Sauce: Combine the butter, sugar, lemon juice and zest, brandy, and eggs in the top of a double boiler pan. Whisk together over boiling water for about 5 minutes, or until the mixture thickens. Cut the torte into slices and serve with the warm brandy sauce.

 $\mathscr{S}$TEAMED CHOCOLATE CAKE

SERVES 12 TO 16

*Steamed puddings and cakes have always been popular dishes all over the United States
with a history reaching back to Colonial days. The cooks were always there in the kitchen to tend the steamers, and
the wood or coal stove was always heated. Also, steamed puddings and cakes were
frequently made in large batches with suet and dried fruit and would keep a long time in cold storage.
But this one, ah, this one from a German cook in Cincinnati is another story.
It is more like a delicate chocolate buttercake, winningly moist. She served it with hard sauce, well-doused with Ohio
sherry, but it is also lovely with crème anglaise or sweetened whipped cream garnished with chocolate leaves.*

½ cup (1 stick) butter, at room temperature	2 cups sifted cake flour
1 cup sugar	2 teaspoons baking powder
2 eggs, at room temperature	1 teaspoon salt
4 squares (4 ounces) unsweetened chocolate, melted	1 cup milk, at room temperature
2 teaspoons vanilla extract	Hard Sauce (page 285), Crème Anglaise (page 286), or Whipped Cream Topping (page 286)

Place a steamer or deep kettle on the stove, fill about ⅓ full of water and bring to a boil.

In a large mixer bowl, cream the butter and sugar together until fluffy, 5 to 7 minutes. Add the eggs to the butter mixture and blend well. Add the melted chocolate and vanilla.

Sift the flour, baking powder, and salt together and add to the batter alternately with the milk, beginning and ending with the flour mixture. Pour the batter into a greased and floured 7-cup mold or tin, cover, and place on a rack in the steamer. Add enough boiling water to come halfway up the side of the mold. Cover the pan and bring the water to a boil, then reduce the heat and simmer for 1 hour and 15 minutes.

Remove from the pot and allow to stand 10 minutes. Loosen the edges of the cake from the pan with a knife, if necessary, and tip the cake out on a rack. Serve hot with Hard Sauce, Crème Anglaise, or Whipped Cream Topping.

PHOTO POST CARD

AMERICA 25

STAN HYWETT HALL AND GARDENS, AKRON, OHIO

Stan Hywett is an extraordinary sixty-five-room English-style manor house built by the Seiberling family in the early 1900s. Fully furnished, the gardens are equally breathtaking! The family entertained lavishly and Gertrude Seiberling's cooks used *Fanny Farmer's Boston Cooking School Cookbook* at her request. Pumpkin pie and steamed chocolate cake, and an unpretentious ham loaf, were among the family's favorite dishes.

M

STEAMED MOLASSES PUDDING

SERVES 8

*This pudding is a lovely thing—moist, rich, and very flavorful. The original recipe called for suet
as the fat and soda as the leavening, for which I have substituted vegetable oil and and baking powder. Prepared
in a few minutes from ingredients you always have on hand, this very good dessert should not be overlooked.
If you don't have a pudding mold or tin, substitute an ovenproof glass bowl.
Molasses was always a sweetening staple in early American cookery, and in the Chesapeake area, it was
readily available since Baltimore was a principal port for the West Indies and the Caribbean. Its popularity lasted
for 150 years, but it is still used in many cornmeal dishes, cakes, and puddings.*

PUDDING
1 cup all-purpose flour
1 teaspoon baking powder
½ teaspoon salt
½ cup golden seedless raisins
1 large egg
½ cup light molasses
½ cup milk
½ cup vegetable oil

ORANGE SAUCE
1 cup sugar
1 tablespoon all-purpose flour
½ cup water
½ cup orange juice
1 tablespoon fresh lemon juice
1 tablespoon butter
½ teaspoon ground cinnamon

Grease and flour a 3-cup pudding mold or ovenproof bowl; set aside. Place a rack and water in the bottom of a vegetable steamer—the water should not touch the pudding mold—and bring to a boil.

In the meantime, in a large bowl, whisk together the flour, baking powder, and salt. Add the raisins and toss together to mix. In a small bowl, beat the egg, then add the molasses, milk, and oil; beat until combined. Pour the molasses mixture over the dry ingredients and blend with a mixing spoon; the batter will be very runny.

Pour into the prepared mold, cover with its lid or foil, place it on the steamer rack, and lower it into the steaming kettle. Cover and steam for 1 hour.

Meanwhile, make the sauce: In a small saucepan, whisk together the sugar and flour. Heat the water and orange juice (I do this in a measuring cup in the microwave) and whisk into the sugar mixture. Cook and stir over medium-high heat until the mixture is thickened, about 2 minutes. Add the lemon juice, butter, and cinnamon and cook 1 minute longer. Keep warm.

Remove the pudding mold from the steamer and allow it to stand for 10 minutes. Loosen the edges with a knife and tip out onto a serving plate. Cut into wedges and serve with the hot orange sauce.

NOTE: *This dessert reheats very well in the microwave.*

BAKED PUMPKIN CUSTARD

SERVES 12

In the fall and early winter, we think of pumpkin and have all sorts of imaginative ways to prepare it.
For entertaining, Baked Pumpkin Custard, smooth and elegant, must be made a day in advance. Sweetened
condensed milk gives this a superb texture. With a touch of orange and spice, this is an
ideal holiday dessert. I use a large foil loaf pan for this recipe.

1 cup sugar	6 large egg yolks
¼ cup water	2 teaspoons grated orange zest
Pinch of cream of tartar	2 teaspoons brandy extract
Three 14-ounce cans sweetened	1 teaspoon ground cinnamon
condensed milk	½ teaspoon ground ginger
One 16-ounce can pumpkin puree	½ teaspoon grated nutmeg
6 large eggs	2 cups milk

Preheat the oven to 325° F.

In a heavy skillet, combine the sugar, water, and cream of tartar. Cook over medium-high heat for 10 to 15 minutes, partially covered, just until the syrup turns a rich golden, tealike brown. Stir the sugar mixture occasionally and watch carefully; it will turn too dark almost instantly. Meanwhile, coat a 12 × 6 × 3-inch foil loaf pan with vegetable oil cooking spray and set aside. When the sugar mixture is dark, pour it immediately into the prepared pan.

In a mixer bowl, on medium speed, combine the condensed milk, pumpkin puree, eggs and egg yolks, orange zest, brandy extract, cinnamon, ginger, and nutmeg. Add the milk and combine, but don't over-beat or foam will form, causing bubbles in the custard as it bakes. Pour the pumpkin mixture over the caramelized sugar. Cover with aluminum foil. Place in a large shallow pan and pour in hot water to a depth of 1 inch. Bake for 2 hours—the center will still be a bit shaky but will firm up as it cools.

Remove the pan from the water and uncover; cool completely, then recover and chill overnight in the refrigerator. To serve, loosen the edges with a knife and invert the custard onto a lipped serving plate. There will be a lovely thin sauce to accompany the creamy custard. Cut in slices and serve with the sauce.

ℱloating Island with Spun Caramel

SERVES 8

*This custard sauce topped with puffs of meringue originated in France and is still a
popular dessert there, where it is called* oeufs à la neige, *or snow eggs. Benjamin Franklin recorded in his letters
(1771) eating this dessert, and we know Thomas Jefferson also relished it. It was known in America
by the late eighteenth century and had become very popular in the nineteenth. I hope it becomes more popular
again in the twentieth, for it is economical, dramatic, and a very satisfactory ending to a meal.
This recipe is from an old cookbook that belonged to "Ma" Sunday, the wife of the early evangelist, Billy Sunday.
There was a check mark beside it, so I have to wonder if it was a family favorite.
If you find the caramel too bothersome, just top each "egg" with a bit of strawberry or raspberry jam, or
even omit the jam and sprinkle some fresh raspberries over the custard. However, I hope you'll try the caramel; it isn't
hard to make and the crunch of it plays off the smoothness of the rest of the ingredients. Make the
custard a day in advance of serving. The egg white puffs can be made eight hours in advance. Make the caramel to
drizzle over the eggs about two hours before serving. Use jumbo eggs. A candy thermometer is helpful.*

CUSTARD
4 cups whole milk
1 cup sugar
2 teaspoons all-purpose flour
8 jumbo egg yolks (reserve
   4 egg whites)
1 tablespoon vanilla extract

ISLANDS
4 egg whites, at room temperature
1 teaspoon vanilla extract
Speck of salt
Speck of cream of tartar
¾ cup sugar
2 teaspoons cornstarch

CARAMEL
¾ cup sugar
3 tablespoons water
¼ teaspoon cream of tartar

Make the custard: Bring the milk almost to a boil in the top of a double boiler pan over direct heat; little bubbles will form about the outside edge of the pan. In a small bowl, whisk together the sugar and flour; set aside. In a mixing bowl, beat the egg yolks slightly, then add the sugar mixture gradually and beat until the egg yolks are creamy and pale yellow. Very slowly add 1 cup of the hot milk mixture to the eggs, with the beater on slow speed, then turn off the beater and add the rest, mixing with a rubber spatula; you do not want bubbles to form.

Transfer the egg-milk mixture back to the double boiler top and cook over simmering water, stirring with a rubber spatula now and then, until the mixture is thickened, about 15 minutes. The temperature should register 165° F.—the mixture will curdle at 180° F., so watch it. (If it does curdle, cool slightly and whiz until smooth in the food processor.) Remove from the hot water pan, add the vanilla, and place a piece of plastic wrap directly on top of the hot custard so a skin does not form. Cool and refrigerate until needed.

Preheat the oven to 325° F.

To make the islands, fill a 10 × 14-inch pan with hot water and set aside. Beat the egg whites, vanilla, salt, and cream of tartar together until the whites form soft peaks. Mix the sugar and cornstarch together and gradually add it to the egg whites, beating until stiff peaks form.

Using a wet tablespoon, dip out a heaping tablespoon of the meringue. With a small rubber spatula, form an oval egg shape and slip the meringue onto the hot water. Repeat to make about 16 "islands." You may have a bit of egg whites left over. Bake the meringues for 15 to 20 minutes, or until they are just light golden. Remove the pan from the oven and with a slotted spoon, place the meringues on a tray lined with paper towels to cool.

Pour the custard onto a deep serving platter (mine is an oval pasta platter, 11 × 15 inches); carefully place the meringues on top of the custard and refrigerate.

Make the caramel: If you are a novice at this, use a candy thermometer. About 2 hours before serving, in a heavy skillet, combine the sugar, water, and cream of tartar. Stir over medium heat for a minute or two, until the mixture begins to boil. Insert the candy thermometer. Wash down any sugar crystals that cling to the side of the pan with a spoon handle wrapped in a wet paper towel. Cook the syrup over medium-high heat until it becomes tea colored and registers 290° F. on the thermometer. To stop its cooking, set the bottom of the pan in cold water, then remove it. Immediately use a spoon to drizzle the hot caramel over the top of the meringues. If the caramel hardens before you are finished, return it briefly to the stove and reheat it. Set the dessert in a cool place until serving time. To serve, place 2 meringues on each dessert plate and surround with several tablespoons of the custard.

A Victorian cookbook illustration

SUGAR BABY WITH CARAMEL ORANGE QUARTERS

Bone-handled fruit set with engraved blades

271

Science Hill Biscuit Pudding with Warm Bourbon Sauce

SERVES 10 TO 12

In Shelbyville, Kentucky, there is a very fine regional restaurant called Science Hill Inn serving Kentucky specialties in what was an old girls' prep school. If you are in the area, you must eat there. It is not too far from the Shaker restoration at Pleasant Hill. The first time I tasted this delicate pudding, which is like a bread pudding only with a bit more character, I swooned with pleasure. Much to my delight, I was able to get the recipe, so when I got back to Indiana, it was one of the first things I made. I do think it is much better if you use the biscuit recipe on page 119 and soft wheat flour (see page 299 for a mail-order sauce). You can make this with regular biscuits too, of course.

PUDDING	SAUCE
Seven 2-inch biscuits, each cut in 8 wedges	1 cup (2 sticks) butter
1 quart whole milk	2 cups sugar
6 large eggs	½ cup water
2 cups sugar	2 large eggs
2 tablespoons vanilla extract	⅔ cup bourbon
Speck of salt	Speck of salt
2 tablespoons (¼ stick) butter, melted	
	Garnish: grated nutmeg

Preheat the oven to 350° F. Fill a 12 × 18-inch pan half full of water and place in the oven.

Place the biscuits in a large bowl and pour the milk over them; let stand for 5 minutes. Meanwhile, in a mixer bowl, beat the eggs, sugar, vanilla, and salt together until well blended but not bubbly. By hand, combine with the biscuit mixture.

Pour the melted butter into a greased deep round casserole (mine is 9½ inches in diameter and 3 inches deep). Pour the biscuit mixture on top of the butter, but do not mix in. Sprinkle the top of the pudding with a bit of nutmeg.

Carefully place the casserole in the pan of hot water and bake the pudding for 1 hour. The center will be a bit quivery when you take it out of the hot water bath, but the pudding will firm up as it cools.

Meanwhile, make the sauce: Melt the butter in a heavy saucepan over low heat. Add the sugar and the water and cook over medium heat, whisking, for 5 minutes. In a mixer bowl, beat the eggs. Remove the butter mixture from the heat and slowly add it to the eggs, beating slowly all the time. Add the bourbon and salt. Serve hot over the warm or cooled pudding.

NOTE: *The creamy rich bourbon sauce reheats well in the microwave. It is heavenly served on vanilla ice cream.*

HONEY CRUST CAKE

MAKES 9 TO 12 PIECES

*Every once in a while a recipe comes along that is so different and delicious that when
you taste it for the first time you sort of want to hop up and down and dance around. (At least some of us
do.) This honey cake is one of those hop-up-and-down recipes. A rich yellow cake layer is halved,
filled with whipped cream, then the top of the cake is drizzled with honey and nuts. It is not a tall thick cake,
but that is perfectly all right; that is the way it is supposed to be. This recipe is adapted from an old Colorado
cookbook, with the help of Jennifer Peterson, of Des Moines, and that's all I know about it—except that I love it.*

CAKE	SYRUP
½ cup (1 stick) unsalted butter, at room temperature	⅔ cup honey
1 cup sugar	1 tablespoon butter
2 large egg yolks	
2⅓ cups sifted all-purpose flour	1 cup Whipped Cream Topping (page 286)
2⅓ teaspoons baking powder	
1 teaspoon salt	Garnish: ¾ cup coarsely chopped walnuts
¾ cup milk, at room temperature	
2 teaspoons vanilla extract	

Preheat the oven to 350° F. Line the bottom of a 8 × 8-inch baking pan with wax paper and grease both the paper and the sides of the pan.

In a large mixer bowl, cream the butter and sugar together for 3 minutes. Add the egg yolks, one at a time, blend, and beat 1 more minute. In a medium mixing bowl, whisk together the flour, baking powder, and salt. In a separate measuring cup, combine the milk and vanilla. Add the dry ingredients to the butter mixture alternately with the milk, beginning and ending with the dry. Blend briefly.

Spread the batter evenly in the prepared pan. Bake for 35 minutes or until the top of the cake is golden brown, and the edges start to pull away from the sides of the pan. Cool the cake for 10 minutes, then tip it out on a serving platter or cooling rack and peel away the wax paper; allow the cake to cool completely.

Make the syrup: Combine the honey with the butter in a small, deep saucepan and simmer over low heat for 2 to 3 minutes (or heat in the microwave); remove from the heat and cool completely.

Meanwhile, after the cake has cooled, use a serrated knife to split the cake into 2 layers. Spread the bottom layer with Whipped Cream Topping; place the other layer on top and drizzle with half the syrup. Top with walnuts, then drizzle on the remaining syrup. Cover and refrigerate until serving time, or at least 4 hours. Cut into squares and serve. Store any leftover cake, covered and refrigerated.

KENTUCKY STACK CAKE
SERVES 16 TO 20

*As I began researching southern recipes, references to "stack cake" (not to be confused with
Stack Pie, page 190; they are two very different recipes) came up over and over again in Kentucky cookbooks. It
turns out to be a scrumptious light gingerbread cake of many layers, filled with a mixture of reconstituted
dried apples and spices. Traditionally, there were seven thin layers, baked in black spider skillets.
A very moist tall cake, this can be made two days in advance of serving and refrigerated,
which is another reason I give it high marks. Make the cake, which only has four layers in this twentieth-century
version, and the dried apple filling a day before you assemble the cake; the cake is easier to
cut then and the spices and apples have time to "marry." Some recipes call for whipped cream as a garnish,
which is very nice but not necessary.
The recipe is from a fellow Hoosier food writer, Marilyn Kluger, whose own cookbook,
The Wild Flavor, is a collection of her work that appeared originally in* Gourmet. *I have changed her recipe
slightly, substituting vegetable shortening for lard and cake pans for iron skillets.*

CAKE	FILLING
1 cup vegetable shortening	1 pound dried apples (available at health
1 cup granulated sugar	food stores and farmer's markets)
1 large egg	Approximately 6½ cups water
1 cup sorghum or light molasses	1 cup granulated sugar
3 cups all-purpose flour	½ cup packed light brown sugar
1 teaspoon baking soda	3 tablespoons butter
1 teaspoon ground ginger	2 teaspoons ground cinnamon
½ teaspoon salt	½ teaspoon ground allspice
1 cup buttermilk, at	¼ teaspoon ground cloves
room temperature	¼ teaspoon ground mace

**Garnish: confectioners' sugar or Whipped
Cream Topping (page 286), optional**

Preheat the oven to 375° F.

In a mixer bowl, cream the shortening and sugar together for 7 minutes. Add the egg and blend, then
add the sorghum or molasses and combine. In a large bowl, whisk together the flour, soda, ginger, and
salt. Add this to the creamed mixture alternating with the buttermilk, beginning and ending with the dry
ingredients. Blend but do not overbeat. Transfer the batter to 2 greased 9-inch layer cake pans and bake
the cake for 35 minutes or until a toothpick inserted in the middle of the cake comes out clean. Remove
the cakes from the oven and allow to cool completely. Wrap them individually in plastic wrap and allow to
stand overnight.

Meanwhile, make the apple filling: Place the apples in a deep kettle and add 6 cups water. Bring to a
boil, lower the heat to medium low, and simmer the apples, uncovered, for 35 to 45 minutes. Stir now
and then and make sure the apples do not burn. When done, the water should be completely absorbed
and the apples very tender. Add more water if necessary. With a potato masher, mash the apples until

the mixture looks like a lumpy puree—it should not be totally smooth. Add the sugars, butter, and spices and continue to cook and stir for 5 minutes longer. Transfer to a storage container, cool, and refrigerate overnight.

Two days before serving, assemble the cake: Cut the 2 layers in half and place one layer on a cake plate. Spread one-third of the apple puree on the cake and top with another cake layer; repeat 2 more times and top with the final cake layer; do not put any of the puree on the top. Cover with plastic wrap and keep chilled until serving time. About an hour before serving, sprinkle with confectioners' sugar, using a doily or a heart cutout as a pattern, if desired. Serve with Whipped Cream Topping, if desired.

DELICATE MINCEMEAT STRUDEL

SERVES 8

I adore mincemeat and always have my own version, made with beef, stored in the freezer. Using it as a filling for phyllo strudel makes a light version of a favorite American dessert. The strudel is better eaten the day it is made and before it is refrigerated.

**5 sheets frozen phyllo dough, defrosted
overnight in the refrigerator
½ cup (1 stick) butter, melted
½ cup fine dry bread crumbs**

**2 cups Amish mincemeat (page 211),
or prepared mincemeat,
fruit or traditional**

Preheat the oven to 350° F.

Unroll the phyllo and cover with a damp towel. Remove one sheet at a time, and place on a 17 × 20-inch piece of foil, keeping the remaining sheets covered. Brush the first sheet with some of the melted butter; sprinkle with some of the bread crumbs. Top with a second sheet; brush with butter and sprinkle with crumbs. Repeat with the remaining sheets and crumbs. Spoon the mincemeat gently over the top of the stack to within 1-inch of the edges. Roll up, jelly-roll style from the long side. Cut the roll in half with a sharp knife.

Transfer the rolls to a foil-lined, greased jelly roll pan and brush with remaining butter. With a very sharp knife, score the top of each roll partly through eight 1-inch slices. Bake for 40 to 45 minutes or until the strudel is golden brown. Remove immediately from the pan to a wire rack to cool. Slice completely through and serve.

CHOCOLATE VELVET CHEESECAKE

*Both the English and the Germans relished cheesecake, and written recipes for this smooth,
unctuous dessert were available in the 1850s, though it was made at least a century earlier in America. The
cakes were much like our cheesecakes are today, except without sugar. These early cheesecakes were
topped instead with sweet jam or jelly or even honey.
Today we have lots of different interpretations of this dessert, and this chocolate one from San Antonio is spectacular.*

CRUST

**One 8-ounce package thin
crisp chocolate wafer cookies
⅓ cup butter, melted
½ teaspoon ground cinnamon
Speck of salt**

FILLING

**12 ounces semisweet chocolate
2 tablespoons (¼ stick) butter
1½ pounds cream cheese, at
room temperature
1 cup sugar
3 large eggs
2 cups heavy cream
1 teaspoon vanilla extract
Speck of salt**

Make the crust: Process the chocolate cookies in the food processor until fine. Add the melted butter, cinnamon, and salt and blend until well combined. Press the mixture firmly onto the bottom and up 2½ inches of the sides of a 10-inch springform pan. (It works best if you do the sides first.) Chill for 30 minutes or overnight.

Preheat the oven to 350° F. and place the rack in the upper third of the oven.

Make the filling: Break the chocolate into squares and melt over hot water with the butter in a double boiler over low heat. Stir now and then, and when melted, set aside. Meanwhile, in a large mixer bowl, beat the cream cheese until softened, then gradually add the sugar, beating until the mixture is fluffy. Add the eggs one a time, just incorporating each one before adding the next. At low speed, add the chocolate, cream, vanilla, and salt. Don't overbeat.

Pour the cheesecake mixture into the crust and smooth the top. Bake for 1 hour; the filling will still be quite soft when you take it out of the oven. Cool completely, cover with plastic wrap, and refrigerate overnight.

MARCIA ADAMS' HEIRLOOM RECIPES

Wooden butter mold

GOLDEN JELLY ROLL WITH ORANGE CURD AND COCONUT

SERVES 8 TO 12

*When selecting desserts for a buffet, consider how they will look together on the table,
and be sure there is a variety in shapes, tastes, and textures. Jelly rolls are nice because of their different form
as well as their spongy cake texture. This roll is filled with a buttery orange curd and coconut filling; I
present it on a long silver tray and garnish it with spurge and yellow flowers.*

ORANGE CURD

⅓ cup granulated sugar

¼ cup cornstarch

1 cup fresh orange juice, about
   3 large oranges

2 tablespoons fresh lemon juice

1 teaspoon grated orange zest

1 large egg

2 tablespoons (¼ stick) butter

One 3-ounce can flaked
   sweetened coconut

ROLL

1 cup all-purpose flour

1 teaspoon baking powder

½ teaspoon salt

3 large eggs, at room temperature

1 teaspoon vanilla extract

1 cup granulated sugar

⅓ cup hot water

Confectioners' sugar

Garnish: Whipped Cream Topping (page 286)

In a medium saucepan, combine the sugar and cornstarch. Blend in the orange juice, lemon juice, and orange zest and cook over medium heat until the mixture is thick, stirring constantly and whisking until smooth, about 5 minutes. Remove from the heat.

In a small bowl, beat the egg well. Add a little of the hot orange mixture to the egg and whisk until smooth. Return the egg mixture, whisking it gradually into the orange juice mixture, and cook over low heat for 2 to 3 minutes longer. Add the butter. Remove from the heat and cool completely. Reserve approximately one-third of the mixture (a little over ½ cup) to frost the roll. To the remainder, add ½ cup coconut. Set this mixture aside while making the cake roll.

Preheat the oven to 375° F. Line a 10 × 15-inch jelly roll pan with foil and grease it lightly.

In a medium bowl, whisk together the flour, baking powder, and salt; set aside. Beat the eggs and vanilla in a large mixer bowl and beat well; add the sugar, 1 tablespoon at a time, beating until the mixture forms a ribbon when the beaters are lifted and is silky and pale yellow, about 1 minute. Reduce the mixer speed to slow and add the flour mixture to the egg mixture, beating only until blended. Add the hot water all at once and mix until the batter is smooth.

Spread the batter evenly in the prepared pan and bake on the middle rack for 12 to 14 minutes.

Immediately loosen the cake from the sides of the pan with a knife; sift confectioners' sugar over the top, cover with a tea towel, and invert the cake on a flat surface. Remove the foil. Cut off the brown edges, for they will keep the cake from rolling well. Use the towel to help roll up the cake. Starting from the short side of the cake, roll the cake and towel up together. Transfer to a rack, seam side down, and allow the roll to cool completely, about 1 hour. Unroll and spread the cake completely with the reserved orange-coconut filling clear to the edges. Gently but tightly roll the cake up again from the short side. Transfer to a serving platter, seam side down, and frost all over with the reserved orange mixture.

Sprinkle 3 tablespoons coconut in a strip down the center of the roll. Cover the cake loosely with plastic wrap and refrigerate. To serve, fold the remaining coconut into the Whipped Cream Topping. Cut the roll in slices and pass the Whipped Cream Topping.

BLUEBERRY GINGERBREAD

MAKES ONE 9 × 9-INCH PAN

Blueberries and gingerbread are a terrific combination, and adding fruit brings
an unexpected texture and flavor to a classic American dessert. Elegant enough for company,
serve this with a clear Orange Sauce (page 287) or warm with Hard Sauce (page 285).
It can be served in shallow fruit bowls (my grandmother called them "nappies") or on dessert plates.

½ cup (1 stick) butter, at
    room temperature (no substitutes)
¾ cup packed light brown sugar
2 large eggs
2 cups all-purpose flour
1 teaspoon salt
1 teaspoon ground ginger

¼ teaspoon ground cinnamon
¼ teaspoon ground mace
1 cup buttermilk, at room temperature
1 teaspoon soda
¼ cup light molasses
1 cup blueberries, fresh or frozen (see Note)

Preheat the oven to 350° F. Grease a 9 × 9-inch square pan and set aside.

In a mixer bowl, beat the butter for a few seconds, then gradually add the brown sugar and beat for 7 minutes. Add the eggs, one at a time, blending well after each addition.

In a mixing bowl, whisk together the flour, salt, ginger, cinnamon, and mace. In a two-cup measure, combine the buttermilk and soda. Begin adding the flour mixture to the butter mixture alternating with the buttermilk mixture, beginning and ending with the flour mixture. Add the molasses and combine quickly; do not overbeat. Fold in the blueberries by hand.

Pour the batter into the pan and bake for 50 to 60 minutes or until the top springs back when touched with your finger. Be careful not to overbake.

NOTE: *If using frozen blueberries, spread them in a single layer on a paper towel and allow to stand for 1 hour.*

DATE-GINGER STEAMED PUDDING

SERVES 8

I adore steamed puddings and they are almost always considered a winter dessert, doubtless because early cooks made them with suet and stored them outside along with other meats that were "put by" for winter. However, this one, made with butter, is lighter than most steamed puddings. A pale yellow cake-type pudding, it is studded with dates and scented with orange. It is so pretty you should present it on a footed glass cake stand and cut it at the table.

1½ cups pitted California dates
½ cup (1 stick) butter, at
    room temperature
¾ cup sugar
3 large eggs
2 tablespoons finely chopped
    crystallized ginger
Juice and zest of 1 orange
Juice and zest of 1 lemon

1 teaspoon vanilla extract
1½ cups all-purpose flour
1 tablespoon ground ginger
2 teaspoons baking powder
Speck of salt
Confectioners' sugar

Crème Anglaise (page 286)

Coarsely chop the dates and set aside. In a large mixer bowl, cream the butter and sugar for 5 minutes, until light and fluffy. Mix in the eggs one at a time, beating well after each addition. Stir in the dates, crystallized ginger, orange juice and zest, lemon juice and zest, and the vanilla. In a small bowl, whisk together the flour, ginger, baking powder, and salt; blend well. Add the flour mixture to the date mixture and stir until well combined.

Grease a 1½-quart metal mold—a vegetable oil cooking spray works well. Pour in the batter, run a knife or spatula through the batter to remove any air pockets, and cover tightly with a greased lid or foil. Place the mold on a rack (if you don't have a rack, canning jar rings work wonderfully) in a deep pot with a tight-fitting lid. Add enough hot water to reach two-thirds up the sides of the mold and cover the pot. Bring the water temperature to a simmer (over approximately medium to medium-high heat) and steam for 2 hours. Remove the mold from the pot, uncover, and let stand on a cooling rack for 15 minutes. Gently unmold onto a serving plate and dust with confectioners' sugar. Serve with Crème Anglaise.

NOTE: *An attractive mold can be ordered from Fantes (page 299). It is a 1½-quart tin mold, with fluted sides and a lid.*

travel Notes
THE END OF THE JOURNEY

To have been able to write this book has been a privilege; the research was fascinating and Dick and I learned so much as we traveled about. Over and over again, I was reminded how critically important women were in settling this country. In the final analysis, the West was won without fanfare or flourishes, by the homesteader and his wife, the mother of that first generation raised on the plains, in the mountains, on the fringes of the desert. Leaving from Independence, Missouri, the starting point for the long trail West, she entered the wilderness and the Middle Ages. Ahead of her and her family was a two-thousand-mile walk. What courage and ignorance led them to an obscure destiny. She was wife, nanny, teacher, minister, doctor, cook, gardener, and seamstress. She was the motivating force to move her brood from the soddy or tent into a frame house with carpets on the floor, to have a piano and Bible in the living room and roses in the yard. She insisted on one-room schoolhouses, libraries, the organization of church choirs and reading clubs. Gradually, she turned a wilderness into a civilization.

Admirable men's names move across the pages of the history books—Jefferson, Boone, Seward, and Captain Cook—yet it's to the legacy of unrecorded women I find myself drawn. How I admire their determination, their bravery, their discipline. And they left something else behind that is very tangible—their recipes.

The BASICS

EVERYTHING YOU FIND in this chapter has been called for or referred to in other recipes in this cookbook. It might more aptly be called the go-with chapter. You will use these recipes frequently and you shouldn't have to go looking through other cookbooks to find them.

The pie pastry is a classic; if you keep it frozen in your freezer all the time you need never resort to storebought. Not only is it perfect for pie, it can be patted into jelly tart pans and used as a base for hors d'oeuvres or made into turnovers. The Whipped Cream Topping, with its addition of corn syrup, keeps its shape for a long time—use it on pies instead of meringue. Hard Sauce is the classic accompaniment for steamed puddings, but you could also use the Brown Sugar Sauce or the Orange Sauce with Grand Marnier. Crème Anglaise is eminently adaptable; add flavorings to suit your dessert.

Since most of us cook southwestern foods from time to time, you'll find a truly good Green Tomatillo Salsa recipe and one for my favorite accompaniment for cold meats, Salsa Mayonnaise. And for those who have fond memories of dumplings simmering on tops of soups, there are two kinds: Cornmeal and Butter Dumplings. Here are the recipes you need to make your menu planning easier; I know you will rely on them as I do.

Cornmeal Dumplings Butter Dumplings Perfect Pie Pastry
Basic White Sauce Crème Fraîche Hard Sauce Orange Frosting for Cookies Whipped Cream
Topping Crème Anglaise Brown Sugar Sauce Orange Sauce with Grand Marnier
Salsa Mayonnaise Green Tomatillo Salsa Red Salsa with Chipolte Chili

CORNMEAL DUMPLINGS

SERVES 4 TO 6

Early cooks made dumplings much more often than we do today; they were probably intended to expand a dish so it would serve more people. But how good they were! For those who yearn for dumplings now and then, these fluffy yellow cornmeal dumplings are substantial, yet very soft and good. Drop them on a large saucepan of chicken broth with some leftover chicken pieces picked off the bone and you will have a filling, luxurious dish.

1 cup all-purpose flour	**1 teaspoon salt**
1 cup yellow cornmeal	**1 large egg**
2 teaspoons baking powder	**¾ cup milk**
1 teaspoon sugar	**1 tablespoon vegetable oil**

In a large bowl, whisk together the flour, cornmeal, baking powder, sugar, and salt. In a small bowl, beat the egg well and then beat in the milk and oil. Pour the egg mixture over the flour mixture and combine the two by hand.

Drop by tablespoons onto hot simmering broth or liquid. You will have about 10 generous dumplings. Cover the pot tightly and simmer over low heat for 25 minutes; do not lift the lid or the dumplings will fall.

BUTTER DUMPLINGS

SERVES 4 TO 6

What a wonderful recipe this is! These puffy light dumplings can be simmered on top of any liquid, such as stews or soups.

1 cup all-purpose flour	**6 tablespoons milk**
1½ teaspoons baking powder	**1 heaping tablespoon finely**
½ teaspoon salt	**minced parsley**
1 tablespoon cold butter	
1 large egg, beaten	**Butter**

In a medium bowl, whisk together the flour, baking powder, and salt. Cut in the cold butter with a pastry blender or 2 knives until the mixture resembles coarse oatmeal. Add the egg, milk, and parsley. Blend lightly; don't overmix. Drop by approximately 6 tablespoonfuls on top of the simmering liquid. Cover tightly and cook over medium-low heat for 20 minutes; do not lift the cover during the cooking period. Serve in bowls, topped with butter.

PERFECT PIE PASTRY

MAKES ENOUGH FOR 8 OR 9-INCH PIE SHELLS
OR TWO 2-CRUST PIES

*This is a flavorful golden pastry, made with an electric mixer. It is ideal for the cook who has
always been apprehensive about making piecrust, for it handles beautifully and comes out perfect every time;
make a double recipe and freeze the extra.*

4 cups all-purpose flour	**1 large egg**
1 tablespoon sugar	**1 tablespoon cider vinegar**
2 teaspoons salt	**½ cup water**
1¾ cups butter-flavored solid	
vegetable shortening	

Combine the flour, sugar, salt, and shortening in a large mixer bowl and blend until it has the texture of coarse crumbs. In a small bowl, beat together the egg, vinegar, and water. Drizzle over the flour mixture and mix thoroughly. Shape the dough into a patty, wrap in plastic wrap, and place in the freezer for 45 minutes, or refrigerate overnight.

To prepare the dough for pies, form it into a long roll, divide into fourths, and wrap each portion separately and refrigerate or freeze. One-fourth of this recipe is enough pastry for one 8- or 9-inch shell; one half of this recipe is enough for a shell and a top crust.

BASIC WHITE SAUCE

MAKES 2¼ CUPS

*This basic white or béchamel sauce is one that is still taught in all high-school home economics
classes, or should be, for this is a recipe that cooks use over and over again. I look back and marvel at all the skills Mrs.
Heiny, my home ec teacher, introduced to us. We learned to bake quick breads, yeast breads, prepare an
assortment of sauces, meat dishes, vegetables, butter cakes, and pies. Plus baby care. And her sewing classes were
legendary; all her students won the blue and purple ribbons at the county 4-H fair.*

¼ cup (½ stick) butter	**⅛ teaspoon grated nutmeg**
¼ cup all-purpose flour	**Salt and white pepper to taste**
2 cups milk	

In a medium saucepan, melt the butter over moderate heat; do not allow it to brown. Add the flour all at once, whisking and cooking until the mixture bubbles up in the center of the pan, about 3 minutes. Add the milk all at once, whisking vigorously and cooking until the mixture thickens, about 5 minutes. Add the nutmeg and salt and pepper to taste. (If using the sauce as part of a meat or vegetable dish, my mother always added a dash of Worcestershire sauce and ground mustard, which gave some extra zip to this sauce.)

CRÈME FRAÎCHE

MAKES 1 CUP

*This is a good topping or garnish on very sweet desserts. Spoon it over fresh fruit, warm cobblers,
puddings, and pies. It can also be used in sauces and soups since it won't curdle when heated.*

1 cup heavy cream **2 tablespoons sour cream or buttermilk**

Combine the ingredients in a glass container, cover, and let stand at room temperature for 8 to 24 hours,
or until very thick. Stir well, cover, and refrigerate for up to 10 days.

HARD SAUCE

MAKES 2 CUPS

*This is a buttery nutmeg-flavored sauce that is traditionally served on top of steamed puddings.
As the butter melts, the rum and nutmeg flavor seep down into the hot pudding, a very satisfactory state of affairs.*

**½ cup (1 stick) butter, at
room temperature
2 cups confectioners' sugar
Speck of salt** **1 teaspoon rum extract or 2
tablespoons rum, sherry, or brandy
½ teaspoon grated nutmeg**

In a mixer bowl, beat the butter until creamy, then blend in the rest of the ingredients and continue beating until the mixture is smooth. Transfer to a covered container and refrigerate. Remove from the refrigerator to soften slightly about 1 hour before serving.

ORANGE FROSTING FOR COOKIES

MAKES 2 CUPS FROSTING

*Frequently a very good cookie can be elevated to something really special by the addition
of a frosting. I have used this particular recipe for just that purpose many times over. If you want an even thinner
frosting to make a glaze-type finish, add up to three tablespoons of milk to the finished frosting.*

**2 cups confectioners' sugar
1 tablespoon very soft butter
¼ cup orange juice** **2 teaspoons grated orange zest
½ teaspoon vanilla extract
Speck of salt**

Combine all of the ingredients in a mixer bowl and beat until well blended. Frost the cookies while warm
for a crackly finish, but if you want a more frosting-on-top-of-a-cookie texture, cool the cookies first.

WHIPPED CREAM TOPPING

MAKES 2 CUPS

The addition of white corn syrup to whipped cream helps stabilize it and the
cream does not go flat, but stays nice and perky for a couple of days (though most pies don't last that long).
Sometimes cooks will complain that their cream doesn't whip. An older cream (check the
date on the box) whips better than a newer cream, and the bowl and beater should be well chilled.

1 cup very cold heavy cream	2 teaspoons white corn syrup
¼ cup confectioners' sugar	Speck of salt
1 teaspoon vanilla extract	

Combine all of the ingredients in a mixer bowl and whip until the cream is stiff, with well-defined peaks. Don't walk away and leave this while it is beating, though, for the mixture can turn to butter in a matter of seconds.

CRÈME ANGLAISE

MAKES 1 ¼ CUPS

Sometimes called "English pouring sauce," this classic accompaniment enhances any number of desserts.

3 large egg yolks	Speck of salt
3 tablespoons sugar	1 teaspoon vanilla extract
1 teaspoon cornstarch	
1 cup milk	Garnish: freshly grated nutmeg

In a mixer bowl, beat the egg yolks well. Gradually add the sugar and beat 3 minutes. Add the cornstarch. In a medium saucepan, scald the milk over medium heat until bubbles form around the edges of the pan, about 4 minutes; do not boil. Gradually add the hot milk to the egg mixture, stirring with a wooden spoon, not a whisk.

Transfer the mixture back to the saucepan and cook over low heat, stirring constantly with the spoon, until the mixture thickens, about 6 minutes. Remove from the heat and add the salt and vanilla. Transfer to a storage container. Place a piece of plastic wrap or wax paper directly on the surface of the hot sauce and allow to cool completely. Cover tightly, leaving the plastic wrap on top. (This keeps a skin from forming on top of the custard.) Refrigerate until needed. To serve, transfer to a bowl and sprinkle freshly grated nutmeg over the top. This sauce can be made 2 days in advance.

ℬROWN SUGAR SAUCE

MAKES 2 CUPS

*This easy sauce can be made either in a saucepan or in
the microwave. Either way, it is one of the classic sauces for steamed puddings.*

½ cup granulated sugar
½ cup packed light brown sugar
2 tablespoons cornstarch
½ teaspoon ground cinnamon
¼ teaspoon ground mace
Speck of salt

2 cups water
2 tablespoons fresh lemon juice
1 teaspoon grated lemon zest
½ teaspoon brandy extract or 2
   tablespoons brandy

In a saucepan, combine the sugars, cornstarch, cinnamon, mace, and salt. Whisk in the water, then add the remaining ingredients. Cook over medium heat, stirring, until the mixture boils and thickens, about 4 to 5 minutes. Serve hot over steamed pudding.

   Microwave method: In an 8-cup glass measure, combine the sugars, cornstarch, cinnamon, mace, and salt. Whisk in the water, then the remaining ingredients. Cover tightly with plastic wrap. Microwave 3 minutes on High, whisk, and microwave 3 minutes longer.

𝒪RANGE SAUCE WITH GRAND MARNIER

MAKES 1 ¼ CUPS

This lightly thickened sauce is good on many things—gingerbread, pie, fruit, or even ice cream.

½ cup sugar
1 tablespoon cornstarch
Speck of salt
1 cup fresh orange juice, about
   2 to 3 large oranges

2 tablespoons butter
2 to 3 tablespoons Grand Marnier or
   other orange-flavored liqueur

In a medium saucepan, mix the sugar, cornstarch, and salt. Gradually whisk in the orange juice and cook over medium heat until the sauce has thickened and is transparent, about 3 minutes. Remove from the heat and add the butter and Grand Marnier. Serve warm or cold.

SALSA MAYONNAISE

MAKES 1 CUP

Tired of mustard on your sandwiches? Substitute this mayonnaise, zapped with chilies, garlic, cilantro, and cumin. Serve it with roast beef, cold chicken or turkey, or even aspic. It can be made in advance and refrigerated. Chipotles are smoked chilies often sold in a spicy sauce called adobo. They are available canned at Mexican groceries.

1 cup mayonnaise

2 canned chipotle chilies,
    very finely minced

1 garlic clove, very finely minced

1 heaping tablespoon chopped
    fresh cilantro

¼ teaspoon of cumin

In a small bowl, combine the mayonnaise, chilies, garlic, cilantro, and cumin. Blend and allow to stand for at least 1 hour before serving.

GREEN TOMATILLO SALSA

MAKES 2 ½ CUPS

This recipe was given to me by the proprietor of a little Mexican grocery where I used to shop. He suggested adding cumin only if the salsa was to be used for a dip with tortilla chips; it should be omitted if I was going to serve the salsa with other highly seasoned Mexican dishes. I have always followed his advice. Cooked tomatillos do not keep well, so make this no more than a day in advance.

¾ pound fresh tomatillos,
    papery husks removed

1 small onion, chopped

2 fresh jalapeño chilies, seeded and finely
    chopped (use canned, if necessary)

2 teaspoons fresh lemon juice

2 garlic cloves, minced

¾ cup chopped fresh cilantro

Salt and pepper to taste

2 teaspoons ground cumin (optional)

Place the tomatillos in a medium saucepan with water to cover. Bring to a boil and simmer, covered, for 10 minutes, or until they split open and began to "cook up." Drain, reserving about ½ cup of the liquid. Transfer the tomatillos to a food processor and process until finely chopped.

Transfer the mixture to a nonreactive bowl and add the onions, chilies, lemon juice, garlic, cilantro, salt and pepper, and enough of the reserved liquid to give the mixture a saucelike consistency. Add the cumin, if desired.

RED SALSA WITH CHIPOTLE CHILI

MAKES 2 CUPS

This tomato salsa is a tad different because of the addition of a smoky chipotle chili. Chipotles are smoked jalapeños and are available dried or canned in adobe sauce.

1 small onion, chopped
½ green bell pepper, chopped
1 chipotle chili, finely minced
2 cups fresh tomatoes, peeled, seeded,
    and coarsely chopped, or one
    14-ounce can, drained and chopped

½ cup minced fresh cilantro
Salt to taste

In a medium bowl, combine all of the ingredients. This will keep 2 days in the refrigerator.

Wooden buckets stored on pegs

Guide to Places to
VISIT

THE EAST

Chesterwood
Stockbridge, MA 01266
413/298-3579
Summer residence and studio of sculptor Daniel Chester French, sculptor of Lincoln in the Memorial at Washington, DC. There is also a museum, nice gardens, and a woodland walk. Open May through October.

The Schlesinger Library
Radcliffe College
10 Garden Street
Cambridge, MA 02138
617/495-8608
Collection of 7,000 cookbooks as well as a collection of the History of Women in America. Call or write for information regarding library hours.

The Mount/Edith Wharton
    Restoration, Inc.
P.O. Box 974
Lenox, MA 01240
413/637-1899
A National Historic Landmark, this former home of American author Edith Wharton is a turn-of-the-century Berkshire summer estate. It is undergoing restoration, but tours of the house and garden are available summer through fall. Call or write in advance. Note: While in the area, be sure to see the Hancock Shaker Village, Chesterwood, Naumkeag, and the charming town of Stockbridge. Also, the Boston Symphony Orchestra performs all summer at nearby Tanglewood.

Naumkeag
Prospect Hill
Stockbridge, MA 01266
413/298-3239
Designed by Stanford White in 1886, this Norman-style summer home of New York lawyer Joseph Coates (who prosecuted the Boss Tweed Ring in New York City as well as Standard Oil antitrust cases) overlooks the Berkshire Hills. The interior features antiques, Oriental rugs, and Chinese porcelain. The extensive gardens include many terraces and fountains, and show a strong affection for Chinese design. It is quite splendid. Guided tours late June through Memorial Day. Call or write for information.

Historic Deerfield
Hall Tavern Information
    Center
Deerfield, MA 01342
413/774-5581
Originally, New England's northernmost outpost, more than fifty of the town's first houses still stand and twelve of them are open to the public. A quiet beautiful town, impeccably restored.

The Orchard House
399 Lexington Road
Concord, MA 01742
508/369-4118
Louisa May Alcott's house and garden, excellent docents. Be sure also to visit The Wayside, home of Nathaniel Hawthorne, and later Margaret Sidney, author of *Five Little Peppers*. There is much to see in Concord, including The Old Manse, the Ralph Waldo Emerson House, The Gropious House, and the Fruitlands Museums, so allow enough time.

The Hancock Shaker Village
Pittsfield, MA 01201
413/443-0188
An original (1790–1960) Shaker site, it is now a living history museum, featuring an extraordinary round stone barn. Large collection of Shaker furniture in twenty restored buildings. Write or phone for visiting hours.

The Homestead
280 Main Street
Amherst, MA 01002
413/542-8161
Emily Dickinson's house, with selected rooms open for guided tours May to October. Reservations recommended.

Plimoth Plantation
Route 3
Plymouth, MA 02360
508/746-1622
Recreated 1627 Pilgrim village and
the *Mayflower II*. Open April
through November.

Barnacle Billy's Dock
Perkins Cove
Ogunquit, ME 03907
207/646-5227
Fifty-minute lobster harvesting trips,
seeing lobster traps hauled out of
the water, and an explanation of the
industry and lobster lore. Boats run
May through mid-October. Write
or phone for precise information.

THE MID-ATLANTIC

Pearl S. Buck House
520 Dublin Road
Dublin, PA 18917
215/249-0100
An 1835 stone farmhouse situated
in a handsome rolling countryside,
the Pearl Buck Foundation sponsors
many events year-round. Write or
phone for information.

Ephrata Cloister
632 West Main Street
Ephrata, PA 17522
717/733-6600
A dozen of the original buildings
built between 1732 and 1750 are
open to the public. Some of the
original manuscripts are also dis-
played. Write or call for information
regarding hours open to the public.
There are craft demonstrations in
the summer.

Fonthill
East Court Street
Doylestown, PA 18901
215/348-9461
Estate/museum of Henry Mercer,
one of the leaders of the arts and
crafts movement. Guided tours.

Hershey
Hershey Information
300 Park Boulevard
Hershey, PA 17033
800/437-7439
A diverse entertainment area built
around the Hershey Chocolate
industry. Write for information.

James A. Michener Art
Museum
138 South Pine Street
Doylestown, PA 18901
215/340-9800
Once an old country jail, the struc-
ture now houses changing exhibi-
tions of twentieth-century American
art and contemporary crafts; there is
also a sculpture garden.

The Moravian Pottery and
Tile Works
130 Swamp Road
Doylestown, PA 18901
215/345-6722
Restored as a living history museum,
tiles are still hand-crafted on the
premises.

The Mushroom Festival
P. O. Box 1000
Kennett Square, PA 19348
215/444-4951
September is American Mushroom
Month and Kennett Square spon-
sors many activities, including a
cook-off. Write for information.

Peddlar's Village
Routes 202 & 263
Lahaska, PA 18931
215/794-4000
Located in historic Bucks County,
with seventy specialty shops in a
country setting; *good* shopping.

The Henry Francis du Pont
Winterthur Museum
Winterthur, DE 19735
302/888-4600
A breathtaking collection of
American antiques placed in
authentic period rooms, plus an
unforgettable garden. This is one of
the great museums in America;
don't miss it.

THE MIDWEST

Daniel Boone Home
Defiance, MI 63341
314/987-2221
Restored home, thirty-five miles
west of St. Louis, of this well-known
explorer of the West, it is open
March through December. Call or
write for information.

Newburgh Country Store
224 West Jennings
Newburgh, IN 47630
800/382-0938
A real country store in a quaint small
town on the banks of the Ohio
river, noted for its weekend April
Herb Festival, featuring excellent
speakers, box lunches, and a superb
collection of herbs for your garden.

The Ohio Sauerkraut Festival
Chamber of Commerce
P. O. Box 201
Waynesville, OH 45068
A real hometown festival held the second weekend of every October; send for a brochure. Lots of great antique shops here too. Be sure to pick up a copy of the local recipe book, One Nation Under Sauerkraut, by Dennis Dalton, or write him at P. O. Box 419. It's $6.00 prepaid if you can't make it to the festival.

Schoenbrunn Village State
Memorial
P.O. Box 129
New Philadelphia, OH 44663
216/339-3636
Restored 1772 Moravian mission/village and museum, costumed interpreters, many planned activities.

Stan Hywett Hall and Gardens
714 Portage Path
Akron, OH 44303
216/836-5533
Sixty-five-room Seilberling mansion, open year-round, seventy acres landscaped gardens, conservatory, greenhouse. A very special place, marvelously furnished.

The Pella Historical Village
507 Franklin Street
Pella, IA 50219
515/628-4311
Over twenty restored old Dutch buildings, plus the Wyatt Earp house.

Seed Saver's Exchange
R. R. #3, Box 239
Decorah, IA 52101
Send for brochure and information on the garden seed inventory.

Include $1.00 and a self-addressed stamped envelope.

Prairie Homestead Site
Badlands National Park
Interior, SD 57750
605/433-5361
The park and visitor's center, with planned activities, is open year-round, the "soddy" is open May through September.

THE MOUNTAIN STATES

Golden Spike National Historic
Site
Chamber of Commerce
6 North Main Street
Brigham City, UT 84302
801/471-2209
Meeting site of the first transcontinental railroad; visitor's center, film, summer programs, and interpretive presentations.

Sundance
R. R. #3, Box A-1
Sundance, UT 86404
800/892-1600
A first-class summer and winter resort open to the public, with summer theater for adults and children and skiing in winter. Features the Sundance Film Festival. Write for information regarding rates.

THE SOUTH

The Biltmore Estate
One North Pack Square
Asheville, NC 28801
800/543-2961
A visit to the 8,000 acre Vanderbilt estate gives us a glimpse of the 250-room chateau and 35 acres of formal gardens. Tours include the

winery and wine tasting, greenhouses, house, and gardens. It is a fantastic experience, well planned for the tourists. Two restaurants. You'll be dazzled. Send for information.

The Carl Sandburg Home
National Historic Site
1928 Little River Road
Flat Rock, NC 28731
704/693-4178
Called "Connemara," the farm-residence of poet Carl Sandburg is open to the public. It is close to Asheville; write ahead, however, for instructions on how to reach it.

Grove Park Inn
290 Macon Avenue
Asheville, NC 28804
704/252-2711
A superb resort overlooking the Blue Ridge Mountains, complete with golf course and tennis courts. Outstanding collection of furniture from the arts and crafts movement. Fine dining, reservations necessary.

The Thomas Wolfe
Memorial
48 Spruce Street
Asheville, NC 28802
704/253-8304
The original Wolfe boardinghouse depicted in Look Homeward, Angel as The Old Kentucky Home and where Wolfe grew up. The house is furnished to appear as it did in 1906 when Wolfe wrote about it.

Cheeca Lodge
Box 527
Islamorada, FL 33036
305/664-4651
An outstanding resort hotel where sports fishing is the thing to do, this lodge has an outstanding dining room. It is a good overnight stop on your way to Key West.

**Ernest Hemingway House
and Museum
907 Whitehead Street
Key West, FL 33040
305/294-1575**

Spanish Colonial house of author
Ernest Hemingway. Original furnishings, memorabilia, and guided tours.

**International Bar-B-Q
Festival
Owensboro, KY 42301
502/926-6938**

During this festival, held the first
weekend in May, the town cooks up
more than 10,000 pounds of mutton, 3,000 chickens, and 1,500 gallons of burgoo. Free admission.

**Museum of the American
Quilter's Society
215 Jefferson Street
Paducah, KY 42001
502/442-8856**

Brand-new quilt museum, with
rotating selections, plus guest quilt-
makers present workshops and
seminars year-round. Write the
museum for a current schedule of
events.

**Science Hill Inn
525 Washington Street
Shelbyville, KY 40065
502/633-2825**

This very fine regional Kentucky
restaurant is close to Shaker Village
and is located next to Wakefield-
Scearce Galleries (502/633-4382)
in an outstanding boutique-type
group of shops, including European
antiques. Downtown Shelbyville
also has many antique shops.

**Shaker Village of Pleasant
Hill
3500 Lexington Road
Harrodsburg, KY 40330
606/734-5411**

A marvelous restoration of an
authentic Shaker community.
Lodging available, and the dining
room is excellent. Activities planned
on weekends.

THE SOUTHWEST

**Banner Day Studio
Mettje Swift
850½ Main Avenue
Durango, CO 81302-1576
303/259-2947**

Artist Mettje Swift fashions marvelous banners and other fiber art
inspired by the Anasazi. Call first
regarding gallery hours.

**Acoma Pueblo
Tourist Visitation Center
P. O. Box 309
Pueblo of Acoma
Acoma, NM 87034
505/252-1139**

A fascinating glimpse into the lives of
an early Indian civilization on top of
a mesa. A shuttle bus takes you to
the top.

**Institute of American Indian
Arts Museum
108 Cathedral Place
Santa Fe, NM 87504
505/988-6486**

An extensive collection of Indian
art, plus well-stocked gift shop.

**Museum of International
Folk Art
706 Camino Lejo
Santa Fe, NM 87504
505/827-6350**

A division of the Museum of New
Mexico, this is the largest collection
of folk art in the world; do see it and
be enchanted.

**Santa Fe School of Cooking
and Market
Upper Level, Plaza Mercado
116 West San Francisco St.
Santa Fe, NM 87501
505/983-4511**

An outstanding cooking school
teaching Santa Fe cookery. Write
for information.

**The Santa Fe Opera
The Opera Association of
New Mexico
Box 2408
Santa Fe, NM 87501
505/982-3851**

Write for information regarding the
season, which is in the summer.

**King Ranch
P. O. Box 1594
Kingsville, TX 78363
800/333-5032**

A ninety-minute tour of the famous
King Ranch. There is also a museum
with a twenty-minute film of the
King Ranch history.

**Marion Koogler McNay Art
Museum
6000 North New Braunfels
San Antonio, TX 78205
210/824-5368**

Attractive museum with patio and
gardens. Includes New Mexican arts
and crafts, plus Gothic, medieval,
late nineteenth to twentieth-century paintings.

**Navajo National Monument
The Superintendent's Office
HC-71, Box 3
Tonalea, AZ 86044
602/672-2366**

This monument is in three scattered
areas and part of the Navajo Indian
Reservation. Guided tours are limited to twenty-four people on a first-
come, first- serve basis. Write for
information.

Taliesin West/Frank Lloyd
    Wright Foundation
108th Street
Scottsdale, AZ 85253
602/860-2700

Winter campus of the Frank Lloyd
Wright Foundation. Tours and
bookstore. Open October through
May with limited hours the rest of
the year. Phone for information.

THE FAR WEST

Pike Place Market
First Avenue and Pike Street
Seattle, WA 98104
206/682-7453

Seven-acre market and the oldest
continuously operating farmer's
market in the country. More than
225 permanent shops and restaurants. It is real street theater.

Pioneer Square
1st Avenue, James Street and
    Yesier Way
Seattle, WA 98104

The city was founded here in 1852.
Restored buildings of early Seattle
now house restaurants, shops, and
an excellent bookstore, the Elliot
Bay Book Company.

Seattle Art Museum
100 University Street
Seattle, WA 98101
206/625-8900

New building; permanent collection
includes Oriental, Alaskan, Asian,
and African art.

Tillicum Village
Excursion from Pier 56, at
    the foot of Seneca Street
2200 Sixth Avenue, Suite 804
Seattle, WA 98121
206/329-5700

Go by luxurious boat out to Blake
Island for an Indian-baked salmon
dinner. Northwest Coast Native
dancing adds to the experience. The
fish is delicious!

Guide to
RESTAURANTS, BED AND BREAKFASTS, AND INNS

Listed below is information on regions visited and/or mentioned in the text. (R) indicates a restaurant only. (R,A) signifies both food and accommodations available.

THE EAST

Deerfield Inn
Box 305, The Street
Deerfield, MA 01342
413/774-5587 (R,A)

Durgin Park
30 North Market Street
Boston, MA 02199
617/227-2038 (R)

The Equinox
Historic Route 7A
Manchester Village, VT 05254
800/362-4747 (R, A)

Jasper's
240 Commercial Street
Boston, MA 02109
617/523-1126 (R)

Kathy Ann's Bakery
350 Marrimac Street
Newburyport, MA 01950
508/462-7415 (R)

Red Lion Inn
Main Street
Stockbridge, MA 01266
413/298-5545 (R,A)

THE MID-ATLANTIC

Hollileif Bed and Breakfast
677 Durham Road (Route 413)
Wrightstown, PA
215/598-3100 (A)

The Inn at Perry Cabin
308 Watkins Lane
St. Michael's, MD 21663
800/722-2949

THE MIDWEST

**Clarinda's Cottage Tea Room and
   Gift Shoppe**
Number 3 Market Street
Newburgh, IN 47630
812/853-2323 (R)

Classic Kitchen
13400 Allisonville Road
Noblesville, IN 46060
317/773-7385 (R)

Fairchild House Bed and Breakfast
606 Butler Street
Saugatuck, MI 49453
616/857-5985

Misty Meadow Farm
64878 Slaughter Hill Road
Cambridge, OH 43725
614/439-5135 (R.A.)

Phelps Mansion Inn
208 State Street
Newburgh, IN 47630
812/853-7766 (A)

Strawtown Inn
1111 Washington Street
Pella, IA 50219
515/628-4043(R)

Teetor House
300 West Main Street
Hagerstown, IN 47346
800/824-4319 (A)

Tony Packo's Cafe
1902 Front Street
Toledo, OH 43604
419/691-6054

THE SOUTH

Cheeca Lodge
Box 527, Overseas Highway (US 1)
Islamorada, FL 33036
305/664-4651 (R,A)

Dooky Chase
2301 Orleans Avenue
New Orleans, LA 70112
504/821-2294 (R)

The Greenbriar
White Sulphur Springs, WV 24986
800/624-6070 (R,A)

Grove Park Inn and Country Club
290 Macon Avenue
Asheville, NC 28804
704/252-2711 (R,A)

The Inn at Pleasant Hill
3500 Lexington Road
Shakertown of Pleasant Hill
Harrodsburg, KY 40330
606/734-5411 (R,A)

Louie's Backyard
700 Wadell Street
Key West, FL 33040
305/292-1919 (R)

Marquesa Hotel and Cafe Marquesa
600 Fleming Street
Key West, FL 33040
305/292-1919 (R,A)

Moonlite Bar-B-Q Inn
2840 West Parrish Avenue
Owensboro, KY 42301
502/684-8143 (R)

Science Hill Inn
525 Washington Street
Shelbyville, KY 40065
502/633-2825 (R)

Soniat House
1133 Chartres Street
New Orleans, LA 70112
800/544-8808 (A)

Williamsburg Inn
Francis Street
Williamsburg, VA 23185
804/229-1000 (R, A)

THE SOUTHWEST

Arizona Biltmore Resort
24th and Missouri Avenue
Phoenix, AZ 85016
602/955-6600 (R,A)

Bishop's Lodge
Box 2367, Bishop's Lodge Road
Santa Fe, NM 87505
505/983-6377 (R, A)

Cafe Y Panaderia Mi Tiera
218 Produce Row
San Antonio, TX 78298
210/225-1262 (R)

Coyote Cafe
132 Water Street
Santa Fe, NM 87505
505/983-1615 (R)

El Mirador
722 South Saint Mary's Street
San Antonio, TX 78298
210/225-9444 (R)

The Fairmount Hotel
401 South Alamo Street
San Antonio, TX 78205
800/642-3363 (R, A)

The Inn of the Anasazi
113 Washington Avenue
Santa Fe, NM 87504
800/688-8100 (R, A)

THE FAR WEST

Alexis Hotel
1007 1st Avenue
Seattle, WA 98104
800/426-7033 (R, A)

The Archbishop's Mansion
1000 Fulton Street
San Francisco, CA 94117
800/543-5820

Brigham Street Inn
1135 East South Temple
Salt Lake City, UT 84102
801/364-4461 (A)

Brown's Palace Hotel
321 17th Street
Denver, CO 80202
303/297-3111 (R, A)

The Chimney Sweep Inn
1154 Copenhaven Drive
Solvang, CA 93463
800/824-6444 (A)

The Fort
19192 County Road 8
Morrison, CO 80465
303/697/4771 (R)

Furnace Creek Inn
Box 1
Death Valley, CA 92338
619/786-2345 (R, A)

Kailua Plantation House
75-5948 Alii De Kailui
Kailua, Koona, HI 96740
808/329-3727 (A)

Sundance
RR 3, Box A-1 North Fork Provo
   Canyon
Sundance, UT 84604
801/225-4107 (R,A)

Old Monterey Inn
500 Martin Street
Monterey, CA 93940
800/350-2344 (A)

The Sylvia Beach Hotel
267 N.W. Cliff Street
Newport, OR 97365
503/265-5428 (R,A)

Cliff Harbor Guest House
P. O. Box 769
Brandon, OR 97411
503/347-3956 (A)

Mail-Order
DIRECTORY

Resources for the specialty foods and cooking implements and accessories mentioned in the text.

ANTIQUES

Antiques at the Sign of the Gas Light
P.O. Box 405
130 North First Street
Pierceton, IN 46562
219/594-2457
General line of antiques, large selection of glass, porcelain, flow blue, collectibles, etc.

Antiques from BC
3641 Sandpoint Road
Fort Wayne, IN 46809
219/747-0043
American eighteenth- and nineteenth-century formal, country, and primitive furniture and accessories.

Candlelight Antiques
3205 Broadway
Fort Wayne, IN 46807
219/456-3150
Very fine furniture and china, including Haviland.

Karen's Antique Mall
1510 Fairfield Avenue
Fort Wayne, IN 46802
219/422-4030
Large two-story building full of American collectibles and antiques; good values.

APPLES

Doud Orchards
Route 1
Denver, IN 62628
317/275-6100
Fresh antique apple varieties, fruit only, no trees. Write or call for information. Gift packs available. Apple festival last weekend in September.

CHEESE

Loomis Cheese Company
220 Felch Street
Ann Arbor, MI 48103
313/741-8512
Artisan cheshire cheeses, made in small quantities from an original nutty, tangy English recipe, handpressed ten-pound molds in antique Welsch cheese press. Three varieties: Great Lakes Cheshire Cheese, Ann Arbor Aged Gold, and Garden Garlic & Chive.

CHÈVRE

Capriole, Inc.
Judith Schad
P. O. Box 117
Greenville, IN 47124
Write for information and recipes regarding this superb goat cheese; several varieties.

CONDIMENTS

Ralph Sechler and Sons
St. Joe, IN 46785
Delicious crispy pickles and relishes, made in small batches. Mail order; write for information.

The Tony Packo Food Company
1902 Front Street
Toledo, OH 43605
800/366-4218
Hungarian hot dogs, chili dog sauce, relishes, spoonable ketchup, sauces, etc.

COOKIE MOLDS

Brown Bag Cookie Art Cookie Molds
Hill Design Inc.
7 Eagle Square
Concord, NH 03301
These clay molds are accompanied by a recipe booklet with instructions on how to make these charming cookies in various shapes.

COOKIES AND DANISH PASTRIES

The Solvang Bakery
460 Alisal Road
Solvang, CA 93463
805/688-5713
Danish cookies, kringle, and pastries. Write for information.

COOKWARE AND CHINA

Amelia's Fine Things
3013 East State
Fort Wayne, IN 46805
219/482-8455
A superb collection of fine china, crystal, linens, and exciting tabletop accessories. Full Vera Bradley collection. Bridal registry.

Fantes
1006 South Ninth Street
Philadelphia, PA 19147
800/878-5557
I have yet to call Fantes and be told they don't have what I want, no matter how esoteric. There apparently is nothing that Fantes cannot supply, from unusual flavoring extracts to peculiar baking pans. If you are in Philadelphia, this is one of the places you must visit. The service is as good as the merchandise.

Sur La Table
84 Pine Street
Pike Place Farmer's Market
Seattle, WA 98101
800/243-0852
Right across from the market, this shop is jammed full of dishes, cookware, cookbooks, and helpful people who can answer your cooking questions. A "must-see" when in Seattle.

FLOUR

White Lily Foods Company
P. O. Box 871
Knoxville, TN 37901
This fine southern soft wheat flour, perfect for biscuits and other southern bread, can be ordered by mail. Write the above address for information.

GOURMET FOODS

Dean and DeLuca
560 Broadway
New York, NY 10012
212/431-1691
Need rosewater? Need jerk sauce? Dean and DeLuca will send it to you. Be sure to visit the place when you are in New York.

West Point Market
1711 West Market Street
Akron, OH 44313
216/864-2251
This is one of the top grocery stores in the United States, stocked with everything under the sun, including a huge bakery (their killer brownies are sent all over the country), cheese shop, and on and on. Go there!

Zingerman's
422 Detroit Street
Ann Arbor, MI 48104
313/663-3400
Fantastic bakery, deli, specialty food items, and informative newsletter.

HONEY

Dave Laney Family Company
25725 New Road
New Liberty, IN 25725
219/656-8701
Wildflower, Michigan star thistle, blueberry blossom, trefoil, dune country honeys, as well as fruit honeys. Write for information.

OLIVE OIL

Nick Sciabica & Sons
P. O. Box 1246
Modesto, CA 95353-1246
Fragrant California olive oils, several blends. Write for price list.

PERSIMMON PULP

Dymple's Delight
Route 4, Box 53
Mitchell, IN 47466
Minimum order is two cans of pulp for $8.

PRALINES

St. Clare's Monastary Gift Shop
720 Henry Clay Avenue
New Orleans, LA 70140
504/895-2019
Open daily 9–6. Call first to make sure pra-
lines are available. You can also buy The
New Orleans Monastery Cookbook,
Recipes from St. Clare's Kitchen, *Paper,*
$11.05 prepaid, a warm and intimate
glimpse of the Poor Clare Nuns of New
Orleans, with photographs and recipes
from all the sisters.

RICE

Konriko
301 Ann Street
New Iberia, LA 70560
318/367-6161
Mail-order catalog available.

Nature's Best Wild Rice Company
2579 Old University Avenue
Madison, WI 53705
800/369-7423
Wild rice, plus wild rice soup mixes, dried
cranberries, etc.

SWEETENERS

Veron Miller
The Cider Press
55514 Country Road 8
Middlebury, IN 46540
219/825-2010
Sorghum, boiled cider, and maple syrup.

BIBLIOGRAPHY

Arnold, Samuel, P.
Eating Up the Santa Fe Trail.
Niwot, Col.: University Press of
Colorado, 1990.
American Heritage Editors.
*The American Heritage Cookbook and
Illustrated History of American Eating and
Drinking.*
New York: American Heritage
Publishing Co., Inc., 1964.
Belsinger, Susan, and Carolyn Dille.
The Chesapeake Cookbook.
New York: Clarkson N. Potter, Inc.,
1990.
Berolzheimer, Ruth.
The United States Regional Cookbook.
Halycon House, 1930.
Brack, Fred, and Tina Bell.
Tastes of the Pacific Northwest.
New York: Doubleday, 1988.
Brown, Dale.
American Cooking: The Northwest.
New York: Time-Life Books, 1970.
**Clements, Carole; Martha Lomask,
and Norma MacMillan.**
*American Tradition, a Classic Guide to
Regional Cooking.*
United Kingdom: The Hamlyn
Publishing Group Ltd., 1989.
Cleveland, Bess A.
California Mission Recipes.
Boston: Charles E. Tuttle Company,
1965.
**De Rochemont, Richard and
Waverly Lewis Root.**
Eating in America, A History.
New York: The Ecco Press, 1981.
Dille, Carolyn, and Susan Belsinger.
New Southwestern Cooking.
New York: Macmillan, 1985.

Glenn, Camille.
The Heritage of Southern Cooking.
New York: Workman, 1986.
Idone, Christopher.
Glorious American Food.
New York: Random House, Inc., 1985.
Jones, Evan.
American Food: The Gastronomic Story.
New York: Random House, Inc., 1981.
Kent, Louise Andrews.
Mrs. Appleyard's Kitchen.
Boston: Houghton Mifflin, 1942.
Kerr, Mary Brandt.
*America, Regional Recipes from the Land
of Plenty.*
Secaucus, NJ: Chartwell Books, Inc.,
n.d.
Lee, Hilde Gabriel.
*Taste of the States: A Food History of
America.*
Charlottesville, Va.: Howell Press, 1992.
Leonard, Jonathan Norton.
American Cooking: The Great West.
New York: Time-Life Books, 1971.
Longstreet, Stephen and Ethel.
A Salute to American Cooking.
New York: Hawthorn Books, 1968.
Madison, James H.
Heart Land.
Bloomington, Ind.: Indiana University
Press, 1988.
McBride, Mary Margaret.
Harvest of American Cooking.
New York: G. P. Putnam's Sons, 1956.
Minear, Tish, and Janet Limon.
The Southwest; Hippocrene Guide.
New York: Hippocrene Books, 1990.
Perl, Lila.
Red-Flannel Hash and Shoo-Fly Pie.
Cleveland: World Publishing Co., 1965.

Platt, June.
June Platt's New England Cookbook.
New York: Atheneum, 1971.
Ricardo, Don.
Early California and Mexico Cook Book.
Toluca Lake, CA: Pacifica House, Inc.,
1968.
Schulz, Phillip Stephen.
America the Beautiful Cookbook.
San Francisco: Collins Publishers, Inc.,
1990.
Tolley, Lynne and Pat Mitchamore.
*Jack Daniel's The Spirit of Tennessee
Cookbook.*
Nashville: Rutledge Hill Press, 1988.
Vaughan, Beatrice.
Yankee Hill-Country Cooking.
Brattleboro, VT: The Stephen Greene
Press, 1963.
Waldman, Carl.
Atlas of the North American Indian.
New York: Facts on File, 1985.
Weisser, Henry.
*Rocky Mountain States; Hippocrene
U.S.A. Guide.*
New York: Hippocrene Books, 1992.
White, Jasper.
*Jasper White's Cooking from New
England.*
New York: Harper Row, 1989.
Whitman, Herbert S.
Exploring the Berkshires.
New York: Hippocrene Books, 1991.

CREDITS

This book drew on the knowledge and skills of many people who gave generously of themselves. As always, I do appreciate it so very much; without them, the book would have never come into existence. Kudos!

Mike Acosta

Hazel Adams

Allen County Public Library, Fort Wayne, Indiana

Mary Ellen Beitman

Bell Memorial Public Library, Mentone, Indiana

Kathy Bertz

Eva Bonitati

Jim Brubaker

Harry and Jenny Bryan

Howard and Betsy Chapman

Julia Child

Sandy Thorne Clark

Clare Clemens

Kim Colby

Sara Corrigan

Yvonne Diamond

Mary Dora

Steve Doud

Todd Downs

George Finley

Madeleine Fisher

Jeff Frank

Randy and Mary Jo Frane

Sue Fuson

Gallatin County Historical Society, Bozeman, Montana

Ina German

Camille Glenn

Irwin Glusker

Luis Goena

Esther Grabill

Phyllis Grabill

Kim Grant

Patty Grant

Sally Gutting

Bill and Suzanne Hall

Michael Hawfield

Carole Hawkins

Max and Holley Hobbs

The Journal-Gazette, Fort Wayne, Indiana

Pat Keenan

Terry and Beth Keenan

Mary Kessner

Marilyn Kluger

Sally Krouse

Pietra LaRotonda, California Date Administrative Committee

Jane Lengacher

Grace Leong

Dave Lewis

Cindy Lorbach

Ella Lucas

Jane Lundy

Tommie Manny

Laura McCaffrey

Bob McCandless

Kathleen McClary, chief curator of textiles, Indiana State Museum

Conie McCoy

Marjorie Meyer

Lou Jane Miller

Jan Montieth

Doris Mooney

Rosemary Noecker

Mary Norton

Evelyn Oechsle

Shirley Partner

Carol Piecuch

Sue Reichert

Lois Rothert

Laurette Ryan

Santa Barbara Public Library

Cliff and Elaine Shultz

Bill Shoaf

Anita Shupe

Barbara Sims-Bell

Louella Snow

Carol Spears

Mettje Swift

Marla Tambellini

Dori Toepfer, Sacramento State Parks Docent Association

Dolores Tomusk

Lynn Trulock

Josephine Van Shaick

Richard Ver Wiebe

Pauline and Carol Watkins

Lou Ann Westlake

Catherine Wolken

Wilmer Zehr

Mary Ellen Zeiger

INDEX

Conversion Chart
EQUIVALENT IMPERIAL AND METRIC MEASUREMENTS

American cooks use standard containers, the 8-ounce cup and a tablespoon that takes exactly 16 level fillings to fill that cup level. Measuring by cup makes it very difficult to give weight equivalents, as a cup of densely packed butter will weigh considerably more than a cup of flour. The easiest way therefore to deal with cup measurements in recipes is to take the amount by volume rather than by weight. Thus the equation reads:

1 cup = 240 ml = 8 fl. oz. $\frac{1}{2}$ cup = 120 ml = 4 fl. oz.

It is possible to buy a set of American cup measures in major stores around the world.

In the States, butter is often measured in sticks. One stick is the equivalent of 8 tablespoons. One tablespoon of butter is therefore the equivalent to $\frac{1}{2}$ ounce/15 grams.

LIQUID MEASURES

Fluid ounces	U.S.	Imperial	Milliliters
	1 teaspoon	1 teaspoon	5
$\frac{1}{4}$	2 teaspoons	1 dessertspoon	10
$\frac{1}{2}$	1 tablespoon	1 tablespoon	14
1	2 tablespoons	2 tablespoons	28
2	$\frac{1}{4}$ cup	4 tablespoons	56
4	$\frac{1}{2}$ cup		110
5		$\frac{1}{4}$ pint or 1 gill	140
6	$\frac{3}{4}$ cup		170
8	1 cup		225
9			250, $\frac{1}{4}$ liter
10	$1\frac{1}{4}$ cups	$\frac{1}{2}$ pint	280
12	$1\frac{1}{2}$ cups		340
15		$\frac{3}{4}$ pint	420
16	2 cups		450
18	$2\frac{1}{4}$ cups		500, $\frac{1}{2}$ liter
20	$2\frac{1}{2}$ cups	1 pint	560
24	3 cups		675
25		$1\frac{1}{4}$ pints	700
27	$3\frac{1}{2}$ cups		750
30	$3\frac{3}{4}$ cups	$1\frac{1}{2}$ pints	840
32	4 cups or 1 quart		900
35		$1\frac{3}{4}$ pints	980
36	$4\frac{1}{2}$ cups		1000, 1 liter
40	5 cups	2 pints or 1 quart	1120
48	6 cups		1350
50		$2\frac{1}{2}$ pints	1400
60	$7\frac{1}{2}$ cups	3 pints	1680
64	8 cups or 2 quarts		1800
72	9 cups		2000, 2 liters

SOLID MEASURES

U.S. and Imperial Measures		Metric Measures	
ounces	pounds	grams	kilos
1		28	
2		56	
$3\frac{1}{2}$		100	
4	$\frac{1}{4}$	112	
5		140	
6		168	
8	$\frac{1}{2}$	225	
9		250	$\frac{1}{4}$
12	$\frac{3}{4}$	340	
16	1	450	
18		500	$\frac{1}{2}$
20	$1\frac{1}{4}$	560	
24	$1\frac{1}{2}$	675	
27		750	$\frac{3}{4}$
28	$1\frac{3}{4}$	780	
32	2	900	
36	$2\frac{1}{4}$	1000	1
40	$2\frac{1}{2}$	1100	
48	3	1350	
54		1500	$1\frac{1}{2}$
64	4	1800	
72	$4\frac{1}{2}$	2000	2
80	5	2250	$2\frac{1}{4}$
90		2500	$2\frac{1}{2}$
100	6	2800	$2\frac{3}{4}$

OVEN TEMPERATURE EQUIVALENTS

Fahrenheit	Celsius	Gas Mark	Description
225	110	$\frac{1}{4}$	Cool
250	130	$\frac{1}{2}$	
275	140	1	Very Slow
300	150	2	
325	170	3	Slow
350	180	4	Moderate
375	190	5	
400	200	6	Moderately Hot
425	220	7	Fairly Hot
450	230	8	Hot
475	240	9	Very Hot
500	250	10	Extremely Hot

EQUIVALENTS FOR INGREDIENTS

all-purpose flour—plain flour
arugula—rocket
baking sheet—oven tray
buttermilk—ordinary milk
cheesecloth—muslin
coarse salt—kitchen salt
confectioners' sugar—icing sugar
cornstarch—cornflour

eggplant—aubergine
granulated sugar—caster sugar
half and half—12% fat milk
heavy cream—double cream
light cream—single cream
lima beans—broad beans
parchment paper—greaseproof paper
plastic wrap—cling film

scallion—spring onion
sour cherry—morello cherry
unbleached flour—strong, white flour
vanilla bean—vanilla pod
zest—rind
zucchini—courgettes or marrow